PARAMUS

Bergen County, New Jersey

REFORMED DUTCH CHURCH BAPTISMS

1740-1850

From a copy made by Dingman Versteeg
under the direction of William Nelson

Together with
Records from the Gravestones
in the Church Yard
and
A List of Church Members

Edited, Indexed and Published
by
Howard S. F. Randolph
and
Russell Bruce Rankin

Southern Historical Press, Inc.
Greenville, South Carolina

This volume was reproduced
from a personal copy located in
the Publishers private library

Please direct all correspondence and book orders to:
SOUTHERN HISTORICAL PRESS, Inc.
PO Box 1267
Greenville, SC   29602-1267

Originally published 1935
Newark, New Jersey
ISBN #978-1-63914-232-3
Printed in the United States of America

Baptisms reprinted from

The Proceedings of the New Jersey

Historical Society

Gravestone Records reprinted from

The Genealogical Magazine of New Jersey

FOREWORD

The Reformed Dutch Church of Paramus is located on the outskirts of the present Village of Ridgewood in Bergen County. The exact date of its organization is unknown, but from 1725 to 1728 the congregation, together with those of Schraalenburgh and Hackensack, was under the pastorate of the Rev. Reinhardt Erickzon. In 1731 and 1732 the Rev. Georgius Wilhelmus Mancius was minister at Paramus and Schraalenburgh. During the next sixteen years there was no settled pastor, and the church was cared for by the Rev. Antonius Curtenius, pastor at Hackensack and Schraalenburgh, by the Rev. Johannes Van Driessen of Acquackanonk, and the Rev. Frederic Muzelius of Tappan, all within ten miles. It is therefore necessary to consult the records of those churches for Paramus baptisms and marriages, especially prior to 1748. The ministers who served the church from that time until 1850 were: Benjamin Van der Linde, 1748-1789; Gerardus Arentse Kuypers, 1788-1789; Isaac Blauvelt, 1790-1791; William Provost Kuypers, 1793-1796; Wilhelmus Eltinge, 1799-1850.

The first reference to a church building occurs on the fly leaf of the *Doop* (or baptismal) Book, and reads as follows: "Den 21 Dagh van April, 1735, is de Eerste Steen van de Kirk Gelegt." It was erected on a three-acre tract donated for the purpose by Peter Fauconier. The building was remodeled in 1785, and entirely rebuilt in 1800.

The baptisms of this church were recorded in a manner peculiar to but few Dutch churches of the period, and so far as we are aware no other New Jersey church employed this system. With the exception of the first four years the records were entered semi-alphabetically according to the baptismal names of the children. Names beginning with "A" were recorded chronologically, followed by those beginning with "B", then "C", etc. Such an arrangement is the despair of the genealogist who must necessarily read through the entire list in order to find all records of a given family or surname. Each of these alphabetical groups has been appropriately designated in this volume and indexed in the table of Contents.

The index presented at the end of the volume gives for the first time a complete analytical index to these baptismal records, with references to fathers, mothers, children and witnesses, as well as to the names in the list of church members, and in the gravestone records.

The earliest marriage records of the Paramus church begin in 1799 with the pastorate of the Rev. Wilhelmus Eltinge. For these records the reader is referred to Volume 22 of the *New Jersey Archives,* page 549, and *Bergen County, N. J., Marriage Records,* by Frances A. Westervelt, 1929, page 70.

Grateful acknowledgment is made to the Board of Trustees of the New Jersey Historical Society for permission to reprint the Baptismal Records from the *Proceedings* of that Society, and to the Board of Trustees of the Genealogical Society of New Jersey for permission to reprint the Gravestone Records from *The Genealogical Magazine of New Jersey.*

HOWARD S. F. RANDOLPH,
RUSSELL BRUCE RANKIN.

CONTENTS

CORRECTIONS

p. 13. 9th line. Write, Albert and Geertje—Aaltje, b. May 28—June 21.

p. 17. 3rd line from bottom. Christopher, John and Altje—Anna, b. July 20—Sept. 25.

p. 19. 4th line. Hopper, Andries H. and Maria—Antje, Sept. 25—Oct. 30.

p. 19. 30th line. Christopher, Jacob and Geesje—Aaltje, b. Mar. 24—Apr. 14.

p. 42. Last line. Sisco, Willem and Elisabeth—Elisabeth, b. Feb. 12—Apr. 1.

p. 66. 23rd line. Lesre [Lozier], Pieter—Isaac—Mar. 7.

p. 68. 18th line. Fesyeur, Abraham and Elisabeth—Jacob, b. Sep. 11—Sep. 28.

p. 74. 13th line. Dey, Solomon and Sally—John, b. Oct. 16—Nov. 14.

BAPTISMAL RECORDS FROM THE REFORMED DUTCH CHURCH OF PARAMUS, BERGEN COUNTY, NEW JERSEY, 1740-1850

Unless otherwise noted dates refer to baptisms.

1740

VAN ALEN, Gerrit and Eefje Neefje—Lea—Feb. 4.
Wit: Christiaan and Lea Zabriskie.

BEERMOOR, Lieven and Rachel Beermoor—Johannis—June 28.
Wit: Gerrit and Hillegont Van Blercom.

PIETERSEN, Salomon and Elisabeth—Susanna—June 28.
Wit: Salomon Dey and wife.

TYSE, Filip and Antje Worms—Pieter—June 29.
Wit: Diederik Wannemaker and wife.

BONGAERT, Lukas and Dorothie—Willempje—June 29.
Wit: Jan and Antje Bongaert.

VAN GELDER, Abraham and Rachel—Jacobus—Oct. 25.
Wit: Jacobus Van Gelder and wife.

RATAN, Paulus and Lybetje—David—Oct. 25.
Wit: Willem and Marytje Stevense.

RYERSE, Jacob and Marytje—Rebecka—Oct. 25.
Wit: Ryer and Betje Ryerse.

1741

WESTERVELT, Steven and Johannis (sic) Ackerman—Jannitje—Feb. 25.
Wit: Hillegont Westervelt; Jannitje Ackerman.

ODEL, Benjamin and Neeltje—Hendrik—Feb. 25.
Wit: Jacobus and Sara Stedg.

VERWEY, Laurens and Tryntje—Catryntje—Feb. 25.
Wit: Jan and Tryntje Verwey.

MEEKS, Joseph and Sara—Catryntje—Feb. 25.
Wit: Abraham Ratan; Sara Rutan.

DUGRAU, Arend and Angonietje—Molly—Feb. 25.
Wit: Jacobus Verwey; Molly Bon.

VANDEUSEN, Isack and Elisabeth—Jannitje—Feb. 26.
Wit: Willem and Jannitje Van Allen.

DEGREA, John and Hannah—Willem—Feb. 26.
Wit: Niclaas and Metje Volk.

WANNAMAKER, Coenraad and Diederik (sic)—Diederik—Feb. 26.
Wit: Marytje (probably the mother) and Anneke Wannamaker.

VOES, Hendrick and Grietje—Anna Marya—Nov. 2.
Wit: Niklaas and Marytje Muiseger.

ACKERMAN, Cobus and Dirkje—Marytje—Nov. 2.
Wit: Albert and Marytje Sabrisko.

MEAKS, Samuel and Yemyme—Joseph—Nov. 27.
Wit: Luwes and Mehetabel Konkele.

1742

VAN BLERKOM, Jan and Jannitje—Annatje—Feb. 13.
Wit: Jimmy and Annatje Johnson.

DUBOU, Andries and Jannitje—Pieter—June 26.
Wit: Pieter and Margrietje Dubou.

ACKERMAN, Johannis and Betje—Petrus—June 26.
Wit: Hendrik and Marytje Laroe.

BAARMOEL, Lieven and Rachel—Hendrikus—June 26.
Wit: Hendrik and Maretje Bertholf.

HOPPE, Hendrik and Catryntje—Rachel—June 26.
Wit: Pieter and Antje Ackerman.

GRUNIG, Abraham and Margryt—Obadia—Oct. 23.
Wit: Barend VanHorn and wife.

VOLCK, Nikolaas and Metje—Ariaantje—Oct. 23.
Wit: Hendrik and Ariaantje Volck.

STOR, Jacob and P. Wannemaker—Machiel—Oct. 23.
Wit: Klaartje Wannemaker; Maragriet Stor.

1743

ODEL, Benjamin and Nellie—Hannes—Feb. 6.
Wit: Hendrik and Tryntje Hoppe.

BOGERT, Cornelis and Lysabeth—Carstyna—Feb. 6.
Wit: Joost and Carstyntje Zabrisko.

BROUWER, Isack and Rachel—Marytje—Feb. 6.
Wit: Adolf and Maragriet Secoort.

ZABRISKO, Steven and Tryntje—Antje[1]—Feb. 6.
Wit: Abram and Jannitje Hoppe.

"A"

1749

ZABROWISKE, Jacob and Aaltje—Antje—Jan. 22.
Wit: Abram and Jannitje Hoppe.

VAN DIEN, Dirk and Catryntje—Andries, b. Jan. 9—Jan. 22.
Wit: Jan and Lisabeth Hoppe.

BANTA, Abram and Annatie—Abram—Aug. 31.
Wit: Teunis and Grietje Helm.

HOPPE, Gerrit and Hendrikje—Abigail, b. Sept. 14.
Wit: Jan and Aaltje Zabrowiske.

VAN HOUTE, Gerrit and Jannitje—Adriaan—Nov. 26.
Wit: Adriaan and Angonietje Van Houte.

TERHUYN, Dirk and Lea—Albert—Dec. 10.
Wit: Albert A. and Weyntje Terhuyn.

RIDDENAER, Hendrik and Grietje—Abel—Dec. 13.
Wit: Hermanus and Janneke Dugrau.

1750

WESTERVELT, Roelof and Tryntje—Abram, b. Feb. 7, 1750.
Wit: Cobus and Jannitje Van Voorhees.

VOLK, Abram and Rachel—Abram—May 24.
Wit: Abram and Caartie Rutan.

MEYER, Marten and Geertje—Abram—Nov. 18.
Wit: Abram Meyer; Rachel Labbagh.

DOREMUS, Hessel and Geesje—Annitie—Nov. 4.
Wit: Teunis and Annatie Hennion.

---

[1]It will be noted that from this point on the records were kept alphabetically in accordance with the name of the child.—EDITOR.

TERHUYN, Dirk and Lea—Abigail—Sept. 23.
Wit: Jan and Aaltje Zabriske.
HOPPE, Jan and Lisabeth—Abram, b. Feb. 3, 1750—Sept. 23.
Wit: Abram and Jannitje Hoppe.

1751

VANDELINDE, D⁰ Benjamin and Lisabeth—Ariaantje, b. June 18—June 23.
Wit: Hendrik and Ariaantje Vandelinde.

1752

VOLK, Nikolaas and Mettie—Arie—Apr. 5.
Wit: Paulus and Annatie Vanderbeek.
SPIER, Teunis and Cathalyntje—Annatje, b. Apr. 24.
Wit: Jan and Eva Amelman.
PILISFELT, Hannis and Marytje—Antje, b. June 14.
Wit: Andries and Antje Pilisfelt.
HOPPE, Hendrik and Wyntje—Aaltje—June 28.
Wit: Jan and Aaltje Zobriske.
ZOBRISKIE, Albert H. and Thellitie—Abram—Sept. 24.
Wit: Abram Ackerman; Marytje Zabriske.
BOGERT, Lucas and Dorotie—Antje—Dec. 17.
Wit: Cobus and Willempje Bogert.

1753

DEBOUW, Reyer and Abigail—Annatje—Jan. 1.
Wit: Cobus and Catryn Dubaen.
VAN BLERCUM, Lucas and Lisabeth—Annatje—Jan. 21.
Wit: David and Annatje Ackerman.
ZABRISKIE, Jacob I. and Aaltje—Albert—Apr. 19.
Wit: Marytje, wid. of Jacob Jan Zabriskie.
VAN SCHYVEN, Hannes and Vrouwtje—Annatje—July 1.
Wit: Wyntje and Hendrik Hoppe.

1754

VANDERBEEK, Abram and Saartje—Coenraad—Feb. 18.
Wit: Coenraad and Marytje Vanderbeek.
RUTAN, Johannes and Aaltje—Abraham—Feb. 18.
Wit: Abram and Saartje Rutan.
VAN BLERCOM, Gerit and Hillegont—Albert—Mar. 24.
Wit: Albert and Saartje Terhuyn.
DOREMUS, Cornelis and Rachel—Aaltje—Mar. 30.
Wit: Albert A. and Lisabeth Terhuyn.
CRIM, Fredrik and Barbara Krim—Adam—June 3.
Wit: Adam Aal; Antje Salomonse.
ACKERMAN, David and Saartje—Arie—July 5.
Wit: Hannes and Jacomyntje Ackerman.
STOR, Jacob and Grietje—Antje, b. July 10—July 28.
Wit: Andries and Antje Pulisfelt.
ACKERMAN, David D. and Annatje—Abraham—Jan. 26.
Wit: Albert A. and Lisabeth Terhuyn.

1755

TERHUYN, Albert A. and Lisabeth—Aaltje—Apr. 20.
Wit: Jacob J. and Aaltje Zabriske.

HOPPE, Hendrik I. and Trientje—Andries, b. July 5—July 20.
    Wit: Andries Hoppe; Aaltje Ackerman.
DENYK, Andries and Marytje—Andries—Aug. 17.
    Wit: Hessel and Geesje Duremus.
TERHUYN, Abram and Marytje—Albert—Oct. 5.
    Wit: Albertus and Anna Maria Terhuyn.
DUBAEN, Jacob and Marytje—Andries—Dec. 14.
    Wit: Andries and Jannitje Debouw.
STORM, Staets S. and Belitje—Abraham—Dec. 4.
    Wit: Abram and Aaltje Storm.

1756

TERHUYN, Dirk A. and Lea—Aaltje—Feb. 15.
    Wit: Jacob J. and Aaltje Zabrowiskie.
DEBAEN, Jacob and Rachel—Abraham, b. Jan. 25—Feb. 15.
    Wit: Barend and Christina Kool.
KIP, Nicasie and Grietje—Antje—May 9.
    Wit: Reinier and Antje Berdan.
WESTERVELT, Casparus and Martyntje—Angenietje, b. Aug. 14—Sept. 5.
    Wit: Jan and Maria Westervelt.
HOPPE, David and Rachel—Andries—Sept. 30.
    Wit: Hendrik and Wyntje Hoppe.
HOPPE, Gerrit and Elsje—Antje—Dec. 25.
    Wit: Pieter and Antje Ackerman.
DEBAEN, Jacob and Marytje—Andries—Dec. 25.
    Wit: Andries and Jannitje Debouw.

1757

DEMAREST, Benjamin and Wybrecht—Angenietje, b. Jan. 9—Jan. 26.
    Wit: Samuel and Angenietje Sidman.
DEMAREST, Petrus and Maria—Annatje, b. Mar. 8—Mar. 20.
    Wit: David and Maria Demarest.
TERHUYN, Dirk and Lea—Albert—Aug. 7.
    Wit: Albert and Lisabeth Terhuyn.
ACKERMAN, Jan—Albert, b. Mar. 9—Mar. 19.
    Wit: Gerrit and Rachel Vandien.

1758

GERRITSE, Hendrik and Neesje—Abraham—Sept. 10.
    Wit: Jacob and Rachel Gerritse.
VANDERBEEK, Jurrien and Marietje—Arie—Nov. 12.
    Wit: Hans A. and Jacomyn Ackerman.
HOPPE, Albert and Rachel—Abraham—Nov. 9.
    Wit: Abram and Jacomyntje Alyie.
ACKERMAN, David D. and Annatje—Annatje—Nov. 19.
    Wit: Gerrit D. and Lena Ackerman.
ZABRISKIE, Jacob H. and Wyntje—Antje—Feb. 5.
    Wit: Dirk and Antje Terhuyn.

1759

HOPPE, Andries J. and Marytje—Antje—Apr. 9.
    Wit: Nicklaas and Semme (?) Demarest.
STORM, Abram and Aaltje—Annatje, b. June 21—July 22.
    Wit: David H. Ackerman; Annatje C. Demarest.

VANDERBEEK, Abram and Sara—Abram, b. June 26.
Wit: Abram A. and Lena Ackerman.

ACKERMAN, Gerrit D. and Lena—Abraham—Sept. 3.
Wit: Hannes H. and Lena Ackerman.

TERHUYN, Dirk and Lea—Andries—Sept. 23.
Wit: Andries H. and Antje Hoppe.

CADMUS, Fredrik and Saartje—Abram, b. Nov. 27—Dec. 25.
Wit: Abram and Lea (?) Cadmus.

1760

VANDIEN, Gerrit and Saartje—Albert—Feb. 17.
Wit: Jan Ackerman; Rachel Vandien.

SIDMAN, Samuel and Angonietje—Angonietje—Mar. 30.
Wit: Willem and Catrina Syourt.

POST, Frans A. and Rachel—Aaltje, b. Feb. 7.—Apr. 13.
Wit: Cornelis Y. and Janneke Westervelt.

ZABRISKIE, Jacob H. and Wyntje—Albert—Oct. 18.
Wit: Albert H. and Thellitie Zabriskie.

LUTKENS, Hendrik and Lybe—Antje—Dec. 4.
Wit: Jan and Belitje Deremus.

1761

BOGART, Cobus and Cornelia—Antje—Jan. 24.
Wit: Antje and Steven Bogert.

STORM, Hendrik and Cornelia—Angonietje—Mar. 29.
Wit: Jacob and Saartje Hoppe.

HOPPE, Marytje—Andries—Apr. 12.
Wit: Hendrik I. and Trientje Hoppe.

ZABRISKIE, Jacob I. and Jannitje—Aaltje—June 14.
Wit: Jan and Aaltje Zabriskie.

VERSEUR, Johannis and Lena—Abraham, b. June 26—Aug. 2.
Wit: Abram and Annatje Banta.

ACKERMAN, Hannes and Jacomyntje—Arie—Sept. 1.
Wit: Arie and Ariaantje Ackerman.

ACKERMAN, Gerrit D. and Lena—Abigael—Dec. 20.
Wit: Lambertus and Lybe Laroi.

1762

WRITE, Willem and Aaltje—Albert—Feb. 14.
Wit: Albert C. and Aaltje Zabriske.

POST, Hannes and Catrintje—Abram—Feb. 14.
Wit: Abram and Saartje Rutan.

TERHUYN, Dirk and Lea—Abraham—Mar. 20.
Wit: Abram and Marytje Terhuyn.

HOPPE, David and Rachel—Ariaantje, b. Apr. 6—Apr. 25.
Wit: Hannes and Ariaantje Van Emburgh.

VANDIEN, Gerrit and Sara—Antje—Oct. 17.
Wit: Hendrik and Lybe Lutkens.

ZABRISKE, Jacob H. and Wyntje—Aaltje—Oct. 31.
Wit: Jacob I. and Aaltje Zabriske.

1763

BOGERT, Steven and Rachel—Antje—Jan. 9.
Wit: Cobus and Cornelia Bogert.

WESTERVELT, Roelof and Tryntje—Albert—Apr. 17.
Wit: Albert and Rachel Ackerman.

PILESFELT, Willem and Lisabeth—Abram, b. Aug. 1—Aug. 21.
Wit: Abram A. and Lena Ackerman.

1764

HOPPE, Jacob and Saartje—Abram, b. Jan. 11—Feb. 19.
Wit: Abram and Rebecka Hoppe.

SYOURT, Willem and Catrina—Adolf, b. June 8—July 8.
Wit: Hannes and Lisabeth Syourt.

DUBAEN, Jacob and Marietje—Antje—Oct. 28.
Wit: David D. and Annatje Ackerman.

ECKERSEN, David and Angenietje—Annatje, b. Aug. 15—Sept. 2.

1765

TOIRS, Laurens and Lisabeth—Arie, b. Jan. 6—Jan. 10.
Wit: Jurrien and Marytje Vanderbeek.

WRITE, Willem and Aaltje—Abram—Apr. 28.
Wit: Gerrit and Sara Van Dien.

VAN ZEYL, Petrus and Jannitje—Abram—Apr. 28.
Wit: Hendrik and Marytje Messiker.

FERSEUR, Hannes and Lena—Annatje, b. May 4—May 26.
Wit: Abram and Annatje Banta.

HOPPE, Andries A. and Lisbeth—Abraham—June 23.
Wit: Abram and Rebecka Hoppe.

ACKERMAN, Abram and Marytje—Antje—Oct. 22.
Wit: Jan J. Zabriske; Wyntje Hoppe.

BANTA, Cornelis A. and Maria—Annatje—Nov. —.
Wit: Jacob and Annaatje Banta.

BOGERT, Jacob and Marytje—Annatje—Nov. 24.
Wit: Cobus and Willempje Rutan.

TERHUYN, Samuel and Lea—Antje—Dec. 19.
Wit: Albert and Sara Terhuyn.

KUYPER, Abram and Sara—Abram, b. Mar. 26—Apr. 27.
Wit: Daniel and Lisabeth Blauvelt.

ACKERMAN, David A. and Myntje—Abram, b. June 15—June 29.
Wit: Abram J. and Brechtje Ackerman.

BANTA, Jan and Lena—Antje, b. Oct. 21—Nov. 16.
Wit: Paulus and Jannitje Rutan.

1767

VAN ORDEN, Jan and Jannetje—Aaltje—Jan. 4.
Wit: Hendrik and Marietje Oldes.

ACKERMAN, David J. and Nietie—Antje—Jan. 18.
Wit: Cobus and Cornelia Bogert.

BANTA, Samuel and Lisabeth—Abram, b. Apr. 13—May 3.
Wit: Johannis and Lena Verscheur.

PIETERSE, Niklaas and Maria—Andries, b. Apr. 18—May 17.
Wit: Andries and Saartje Pieterse.

ACKERMAN, Willem and Grietje—Albert—Apr. 24.
Wit: Albert V. and Marytje Voorhees.

BROUWER, Abram D.—Abram—July 19.
Wit: Abram and Saartje Rutan.

WOERTENDYK, Rynier and wife—Aaltje—July 19.
Wit: Frederik and Jemyma Woertendyk.

HOPPE, Albert and Rachel—Andries—Sept. 27.
Wit: Johannes J. and Lena Ackerman.

BOGERT, Petrus P. and Maria—Abram—Nov. 15.
Wit: Abram J. and Brechje Ackerman.

VAN BLERCOM, Pieter H. and Jannitje—Aaltje—Nov. 15.
Wit: David H. and Antje P. Van blerkom.

1768

TERHUYN, Dirk A. and Lea—Andries—Mar. 6.
Wit: Andries J. and Cristina Zabriske.

HOPPE, Abram H. and Antje—Aaltje—Aug. 7.
Wit: Jacob J. and Aaltje Zabriske.

JACOBUSSE, Brand B. and Geertje—Antje—Sept. 19.
Wit: Pieter and Trientje Van Wagene.

1767

DEVOE, Jan and Aaltje—Abraham—May 3.

1768

STORM, Hendrik and Cornelia—Abram—Nov. 13.
Wit: Andries A. Hoppe and Marytje Hoppe.

CHRISTIE, Andries and Abigail—Antje, b. Nov. 26—Dec. 25.
Wit: Willem and Antje Hoppe.

WESSELS, Joseph and Ariaantje—Ariaantje—Dec. 25.
Wit: Hendrik and Marytje Oldes.

VESEUR, Barend and Syntje—Annatje—Dec. 25.
Wit: Gerrit and Annatje Blauvelt.

1769

WOERTENDYK, Rynier and his 2nd wife—Albert, b. Jan. 23—Feb. 5.

ECKERSEN, David and Angonietje—Angonietje, b. Jan. 11—Feb. 26.
Wit: Paulus C. and Annatje Vanderbeek.

ALYE, Albert and Maria—Albert—Mar. 12.
Wit: Albert and Rachel Hoppe.

BOGERT, Steven and Rachel—Antje, b. June 20—July 2.
Wit: Jan and Willempje Dumaree.

STAGG, Isaac and Helena—Abraham—Aug. 27.
Wit: Thomas and Geertje Banta.

HOPPE, Andries A. and Marytje—Andries—Sept. 3.
Wit: Andries I. and Elisabeth Hoppe.

RUTAN, Johannis P. and Cathalyntje—Abraham—Sept. 1.
Wit: Abraham and Saartje Rutan.

HENNION, David D. and Tryntje—Andries—Oct. 15.
Wit: Elisabeth and Johannis Hennion.

ZABRISKE, Jacob J. and Jannitje—Antje—Nov. 5.
Wit: Jan J. and Lea Zabriskie.

HOPPE, David and Rachel—Abigail, b. Nov. 26—Nov. 30.
Wit: Jan and Aaltje Zabriske.

RUTAN, Pieter and Jannetje—Abraham—Dec. 24.
Wit: Abram W. and Grietje Rutan.

HOPPE, Gerret H. and Antje—Albert—Dec. 24.
Wit: Andries A. and Jannetje Zabriskie.

1770

RYKER, Hendrik and Grace—Abraham—Jan. 14.
Wit: Abraham and Polly Bricker.

BANTA, Jacob and Rachel—Abram, Jan. 14.

HOPPE, Jan J. and Geertje—Andries—Mar. 25.
Wit: Abram and Marytje Ackerman.

DUMAREE, Albert C. and Rachel—Albert, b. June 19—July 8.
Wit: Albert and Lea Deryie.

DUBAEN, Abram and Brechje—Abraham, b. June 14—July 8.
Wit: Christiaen and Rachel Dubaen.

TERHUYN, Dirk and Lea—Albert—July 29.
Wit: Albert A. and Betje Terhuyn.

RUTAN, Cobus and Willempje—Albert—Aug. 24.
Wit: Albert and Machtel Bogert.

ZABRISKIE, Jan J. and Lea—Aaltje—Sept. 30.
Wit: Jan and Aaltje Zabriske.

LUTKENS, Pieter and Lisabeth—Antje—Sept. 30.
Wit: Harme H. and Antie Lutkens.

SUDDERLAND, James and Marietje—Antje—Dec. 6.
Wit: Jan and Lea Maybe.

WINTER, Hannes and Sara—Abram—Dec. 9.
Wit: Abram V. Voorheesen.

1771

PERRIE, Cobus and Annatje—Annatje—Feb. 24.
Wit: Daniel and Jannetje Perrie.

VAN BLERKOM, Isaac and Saartje—Annatje—Feb. 24.
Wit: Jonathan and Annatje Wealer.

QUACKENBOS, Abram and Gerritie—Anna Elisabeth, b. May 23—June 23.
Wit: Abram C. Herring; Wyntje Quackenbos.

DUMAREE, Samuel B. and Rebecka—Annatje—June 30.
Wit: David and Annatje Dumaree.

DUREMES, Johannes and Jannitje—Abraham, b. Oct. 3—Nov. 3.
Wit: Jonathan and Trientje Traphagen.

MYER, Jacob D. and Abigail—Annatje—Nov. 3.
Wit: Abel and Annatje Riddenaar.

CHRISTIE, Andries and Abigail—Antje, b. Nov. 3—Dec. 22.
Wit: Willem and Antje Hoppe.

1772

ZABRISKE, Hendrik C. and Maria—Abram—Jan. 2.
Wit: Petrus A. and Catrina Haring.

ACKERMAN, David D. and Jannetje—Aaltje—June 9.
Wit: Jacobus and Tittie Pilesfelt.

ALYEE, Albert and Maria—Albert—June 28.
Wit: Albert and Rachel Hoppe.

POST, Isaac and Jannetje—Abram—Sept. 6.
Wit: Abram and Sara Post.

MARIE, Jan and Lea—Abram—Dec. 6.
Wit: Abram W. and Grietje Rutan.

TRAPHAGEN, Jonathan and Trientje—Annatje, b. Nov. 2—Dec. 6.

DOBBS, William and Rachel—Abigael, Dec. 6.

1773

VAN VOORHEESE, Jan W. and Lea—Albert and Jacobus (twins)—Feb. 21.
Wit: Albert W. and Jannitje Van Voorhees; Petrus J. and Marietje
Van Blerkom.

TOIRS, Laurens and Lisabeth—Annaatje—Mar. 7.
Wit: Arie and Annatje Vanderbeek.

HERRING, Jan D. and Lisabeth—Ariaantje, b. Feb. 22—Mar. 21.

CHRISTIE, James and Bethsie—Antje—Apr. 11.
Wit: Abram and Marytje Ackerman.

GARDENIER, Hans and Jacomyntje—Annatje—June 6.
Wit: Abram and Annatje Banta.

TERHUYN, Steven D. and Jannetje—Albert—June 6.
Wit: Albert C. and Aaltje Zabriske.

ZABRISKE, Abram and Marietje—Albert—July 11.
Wit: Albert H. and Jannitje A. Zabriske.

TERHUYN, Abram and Marytje—Abraham—Aug. 29.
Wit: Hannes and Antje Westervelt.

1774

BANTA, Jacob A. and Rachel—Annatje—Jan. 3.
Wit: Abram and Annatje Banta.

DUBOUW, Pieter A. and Gerrebrecht—Andries—Jan. 23.
Wit: Andries and Jannitje Dubow.

TERHUYN, Samuel and Lea—Albert—Apr. 29.
Wit: Albert and Sara Terhuyn.

POST, Abram and Jannitje—Annaatje—Sept. 4.
Pieter and Annatje Jersie.

SMITH, Willem and Grietje—Annatje—Sept. 12.
Wit: Frans Smith; Annatje Dumaree.

HOPPE, Andries and Maria—Antje—Oct. 9.
Wit: Abram G. and Lea Gerritse.

WARENT, John and Elisabeth—Antje—Nov. 6.
Wit: Cornelis and Lisabeth Ackerman.

HELM, Samuel and Trina—Annatje, b. Nov. 31—Dec. 18.
Wit: Benjamin and Annatje Zabriske.

1775

VANDERBEEK, Abram J. and Susanna—Abraham—Jan. 22.
Wit: Hannes and Abigael Vanderbeek.

VANGELDER, Cobus and Jannitje—Annatje, b. Jan. 30—Feb. 19.
Wit: Abram D. and Annatje Ackerman.

V[AN] BLERKOM, Devid J. and Gerritje—Abram—Mar. 12.
Wit: Jan and Lea Maybe.

BOGERT, Steven and Geesje—Angonietje—Apr. 23.
Wit: David J. and Antje Ackerman.

BOGERT, Joost C. and Marietje—Aaltje—May 14.
Wit: Jan I. and Lea Zabriske.

VANHOREN, Cornelis C. and Geesje—Adam, b. Aug. 14—Sept. 10.
Wit: Adam and Grietje Van Orden.

BONGERT, Andries and Trientje—Andries—Oct. 1.
Wit: Cristiaan I. and Marietje Zobriskie.

STEGG, Isaac and Lena—Angonietje—Oct. 22.
Wit: David J. and Antje Ackerman.

ZABRISKE, Joost C. and Polly—Antje—Dec. 26.
Wit: Jan A. and Antje G. Hoppe.

1776

ZOBRISKE, Jacob H. and Wyntje—Abraham—Jan. 14.
Wit: Albert A. Terhuyn; Marietje I. Zobriske.

VAN GELDER, Hendrik and Antje—Antje—Feb. 4.
Wit: Abram and Grietje Van Voorhese.

RIDNAER, Coenraad and Elisabeth—Abel, b. Jan. 28—Feb. 18.
Wit: Abel and Susanna Ridnaer.

MEYER, Martin J. and Gerrebrecht—Aaltje, b. Feb. 19—Mar. 9.
Wit: Hannes D. and Aaltje Ackerman.

VAN VOORHESE, Isaac L. and Pryntje—Albert, b. Feb. 19—Mar. 17.
Wit: Albert and Rachel Ackerman.

HOPPE, Gerret H. and Antje—Andries—Apr. 21.
Wit: Jan J. and Lea Zabriske.

BOGERT, Cobus J. and Cornelia—Angonietje—May 5.
Wit: David H. and Antje Ackerman.

HOPPE, Abram H. and Antje—Antje—June 16.
Wit: Jan J. and Lea Zabriske.

DEGROOT, David and Elsje—Angonietje—Aug. 25.
Wit: Isaac and Syntje Dey.

LUTKENS, Jan and Grietje—Antje—Sept. 15.
Wit: Cornelis and Sara Vandien.

DOREMES, Hannis and Jannitje—Andries, b. Sept. 4—Oct. 6.
Wit: Andries A. and Annatje Van Boskerk.

POST, Jacob and Saartje—Abram, b. Sept. 11—Oct. 6.
Wit: Abram and Jannitje Post.

HOPPE, Jonathan and Grietje—Albert—Oct. 6.
Wit: Albert and Rachel Hoppe.

1778

TERHUYN, Steve D. and Jannitje—Albert—Aug. 2.
Wit: Jan J. and Lea Zabriske.

VAN BLERCUM, Pieter and Jannitje—Antje, b. Dec. 9—Dec. 20.
Wit: Isaac and Antje Bogert.

1779

VAN BLERCOM, Lena—Antje—Sept. 2.
Wit: William and Grietje Smith.

ZABRISKIE, Christian and Martyntje—Andries—Dec. 24.
Wit: Andries and Lisabeth Zabriskie.

1780

VAN ORDER, Jannitje—Abel—Apr. 9.
Wit: David and Pollie Van Blercom.

PULISFELT, Andries—Andries—Apr. 8.

ACKERMAN, David G. and Aaltje—Albert—Nov. 19.
Wit: Albert and Lisabeth Terhuyn.

1781

ZABRISKIE, Albert J. and Matje—Aaltje—Sept. 2.
Wit: Abraham H. and Antje Hopper.

HOPPER, Jan H. and Fytje—Annetje—Sept. 2.
Wit: Hendrik and Margriet Doremus.

VALENTYNE, Jacob and Grietje—Abraham—Nov. 1.

VAN BLERCOM, Hannes and Rebecca—Albert—Nov. 10.
Wit: Albert W. and Jannitje Van Voorhese.

1782

V[AN] BOSKERCK, Thomas A. and Maria—Annatje—Feb. 17.

1783

VAN HOORN, Cornelis—Andois—Feb. 16.

1782

ZABRISKE, Andries and Carstina—Aaltje—Dec. 11.
Wit: Albert and Geesje Zabriske.

1783?

VAN BEECK, Arie—Annatje—Aug. 25.
Wit: Jacobus Bogert and wife.

HOPPE, Gerrit—Albert—Sept. 1.
Wit: Albert and Rachel Banta.

1783

LUTKENS, Harmen—Antje—Sept. 7.
Wit: Jan Vandebeek and wife.

ACKERMAN, Jan—Antje—Dec. 7.
Wit: Johannis Ratan and wife.

WILSEN, Albert—Antje—Dec. 15.
Wit: Abraham Hoppe and wife.

1784

VAN BLERCOM, Pieter—Andries—Aug. 8.

TERHUNE, Steven and Jannitje—Annatje—Aug. 22.
Wit: David and Annatje Terhune.

HOPPE, Abraham—Andries—Aug. 22.
Wit: Andries Hoppe and wife.

1785

MEYER, Marte—Abraham—Jan. 1.

VAN BLERCOM, Pieter—Annatje—Feb. 20.
Wit: Lewis Meltenberrie and wife.

POST, Pieter—Abram—Mar. 20.
Wit: Laurens Van Orden and wife.

McPHERSON, Abraham and Jennie—Antje, b. Apr. 15—May 22.

1786

GERRITSE, Johannis and Maria—Albert, b. Mar. 26—Apr. 16.
Wit: Wyntje Zabriske.

HOPPE, Hendrik and Jacomyntje—Andreas, b. Aug. 5—Sept. 10.
Wit: Pieter and Antje Hoppe.

1789

BERTOLF, Jacobus and Lea—Abraham, b. Feb. 10—Mar. 1.
Wit: Abraham and Grietje Rotan.

Hoppe, Isaac and Rachel—Albert, b. Feb. 14—Mar. 15.

Hoppe, Gerrit J. and Maria—Arie, b. Feb. 26—Mar. 22.

Van Blercom, Johannis and Rebecka—Annaatje, b. Mar. 2—Apr. 4.
Wit: William and Annaatje Van Voorhesen.

Woertendyk, Cornelis and Sophia—Abraham, b. July 3—July 19.

Ackerman, Arie and Christina—Aart Cuyper, b. Aug. 2—Aug. 23.

1790

Van Boskerk, Jan and Sara—Annaatje, b. Dec. 12, 1789—Jan. 24.
Wit: Jacob and Annaatje Servent.

Van Hoorn, Daniel and Annatje—Antje—Jan. 31.
Wit: Pieter and Antje Demarest.

Messeker, Lodewyk and Sara—Abraham—Mar. 14.

Durie, Petrus and Osseltje—Annatje, b. Feb. 13—Mar. 15.
Wit: Daniel and Annatje Demarest.

Hoppe, Hendrik G. and Rachel—Albert, b. June 12—Aug. 4.
Wit: Albert G. and Rachel Hoppe.

Eckerson, Edward and Catrina—Angonietje, b. May 18—Aug. —.
Wit: David and Angenietje Eckerson.

Fesyuer, Abraham and Elisabeth—Annatje—Oct. —.

Debaen, Petrus and Maria—Angonietje, b. Sept. 6—Oct. —.
Wit: David and Angonietje Eckerson.

Gerritsen, Johannis and Maria—Antje, b. Dec. 1—Dec. 5.
Wit: Abraham and Antje Hoppe.

1791

Snyder, Jacob and Grietje—Adam, b. Dec. 13, 1790—Jan. 3.

Vanderbeek, Coenradus and Annaatje—Angenietje, b. Dec. 15, 1790.
Jan. 3.
Wit: Jurrie and Maria Vanderbeek.

Banta, Hendrik and Margrietje—Angenietje, b. Jan. 2—Feb. —.
Wit: Jacob and Hester Banta.

Ackerman, David and Jannitje—Abraham, b. Feb. 6—Feb. 24.?
Wit: Abraham and Maria Blauvelt.

Zabriskie, Christiaan A. and Maria—Abraham, b. May 3.

VenderBeck, Jan and Aaltje—Abraham, b. May 27.
Wit: Abraham H. and Antje Hoppe.

Smyth, John and Sara—Antje, b. Apr. 10—June 29.
Wit: David and Jacomyntje Ackerman.

Schuyler, Adonia and Elisabeth—Arend, b. Apr. 26—June 12.

Hoppe, Jan J. and Catrina—Antje, b. July 12—Aug. 4.
Wit: Gerrit H. and Antje Hoppe.

Eckerson, Edward P. and Hetty—Annatje, b. July 29—Aug. 21.
Wit: Jacob and Annatje Servent.

Bos, Pieter and Frone—Annatje, b. Aug. 27—Oct. 2.
Wit: Edward P. and Hette Eckerson.

1786

Janse, Abraham and Elisabeth—Aaltje, b. Sept. 23—Oct. —.
Wit: Cornelis and Sara Van Hoorn.

V[an] Blerkom, Johannis and Rebecka—Abigail, b. Sept. 15—Oct. 8.

1787

BLAUVELT, Abraham and Margrietje—Abraham, b. July 9, 1786—Jan. 2.

DEBOW, Andreas and Francyntje—Abraham, b. Oct. 6.
Wit: Hendrik and Jannitje Terhuun.

HORN, Joseph and Maria—Andreas, b. Jan. 17—Mar. 4.
Wit: Andreas and Catrina Hoppe.

BOGERT, Albert I. and Maria—Aaltje, b. Jan. 27—Mar. 11.
Wit: Hendrik and Aaltje Storm.

WRITE, Albert and Geertje—Aaltje—Aaltje, b. May 28—June 21.
Wit: Jan J. and Lea Zabriskie.

ZABRISKE, Abraham and Maria—Aaltje, b. July 3—July 15.
Wit: David G. and Aaltje Ackerman.

HOPPE, Hendrik G. and Rachel—Aaltje, b. Aug. 14—Sept. 9.
Wit: Abraham and Antje Hoppe.

DEBOW, Pieter and Susanna—Annatje—Oct. 28.
Wit: William and Annatje Van Voorhesen.

1788

HOPPE, Gerrit I. and Maria—Abraham—Feb. 3.
Wit: Abraham I. and Geertje Hoppe.

BERTOLF, Samuel and Elsje—Albert—Feb. 3.

ECKERSON, Thomas and Susanna—Angenietje, b. Jan. 4—Feb. 3.
Wit: David and Angenietje Eckerson.

VAN HOORN, Cornelis B. and Sara—Antje, b. Apr. 1—Apr. 20.
Wit: David and Antje Ackerman.

SMITH, Albert and Susanna—Albert, b. Mar. 15—Apr. 20.

HOPPE, Petrus and Elisabeth—Albert—May 4.

BROWER, Petrus and Rachel—Abraham, b. June 8—June 22.
Wit: Johannes and Annatje Ackerman.

CUYPER, Hendrik and Antje—Andrew—July 20.
Wit: Andrew and Maritje Van Orden.

BROWN, James and Anna—Anna—July 20.

VAN RYPEN, Johannis and Geertje—Antje, b. Sept. 13—Sept. 28.
Wit: Gerrit and Abigail Van Rypen.

MEBIE, Isaac and Sara—Abraham, b. Sept. 19—Oct. 19.
Wit: Jacob and Sara Post.

ACKERMAN, Johannis and Elisabeth—Annatje—Nov. 16.
Wit: Jacobus and Annatje Perry.

JANSE, Abraham and Elisabeth—Abraham, b. Dec. 6—Dec. 21.
Wit: Abraham and Maria Blauvelt.

1789

VANDERBEEK, Jacob and Maria—Abraham, b. Dec. 16, 1788—Jan. 18.
Wit: Abraham and Jannetje Vanderbeek.

SMIT, Abraham and Grietje—Aaltje, b. Oct. 17, 1788—Jan. 18.
Wit: Arie and Aaltje Blauvelt.

ACKERMAN, John and Annatje—Abraham, b. Jan. 4—Jan. 29.
Wit: Petrus and Rachel Brower.

VANDERBEEK, Cornelis and Hilletje—Abram, b. Sept. 12—Oct. 9.
Wit: Abraham and Susanna Vanderbeek.

1792

ZABRISKE, Abraham and Maria—Abraham, b. Feb. 17—Feb. 26.
  Wit: Albert and Aaltje Terhuen.

ZABRISKE, Albert and Metje—Albert, b. Mar. 25—Apr. 10.

ECKERSON, Thomas and Susanna—Annatje, b. Mar. 25—June 16.
  Wit: Abraham and Annaatje Lesyer.

DEBAEN, Joost—Antje, b. May 27—June 16.
  Wit: Jacob and Antje Debaen.

FOLLE, Willem and Antje—Adam, b. May 29—June 16.
  Wit: Thomas and Hester Stag.

VANDERBEEK, Arie and Lena—Angenietje, b. Apr. 24—June 21.

BROUWER, Petrus and Rachel—Antje—Nov. 11.
  Wit: Harman and Antje Vanderbeek.

1793

BOGERT, Albert and Maria—Abraham, b. Oct. 18, 1792—Feb. 10.

ACKERMAN, Jacobus and Annatje—Abraham, b. Mar. 8—Mar. 31.
  Wit: Paulus and Rachel Vanboskerk.

VAN IMBURG, Hendrik and Maria—Albert, b. June 25—July 7.
  Wit: Albert and Maritje Van Voorhesen.

McCALL, John and Geertrui—Archibald, b. Apr. 28—July 7.

VAN VOORHESEN, Jan and Tryntje—Abraham—Aug. 4.
  Wit: Jacobus and Maria Ackerman.

VANDEVOTE, Paul and Elisabeth—Abraham, b. July 10—Aug. 4.
  Wit: John and Lena Romyn.

POOST, John and Annatje—Abraham and Elisabeth (twins), b. Aug. 26—
  Sept. 22.
  Wit: Isaak and Sara Mebe.

CAMPBELL, John and Jane—Archibold, b. Aug. 28—Sept. 15.

HORN, Jacob and Femmetje—Abraham, b. Sept. 11—Oct. 20.
  Wit: Johannes and Jannitje Dremus.

DEBAEN, Petrus and Maria—Antje, b. Oct. 23—Nov. 17.
  Wit: Jacob and Antje Debaan.

BOS, Dirk and Antje—Antje, b. Nov. 22—Dec. 15.
  Wit: Lodewyck and Leentje Bos.

1794

HOPPE, Stephen and Geertje—Abraham, b. Jan. 6—Jan. 19.
  Wit: Albert and Aaltje Terhune.

WESTERVELT, Abraham and Antje—Abraham, b. Jan. 6—Jan. 14.

POTTER, John and Maria—Adam, b. Jan. 7.—Jan. 26.

ACKERMAN, David and Aaltje—Abraham, b. Jan. 30—Feb. 9.
  Wit: Abraham and Margrietje Rotan.

ACKERMAN, Abraham and Elisabeth—Albert, b. Jan. 10—Feb. 9.
  Wit: Johannis and Lena Pecker.

ACKERMAN, Jacobus G. and Rachel—Annatje, b. Jan. 28—Feb. 23.
  Wit: Cornelis and Hester Van Saan.

WOERTENDYK, Albert and Grietje—Abraham, b. Feb. 16—Mar. 16.
  Wit: Abraham and Lea Debaan.

VAN ORDEN, Thomas and Lea—Aaltje, b. Feb. 13—Mar. 20.
  Wit: David D. and Metje Ackerman.

WOERTENDYK, Cornelius and Sophia—Abraham, b. Apr. 17—May 18.
HOPPE, Hendrik and Aaltje—Aaltje, b. June 29—July 27.
Wit: Andrias and Elisabeth Hoppe.
VAN RYPEN, Johannis and Geertje—Adriaan, b. July 9—July 27.
Wit: Abraham and Catrina Cadmus.
BLAUVELT, Frederick and Elisabeth—Aaltje, b. July 30—Aug. 31.
Wit: Aaltje Blauvelt.
RIDDENAAR, John and Catrina Van Houten—Abel, b. Mar. 14—Aug. 31.
V[AN]D BEEK, Cornelis and Hilletje—Andreas, b. Sept. 23—Oct. 26.
FESJEUR, Abraham and Elisabeth—Abraham, b. Sept. 25—Nov. 2.
BOGERT, Casparus and Jannitje—Andreas, b. Oct. 8—Nov. 9.
Wit: Christiaan and Maria Zabriske.
ZABRISKE, Jan and Jannetje—Andreas, b. Nov. 1—Nov. 23.
Wit: Andreas and Christina Zabriske.
VAN RYPE, Frederick and Maria—Angenietje, b. Oct. 1—Nov. 23.
Wit: Maria V. d. Beek.

1795

ACKERMAN, Johannis and Annatje—Arie, b. Dec. 27, 1794—Feb. 11.
Wit: David and Metje Ackerman.
VANHOORN, John and Elisabeth—Abraham, b. Jan. 31—Feb. 19.
Wit: Abraham and Geertje Hoppe.
ACKERMAN, Gerrit and Geertje—Aaltje, b. Feb. 15—Mar. 5.
Wit: David and Aaltje Ackerman.
TERHUNE, Jacob and Maria—Abraham, Feb. 22—Mar. 15.
Wit: Abraham Terhune.
WRIGHT, John and Abigail—Aaltje, b. May 18—June 28.
Wit: Cornelis and Aaltje Bogert.
Bos, Dirk and Antje—Antje, b. July 11—July 19.
Wit: Lodewyk and Leentje Bos.
TERHUNE, Albert and Aaltje—Abraham, b. July 4—Aug. 9.
Wit: Hendrik and Rachel Terhune.
VAN KLEEFT, Joseph and Elisabeth—Abraham, b. Aug. 5—Sept. 20.
BEYERD, David and Grietje—Adam—Oct. 18.
Wit: Coenraad and Maria Wannemaker.
WOERTENDYCK, Reinier and Annaatje—Abraham, b. Nov. 3—Nov. 22.
Wit: Abraham and Elisabeth Fesjeur.
ACKERMAN, Johannis and Maria—Angenietje, b. Oct. 27—Nov. 22.

1796

ACKERMAN, Daniel and Cathalyntje—Annatje, b. Jan. 6—Jan. 24.
Wit: John and Annaatje Christe.
VANDERBEEK, Coenraad and Annatje—Angenietje, b. Mar. 3—Mar. 27.
LESIER, Abraham and Annaatje—Angenietje and Maria, b. Jan. 18—Mar. 28.
Wit: David and Angenietje Eckersen; Petrus and Maria Debaan.
MASSEKER, Dirk and Lena—Aaltje, b. Dec. 8, 1795—Apr. 3.
ROTAN, Jan and Rachel—Abram, b. July 4—Aug. 7.
Wit: Abraham and Susanna V. d. Beek.
DECKER, Cornelius and Lea—Antje, b. June 4—Aug. 7.
Wit: Elizabeth Carlough.

DOREMUS, Andries and Abigael—Annaatje, b. Sept. 11—Sept. 25.
Wit: Johannes and Jannetje Doremus.

BROUWER, John and Catrina—Abraham, b. Nov. 9—Dec. 25.

TERHUEN, Albert and Rachel—Abraham, b. Oct. 15.

1797

ZABRISKE, Albert and Metje—Antje, b. Jan. 17—Feb. 19.

WRIGHT, Abraham and Annatje—Aaltje, b. Mar. 25—Apr. 23.

HOPPE, Hendrik A. and Charity—Abraham, b. Apr. 26—May 21.
Wit: Abraham H. and Antje Hoppe.

ROTAN, Daniel and Jannetje—Abram, b. July 5—Aug. 20.
Wit: Abram and Angenietje Van Voorhesen.

DEBAEN, Jacob and Geesje—Annaatje, b. July 4—Sept. 2.
Wit: Thomas and Geertje Banta.

MEBE, Pieter and Jannitje—Annatje, b. Aug. 25—Sept. 2.

BANTA, Abraham and Dievertje—Abraham, b. Sept. 17—Dec. 24.

1798

RIDMAN, Abraham and Elisabeth—Abraham, b. Jan. 28—Feb. 11.
Wit: Gerritje Van Blercum.

HOPPE, Adries and Sara—Albert, b. Mar. 22—Apr. 15.

ACKERMAN, Gerrit and Geertje—Andreas, b. May 5—May 29.

DEBAEN, Petrus and Maria—Annaatje, b. May 17—June 3.
Wit: Abraham and Annatje Lesier.

FESYEUR, Abraham and Elisabeth—Antje, b. Jan. 27—June 20.
Wit: Jacob and Antje Debaan.

DURIE, John and Rachel—Annaatje, b. May 25—June 20.

POULISVELT, Pieter and Nansje—Annaatje, b. May 24—June 20.

1799

VAN BOSKERCK, Pieter and Selle—Abraham, b. Nov. 21, 1798—Apr. 14.
Wit: Abraham and Jennie Van Boskerck.

HEDDE, Jesaia and Elisabeth—Antje—Mar. 15.
Wit: Jose and Aaltje Poost.

ZABRISKE, Jacob and Elisabeth—Aaltje, b. Apr. 16—July 7.
Wit: Hendrik and Aaltje Hopper.

Bos, Lodewyk and Leentje—Andrias, b. May 6—July 7.
Wit: Andrias and Jannetje Debaan.

ACKERMAN, Daniel and Teyne—Antje, b. Aug. 24—Sept. 8.
Wit: Willem and Antje Christie.

ECKERSON, Paulus and Maria—Angenietje, b. Aug. 6—Oct. 6.
Wit: David and Angenietje Eckerson.

TERHUNE, John and Egje—Annatje, b. Sept. 25—Oct. 27.
Wit: Christiaan A. and Maria Zabriske.

ZABRISKE, Nicholas and Annatje—Annatje, b. Oct. 19—Nov. 10.
Wit: Benjamin and Annatje Zabriskie.

MORE, John and Jane—Anna, b. Oct. 23—Dec. 15.

1800

HOPPER, Andrew and Antie—Albert, b. Dec. 30, 1799—Jan. 23.
Wit: Albert and Marytje Van Voorhees.

BANTA, Thomas and Peggy—Antje, b. Oct. 10, 1799—Feb. 2.

ZABRISKIE, Albert and Aaltje—Albert, b. Jan. 11—Feb. 16.

VAN SCHYVEN, William and Saartje—Abraham, b. Feb. 20—Apr. 6.
Wit: John and Aaltje Debaen.

ZABRISKIE, Jacob and Wyntje—Aaltje, b. May 21—July 17.
Wit: Albert and Aaltje Terhune.

ACKERMAN, Gerrit and Geertje—Andreas, b. Aug. 7—Aug. 24.

LESIER, Abraham and Annatje—Abraham, b. Sept. 25—Nov. 30.

1801

DEMAREST, Nicholas and Maria—Abraham, b. Sept. 14, 1800—Feb. 22.

DEMAREST, David and Grietje—Annatje, b. Apr. 22, 1800—Feb. 22.

ALYEA, Hendrik and Sara—Annatje, b. Mar. 25, 1799—Feb. 22.

DOREMUS, Jacobus and Polly—Annatje, b. Jan. 26—March 1.

SNYDER, Andries and Rachel—Andreas, b. Apr. 2—April 26.

STORM, Staats and Margrietje—Abraham, b. Apr. 14—May 3.

ECKERSON, John and Geertje—Angenietje, b. Apr. 16—May 20.
Wit: David and Angenietje Eckerson.

BLAUVELT, Fredrik and Elisabeth—Annatje, b. May 30—June 12.

WESTERVELT, Petrus and Martyntje—Angenietje, b. June 3—June 21.
Wit: John and Angenietje Westervelt.

TERHUNE, Abraham and Tryntje—Abraham, b. Nov 16—Dec. 13.

HOPPER, Isaac and Rachel—Albert, b. Jan. 29—Feb. 14.

DEBAEN, Andries and Jannitje—Antje, b. Apr. 5—Apr. 7.
Wit: Jacob and Antje Debaan.

WESTERVELT, Lukas and Maria—Antje, b. Sept. 8—Oct. 3.

QUACKENBOSH, Teunis and Maria—Annatje, b. Aug. 19—Oct. 3.
Wit: John and Elisabeth Quackenbush.

1802

VAN RYPEN, Cornelius and Elisabeth—Antje, b. Sept. 14—Oct. 17.

QUACKENBUSH, Barend and Catrina—Abraham, b. Sept. 26—Oct. 24.

LEZIER, Abraham and Annatje—Annatje, b. Sept. 5—Oct. 31.
Wit: Thomas and Angenietje Tours.

ZABRISKIE, Jacob and Elisabeth—Albert, b. Oct. 30—Nov. 28.

GROAVELT, Joseph A. and Sally—Anny, b. Oct. 4—Dec. 12.

1803

HOPPER, Nacasie and Mary—Andreas, b. Dec. 23, 1802—Jan. 23.

ECKERSON, Thomas and Susanna—Abraham, b. Dec. 25, 1802—Jan. 23.
Wit: Abraham and Margaret Demarest.

TERHUNE, Jacob and Angenietje—Albert, b. Jan. 7—Feb. 13.

HIGGINSON, Samuel and Willemyntje—Antje, b. Oct. 19, 1802—Mar. 6.

QUACKENBUSH, Hendrikje—Annatje, b. Dec. 11, 1802—Apr. 11.

HEDDEN, William and Antje—Antje, b. Mar. 3—Apr. 11.

WESTERVELT, Albert and Elisabeth—Angenietje, b. June 13—July 3.

HARING, Garrit and Maria—Abram, b. July 16—Aug. 14.

CHRISTOPHER, John and Aaltjo—Anna, b. July 20—Sept. 25.

QUACKINBUSH, Teunis and Maria—Annatje, b. Sept. 2—Oct. 2.
Wit: Jacob and Annatje Eckerson.

BUSH, Lodewyk and Magdalen—Annatje, b. Sept. 22—Oct. 2.
DOREMUS, James and Polly—Abraham, b. Oct. 11—Nov. 27.

1804

DEBAUN, David and Annatje—Abram, b. Mar. 22—Apr. 15.
YEOMANS, John and Trientje—Abby, b. Aug. 12—Oct. 7.
ECKERSON, Cornelius and Marytje—Annatje, b. Aug. 27—Oct. 7.
GARRISON, Jacob and Rachel—Antje, b. Nov. 4—Nov. 25.

1805

HOPPER, Jacob A. and Geesje—Abraham, b. Mar. 22—Apr. 14.
JERSEY, John and Maria—Annatje, b. June 3—June 20.
TOMSEN, James and Sara—Annatje, b. June 3—July 7.
TERHUNE, Abraham and Susanna—Abraham and Hendrik, b. May 1—July 21.
RUTAN, Abraham and Lydia—Antje, b. Apr. 23—July 28.
HOPPER, Garret and Maria—Andrew, b. July 22—Aug. 4.

1806

WESTERVELT, Hendrik and Aaltje—Aury, b. Dec. 17, 1805—Jan. 19.
ECKERSON, John and Geertje—Annatje, b. Feb. 3—Mar. 2.
BUSH, Reinard and Elisabeth—Abram, b. Mar. 12—Mar. 16.
VANDERBEEK, Arie and Lenah—Annatje, b. Mar. 28—June 8.
ALLER, Peter and Cornelia—Antje Demarest, b. Apr. 29—June 8.
ACKERMAN, Albert and Elisabeth—Aaltje, b. May 22—June 2.
CHRISTOPHER, Joseph and Eva—Aaltje, b. May 24—June 22.
DEBAUN, John and Aaltje—Abraham, b. July 8—July 27.
HOPPER, Garrit and Maria—Abram, b. Aug. 31—Sept. 28.
HOPPER, Henry A. and Annatje—Andries, b. Oct. 3—Nov. 16.

1807

ACKERMAN, John A. and Maria—Abraham, b. Dec. 14, 1806—Feb. 1.
MABEE, Peter and Jannitje—Abraham, b. Dec. 10, 1806—Feb. 8.
  Wit: Abram and Leentje Vlierboom.
LUTKINS, Harmen and Elisabeth—Antje, b. Jan. 17—Feb. 15.
HOPPER, Andries and Peggy—Anna, b. Jan. 1—Feb. 22.
HARING, Jacob and Femmetje—Annatje, b. Feb. 10—Mar. 1.
ACKERMAN, John and Annatje—Aaltje, b. Apr. 5—Apr. 26.
  Wit: Elizabeth Ackerman.
TERHUNE, Albert G. and Martyntje—Annatje, b. May 6—May 31.
ACKERMAN, Gerrit and Jannetje—Abraham, b. July 10—Aug. 2.
ZABRISKE, Jacob and Antje—Annatje, b. July 30—Aug. 16.
HOPPER, Hendrik and Elisabeth—Abraham, b. Sept. 20—Oct. 11.
HOPPER, Thomas and Elisabeth—Abram, b. Aug. 28—Oct. 4.

1808

ECKERSON, Aaron and Katelyntje—Angenietje, b. Dec. 18, 1807—Jan. 10.
ZABRISKIE, Jacob and Lea—Aaltje, b. Jan. 27—Mar. 13.
VAN RIPEN, Frederik and Maria—Annaatje, b. Feb. 19—Apr. 18.
TERHUNE, Richard and Anna—Abraham, b. Mar. 23—Apr. 24.

COLE, Abraham and Annatje—Abraham, b. Mar. 11—Apr. 24.

ACKERMAN, Gerrit and Geertje—Antje, b. Sept. 9—Oct. 23.

BUSH, Peter and Grietje—Antje, b. Oct. 15—Oct. 23.

HOPPER, Audries H. and Maria—Antje, b. Sept. 25—Oct. 30.
  Wit: Jores and Antje Doremes.

ACKERMAN, John A. and Polly—Aron, b. Oct. 18—Nov. 17.

1809

CROUTER, James and Margriet—Albert, b. Nov. 9, 1808—Jan. 1.

SMITH, George and Geertje—Abram, b. Dec. 7, 1808—Jan. 22.

ACKERMAN, Jacobus and Annatje—Abraham, b. Jan. 20—Feb. 19.

WESTERVELT, Peter and Caty—Abraham, b. Mar. 14—Apr. 9.

DEBAUN, Isaac and Elizabeth—Abram, b. Feb. 7—Feb. 26.

BOSCH, John and Maria—Abraham, b. May 7—July 2.

DOREMUS, Andrew and Abby—Ariaantje, b. July 24—Aug. 31.

ZABRISKE, Jacob A. and Antje—Annatje, b. Nov. 8—Dec. 9.

HOPPER, John and Maretje—Albert, b. Nov. 7—Dec. 17.

ECKERSON, John and Geertje—Annatje, b. Nov. 9—Dec. 10.

TOLLMAN, John and Geertje—Andries, b. Nov. 30—Dec. 21.

VAN RYPEN, Frederik and Maria—Adriaan, b. Nov. 9—Dec. 21.

1810

STORM, Isaac and Rachel—Antje, b. Dec. 9, 1809—Jan. 1.

TOERS, Laurens and Jannitje—Arie, b. July 17—Aug. 26.

SNYDER, Gerrit and Trientje—Andrew, b. July 29—Aug. 26.

MAURISSEN, Jacob and Maretje—Abraham, b. Oct. 14—Dec. 9.

1811

MACLAIN, William and Dolla—Andrew, b. Dec. 22, 1810—Feb. 3.

HOPPER, John and Maretje—Andreas, b. Jan. 20—Feb. 17.

VAN WINCIL (?), John and Sylettje (?) Van Wincil (?)—Abraham,
  b. Feb. 27—Mar. 31.

CURISTOPHER, Jacob and Geesje—Aaltje, b. Mar. 24—Apr. 14.

STORM, Isaac and Rachel—Abraham, b. Apr. 9—Apr. 22.

TERHUNE, Albert and Antje—Antje, b. June 10—July 21.
  Wit: Dolla Snyder.

ZABRISKE, Gerrit and Martyntje—Albert, b. July 23—Sept. 1.

ACKERMAN, Albert and Elizabeth—Aaltje, b. July 27—Aug. 25.

HOPPER, Michael and Jennitje—Andreas, b. Oct. 3—Oct. 20.

ACKERMAN, John and Bridget—Abraham, b. Sept. 15—Dec. 11.

VAN NORDEN, David and Ally—Adam, b. Nov. 2—Dec. 20.

1813

SNYDER, Garrit and Caty—Ally, b. Feb. 16—Mar. 7.

DEMAREST, James S. (?) and Leah—Abigael, b. Sept. 26—Oct. 24.

EARL, Gerrit and Sally—Abby, b. Sept. 16—Nov. 21.

GERRITSON, Albert and Jemima—Aaron, b. Oct. 9—Dec. 26.

1814

HOPPER, Henry P. and Elisabeth—Anne, b. May 10—May 29.

1815

LUTKINS, Harman I. and Elisabeth—Albert, b. Dec. 11, 1814—Feb. 5.
VANDERBEEK, James and Peggy—Ally, b. June 5—July 2.
HOPPER, Andrew P. and Anne—Andrew, b. Oct. 10—Nov. 12.

1816

ZABRISKE, Jacob H. and Anne—Abraham, b. Aug. 28—Oct. 6.
CHRISTOPHER, Jacob and Kizia—Abraham Quacenbush, b. Nov. 28—Dec. 26.

1817

BOGERT, Cornelius and Jane—Albert Zabriskie, b. March 29—May 11.
ROSEGRANT, Eliza (?) and Cornelia—Andrew, b. April 31—June 29.
WESTERVELT, Peter A. and Martha—Albert, b. Sept. 18—Oct. 12.
RETAN, Abraham D. and Leah—Abraham, b. Apr. 25—June 28.

1819

KIPP, Roelof and Charity—Albert, b. Dec. 17, 1818—Jan. 24.
TERHUNE, Martha[1] (?) and Caty—Albert, b. Feb. 21—Mar. 21.
TOURS, Lawrence and Hannah—Aletta, b. March 23—April 18.
ZABRISKIE, Abraham A. and Jane—Anne, b. May 25—June 27.
HOPPER, Garrit A. and Betsey—Albert, b. Sept. 7—Oct. 3.
ZABRISKIE, John J. and Maria—Anne, b. Sept. 27—Oct. 30.
TERHUNE, Hester—Anne, b. Sept. 28—Dec. 6.

1820

ZABRISKIE, John A. and Betsy—Albert, b. Dec. 31, 1819—Feb. 6.
WESTERVELT, Peter Ab. and Martha—Agnes, b. March 12—April 16.
ACKERMAN, Henry and Betsy—Abraham, b. May 22—June 25.

1821

SNYDER, John A. and Allena—Andrew, b. May 13—June 3.

1822

VANDERBEEK, Abraham C. and Elisabeth—Andrew, b. Aug. 19—Oct. 6.
HOPPER, Andrew P. and Anna—Albert, Jr., b. Nov. 18—Dec. 12.

1823

VANDERBEEK, Paul P. and Hannah—Abraham, b. March 25—May 18.
VAN BLARCOM, Henry and Peggy—Abraham, b. June 30—Aug. 9.
ACKERMAN, Abraham D. and Rachel—Abraham, b. Aug. 25—Sept. 7.

1825

VAN RIPER, Harmen and Caty—Abraham, b. Feb. 20—March 20.
VANDERBEEK, John C. and Peggy—Ann Maria, b. May 16—Sept. 4.
HOPPER, Nicholas and Wibie—Albert, b. Oct. 12—Nov. 12.
ZABRISKIE, Casparus and Caty—Andrew, b. Oct. 25—Nov. 12.
VANDIEN, Richard A. and Ally—Andrew, b. Oct. 19—Nov. 27.

1826

WESTERVELT, Peter A. and Mathilda—Albert, b. July 30—Aug. 19.

---

[1]Probably Martin—Editor.

1827

QUACKINBUSH, John J. and Susan—Abraham, b. Sept. 17—Nov. 18.
STORMS, Cornelius and Sally—Abraham, b. Oct. 26—Dec. 2.
TERHUNE, Martin and Caty—Abraham, b. Nov. 25—Dec. 30.

1828

WESTERVELT, Peter and Tyna—Agnes, b. April 9—May 11.
ZABRISKIE, Peter A. and Anna—Albert, b. Oct. 8—Nov. 30.

1829

ACKERMAN, Abraham I. and Caty—Annet, b. Dec. 5, 1828—Jan. 11.
VANDERBEEK, Jerry and Hannah—Aaron, b. April 29—June 7.
ZABRISKIE, Gilliam and Tyna—Albert, b. July 9—July 19.

1830

ACKERMAN, John J. and Maria—Albert, b. Nov. 26, 1829—Jan. 24.
VAN DALSEN, John and Jane—Albert, b. Jan. 1—Jan. 24.
HOPPER, Cornelius A. and Elisabeth—Albert, b. March 15—April 17.
DERONDA, George and Phebe—Asa, b. June 4—July 4.
HOPPER, Garrit A. and Sophia—Albert, b. June 29—July 25.
SNYDER, Garrit and Caty—Andries, b. Nov. 8—Dec. 16.

1831

ZABRISKIE, Cornelius J. and Jane—Abram Van Buskirk, b. May 14—
June 26.

1832

TERHUNE, Henry P. and Maria—Abraham Romine, b. April 16—May 27.
ZABRISKIE, Casparus J. and Caty—Aletta Levina, b. Aug. 23—Sept. 23.
ZABRISKIE, John J. and Sally—Abraham Stephens, b. Aug. 16—Sept. 23.

1833

ZABRISKIE, Guilliam and Levina Maria—Ann Maria, b. March 7—Apr. 21.

1834

STORMS, Conrad H. and Hetty—Albert, b. June 7—July 6.
ACKERMAN, Abraham U. and Peggy—Ann Maria, b. Aug. 3—Sept. 28.

1836

HASBROOK, Augustus and Jane—Abraham Houseman, b. Dec. 29, 1835—
April 30.
BLAUVELT, James and Hannah—Abraham, b. March 18—July 10.
VOORHIS, John H. and Elizabeth—Albert Bogart, b. Aug. 17—Sept. 11.
BANTA, Thomas, Jr., and Ellen—Ann Elisabeth, b. Sept. 22—Nov. 3.

1837

HOPPER, Henry A. and Margarit Ann—Andrew, b. March 30—May 7.
ZABRISKIE, Henry A. and Petty—Albert, b. Oct. 12—Nov. 26.

1838

VAN DIEN, John and Hannah—Aletta, b. Jan. 31—April 15.

1839

ACKERMAN, Ralph and Hester—Agnes, b. July 16—Aug. 11.

1835

ACKERMAN, John G. and Maria—Andrew Hopper, b. Aug. 11—Sept. 7.

1840
HOPPER, Jacob H. and Caty—Albert, b. Aug. 1—Sept. 20.

1841
ZABRISKIE, Christian J. and Hannah—Anna, b. June 13, 1834—March 28.
VAN VOORHIS, John H. and Elizabeth—Albert Bogart, b. July 24—Aug. 28.
———— ———— ———— Abraham Terhune, b. May 6, 1833—Aug. 29.
   Wit: Abraham A. and Tyna Terhune.
VANDERBEEK, Jacob A. and Maria—Abraham, b. July 8—Sept. 12.
RATHBONE, John Carstella and Eliza—Abraham, b. Sept. 22—Nov. 21.

1842
BOGART, Isaac and Rachel—Albert James, b. May 28—July 31.
ZABRISKIE, John T. and Ann—Anne, b. June 9—Aug. 28.

1843
TERHUNE, Henry Z. and Maria—Alexander, b. July 1—Aug. 20.

1844
BOGERT, Albert and Jane—Albert, b. Jan. 17—Aprl 6.
ACKERMAN, Abraham and Dorcas—Abraham Rutan, b. Mar. 10—Apr. 6.
HERRING, John and Eliza—Abraham John, b. Aug. 13—Sept. 8.

1845
TERHUNE, Henry Z. and Maria—Ann Amelia, b. April 8—June 1.
ACKERMAN, Garrit A. and Maria Jemima—Andrew, b. Oct. 11—Dec. 28.
ZABRISKIE, John C. and Eliza Maria—Andrew, b. June 7—July 13.

1846
ACKERMAN, Garrit D. and Eliza—Adoline, b. Oct. 27, 1845—March 1.

1847
BANTA, Thomas, Jr., and Ellen—Aaron Vanderbeek, b. Feb. 7—Mar. 21.

1848
VANDIEN, John Z. and Maria—Anna, b. Jan. 27—March 18.
BOGART, Albert and Martha—Aletta Jane, b. April 15—May 13.
VANDIEN, Andrew and Sarah Catharina—Aletta Paulina, b. June 14—
   Sept. 16.

1849
DEVOIE, Harmanus and Eliza Jane—Albert, b. July 21—Aug. 19.
GOW, Robert and Joanne Rutherford—Augustus Horsbrook, b. Oct. 8
   —Dec. 27.

1850
HORSBROOK, Augustus and Jane W.—Augustus, b. Feb. 28—April 25.

1852
HORSBROOK, Augustus and Jane W.—Aaron Hasseth, b. Sept. 14, 1851—
   Feb. 16.

1854
ZABRISKIE, Andrew C. and Sarah Margaret—Andrew Hoppe, b. Jan.
   7—April 8.

"B"

1753
Bos, Samuel and Rebecka—Benjamin—March 18.
Wit: Dom. Benj. and Lisabeth Vandelinde.
1768
VESEUR, Hannes and Lena—Barend—May 15.
Wit: Barend and Francyntje Veseur.
1770
QUACKENBOS, Hannes and Margrita—Barend—Feb. 25.
Wit: Klaas and Marietje Haledrom.
1771
DUMAREE, Daniel D. and Cornelia—Belitie—June 23.
Wit: Pieter and Belitie Outwater.
1772
ZABRISKE, Jacob J. and Jannitje—Belitie—Jan. 12.
Wit: Albert J. and Geesje Zabriske.
1773
PIETERIE, Willem and Santje—Barend, b. April 12—May 2.
AYCRIGG, John and Rachel—Benjamin—Oct. 10.
From the Parish of Upton upon Severn, Worcestershire O. England.
Wit: Albert A. Terhuyn and Lisabeth Leydecker.
1774
VERSEUR, Pieter and Maria—Barend, b. March 29—April 24.
Wit: Barent and Syntje Verseur.
1775
WESSELS, Joseph and Ariaantje—Benjamin—April 2.
Wit: Hannes Smith and wife.
GARDENIER, Johannis and Jacomyntje—Barend—April 17.
Wit: Barend and Francyntje Veseur.
1780
ZABRISKE, Jacob J. and Jannitje—Belitie—Oct. 15.
Wit Albert and Geesje Zabriske.
1785
ODEL, Gerrit and Rebecka—Benjamin—March 20.
Wit: Hendrik and Maria Odel.
1786
RYER, Jan and Maria—Barend, b. March 7—April 1.
Wit: Barent and Francyntje Fesyeur.
1788
MAURUSSEN, Nathaniel and Elisabeth—Brechje, b. Aug. 8—Aug. 31.
1789
SHURTE, Adolph and Elisabeth—Benjamin, b. Feb. 22—March 29.
Wit: Jacobus and Jannitje Demarest.
1790
RIGWAY, John and Grietje—Betsey—March 14.
DEBAAN, Jacob and Antje—Brechje, b. Feb. 19—March 15.
Wit: Abraham and Brechje Debaan.

Bos, Lodewyk and Leentje—Barend, b. May 7—Aug. 3.
  Wit: Barend and Francyntje Fesyeur.

1791
Janse, Abraham and Elisabeth—Barend, b. March 23—April 24.
  Wit: Daniel and Margrietje Ackerman.

1794
Van Wert, Isaac and Elisabeth—Betsey, b. July 20—Aug. 24.
  Wit: David Paulisvelt and Bethsy Shoemaker.

1797
Cole, Adriaan and Elisabeth—Barend, b. June 30—Aug. 20.

1807
Banta, Thomas and Elisabeth—Brechje, b. Nov. 1—Dec. 1.

1818
Voorhis, John A. and Rachel—Betsey, b. May 27—June 28.

1822
Van Emburgh, Albert and Hannah—Benjamin Zabriskie, b. Sep. 4—
  Oct. 6.

1823
Van Saun, Cornelius and Rachel—Betsey, b. Dec. 10, 1822—Feb. 18.

1829
Hover, Benjamin and Jemima—Benjamin, b. Feb. 5—April 5.

1837
Ackerman, Abraham J. and Lavina—Bridget Westervelt, b. Aug. 28—
  Oct. 15.

1838
Maurus, John D. and Eliza—Bridget Maria, b. Jan. 21—March 11.

"C"

1749
Walli, Elias and Anna—Claartje—Aug. 13.
  Wit: Pieter and Claartje Wannemaker.

1750
Mabe, Pieter and Rachel—Casparus—Feb. 4.
  Wit: Casparus and Willempje Mebe.
Duremus, Abram and Annatje—Catrina, b. Jan. 22.
  Wit: Samuel and Rebecka Bos.
Storm, Hendrik and Cornelia—Coenradus, b. March 26.
  Wit: Coenradus and Angenietje Vanderbeek.
Zabriske, Albert and Aaltje—Cristiaan—Nov. 28.
  Wit: Hendrik and Neesje Zabriske.

1751
Zabriskie, Andries and Lisabeth—Cristiaan—Feb. 24.
  Wit: Albert and Aaltje Zabriske.
Van Bosse, Hermanus and Abigail—Catharina—Aug. 18.
  Wit: Isaac and Janneke Kingsland.

DERYIE, Daniel and Vrouwtje—Catharina—Oct. 20.
Wit: Dirk and Catryntje Vandien.
SLINGERLAND, Teunis and Hendrika—Casparus—Oct. 27.
Wit: Hermanus and Jenneke Degrau.

1752

USTERLI, Marten and Grouda—Catrientje, b. Dec. 16, 1751—Jan. 19.
Wit: Pieter and Margrietje Dubou.
RIDDENAAR, Hendrik and Grietje—Coenraad—June 28.
Wit: Abram and Rachel Van Gelder.

1753

BALLDIN, Steven and Antje—Carstina—April 23.
Wit: Joost and Carstine Zabriske.
HOPPE, David—Cornelia—July 22.
Wit: Jan and Antje Bogert.

1754

KUYPER, Cornelis and Mettie—Catharina—Feb. 9.
Wit: Dirk and Tryntje Vandien.
VANDERBEEK, Jurrien and Marytje—Coenradus—March 10.
Wit: Paulus and Annatje Vanderbeek.
VOLLIK, Niklaas and Metje—Sara—Sept. 8.
Wit: Benjamin and Nellie Odel.
ZOBRISKE, Hendrik C. and Maria—Christiaan—Sept. 29.
Wit: Albert C. and Aaltje Zobriske.

1755

VAN RYPE, Fredrik and Antje—Cornelis, b. June 27—July 13.
Wit: Cornelis and Antje Van Vorst.

1756

DEGRAU, Hermanus and Jannike—Casparus—July 11.
Wit: Andries and Jannitie Debouw.

1758

VAN BLERCOM, Isaac and Sara—Cornelia—March 5.
Wit: Egbert and Sara Van Zeyl.
BONGAERT, Cornelis Y. and Elisabeth—Casparus—April 9.
Wit: Silvester and Mechtel Earl.

1760

FOCHI,[1] Barend and Francyntje—Catharina, b. June 24—Aug. 9.
Wit: Jan and Catharina Fochi.
MEYER, Hannes I. and Leentje—Cornelis—Aug. 5.
Wit: Hermanus and Aaltje V[an] Blercom.

1761

KOGH, Casper and Lidea—Casparus—Oct. 18.
Wit: Anna Maria and Elias Kogh.
BANTA, Jan Jo. and Sara—Catrientje, b. Nov. 17—Nov. 29.
Wit: Jan H. and Tryntje Banta.

---

[1]This Fochi is doubtless a corruption of Verschuur, Fresheur, etc.

1762

LUTKENS, Harme and Antje—Catrientje—May 2.
  Wit: Steven and Catryntje Zabriske.
VAN BLERKOM, Pieter and Sucke—Carstyntje—Oct. 24.
  Wit: Jan and Carstyntje Ackerman.
PERRY, Daniel and Jannitje—Catrina, b. Nov. 16—Dec. 12.
  Wit: Jan and Catrina Voseur.
QUACKENBUSH, Reinier and Catrina—Catrina, b. Nov. 15—Dec. 12.
  Wit: Abram and Gerritje Quackinbush.
VAN ZEYL, Pieter and Lena—Saartje—Nov. 12.
  Wit: Egbert and Saartje Van Zeyl.

1764

DOREMES, Hendrik and Aagje—Catrina, b. Jan. 24—Feb. 9.
  Wit: Johannes and Pryntje Van Houten.
CAERLOG, Hendrik and Grietje—Coenraad—July 8.
  Wit: Coenraad and Antje Bruyn.

1765

PERRY, Daniel and Jannitje—Catharina—Jan. 27.
  Wit: Jan and Catrina Voseur.
STRAET, Dirk and Rebecka—Catharina, b. Mar. 1—April 14.
  Wit: Jacob and Sara Straet.
MAGDANEL, Cornelis and Catrina—Cornelis, b. April 7—May 5.
  Wit: John J. and Maria Eckersen.
PIELESFELT, Coenraad and Eva—Cornelis and Petrus, (twins)—Nov. 3.
  Wit: Cornelis and Cornelia Pielesfelt.

1766

PERRY, Cobus and Annatje—Catrina—March 16.
  Wit: Isaac and Maragriet Perry.
VOSEUR, Willem ———————— —Cornelis—March 23.
  Wit: Cornelis Blauvelt.
NIX, Hermanus ———————— —Catrina—April 27.
  Wit: Andries and Jannitje Debouw.
MOURUSSE, Jacobus and Lena—Catrina—June 22.
  Wit: Pieter A. Debouw and Catrina Duremus.
HARING, ———————— Lea—Christiana, b. May 21—June 29.
  Wit: Cornelis and Catrina Haring.
HOPPE, Gerrit H. and Antje—Catryntje—May 9.
  Wit: Hendrik and Claartje Traphage.

1767

TERHUYN, Steven D. and Jannitje—David—Nov 15.
  Wit: David and Sara Terhuyn.

1768

RUTAN, Cobus and Willampje—Saartje—Jan. 4.
  Wit: Saartje and Abram Rutan.
BOGERT, Jacobus and Cornelia—Cornelia—April 3.
  Wit: David and Rachel Hoppe.
JERSEY, Hendrik ———————— —Catrina—Aug. 28.
  Wit: Jacob and Maria Bogert.

SYMESSE, Walter and Rachel—Catrina—Oct. 7.
DAVENPOORT, Pieter and Lea—Catrina—Mar. 16.
1769
PILISFELT, Willem and Elisabeth—Coenraad—Nov. 5.
1770
VERSEUR, Hannes and Lena—Cornelis, b. June 6—July 1.
Wit: Cornelis A. and Maria Banta.
SYOURT, Willem and Catrina—Christiaan—July 29.
TERHUYN, Steven D. and Jannitje—Christiaan—Sept. 30.
Wit: Christiaan A. and Martyntje Zabriskie.
1771
VANDIEN, Gerrit and Sara—Cornelis—Feb. 24.
Wit: Thomas and Polly Vandien.
BLAUVELT, David and Rachel—Cornelis, b. Jan. 25—Feb. 24.
Wit: Willem and Lisabeth Verseur.
BAELDIN, Steven and Antje—Cristina, b. Apr. 6, 1756—Feb. 24.
HELM, Samuel and Catrina—Cornelis, b. July 6—July 21.
Wit: Cornelis and Grietje Helm.
1772
ZABRISKE, Joost and Marytje—Casparus—July 19.
Wit: John T. Earl and Antje Baldwin.
VAN BLERKOM, Frans and Jacomyntje—Cornelis—Oct. 25.
Wit: Pieter H. and Jannetje Van Blerkom.
CARNS, Duglas and Geesje—Cornelia—Sept. 6.
Wit: David Carns and Rachel Van Horen.
1773
BOGERT, Joost and Marietje—Cornelis—Jan. 10.
Wit: Cornelis and Elisabeth Bogert.
VAN BLERKOM, Pieter H. and Jannitje—Cornelis—May 16.
Wit: Frans and Jacomyntje Van Blerkom.
1774
COEL, Jacob J. and Geertrui—Catrina, b. Jan. 30—June 28.
Wit: Joannes and Catrina Coel.
RYKER, Pieter and Lea—Cornelis, b. Feb. 28, 1773—June 28.
1775
MILTENBERRY, Luwes and Lisabeth—Crastina—July 2.
VAN BOSKERCK, Joost and Marytje—Cornelia—July 9.
Wit: Willem and Cornelia Verburgh.
PULLES, Hendrik and Cathalyntje—Cornelis, b. Aug. 9—Sept. 10.
Wit: Christiaan and Claartje Pulles.
1776
ZABRISKE, Hendrik I. and Willempje—Cornelis—July 14.
1782
SMITH, Jacob and Rachel—Catrina, b. Apr. 8—Nov. 3.
Wit: Albert J. and Annatje Bogert.
1780
MEYER, Andrew and Pegge—Cornelia—May 16.
Wit: Cornelis and Cornelia Meyer.

1784

ZABRISKE, Christiaan and Marytje—Cornelis—April 25.

BERKHOF, Hendrik and Maria—Catrina, b. March 13—May 22.
Wit: Jan and Catrina Rose.

BLAUVELT, Cornelis and Catrina—Cathalyntje, b. Nov. 8—Dec. 5.
Wit: Christaan and Cathalyntje Blauvelt.

1785

DEBAAN, Joost and Margrietje—Catrina, b. Dec. 7—Dec. 11.
Wit: Jan and Elisabeth Debaan.

1787

FRERIKSE, Coenraad and Elisabeth—Catrina, b. Dec. 30, 1786—Aug. 9.
Wit: Robert and Catrina Frerikse.

ODEL, Gerrit and Rebecka—Catrina, b. May 6—May 27.

FERSYEUR, Jan W. and Wyntje—Catrientje, b. June 21—July 15.
Wit: Cornelis and Trientje Fersyeur.

1788

BERTOLF, Jillis and Sally—Catriena, b. Dec. 15, 1787—Jan. 20.
Wit: Christiaan A. and Marytje A. Zabriske.

HALDEROM, Cornelius and Margrietje—Catriena, b. Jan. 31—Feb. 24.
Wit: Steven T. Bogert and Elisabeth Krom.

HENNION, William and Eva—Cornelis—April 27.

MICHLER, Lodewyk and Antje—Catriena—July 13.
Wit: Catriena Hofman.

VAN HOORN, Jacobus and Lea—Cornelis—Nov. 23.
Wit: Daniel and Annaatje Van Hoorn.

BOGERT, Casparus and Jannitje—Cornelis, b. Nov. 7—Nov. 30.
Wit: Joost and Maria Bogert.

1789

PULISFELT, Jan and Elisabeth—Coenraad, b. Dec. 10, 1788—Jan. 1.

GOETSCHIUS, Piatus and Catriena—Catriena, b. June 1—July 19.

BERTOLF, Jan and Susanna—Catriena, b. June 19—Aug. 9.
Wit: Hendrik and Marytje Storm.

STORM, Staats and Margrietje—Cornelia, b. Oct. 6—Oct. 25.
Wit: Hendrik and Cornelia Storm.

1790

POTTER, John and Maria—Caty—Aug. 15.
Wit: Thomas and Polly Snyder.

KOGH, Casparus C. and Margrietje—Casparus—Oct. 17.
Wit: Sara Kogh.

HOPPE, Petrus and Elisabeth—Cornelis, b. Nov. 9—Dec. 12.

KING, William and Myntje—Catriena, b. Nov. 21—Dec. 25.
Wit: Jan and Leentje Eckerson.

1791

HORN, Joseph and Maria—Catrina, b. July 10—Aug. 9.

1793

WESTERVELT, Albert C. and Maria—Cornelius, b. June 12—June 23.

SERVENT, Jacobus and Polly—Catrina, b. May 9—June 16.
Wit: Martyntje Van Boskerk.

SMITH, Gerrit and Hetty—Cornelius, b. Nov. 2—Nov. 17.
Wit: Cornelius and Becke Blauvelt.

1794

BERVOORT, Samuel and Martyntje—Christiaan, b. Feb. 19—March 20.
Wit: Christiaan J. and Maria Zabriskie.
Bos, Hendrik and Maritje—Coenraad, b. March 10—March 30.
Wit: Pieter Van Vlerkom and Elizabeth Bos.
AUSBON, John and Martyntje—Catriena and David (twins) b. Mar. 27
—March 30.
Wit: David Ausbon and Maria Van Boskerk.
ACKERMAN, Johannis and Elisabeth—Cornelius, b. June 8—July 6.
Wit: Cornelis and Maria Demarest.
ACKERMAN, Jacobus and Maria—Cornelia, b. July 12—Aug. 3.
Wit: Jacobus and Cornelia Bogert.
ACKERMAN, Petrus and Maria—Catriena, b. May 26—Aug. 24.
Wit: Joseph and Catriena Blauvelt.
MEYER, Marten and Brechje—Cornelis, b. Sept. 24—Nov. 9.
WANNEMAKER, Abraham and Annatje—Catriena, b. Dec. 1—Dec. 25.
Wit: Lourens and Maria Van Boskerk.

1795

SCHUYLER, Adonia and Elisabeth—Cornelis, b. April 30—June 14.
Wit: Andreas and Christina Zabriske.
VAN BLERCOM, John and Geertje—Catriena, b. July 13—Aug. 2.
Wit: Steven and Claartje Campbel.
VEIL, Enos and Nellie—Catharina, b. Aug. 24—Sept. 20.
TAALMAN, John and Margrietje—Catriena, b. Sept. 15—Oct. 25.
DODS, James and Maria—Catriena, b. Oct. 14—Nov. 22.
YOOMENS, John and Catriena—Coenraad, b. Nov. 3—Nov. 22.

1796

DEMAREST, David and Geesje—Cornelis, b. Dec. 7, 1795—Jan. 31.
Wit: Cornelis and Elisabeth Demarest.
PERRY, John and Charity—Cecilia, b. Oct. 26, 1795—March 13.
POULISVELT, Pieter and Nancy—Cornelia, b. Feb. 4—March 6.
POST, Gerrit A. and Nelly—Cornelis, b. March 11—March 27.
PECKER, William and Sally—Catriena, b. Aug. 2—Sept. 18.
SJOERT, Adolph and Aaltje—Catriena, b. Sept. 19—Sept. 25.
Wit: John and Catriena Youmens.

1797

ECKERSON, Cornelius and Catriena—Catriena, b. April 8—June 4.
HOPPE, Abraham and Elisabeth—Cornelius, b. Aug. 2—Aug. 20.
Wit: Jan G. and Rachel Hoppe.

1798

ZABRISKE, Jacob C. and Elisabeth—Christiaan, b. Jan. 6—Feb. 5.
Wit: Christiaan and Maria Zabriske.
CROUTER, Jacob and Maria—Cornelia, b. April 25—June 3.
Wit: Thomas and Cornelia Eckerson.
WESTERVELT, Petrus and Martyntje—Casparus, b. Aug. 21—Sept. 9.

1799

RIDDENAAR, Hendrick and Sally—Coen, b. July 6—July 21.

ACKERMAN, David and Metje—Catriena, b. Aug. 18—Sept. 1.

HALDEROM, William and Catriena—Catriena, b. Sept. 16—Oct. 6.
  Wit: Andries and Catriena Halderom.

1800

DEBAAN, Andries and Jannitje—Catriena, b. Feb. 8—Feb. 23.
  Wit: Samuel and Catriena Durie.

WESTERVELT, Albert and Maria—Casparus, b. April 5—April 10.

VAN BLERCOM, John and Geertje—Catriena, b. April 21—May 11.

WILLS, Thomas and Rachel—Catharina, b. June 14—June 29.
  Wit: John Marinus and Jane Ackerman.

RIDDENAAR, Coenraad and Elisabeth—Catriena, b. July 13—Aug. 10.

STORM, Hendrik and Margrietje—Cornelius, b. July 28—Aug. 17.
  Wit: Cornelius and Margrietje Halderom.

VANHORN, John and Elisabeth—Cornelius, b. Aug. 18—Sept. 7.

1801

ECKERSON, Thomas and Polly—Cornelia, b. Jan. 12—March 1.
  Wit: Thomas and Cornelia Eckerson.

BLAUVELT, Aurie and Jacomyntje—Cathalyntje, b. Nov. 25, 1800—
  March 8.
  Wit: Christian and Cathalyntje Blauvelt.

TERHUNE, David and Trientje—Casparus, b. Feb. 2—March 11.
  Wit: Casparus and Grietje Cogh.

ECKERSON, Edward and Hettie—Charity, b. April 10—May 3.

1802

LEMATER, Abraham and Sarah—Catriena, b. April 1—May 16.
  Wit: Catriena Cadmus.

ZABRISKE, Jacob J. and Antje—Cornelius, b. Oct. 3, 1801(?), Sept. 24.

STORM, Hendrik and Margrietje—Coenradus, b. Nov. 23—Dec. 26.
  Wit: Coenradus and Maria Storm.

1803

ACKERMAN, Laurens and Hester—Cornelius, b. April 2—April 17.

1804

ZABRISKIE, Cornelius and Maria—Christian Andrew, b. Feb. 25—April 1.

DECKER, Moses and Polly—Caty, b. Jan. 24—April 2.

WESTERVELT, Hendrik and Aaltje—Cathalyntje, b. May 12—May 27.

POTTER, John and Maria—Catriena, b. May 8—May 27.

HOPPER, Hendrik and Hester—Cornelia, b. Oct. 19—Dec. 23.

1805

WORTENDYK, Cornelius and Annatje—Cornelius, b. Dec. 3, 1804—Jan. 13.

BUSH, Dirk and Antje—Catriena, b. Jan. 25—Feb. 17.

DEY, William and Nancy—Caty, b. May 4—June 9.

ECKERSON, David and Maria—Cornelia, b. Sept. 15—Oct. 13.

1806

STUART, Adolph and Aaltje—Christian Abraham, b. Dec. 23, 1805—Jan.
  26.

ELTINGE, Wilhelmus and Jane—Cornelius Houseman, b. Jan. 1—Feb. 2.
ECKERSON, Peter and Margaret—Cornelia, b. Aug. 21—Sept. 14.
ACKERMAN, Lawrence and Hester—Catharina, b. Nov. 2—Nov. 23.

1807
BALDWIN, Thomas and Elisabeth—Cristina, b. Jan. 19—Feb. 22.
ECKERSON, Jacob S. and Leah—Cornelia, b. March 27—April 19.

1808
GARRETSON, Jacob and Rachel—Cate, b. Dec. 9, 1807—Jan. 1.
  Wit: Cornelius Bogert and Antje Gerritse.

1809
VANDIEN, Garret H. and Antje—Catharina Leah, b. March 4—April 2.
CAMPBELL, Samuel and Caty—Caty, b. Feb. 11—April 14.
Vos, Hendrik and Margrietje—Coenraad, b. May 10—May 28.
ZABRISKIE, Albert and Maria—Cathalyntje Myntje, b. July 3—July 30.
  Wit: John and Willemyntje Zabriskie.
CHRISTOPHER, Jacob and Geesje—Caty, b. Sept. 15—Oct. 22.
  Wit: Abraham and Trientje Quackenbush.
BUSH, Peter and Grietje—Coenraad, b. Oct. 19—Nov. 12.

1810
VAN OSTRAND, John and Maria—Charratje Ann, b. Feb. 1—March 18.
  Wit: Dirk and Maria Vandien.
HOPPER, John G. and Rachel—Caty Ann, b. Feb. 26—May 22.
GERRITSEN, Jacob and Rachel—Caty, b. June 25—July 15.
HOPPER, Andrew and Antje—Caty, b. July 2—Aug. 5.
DEBAUN, Antje—Caty, b. July 19—Sept. 11.
  Wit: Joost and Caty Debaun.

1811
COLE, Cornelius and Maria—Caty, b. Jan. 27—Feb. 24.
CHRISTOPHER, Joseph and Eefje—Caty, b. Feb. 28—April 14.
BOGERT, Albert and Aaltje—Cornelia, b. April 15—May 12.
CUYPER, James and Naatje—Cornelius, b. Sept. 4—Sept. 22.

1812
DEMAREST, Jacobus and Lea—Catriena, b. Feb. 14—March 30.

1813
HARRIS, Isaac and Hannah—Cornelius, b. Jan. 9—Feb. 28.
BOMAN, Nicolas and Margaret—Charity, b. July 3—Aug. 1.

1814
BANTA, Dr. Garrit D. and Harriet—Catharina, b. Feb. 27—March 27.
KOUGH, Casparus, Jr. and Tyna—Casparus, b. Jan. 7—Feb. 8.
BERVOORT, Henry and Polly—Christian, b. July 9—Aug. 7.
CHRISTOPHER, Jacob and Kizia—Charity Ann, b. Nov. 1—Dec. 25.

1815
ZABRISKIE, Cornelius C. and Polly—Catharine Law, b. Nov. 22, 1814—
  March 5.
VANDERBEEK, Abraham C. and Elizabeth—Cornelius, b. April 15—May
  14.

1816
VAN EMBURGH, John and Polly—Caty Ann, b. Jan. 7—Feb. 11.

1817
HOPPER, Andrew H. and Maria—Catharina, b. Dec. 22, 1816—Feb. 9.
GARRISON, Peter and Margaret—Caty, b. May 17—July 13.

1818
VANDIEN, Garrit C. and Sophia—Cornelius, b. Jan. 28—March 8.
VAN DALSEM, John and Jane—Caty, b. March 27—Apr. 12.
DOREMUS, George Jr. and Harriet—Caty Ann, b. July 20—Aug. 9.

1819
HOPPER, Henry P. and Elisabeth—Carolina, b. Aug. 29—Sept. 19.
ZABRISKIE, Jacob A. and Jane—Catharina, b. Aug. 31—Sept. 19.

1820
WORTENDYKE, Abraham and Catharina—Cornelius, b. March 9—April 2.
SMITH, Harmen P. and Jane—Charles, b. Oct. 18, 1819—Feb. 24.
CARLOUGH, Jeremiah and Elisabeth—Cornelius, b. July 27—Aug. 6.

1821
VANDIEN, Garrit and Jane—Caty, b. July 22—Aug. 12.
EVERSON, Isaac and Lena—Cornelius Meyres, b. July 8—Dec. 29.

1822
ZABRISKIE, Casparus I. and Caty—Cornelius, b. Jan. 25—Feb. 22.
BELL, Gerrit I. H. and Anne—Charity Ann, b. Feb. 25—April 7.
VANDERBEEK, John C. and Peggy—Cornelius, b. Sept. 11—Dec. 1.
POST, Cornelius I. and Elisabeth—Caty, b. Dec. 8—Dec. 17.

1823
TERHUNE, Abraham A. and Caty—Catharine, b. Aug. 6—Sept. 7.
HOPPER, John H. and Mary—Catharine, b. Dec. 1—Dec. 25.

1824
KOUGH, Casparus and Tyna—Casparus, b. Feb. 9—April 3.
TWICE (TOIRCE), Lawrence and Jane—Charity, b. Feb. 16—March 21.
BERDAN, John, Jr. and Sally—Cornelius, b. Sept. 4—Oct. 30.

1825
VANHOUTEN, Abraham and Abigail—Catharina Ann, b. Nov. 1, 1824—
    March 6.
ACKERMAN, David D. and Effy—Caty Ann, b. Feb. 24—March 20.
BOGAERT, Peter and Jane—Catharine, b. Aug. 11—Oct. 2.

1826
HOPPER, John I. and Mary Ann—Catharine Ann, b. April 24—May 28.
HOPPER, Albert G. and Polly—Christian, b. Aug. 13—Sept. 7.

1827
DEMAREST, James J. and Anne—Catharine Ann, b. Apr. 28—June 17.
HALL, William and Jane—Caroline, b. Nov. 20—Dec. 25.

1828
TAYLOR, John I. and Mary—Catharine Maria, b. Aug. 17—Oct. 12.

1829

SNYDER, James G. and Catharine—Catharine, b. March 10—April 5.

ACKERMAN, Abraham D. and Rachel—Charity Ann, b. March 18—April 19.

VANDERBEEK, Coenradus and Hetty—Caty Ann, b. April 29—June 7.

VANDIEN, Garrit and Jane—Casper Demarest, b. June 14—Aug. 23.

1830

TERHUNE, Abraham A. and Polly Zabriskie, Sponsors (?) Cornelius Zabriskie, b. April 10—May 1.

DAVIS, James and Nancy—Charles De Buard (?), b. Feb. 27—May 23.

1831

ACKERMAN, Abraham and Catarine—Catharine Ann, b. Nov. 23, 1830 —Jan. 29.

ZABRISKIE, John J. and Maria—Cornelius, b. April 25—June 26.

1832

QUACKENBUSH, John J. and Susan—Catharine, b. Aug. 28—Nov. 11.

1833

HOPPER, Garrit A. and Sophia—Catharine, b. Feb. 14—March 24.

PAKE (?), Martin and Betsy—Catharine Ann, b. Oct. 14—Nov. 17.

1834

ACKERMAN, David D. and Agnes—Cornelius, b. Jan. 9—April 5.

ACKERMAN, Abraham D. and Rachel—Catharine Maria, b. April 12— May 11.

1835

QUACKENBUSH, John J. and Susan—Cornelius, b. June 21—Aug. 23.

1836

ACKERMAN, Andrew G. and Caty—Charity, b. Aug. 1—Sept. 10.

1837

HORSBROOK, Augustine and Jane—Cornelia Houseman, b. July 10— Aug. 6.

1839 (Prob. 1838)

BOGERT, Gardener and Peggy—Christiana, b. Dec. 31—Dec. 31.

1839

SNYDER, Isaac and Mary Ann—Catharine, b. April 30—July 21.

BOGART, John C. and Jannette—Cornelius James, b. July 15—Sept. 15.

ACKERMAN, John G. and Maria—Cornelius Henry, b. Sept. 7—Oct. 19.

1840

VAN WAGONER, Garret and Jemima—Cornelius, b. Feb. 4—April 19.

HORSBROOK, Augustine and Jane—Cornelius, b. Aug. 6—Sept. 13.

1841

ZABRISKIE, Guliam and Tina—Christian, b. May 15—July 11.

1842

VAN SAUN, Lucas I. and Jane—Christina, b. July 27—Aug. 28.

1843

ZABRISKIE, John C. and Eliza Maria—Catharine Christina, b. Feb. 25— April 16.

1845

HELMS, Daniel and Catharine—Charles William, b. Oct. 3, 1844—Feb. 1.

BANTA, Thomas Jr. and Ally—Charity Jane, b. May 9, 1844—April 5.

HARRIS, Edward and Rachel Pack—Charles Augustus, b. July 2—Aug. 2.

1846

HORSBROOK, Augustus and Jane—Charles Dudley, b. Sept. 21—Nov. 29.

1847

VAN RYPER, Abraham and Anna—Catharine Maria, b. Feb. 15—April 25.

ZABRISKIE, Guilliam and Tyna—Christian—April 25.

1848

MARINUS, Harmanus and Eliza Jane—Catharina Maria, b. Dec. 10, 1847—March 5.

TERHUNE, Henry Z. and Maria—Charles, b. Sept. 6, 1847—March 12.

HORSBROOK, Augustus and Jane—Cornelia Schooman, b. May 24—Aug. 27.

ACKERMAN, Garrit An. and Maria Jemima—Catharina Mathilda, b. Aug. 18—Sept. 16.

1851

VAN BLARCOM, Jacob Z. and Maria—Cornelius Ackerson, b. March 31, 1850—Feb. 16.

"D"

1750

WANNEMAKER, Christiaan and Grietje—Dirk—Jan. 21.
Wit: Pieter D. and Marytje Wannemaker.

1751

DUREMUS, Cornelius and Rachel—David—March 24.
Wit: Thomas and Marytje Ecker.

1753

JURRIXSE, Cobus and Rachel—David—Jan. 21.
Wit: David and Grietje Ackerman.

1754

VAN ZEYL, Petrus and Jannitje—Divertje—July 28.
Wit: Gerrit and Eva Bense.

1755

DUMAREST, Jacob and Rachel—Daniel, b. June 23—Aug. 17.
Wit: Samuel and Marytje Ecker.

VAN VOORHEES, Jan W. and Lea—Daniel—Aug. 21.
Wit: Daniel D. and Susanna Rutan.

RUTAN, William and Marytje—David—Dec. 14.
Wit: Abram J. and Hester Ackerman.

1756

RUTAN, Johannes and Aaltje—Daniel—April 15.
Wit: Albert and Antje V[an] Voorhees.

ACKERMAN, Niklaas and Maria—Daniel—May 9.
Wit: David Demarest and Fytje D. Westervelt.

1758

CROOFOOT, Elias—Deborah—May 13.
Wit: David Rensford.

1760

DERYIE, David and Vrouwtje—Dirk—Aug. 24.
Wit: Tryntje and Thomas Vandien.

1761

ALYEE, Isaac and Annaatje—David, b. Aug. 28—Nov. 29.
Wit: David and Agnietje Eckersen.

1762

SMITH, Daniel and Nansje—Dunken—Sept. 11.
VANHOREN, Lucas and Grietje—Daniel—Oct. 25.

1765

ACKERMAN, David A. and Jacomyntje—David—Jan. 27.
Wit: Jacobus and Cornelia Bongaart.

1766

ALYIE, Isaac and Annatje—David, b. Feb. 4—Feb. 23.
BOGERT, Margrietje—Dirk Wannemaker, b. Dec. 9, 1765—May 8.
Wit: Pieter and Rachel Bogert.

1768

STEGG, Cornelis and Grietje—David—May 1.
Wit: Guliam and Santje Dumaree.
MACKENNEL, Cornelis and Trientje—Daniel, b. June 22—June 24.
Wit: Philip and Sara Eckersen.
VANDIEN. Thomas and Polly—Dirk—Dec. 22.
Wit: Cornelis and Tryntje Vandien.

1769

V[AN] VOORHEESE, Jan. W. and Lea—Daniel—Feb. 5.
Wit: Abraham and Saartje Rutan.
WOERTENDYK, Frederik and Maseri—Divertje, b. Jan. 21—Feb. 9.
Wit: Jacob and Maria Woertendyk.
PERRY, Daniel and Jannitje—Daniel, b. Feb. 18—March 19.
Wit: Jan and Lisabeth Perry.
WESTERVELT, Johannis and Elisabeth—Dorothea—Sept. 10.
Wit: Cornelis L. and Elisabeth Bogert.
ACKERMAN, Willem and Grietje—Davidt—Dec. 24.
Wit: David J. and Antje Ackerman.

1770?

CHRISTIE, Andries and Abigail—David—March 18.
Wit: David and Wybrech Christe.
VESEUR, Willim and Lisabeth—David, b. Aug. 29—Sept. 9.
Wit: David and Rachel Blauvelt.

1770

ACKERMAN, David D. and Jannitje—Daniel (or David?)—Nov. 4.
Wit: Johannis Blauvelt.

1771

BLINKERHOF, Dirk S. and Osseltje—Dirk—Jan. 13.
BLAUVELT, Johannis and Catriena—David, b. Dec. 26, 1770—Feb. 3.

Post, Cobus and Mettie—David—Aug. 4.
  Wit: Jacob S. and Vrouwtje Van Winkel.

1772

Dumaree, Pieter D. and Marytje—David—Jan. 12.
  Wit: David and Sara Terhuyn.

Van Gelder, Hendrik and Antje—David—Sept. 13.
  Wit: David and Wybrecht Christie.

1773

Berdan, Jacob D. and Sara—Dirk, b. Nov. 24—Dec. 19.
  Wit: Lea Van Wageninge.

1774

Asley, John and Elisabeth—David—May 29.
  Wit: David J. and Antje Ackerman.

1775

Blauvelt, Abram and Maria—Daniel—Jan. 8.
  Wit: Gerrit and Tryntje Blauvelt.

Carns, Duglas and Geesje—Dorothie—April 24.

Vandien, Cornelis and Sara—Dirk—July 20.
  Wit: Andries and Catharyntje Vandien.

1767

Terhune, Steven D.—David—Nov. 15.
  Wit: David and Sara Terhune.

1775

Pulisvelt, Willem and Lisabeth—David, b. Aug. 5—Sept. 10.
  Wit: Pieter Pulisvelt and Widow Coenraad Roiger.

Van Orden, Jan P. and Jannitje—David—Dec. 10.
  Wit: David H. and Polly Van Blerkom.

1776

Hoppe, Hendrik I. and Aaltje—Dirk—June 16.
  Wit: Hendrik D. and Polly Terhuyn.

1778

Bos, Samuel, Jr., and Lena—David—Nov. 15.
  Wit: Pieter Debow and wife.

1781

Christie, John and Elisabeth—David—April 7.
  Wit: David and Wybrech Christie.

Ackerman, Johannis D. and Annatje—David—Sept. 16.
  Wit: David and Rachel Hopper.

1785

Vandien, Cornelis (?) and Sierie—Dirk———.
  Wit: Jan and Hankee Berdan.

1786

Ackerman, David and Jannetje—David, b. March 26—April 9.

Vande Voot, Paulus and Maria—Daniel, b. June 26—Aug. 13.

1787

Myer, Martin and Gerrebrecht—David, b. March 23—April 15.
  Wit: David J. and Margrietje Ackerman.

Messeker, Dirk and Lena—Dirk, b. Oct. 18—Nov. 11.

Spiers, David and Grietje—David—Dec. 30.

1788

EARL, Edward and Abigail—Doosje—May 25.
Wit: Hessel and Catriena Ryerson.
DEFFENDORF, George and Elisabeth—Dolle, b. July 1—Aug. 10.
Wit: Willem and Maragrietje Wannemaker.
DEBAEN, Jacob and Geesje—David, b. Aug. 10—Aug. 31.
HORN, Joseph and Marytje—David, b. Nov. 10—Dec. 21.
Wit: David and Jannetje Ackerman.

1789

DEBAEN, Joost and Grietje—David, b. Jan. 10, 1789————.
Wit: Benjamin and Polle Jero.
MEEBIE, Jan and Lea—David, b. July 15—Aug. 9.
Wit: David and Annaatje Debaen.

1791

HOPPE, Andreas D. and Aaltje—David, b. Sept. 1—Sept. 29.
Wit: David and Rachel Hoppe.

1792

ACKERMAN, David and Metje—David, b. March 17—April 10.
Wit: Gerrit and Elisabeth Ackerman.

1793

LESYIER, Abraham and Annaatje—David, b. Sept. 6, 1792—Feb. 17.
Wit: David and Angenietje Eckerson.
VAN VLERCOM, John and Geertje—David, b. April 24—May 9.
Wit: David and Gerretje Van Vlercom

1794

PERRY, Pieter and Marregrietje—Daniel, b. Jan. 18—Feb. 16.
Wit: Daniel and Jannitje Perry.
VAN WINKEL, Francis and Isabella—David, b. July 13—Sept. 14.
ECKERSON, Paulus and Maria—David, b. Sept. 12—Oct. 5.
Wit: David and Angenietje Eckerson.
SYOURT, Adolf and Aaltje—David, b. July 1—Oct. 5.
Wit: Daniel and Cathalyntje Ackerman.
JERSEY, John and Maria—Daniel, b. Nov. 3—Nov. 30.
Wit: Daniel and Jannitje Perry.

1795

TAYLOR, Aaron and Jannitje—Dirkje, b. Dec. 4, 1794—Jan. 4.
TAALMAN, Isaack and Cornelia—David, b. Jan. 16—Feb. 8.
Wit: David and Cornelia Bogert.
BERDAN, Johannis and Maria—Dirk, b. April 19—May 14.
HOPPE, Hendrik and Hettie—David, b. Oct. 2—Nov. 1.
Wit: David and Rachel Hoppe.
TERHUNE, Albert and Leah—Dirk, b. Oct. 31—Nov. 22.
Wit: Abraham and Soecke Terhune.
TISE, John and Rachel—David, b. Oct. 26—Dec. 6.

1796

DEBAAN, Abraham and Sara—David, b. Feb. 20—March 6.
Wit: David and Annaatje Debaan.
V[AN] D. VOTE, Paul and Elisabeth—David, b. Feb. 6—March 27.

VANSCHYVEN, Willem and Saartje—Dirk, b. June 25—July 31.
  Wit: Dirk and Antje Bos.
VANDIEN, Andries and Saartje—Dirk, b. Aug. 8—Sept. 18.
  Wit: Dirk and Maria Vandien.

1797

ECKERSON, Thomas and Susanna—David, b. Jan. 10—Feb. 19.
  Wit: David and Angenietje Eckerson.
VAN BLERCOM, John and Geertje—David, b. Feb. 14—March 19.
  Wit: David and Gerritje Van Blercom.

1798

BOS, Dirk and Antje—Dirk, b. March 17—April 1.
  Wit: Jacob and Selle Vanderbeeck.
HOPPER, Gerrit and Maria—David, b. May 12—July 7.
POTTER, John and Maria—Dolle, b. Nov. 21—Dec. 8.

1800

POULISSON, John and Charitie—David, b. Jan. 3—March 2.
ECKER, Cornelius and Marytje—David, b. Apr. 15—May 11.
BANTA, Abraham and Dievertje—Dievertje, b. Aug. 18—Sept. 14.
QUACKENBUSH, David and Maria—David, b. Sept. 26—Nov. 2.

1801

BURGESS, Daniel and Grietje—Daniel, b. Aug. 18, 1800—Feb. 22.
STUART, Adolf and Aaltje (?)—Daniel, b. Feb. 1—March 1.
BOSCH, Hendrik and Maretje—David, b. March 12—April 5.
COUPER, Lucas and Martyntje—Dirk, b. March 18—April 19.
DEMAREST, David and Geesje—David, b. March 5—May 3.
BOSCH, Reinhart and Elizabeth—John, b. May 5—May 24.
  Wit: Dirk and Antje Bosch.

1802

BROWER, John and Catriena—David, b. Jan. 24—Feb. 14.
ACKERMAN, Daniel and Cathalyntje—David, b. June 29—July 18.

1803

ACKERMAN, Abraham and Sarah—David, b. April 12—May 1.
ACKER, John and Elisabeth—Doritje, b. Feb. 6—June 19.
PARLMAN, Jacobus and Aime—David, b. May 9—June 20.
ACKERMAN, Garrit and Geertje—David, b. Sept. 27—Oct. 16.
DUREMUS, Andrew and Abby—David, b. Sept. 26—Oct. 16.

1804

VANDIEN, Casparus and Maria—Dirk, b. Nov. 15—Dec. 23.
  Wit: Dirk and Antje Vandien.

1805

DEMAREST, Albert and Annatje—David, b. Dec. 21, 1804—Feb. 3.
ECKERSON, Abraham and Trientje—Dorkus, b. July 15—Aug. 4.

1806

VAN VOORHESEN, Nicasie and Beletje—Dirk, b. Aug. 4—Sept. 11.
  Wit: Dirk and Osseltje Brinkerhof.

1807

VANRYPEN, Frederik and Maria—David Baldwin, b. July 17—Aug. 11.

1808
WORTENDYCK, Albert and Margrietje—David, b. Feb. 5—Feb. 21.
ECKERSON, David and Grietje—David, b. Sept. 7—Oct. 23.
1809
ECKERSON, Peter and Margaret—David, b. Dec. 7, 1808—Jan. 1.
ECKERSON, Aaron and Catryntje—Daniel, b. May 16—June 25.
HORN, Andries and Maria—David and Joseph, b. Feb. 23—July 9.
WESTERVELT, Hendrik and Aaltje—Daniel, b. Aug. 3—Aug. 27.
ECKERSON, John and Geertje—David, b. Aug. 23—Sept. 3.
ACKERMAN, John and Maria—Daniel, b. Oct. 23, 1803—Dec. 8.
1810
BUSH, Hendrik and Antje—Dirk, b. Dec. 25, 1809—Feb. 4.
FORSHUR, Cornelius and Maria—David, b. May 27—June 11.
DURYEA, Albert and Angonietje—David, b. Sept. 9—Sept. 30.
1811
ACKERMAN, Daniel and Cathalyntje—David, b. June 26—July 14.
1813
BUSH, Lodewyk and Magdalena—David—March 5.
BUSH, John and Maria—David, b. Oct. 25—Dec. 13.
1815
HOPPER, Garrit H. and Polly—Dolly, b. Feb. 9—March 27.
1816
ACKERMAN, David and Effy—David, b. Oct. 19—Dec. 1.
1817
VANDERBEEK, Abraham and Elisabeth—Daniel, b. Sept. 4—Dec. 21.
1818
ACKERMAN, John A. and Bridget—Daniel, b. Dec. 7 (1817?)—Jan. 11.
HARRIS, Isaac and Hannah—Dorothy, b. May 28—June 28.
WORTENDYKE, Abraham and Catharina—David Demarest, b. June 11
—July 12.
1819
ACKERMAN, Abraham D. and Rachel—David, b. Nov. 30—Dec. 25.
1820
QUACKENBUSH, John J. and Susan—David, b. May 7—June 25.
1823
WESTERVELT, Peter D. and Maria—Daniel Talman, b. Sept. 5—Oct. 20.
1824
ROMINE, John D. and Mary—David, b. April 11—May 16.
1825
TERHUNE, Martin and Caty—David, b. Nov. 17—Dec. 11.
BUTLER, Thomas C. and Jane Ann—Daniel Dash, b. July 23, 1824—Jan. 8.
1827
SMITH, John S. and Patty—David Ackerman, b. Nov. 12, 1826—Jan. 28.
1831
VAN BLARCOM, Henry and Mary—David, b. Aug. 15—Oct. 30.

1833
HAMMON, Thomas and Patty—David Henry, b. July 22—Sept. 1.
1834
VAN ORDEN, Adam and Rosy—David James, b. Sept. 21—Oct. 19.
MORINUS, John D. and Eliza—David, b. Oct. 2—Nov. 9.
1835
HELMS, Daniel and Catharina—Daniel Perry, b. April 3—April 9.
BALDWIN, David and Catharina—David, b. May 13—July 19.
VOORHIS, William and Maria—David Henry, b. Oct. 10—Nov. 1.
1836
EARLE, Jacob and Maria—Daniel Blauvelt, b. July 16—Aug. 14.
1839
HOPPER, Nicholas and Wibie—David Henry, b. Oct. 3—Oct. 27.
1841
ACKERMAN, Albert and Dorcas—David Henry, b. July 25—Oct. 9.
1842
HELMS, Daniel and Catharine—Daniel Peter, b. Jan. 19—May 21.

"E"

1756
ALYEE, Hannes and Annatje—Elsie, b. May 11—May 30.
    Wit. Cobus and Annatje Alyee.
1758
VANDELINDE, Dom. Benjamin and Elisabeth—Ester, b. Sept. 9—Sept. 18.
    Wit: Isack and Janneke Kingsland.
VANBLERKOM, Garrit and Hillegond—Elisabeth—Sept. 24.
    Wit: Adriaan and Hendrik Post.
VONCK, Pieter and Marytje—Elisabeth, b. Oct. 17—Nov. 19.
    Wit: Joseph and Ariaantje Wessels.
1759
HENNION, David and Willemyntje—Eva, b. Jan. 19—Feb. 18.
    Wit: Roelof H. and Annaatje Van Houte.
1761
VAN ZEYL, Pieter and Lena—Egbert, b. Feb. 1.
    Wit: Egbert and Saartje Van Zeyl.
ACKERMAN, Hannes I. and Lena—Elisabeth—Aug. 9.
    Wit: Willem and Grietje Ackerman.
1764
ACKERMAN, Willem and Grietje—Elisabeth—Feb. 5.
    Wit: David J. and Angenietje Ackerman.
1766
DEPUE, Isaac and Brechje—Elisabeth, b. Jan. 4—Feb. 2.
    Wit: Petrus and Lisabeth Depue.
1768
SWIN, Pieter and Elisabeth—Elisabeth, b. May 8—June 5.
    Wit: Christoffel and Rebecka Sendel.
1769
PERRY, Cobus and Annatje—Elisabeth—Jan. 1.
    Wit: Harme and Maria Van Rype.

HOPPE, Andries I. and Elisabeth—Elisabeth—Mar. 26.
Wit: Jan and Elisabeth Hoppe.

VAN BLERKOM, Pieter H. and Jannitje—Elisabeth—Apr. 9.
Wit: Cornelis and Elisabeth Vanhoren.

1770

MESSEKER, Abram and Rachel—Eva—Jan. 14.
Wit: Coenraad and Eva Pielisfelt.

1771

VANBLERCOM, Frans and Jacomyntje—Elisabeth—Feb. 24.
Wit: Cornelis and Elisabeth Vanhoren.

HOPPE, Albert and Rachel—Elisabeth—June 2.
Wit: Johannis and Antje Westervelt.

BOGERT, Jacob and Marytje—Eva—Nov. 10.
Wit: Hendrik Beer.

1772

ACKERMAN, David D. and Lisabeth—Elsje—Feb. 2.
Wit: Abram R. and Jannitje Westervelt

1774

DAVIS, Nikolaas—Egbert—May 8.
Wit: Egbert Van Zeyl.

ZABRISKE, Hendrik C. and Maria—Elisabeth—Aug. 28.
Wit: Christiaan A. and Marytje Zobriskie.

ACKERMAN, Gerrit J. and Rachel—Elisabeth—Sept. 4.
Wit: Cornelis and Elisabeth Ackerman.

1775

BANTA, Thomas W. and Geertruy—Eefje, b. Feb. 13—Apr. 9.

1779

GERRILL, John and Sara—Elisabeth—Apr. 4.

1781

HERS, Hendrik—Elizabeth—July 1.

HENNION, Willem and Eva—Eva, b. June 20—July 1.
Wit: Christiaan and Eva Pulisvelt.

1785

VANDIEN, Andreas and Sara—Elisabeth—Sept. 4.

1786

ACKERMAN, David and Aaltje—Elisabeth, b. May 8—May 14.
Wit: Albert and Elisabeth Terhune.

1787

KNEGT, Coenraad and Grietje—Elisabeth, b. June 11—July 15.
Wit: Hermanus Van Orden; Elisabeth Swin.

VAN BOSKERK, Laurens and Maria—Elisabeth—Dec. 9.
Wit: Johan Jurrie and Elisabeth Snyder.

1788

BERTOLF, Benjamin and Maria—Elisabeth—May 1.
Wit: Jan and Lea Van Imburgh.

HORN, Jacob and Femmetje—Elisabeth, b. July 19—Aug. 10.
Wit: Thomas and Maria Van Boskerk.

BELL, William and Rachel—Elsje Earl—Sept. 8.

1789

SCHUYLER, Adoniah and Elisabeth—Elisabeth—Feb. 17.

ZABRISKE, John and Cornelia—Elisabeth, b. Feb. 13—Mar. 1.
    Wit: Thomas and Maria Vandien.

WILSON, Albert and Maria—Elisabeth, b. June 6—June 15.

MYER, Marten and Brechje—Elisabeth, b. Sept. 5—Oct. 11.

1790

VANDERBEEK, Arie and Lena—Elisabeth, b. Jan. 8—Jan. 31.
    Wit: Thomas and Angenietje Toers.

EARLE, Edward and Abigael—Enoch—Aug. 15.
    Wit: Jacobus G. and Rachel Ackerman.

ACKERMAN, David and Aaltje—Elisabeth, b. Aug. 24—Sept. 13.
    Wit: Albert and Elisabeth Terhune.

1791

GOETSCHIUS, Samuel and Elisabeth—Elisabeth, b. Dec. 29, 1790—Jan. 30.

JURRIE, John and Elisabeth—Elisabeth—Feb. 6.

DIETER, Adam and Rosina—Elisabeth, b. Sept. 14—Oct. 2.
    Wit: Casparus Berberie; Polla Goetschius.

FISHER, Coenraad and Maria—Elisabeth, b. Aug. 18—Oct. 2.
    Wit: Hendrik and Maritje Bos.

1792

SHARP, Morris and Elisabeth—Elisabeth, b. Sept. 15—Nov. 11.
    Wit: James Stagge; Ariaantje Myer.

1793

BOGERT, Steven and Maria—Effie, b. Feb. 22—Mar. 24.

BANTA, Samuel and Elisabeth—Elisabeth, b. May 12—June 9.
    Wit: David Beyerd; Betsey Bayard.

BOURGEES, Daniel and Maragrietje—Elisabeth, b. Sept. 3—Sept. 22.

SMITH, Pieter and Grietje—Elisabeth, b. Aug. 11—Oct. 20.

1794

WILSON, Albert and Maria—Eliah, b. Dec. 16, 1793—Jan. 26.

GOETSCHIUS, John and Annatje—Elisabeth, b. Jan. 18—Mar. 16.

COLE, Adriaan and Elisabeth—Elisabeth, b. Sept. 7—Oct. 26.

YOUMANS, Daniel and Catrina—Elisabeth, b. Oct. 25—Nov. 16.

DURIE, Jan and Annatje—Elisabeth, b. Oct. 17—Dec. 7.
    Wit: Johannes and Saartje Ackerman.

1795

POLHEMIUS, Theodorus and Elisabeth—Elisabeth, b. Aug. 3—Aug. 23.

SWIN, Hendrik and Rachel—Elisabeth, b. Nov. 22—Dec. 25.

1796

RYERS, Jan and Maria—Elisabeth, b. Jan. 17—Jan. 31.

1797

VAN HOORN, Cornelis and Jannetje—Elisabeth, b. Jan. 8—Feb. 19.

EARL, Edward and Abigail—Elisabeth, b. Sept. 22—Oct. 8.

VANORDEN, John and Tryntje—Elisabeth, b. Nov. 9—Dec. 24.

1798

SISCO, Willem and Elsiabeth—Elisabeth, b. Feb. 12—Apr. 1.

1799

ECKERSON, Edward and Hatty—Elisabeth, b. Oct. 26, 1798—Jan. 6.
WORTENDYK, Jacob and Elisabeth—Elisabeth, b. June 20—July 7.
HOPPER, Nicasie and Maria—Elisabeth, b. May 28—July 7.
VAN AULEN, Gerrit and Geertje—Effie, b. June 1—July 7.

1800

ZABRISKIE, John and Margarit—Elisabeth, b. Dec. 19, 1799—Jan. 23.
HEMMION, Nicholaas and Leentje—Elisabeth, b. Jan. 13—Jan. 26.
DERYEA, Samuel and Catriena—Elisabeth, b. Feb. 18—Mar. 12.
STUDS, Henry and Margaret—Elisabeth, b. May 4—July 20.
BARR, David and Mary—Elisabeth, b. April 13—Sept. 21.

1801

FORSHUR, Cornelius and Maria—Elisabeth, b. Apr. 28—May 24.
HOPPER, Albert and Elisabeth—Elisabeth, b. Ma⸚ ⸚—May 25.
HALDEROM, William and Catriena—Elisabeth, ⸚ ,uly 7—Aug. 2.
HOPPER, Hendrik and Myntje—Elisabeth, b. Aug. 26—Sept. 6.
   Wit: Rachel Hopper.
WATSON, Peter and Margaret—Elisabeth, b. Oct. 7—Nov. 1.
ACKERMAN, Lourens and Hester—Elisabeth, b. Nov. 15—Dec. 13.

1802

BOSCH, Dirk and Antje—Elisabeth, b. Jan. 12—Feb. 4.
TERHUNE, John and Catriena—Elisabeth, b. July 8—July 31.

1804

DEBOW, Andreas and Tyna—Elisabeth, b. Dec. 24, 1803—Jan. 8.
ROMAN, Peter and Louisa—Elisabeth, b. Dec. 23, 1803—Sept. 30.

1805

HOPPER, Isaac and Rachel—Elisabeth, b. Dec. 2, 1804—Jan. 13.
ACKERMAN, Gerrit and Jannetje—Elisabeth, b. Mar. 23—Apr. 14.
SMITH, Cornelius and Maria—Edward, b. Apr. 25—June 3.
BUSH, Peter C. and Grietje—Elisabeth, b. Oct. 10—Oct. 27.
POLHEMUS, John and Caty—Elisabeth, b. Oct. 24—Dec. 1.

1806

LARUE, James and Cathalyne—Eliza Wood, b. Nov. 1, 1805—Feb. 16.

1807

CAMPBLE, William and Jannetje—Elisabeth, b. Aug. 19—Oct. 4.
VANDIEN, Casparus and Polly—Elisa Blanch, b. July 1—Oct. 25.
   Wit: Thomas and Elisabeth Blanch.

1808

HOPPER, Jacob and Fytje—Elisabeth, b. May 31—June 25.
SHUART, Adolf and Aaltje—Elisabeth, b. Oct. 15—Nov. 20.

1809

FREDERICK, William and Wyntje—Elisabeth, b. Nov. 10, 1808—Jan. 1.
TAYLOR, Samuel and Sarah—Elisabeth, b. Mar. 23—Apr. 16.

1810

MESSEKER, John C. and Antje—Elisabeth, b. Mar. 2—Apr. 22.
HARRING, Isaac and Antje—Elisabeth, b. Mar. 7—Apr. 26.
HOPPER, Garrit and Maria—Elisabeth, b. Apr. 24—May 20.
SMITH, Peter and Catriena—Elisabeth, b. June 3—July 1.
DEBOW, Isaac and Elisabeth—Elisabeth, b. Sept. 25—Oct. 11.

1811

MOURISON, Peter and Peggy—Elisabeth, b. Dec. 26, 1810—Feb. 10.
EARL, Gerrit and Salla—Edward, b. Mar. 31—June 1.

1812

STORM, John and Aaltje—Elisabeth, b. Feb. 24—Apr. 5.
VANNORSTRAND, John and Polly—Elisabeth, b. June 19—July 12.

1813

COOPER, James and Agnes—Edward, b. Apr. 7—May 9.

1814

ROSEGRANT, Eliah and Corneliah—Eliah, b. June 25—Aug. 22.

1815

ACKERMAN, John and Bridget—Elisabeth, b. Jan. 3—Feb. 5.

1818

VANDIEN, John H. and Leah—Ellen Zabriskie, b. Feb. 4—Mar. 8.

1819

Row, Peter and Jane—Elisabeth, b. Feb. 2—July 11.
VANDERBEEK, Abraham J. and Letty—Eliza, b. Aug. 30—Sept. 19.
ZABRISKIE, Christian J. and Hannah—Elisabeth, b. Nov. 29—Dec. 12.

1820

ZABRISKIE, Abraham C. and Maria—Elisabeth, b. June 23—Aug. 20.
LEYDACKER, John G. and Caty—Elisabeth, b. Aug. 16—Sept. 3.
PULUS, William and Maria—Elisabeth, b. Aug. 8—Sept. 3.

1821

ACKERMAN, Abrm. D. and Rachel—Eliza, b. Sept. 2—Sept. 23.
HOPPER, Garrit A. and Hannah—Eliza Ann, b. Sept. 28—Oct. 21.

1822

KOUGH, Casparus and Tyna—Elisabeth, b. Jan. 9—Apr. 7.

1823

LUTKINS, Harmen and Rachel—Eliza, b. June 3—June 29.
HOPPER, Andrew H. and Maria—Eliza Maria, b. Sept. 2—Oct. 5.

1824

ACKERMAN, Albert A. and Dorcas—Elisabeth Ann, b. Mar. 19—Apr. 18.
TERHUNE, Henry J. and Sally—Eliza Jane, b. July 19—Nov. 14.

1825

HALL, William and Jane—Eliza Jane, b. Sept. 16—Oct. 16.

1826

EARLE, Jacob and Maria—Edward, b. Dec. 30, 1825—Jan. 22.
DOREMUS, George, Jr. and Harriet—Elisabeth, b. May 10—May 28.
HOPPER, Cornelius A. and Betsy—Elisabeth Jemima, b. Oct. 26—Dec.

1827

DEMAREST, John Ab. and Agnes—Eliza, b. Sept. 2—Sept. 23.

ZABRISKIE, Casparus J. and Caty—Eliza Jane, b. Oct. 3—Nov. 4.

ZABRISKIE, Gilliam and Tyna—Elisabeth, b. Nov. 24—Dec. 30.

1828

VANDIEN, Richard A. and Ellen—Elisabeth, b. Feb. 12—Apr. 7.

VOORHIS, Albert A. and Charity—Eliza Jane, b. Sept. 8—Oct. 12.

ZABRISKIE, Stephen J. and Jane—Elisabeth Maria, b. Oct. 7—Oct. 26.

1829

ACKERMAN, Albert A. and Dorcas—Ellen Maria, b. Sept. 19—Oct. 17.

BERVOORT, Garrit and Maria—Elisabeth Maria, b. Dec. 7—Dec. 31.

1830

POST, James R. and Maria—Elisabeth, b. Jan. 2—May 1.

1831

HOPPER, John H. and Mary—Elisabeth, b. Mar. 13—Apr. 3.

1836

ACKERMAN, John I. and Jane—Elisabeth, b. Jan. 8—Jan. 31.

CARLOUGH, Abraham and Maria—Eliza Ann, b. Oct. 31, 1833—Apr. 22.

ZABRISKIE, John J. and Maria—Ellen, b. July 7—Oct. 1.

HOPPER, Nicholas and Wybee—Eliza Jane, b. Sept. 8—Oct. 9.

1838

BANTA, Betsy—Eliza Margaret, b. Mar. 19—Apr. 15.

1840

TURSE, Polly, widow of Ganut—Elisabeth Ellen, b. Dec. 25, 1839—Feb. 8.

LYDACKER, David and Susan—Evelina Amelia, b. Nov. 19, 1839—Apr. 26.

BANTA, Henry H. and Ann Eliza—Eliza Demarest, b. Sept. 19—Nov. 1.

1842

VAN WAGONER, Albert S. and Cornelia—Elisabeth, b. Sept. 1—Nov. 13.

1843

TERHUNE, Casparus and Gitty—Ellen, b. Jan. 5—Mar. 26.

1844

CARLOUGH, Jacob and Maria—Ellen, b. Sept. 12, 1843—Mar. 11.

1845

BANTA, Cornelius and Catherine—Ellen, b. Sept. 25, 1844—Feb. 2.

BENNET, Samuel and Abbe—Elisabeth, b. Nov. 20, 1844—Apr. 20.

ZABRISKIE, John T. and Anne—Elizabeth Jane, b. Mar. 18—July 20.
  Wit: Jane Moore.

VANDIEN, John Z. and Maria—Elizabeth, b. July 7—Oct. 4.

1846

BOGART, Albert and Martha—Ellen Priscilla, b. Nov. 14, 1845—Jan. 4.

1848

ACKERMAN, Abraham H. and Maria—Elizabeth Maria, b Apr. 2—July 22.

1849

ACKERMAN, Peter, Jr. and Eliza—Ellen Jemima, b. Nov. 2, 1848—Feb. 11.

1851

LEARY, William and Leah Ann—Edward Demscombe, b. July 13—Oct. 11.

1852

ZABRISKIE, Andrew C. and Sarah Margaret—Eliza Maria, b. Mar. 6—
May 9.

1853

HOPPER, Rachel—Eliza Ann, b. Oct. 6, 1849—July 9.

"F"

1751

RYERSE, Hannes W. and Marytje—Frans—Mar. 17.
    Wit: Teunis and Lena Ryerse.

1765

NIX, Christoffel and Sara—Femmitje, b. Mar. 22—May 5.
    Wit: Egbert and Saartje V. Zeyl.

1768

VAN RYPE, Harme and Maria—Frederik—Aug. 28.
    Wit: Frederik and Antje Van Rype.

1773

VAN BLERKOM, David J. and Gerritje—Fytje—June 27.
    Wit: Isaac and Fytje Meaby.
SWAN, Rachel—Frances—July 11.
    Wit: Gerrit J. and Elsje Hoppe.

1775

WESTERVELT, Pieter and Cathalyntje—Fytje, b. Dec. 5, 1774—Jan. 2.

1776

MYER, Jacob D. and Ellie—Fytje—Apr. 7.
ODEL, Gerrit and Rebecka—Frances—Feb. 16.
    Wit: Keetje Hoogland.

1787

DEMAREST, Samuel and Catriena—Francyntje, b. Jan. 13—Feb. 11.
    Wit: Barend and Francyntje Fersyeur.
BLAUVELT, Cornelis and Catriena—Francyntje, b. Aug. 5—Aug. 26.
    Wit: Barend and Francyntje Fersyeur.

1794

TAYLOR, Aaron and Jannetje—Phebe, b. Oct. 23, 1792—Mar. 16.
JUREY, John and Elisabeth—Fredrikus, b. Nov. 15—Dec. 14.
    Wit: William and Susanna Jurey.

1795

CROUT, John and Phebe—Phebe, b. Feb. 7—Apr. 12.

1796

DEBAAN, Andreas and Jannitje—Francyntje, b. Dec. 17, 1795—Jan. 1.
    Wit: Barend and Francyntje Fersyeur.

1798

WOERTENDYK, John and Elisabeth—Fredrik, b. Feb. 6—Feb. 11.
    Wit: Neesje Poost.

1801
BOSCH, Lodewyk and Leentje—Francyntje, b. Sept. 5—Oct. 11.
    Wit: Barend and Francyntje Forshuer (originally Verschuer).
1802
SMITH, George and Geertje—Femmetje, b. Oct. 25—Nov. 23.
1814
ZABRISKIE, Hendrik and Sally—Frances Warren, b. Jan. 26—Feb. 27.
BLAUVELT, Frederik and Elisabeth—Frederick, b. Nov. 11, 1813—Mar. 20.
1817
CROWTER, Cornelius and Agnes—Frederik Van Rypen, b. Dec. 8, 1816—
    Jan. 5.
1821
HALL, William and Jane—Frederik, b. June 3—June 31.
DEMAREST, Barney and Susannah—Frances, b. Aug. 29—Oct. 7.
1825
VANDERBEEK, George (or Jeremiah?) and Elisabeth—Frederik, b. July
    26—Sept. 4.
HOPPER, John A. and Mary Ann—Frederik, b. Oct. 2—Nov. 16.
1830
VANDERBEEK, Jeremiah and Elizabeth—Frederik, b. Aug. 11—Sept 26.
1833
VANBLARCOM, Henry A. and Margaret—Francis, b. Aug. 23—Dec. 15.

"G"

1750
ZABRISKIE, Jacob C. and Lena—Gerrit—Sept. 23.
    Wit: Albert and Rachel Ackerman.
ZABRISKIE, Hendrik C. and Neesje—Geertje—Nov. 11.
    Wit: Hartman and Lea Cadmus.
1752
HARMANUS, Nix[1]—Geertje—Aug. 2.
    Wit: Cornelius C. Dugrau.
1753
SYOURT, Willem and Trintje—Grietje—Dec. 2.
    Wit: Christiaan and Grietje Wannemaker.
1754
ODEL, Benjamin and Nellie—Gerrit—July 28.
    Wit: Gerrit I. and Elsje Hoppe.
WESTERVELT, Cornelius J. and Jannike—Gerrit, b. July 19—Aug. 4.
    Wit: Hendrik and Lisabeth Lutkins.
1755
BONGAERT, Lucas and Doritie—Geertje—Aug. 3.
    Wit: Albert H. and Jannitje Terhuyn.
DUGRAU, Abel and Maaike—Geertje—Sept. 14.
    Wit: Barend and Rachel Vanhoren.
LUTKINS, Hendrik and Lisabeth—Gerrit—Sept. 14.
    Wit: Cornelius I. and Janneke Westervelt.

[1]Probably Nix, Harmanus.—EDITOR.

1756

ACKERMAN, Gerrit and Lena—Gerrit—Feb. 1.
Wit: Adam and Rachel Van Voorhees.

ZABRISKE, Jacob H. and Wyntje—Geertrui—Oct. 17.
Wit: Abram and Marytje Terhuyn.

ACKERMAN, David D. and Annatje—Grietje—Dec. 25.
Wit: Harmanus and Aaltje Vanblerkom.

1757

ALYEE, Isaac and Annaatje—Margrietje, b. Jan. 6—Jan. 16.
Wit: Pieter and Margrietje Alyee.

HOPPE, Albert and Rachel—Gerrit—Feb. 6.
Wit: Gerrit and Elsie Hoppe.

HOPPE, Abram and Rebecka—Gerrit, b. Jan. 29—Mar. 12.
Wit: Jan and Jannitje Dykman.

1758

TERHUYN, Abram and Marytje—Geertrui—Feb. 26.
Wit: Jacob H. and Wyntje Zabriskie.

1759

HOPPE, Willem and Antje—Gerrit—Sept. 30.
Wit: Gerrit A. and Hendrikje Hoppe.

1761

TERHUYN, Abraham and Marytje—Geertje, b. June 5.
Wit: Jacob H. and Wyntje Zabriskie.

1764

HELM, Samuel and Trientje—Geertje, b. Oct. 26—Nov. 25.
Wit: Cornelis and Arianntje Myer.

1765

ACKERMAN, Albert and Rachel—Gerrit—Dec. 15.
Wit: Albert C. and Aaltje Zabriske.

1766

VANHOREN, Lucas and Grietje—Gerrit, b. Apr. 9—May 1.
Wit: Gerrit and Jacomyntje Dumaree.

1767

HOPPE, Jan J. and Geertje—Gerrit—Sept. 27.
Wit: Gerrit and Elsje Hoppe.

HOPPE, Gerrit A. and Margrietje—Gerrit, b. Nov. 11—Dec. 6.
Wit: Hendrik and Wyntje Hoppe.

1768

DUMAREE, Pieter P. and Lydea—Gerrit—June 19.
Wit: Andries G. and Abigail Hoppe.

ZABRISKE, Albert J. and Geesje—Gerrit—Sept. 4.

VANBLERKOM, David and Elisabeth—Gerrit—Sept. 25.
Wit: Cobus and Antje Parrelman.

1769

ACKERMAN, Abram and Marietje—Gerrit—June 25.
Wit: Albert and Rachel Ackerman.

1770

HOPPE, Pieter and Annetje—Gerrit—Feb. 19.
Wit: Gerrit H. and Antje Hoppe.
KIP, Isaac N. and Hendrikje—Grietje, b. Mar. 10—Apr. 8.
Wit: Nicasie and Grietje Kip.
DUMAREE, Pieter P. and Lydea—Gerrit, b. Nov. 28—Dec. 25.
Wit: Gerrit A. and Rachel Hoppe.

1772

VANDIEN, Thomas and Polly—Gerrit—Feb. 16.
Wit: Andries and Sarah Vandien.
PILESFELT, Willem and Lisabeth—Geertje—Nov. 8.
Wit: Jacob and Ebbi Myer.

1773

ACKERMAN, Albert G. and Antje—Grietje—Mar. 7.
Wit: Jacob and Grietje Stor.
HOPPE, Jan. J. A. and Jannitje—Geertje, b. Apr. 1—May 2.
Wit: Jan. Hoppe, Jr., and Alltje Hoppe.
HOPPE, Pieter and Annitje—Geesje—May 2.
Wit: Hessel and Geesje Doremus.
BANTA, Thomas—Geesje—Sept. 26.
Wit: Geertje Banta.

1774

ACKERMAN, Willem and Grietje—Gerrit—Feb. 6.
Wit: Gerrit J. and Rachel Ackerman.
DUMAREE, Samuel B. and Rebecka—Geesje—May 29.
Wit: Jacobus and Geesje Deryee.
HOPPE, Jan. J. and Aaltje—Geertje—Aug. 7.
Wit: Jan Clase and Marytje Zabriskie.
RIDDENAAR, Coenraad and Lisabeth—Grietje, b. July 29—Aug. 7.
Wit: Hans and Antje Ridnaar.
ACKERMAN, David G. and Aaltje—Gerrit—Sept. 4.
Wit: Johannes and Lena Ackerman.
HOPPE, Andries G. and Trientje—Gerrit—Sept. 18.
Wit: Gerrit A. and Rachel Hoppe.
ACKERMAN, David D. and Lisabeth—Gerrit—Sept. 25.
Wit: Gerrit D. and Lena Ackerman.

1775

DUBOW, Pieter A. and Brechje—Gerrit—Apr. 2.
Wit: Jacobus and Antje Parrelman.
HOPPE, Andries I. and Lisabeth—Geertje—Sept. 17.
Wit: Benjamin and Annatje Zabriske.

1776

WESTERVELT, Casparus and Rachel—Geertje, b. Feb. 12—Mar. 10.
STEKER, Nathes and Lisabeth—Grietje—Mar. 17.
Wit: Jacob Valentyne; Grietje Valentyne.
BREVOORT, Samuel and Martynyje—Grietje—Apr. 21.
Wit: Johannis and Grietje Brevoort.
ALLEN, John and Margaret—Guy—Oct. 14.

1780

PERKHOFF, Hendrik and Polly—Geesje—Mar. 19.
    Wit: Cornelis and Geesje Vanhoren.
VANBLERCOM, Samuel and Sucke—Gerrit—Nov. 19.

1782

VANHORN, Daniel and Antje—Grietje—Feb. 25.
HERRING, Cornelis—Gerrit, b Dec. 9, 1781—Jan. 6.
    Wit: Gerrit Ariaanse.

1783

HALDRUM, Nicolaas and Marretje—Geertje.
    Wit: Abraham Haldrum and wife Judik.

1782

BOGERT, Steven—Geesje—Dec. 4.
HOPPE, Steven and Giertje—Gerrit—July 25.
    Wit: Andries and Tryntje Hoppe.

1783

LOURENS—Grietje—Apr. 26.

1784

ECKERSE, Edward—Grietje—Apr. 25.
BEL, Bellie and Rachel—Gerrit Jan Hoppe, b. Apr. 1—May 16.
    Wit: Jan Hoppe and wife.
HOPPE, Jan J. and Catharina— Geertje—Apr. 10.
    Wit: Albert Van Voorhees and wife.

1785

HOPPE, Hendrik and Rachel—Gerrit, b. June 11—July 3.
    Wit. Gerrit and Antje Hoppe.
MOLGRAF, Boljer and Christien—Grietje—Sep. 4.
    Wit: Lodewyk and Grietje Fisher
ZABRISKE, Abraham and Maria—Gerrit—Sept. 11.
    Wit: Gerrit Zabriske.
BELL, Wm. M. and Rachel—Gerard De Peyster—Sep. 25.
    Wit: Gerard De Peyster and Sally Swartwout.
VANDIEN, Albert and Polly—Gerrit—Nov. 13.
    Wit: Cornelis and Sara Vandien.

1786

DE BAAN, Jan and Wyntje—Gerrit, b. Jan. 11—Feb. 5.
    Wit: Gerrit and Cathalyntje Durie.
SMYTH, Albert and Susanna—Gerrit, b. Mar. 11—Apr. 9.
    Wit: Gerrit and Hester Smith.
HOPPE, Gerrit and Maria—Gerrit, b. June 24—July 9.
    Wit: Arie and Christina Ackerman.
QUIN, Tertullian and Elsje—Grietje, b. July 4—Sep. 10.
VAN BLERKOM, Petrus and Jannetje—Gerrit, b. Oct. 10—Oct. 22.
    Wit: Gerrit and Rachel Ackerman.
Bos, Dirk and Antje—Grietje, b. Nov. 13—Dec. 24.
    Wit: Pieter and Grietje Bos.

1787

BERTOLF, Jacobus and Lea—Guliaam, b. Dec. 22, 1786—Jan. 28.

GOETSCHIUS, Piatus and Catriena—Grietje, b. Dec. 28, 1786—Jan. 28.

VAN RYPE, Herman and Maria—Gerrit, b. Mar. 29—May 6.
　Wit: Gerrit and Abigail Van Rype.

DEBAAN, Petrus and Maria—Grietje—Sep. 16.

POST, Pieter I. and Rachel—Grietje, b. Nov. 27—Dec. 25.
　Wit: Pieter and Nellie Davis.

1788

VANDIEN, Harmen and Aaltje—Gerrit—May 1.
　Wit: Albert and Maria Vandien.

ZABRISKIE, Hendrik and Maria—Gerrit—June 22.

POST, Jacob and Sara—Gerrit, b. Aug. 5—Aug. 31.

BOS, Lodewyk and Leentje—Grietje, b. Nov. 22—Dec. 21.
　Wit: Hendrik and Maria Bos.

SERVENT, John and Grietje—Grietje, b. Nov. 20—Dec. 21.

1789

BOS, Pieter and Frone—Grietje, b. Feb. 15—Mar. 1.
　Wit: Pieter and Grietje Watkins.

HOPPE, Jan J. and Catriena—Gerrit and Jan (twins), b. Feb. 7—Mar. 1.

1791

ACKERMAN, Jacobus G. and Rachel—Gerardus, b. Mar. 20—Apr. 3.
　Wit: Gerrit G. Ackerman and wife.

1792

HOPPE, Hendrik and Aaltje—Geertje, b. Mar. 10—Apr. 10.
　Wit: Abraham J. and Geertje Hoppe.

BANTA, Johannis and Tryntje—Gerrit, b. Mar. 10—Apr. 10.
　Wit: Gerrit and Cathalyntje Durie.

1794

OLDIS, Gerrit and Rebecka—Gerrit, b. May 25—June 22.
　Wit: Jan and Rachel Hoppe.

HOPPE, John and Maria—Gerrit, b. July 2—July 27.
　Wit: Gerrit and Maria Hoppe.

1795

ZABRISKE, Jacob and Elisabeth—Geesje, b. Feb. 8—Feb. 19.
　Wit: Gerrit and Maria Zabriske.

CROUTER, John and Maragrietje—George, b. Mar. 11—Apr. 12.

1796

POST, Pieter and Neesje—Gerrit, b. Dec. 16, 1795—Feb. 28.

WREYGHT, Albert and Annaatje—Geertje, b. Aug. 7—Sep. 18.

HOPPE, Abraham and Geertje—Geertje, b. Nov. 3—Dec. 25.

1797

VANDIEN, Cornelis and Margrietje—Gerrit, b. Apr. 8—Apr. 23.

1798

HOPPE, Jan G. (?) and Rachel—Gerrit, b. Apr. 7—May 29.

FLEISCHMAN, Abraham and Sophia Elisabeth—George Scriba, b. July
　29—Sep. 9.

BLAUVELT, Abraham and Elisabeth—Geertje, b. July 24—Aug. 11.
    Wit: Isaac and Geertje Blauvelt.

1799

HOPPER, Albert and Elisabeth—Gerrit, b. Oct. 20—Nov. 10.
ACKERMAN, John and Maria—Gerrit, b. Apr. 24—June 2.

1800

SMITH, Gerrit and Hetty—Gerrit, b. Nov. 30—Dec. 7.

1801

COLE, John and Elisabeth—Grietje, b. Aug. 18, 1799—Feb. 22.
PARLEMAN, James and Aimy—Gilbert, b. Nov. 18, 1800—Feb. 22
DEMAREST, Jacobus and Maria—Gerrit, b. June 6—July 12.
    Wit: Gerrit and Annatje Zabriskie.

1802

POST, John C. and Cornelia—Geertje, b. Jan. 7—Feb. 14.
DEBAUN, Abraham and Saartje—Geertje, b. Feb. 22—Mar. 7.
VAN DIEN, Casparus and Polly—Gerrit, b. Apr. 25—June 7.
HOPPER, Andreas and Aaltje V.—Gerrit—b. June 10—July 11.

1803

VANHOUTEN, John and Antje—Grietje, b. Jan. 1—Jan. 23.
ACKERMAN, John and Elisabeth—Geertje, b. Feb. 18—Apr. 10.
TOLMAN, Jacob and Polly—Garret, b. Apr. 5—Apr. 24.
DEMAREST, Jacob and Geesje—Garret Hopper, b. May 28—June 19.
    Wit: Garret and Dirkje Hopper.
VANHORN, John and Elisabeth—Geertje, b. Aug. 1—Aug. 24.
ZABRISKIE, Jacob C. and Elisabeth—Guiliaam, b. Feb. 13—Mar. 4.

1804

SNYDER, John and Polly—George, b. Apr. 5—June 17.
DEBAAN, Jacob and Maria—Geesje, b. July 13—Aug. 12.
PERVO, Hendrik and Polly—Gerrit Hopper, b. Sept. 1—Sept. 30.
    Wit: Gerrit and Tyne Hopper.
ZABRISKIE, Albert and Aaltje—Gerrit, b. July 14—Nov. 25.
    Wit: Gerrit and Annatje Zabriskie.
HARING, Jacob and Femmetje—Geertje, b. Nov. 19—Dec. 9.

1805

DEY, Solomon and Sally—Ginny, b. Apr. 3—May 5.
HARING, Peter and Elisabeth—Grietje, b. May 29—June 20.

1806

NACHEBACH, Thomas and Antje—George, b. Dec. 18, 1805—Jan. 26.
VANDERBEEK, Coenradus and Annatje—Geesje, b. Apr. 20—July 20.
BOGERT, Elisabeth—Geertje, b. June 16—Aug. 3.
    Wit: Geertje Bogert.
VAN RYPEN, Frederik and Mary—Gerrit, b. Sept. 16—Nov. 16.
DOREMUS, Jacobus and Polly—Ginny, b. Nov. 22—Dec. 14.
QUACKENBUSH, Barend and Catriena—Geertje, b. Apr. 5—Apr. 26.

1807

POTTER (?), John and Maria—Grietje, b. Apr. 14—May 10.

1808

TOLMAN, John and Geertje—Garret, b. Feb. 11—Mar. 6.
  Wit: Gerrit and Maria Hopper.
BREVOORT, John and Jane—Gerrit, b. June 5—July 10.
BLAUVELT, Isaac and Sara—Geertje, b. June 16—July 24.
  Wit: Geertje Blauvelt.
HOPPER, Albert and Maria—Gerrit, b. Aug. 21—Sept. 11.
BREVOORT, Hendrik and Maria—Gerrit, b. Oct. 1—Oct. 30.

1809

BOGERT, John and Jacomyntje—Gerrit, b. Dec. 14, 1808—Jan. 29.

1808

OSBURN, Mathew and Aaltje—Gerrit, b. Nov. 5—Dec. 25.

1809

HOPPER, Henry And. and Annatje—Garret, b. Jan. 4—Feb. 12.
HOPPER, Garret S. and Marytje—Geertje, b. Aug. 16—Aug. 31.
HOPPER, Hendrik and Elisabeth—Gerrit, b. Dec. 2—Dec. 25.
  Wit: Gerrit and Dirkje Hopper.

1811

ACKERMAN, Garrit and Geertje—Garret, Mar. 30—May 19.

1812

ROSEGRANT, Elijah and Cornelia—George Puffern, b. May 24—July 30.
ACKERMAN, David and Matty—Garrit, b. Aug. 18—Sept. 13.

1813

ZABRISKIE, Jacob and Anne—Gillam, b. Oct. 18—Nov. 21.
HOPPER, Andrew C. and Anne—Garrit, b. Nov. 4—Dec. 5.

1816

CLAARWATER, Frederik and Hetty—Garrit, b. May 25—June 16.
TURSE, Lawrence and Jane—Garrit, b. June 15—July 20.
SNYDER, George T. and Charity—Garrit, b. Nov. 30—Dec. 22.

1817

ALGER, William I. and Jane—George, b. Nov. 20, 1816—Apr. 5.
LYDACKER, John G. and Caty—Garrit, b. Sept. 10—Oct. 5.
SNYDER, Garret and Catharina—Garrit, b. Nov. 20—Dec. 14.

1819

BELL, Garrit I. H. and Anne—Garrit, b. July 28—Aug. 22.
SNYDER, Richard and Ally—Garrit, b. Sept. 2—Oct. 3.
HOPPER, Andrew H. and Maria—George Doremus, b. Oct. 24—Nov. 14.

1820

BANTA, Garrit D. and Harriet—Garrit, b. Mar. 1—Apr. 3.
ZABRISKIE, Henry A. and Patty—Garrit, b. Nov. 2—Dec. 17.

1821

ZABRISKIE, Abraham A. and Jane—Garrit, b. Jan. 17—Feb. 25.
HOPPER, John H. and Mary—Garrit, b. July 19—Aug. 12.
ZABRISKIE, John J. and Maria—Gilliam, b. Nov. 14—Dec. 16.
POST, Anne—Gerrit Muculus, b. Oct. 12—Dec. 29.

1822

VANDIEN, Cornelius G. and Jane—Garrit, Nov. 6—Dec. 1.

1823

ACKERMAN, Andrew and Catharine—Garrit, b. Dec. 22, 1822—Jan. 26.

JINKINS, William and Dorothy—Garrit Van Wagoner, b. Oct. 28—Dec. 14.

1825

HOPPER, David and Charity—Garrit, b. Sept. 4—Oct. 2.

1824

DOREMUS, George, Jr. and Harriet—George, b. Jan. 3—Feb. 8.

HOPPER, Henry G. and Margaret—Garrit, b. June 2—July 9.

1826

HOPPER, John H. and Mary—George, b. Dec. 19, 1825—Jan. 22.

HARRIS, Henry and Hannah—George, b. Feb. 9—Mar. 19.

1827

VANDERBEEK, Paul and Hannah—Garrit Van Wagoner, b. May 29—July 1.

ZABRISKIE, Henry J. and Elisabeth—Garrit, b. Nov. 19—Dec. 30.

1828

BANTA, Henry H. and Levina—Garrit Zabriskie, b. Apr. 23—May 11.

HOPPER, Nicholas and Wibie—Garrit, b. Mar. 29—May 11.

1829

LYDACKER, David and Susan—Garrit, b. May 23—Oct. 25.

1831

VANDERBEEK, James and Peggy—Getty, b. Jan. 12—Mar. 6.

1832

BEATY, George and Rachel—George Albert, b. July 29, 1830—Mar. 25.

1834

VANDIEN, Garrit and Jane—Garrit, b. Jan. 27—Apr. 27.

1836

TERHUNE, Casparus and Gettie—Garrit, b. May 28—July 10.

VAN SAUN, John S. and Elsje—Garrit Zabriskie, b. Aug. 7—Sept. 26.

1837

TERHUNE, Casparus and Getty—Garrit, b. June 25—Aug. 6.

1838

HAMMON, Thomas and Patty—Garrit, b. Dec. 15, 1837—Feb. 4.

1842

VAN WAGONER, Garrit and Jemima—Garrit, b. Mar. 16—May 12.

VANDIEN, John Z. and Maria—Garrit Henry, b. June 20—Aug. 14.

1848

LACKY, James and Catharine—Garrit Banta, b. May 7, 1847—Jan. 2.

ACKERMAN, Garrit D. and Eliza—Garrit, b. Dec. 21, 1847—Feb. 20.

WESLEY, Garret and Catharine—Guistica, b. June 4—July 23.

1850

TERHUNE, Abraham and Caty—George Demarest, b. Apr. 5—July 21.

1851

VANDERBEEK, Aaron and Jane Elisabeth—George, b. Mar. 3—Apr. 6.

"H"

1749

STEVENS, Nathaniel and Lea—Hendrik—May 21.
Wit: Hendrik and Grietje Riddenaar.

WANNEMAKER, Pieter and Marytje—Hendrik—Nov. 26.
Wit: Joost and Elisabeth Schyourt.

RUTAN, Hannes and Aaltje—Hannes—Nov. 26.
Wit: Dennis D. and Lea Rutan.

1751

VANDERBEEK, Paulus and Rachel—Hannes—June 14.
Wit: Hannes and Marytje Van Blercom.

1752

ZABRISKIE, Jacob H. and Wyntje—Hendrikus—Mar. 8.
Wit: Hendrik and Geertje Zabriskie.

VOS, Hendrik and Anna Margrit—Hendrik—Aug. 9.
Wit: Coenraad and Marytje Wannemaker.

VOS, Philip and Lisabeth—Hendrik and Coenradus (twins)—Aug. 9.
Wit: Hendrik and Anna Margriet Vos; Coenraad and Catriena
Muyseger.

STORM, Hendrik and Cornelia—Hendrik—Oct. 16.
Wit: Jurrien and Marytje Vanderbeek.

1754

DUREMES, Hessel and Geesje—Hendrik—Apr. 28.
Wit: Hendrik and Lybe Van Ale.

TERHUYN, Dirk and Lea—Hendrikus—May 4.
Wit: Hendrik and Geertje Zobrowiske.

VAN ZEYL, Pieter and Lena—Hannes—May 4.
Wit: Hans and Lena Van Zeyl.

1756

ACKERMAN, Pieter and Antje—Hendrik—Feb. 5.
Wit: Steven and Tryntje Zoberewiske.

WANNEMAKER, Harmanus and Susanna—Hendrik, b. Dec. 23, 1755—
Mar. 7.
Wit: Hendrik and Lisabeth Wannemaker.

SLINGERLAND, Teunis—Hendrik and Abram (twins)—May 9.
Wit: Abel and Maaike Degrau; Joshua S. and Lisabeth Bos.

VAN ZEYL, Pieter and Lena—Hermanus—May 9.
Wit: Hermanus Vanblerkom.

(Name of second witness obliterated).

1757

LAROY, Cobus and Rebecka—Hendrik—Dec. 4.
Wit: Lambert and Lybe Laroy.

1758

LUTKENS, Hendrik and Leybe—Harme—Feb. 12.
Wit: Hannes and Maritje Vanhoren.

1759

HOPPE, Andries and Marytje—Hendrik—Sep. 9.
Wit: Hendrik and Wyntje Hoppe.

1760

HOPPE, Hendrik A. and Wyntje—Hendrik—Feb. 17.
Wit: Jan. A. and Lisabeth Hoppe.

DEGRAU, Klaes and N. N.—Hermanus—Mar. 23.
Wit: Lucas and N. N. Van Blerkum.

1761

BOGERT, Jacob and Marytje—Hendrik—May 24.
Wit: Hendrik and Antje Beer.

1762

BANTA, Jacob and Lena—Hendrik—Sep. 12.
Wit: Hendrik and Sara Banta.

1763

TERHUYN, Abram and Marytje—Hendrikus or Hendrika—Aug. 7.
Wit: Albert H. and Telletje Zabriske.

VAN ZEYL, Hannes A. and Catriena—Hendrik—Aug. 7.
Wit: Hendrik and Marytje Messeker.

1764

TRAPHAGE, Hendrik and Claartje—Hendrik—June 10.
Wit: Gerrit H. and Antje Hoppe.

1765

DERYIE, Daniel and Vrouwtje—Hendrika—Feb. 10.
Wit: Jan R. and Hendrika Berdan.

ALYEE, Abram—Hendrik—Oct. 13.

LUTKENS, Harme and Antje—Hendrik—Nov. 24.
Wit: Hendrik and Lybe Lutkens.

1767

V. DIEN, Gerrit and Sara—Harme—Jan. 25.
Wit: Harme and Antje Lutkins.

BOGERT, Jacob and Marytje—Jannitje—Apr. 24.
Wit: Jacob J. and Jannitje Zobriske.

HOPPE, Abram H. and Antje—Hendrik—July 5.
Wit: Hendrik and Wyntje Hoppe.

HOPPE, David and Rachel—Hendrik—Aug. 30.
Wit: Abram H. and Antje Hoppe.

1768

RITE, Willem and Aaltje—Hendrik—Sep. 19.
Wit: Hendrik Ackerman and Lea A. Zabriske.

1769

BROUWER, Abram D.—Hans—June 4.
Wit: Brechje Van Blercom.

RIDNAER, Hendrik H. and Marytje—Hendrik—July 23.
Wit: Hendrik and Margrit Ridnaer.

TERHUYN, Samuel and Lea—Hendrik—Dec. 3.
Wit: Hendrik C. and Maria Zabriske.

VAN IMBURGH, John and Antje—Hendrik—Dec. 31.
Wit: Hannes and Ariaantje Van Imburgh.

1770

RIDDENAAR, Hannes and Nansje—Hendrik, b. May 5—May 20.
Wit: Hendrik H. and Marytje Riddenaar.

CLERCK, Jacobus D. and Neeltje—Hermanus, b. Apr. 11—May 27.
Wit: Harmanus and Rebecca Taelman.

HOPPE, Abram H. and Antje—Hendrik—June 4.
Wit: Hendrik and Aaltje H. Hoppe.

TRAPHAGE, Hendrik—Hannes—June 4.
Wit: Paulus J. and Rachel Vanderbeek.

V. HOUTEN, Adriaan and Maritje—Helmeg—June 4.
Wit: Abram and Lea Cadmus.

1771
LUTKINS, Jan and Grietje—Harme—June 30.
Wit: Hendrik and Lybe Lutkins.

HOPPE, Andries J. and Lisabeth—Hester—June 30.
Wit: Abram J. and Brechje Ackerman.

SWIN, Pieter and Lisabeth—Hendrik, b. Aug. 14—Sep. 15.
Wit: Hendrik and Crastina Ryke.

1772
HOPPE, Jan H. and Fytje—Hessel—Mar. 15.
Wit: Pieter H. and Antje Hoppe.

VAN RYPE, Gerret and Abigael—Hendrika—Apr. 15.
Wit: Gerrit A. and Rachel Hoppe.

HOPPE, Andries G. and Lea—Hendrika—June 9.
Wit: Gerrit A. and Rachel Hoppe.

1774
LUTKENS, Harme and Antie—Harme—Feb. 26.
Wit: Pieter and Annatje Lutkens.

VAN GELDER, Jonathan and Rachel—Hittie, b. Oct. 23—Nov. 20.

1775
JENKENS, Lambertus and Annatje—Hannes, b. Jan. 24—Feb. 19.
Wit: Cobus H. and Trientje Bertolf.

VALENTYNE, Jacob and Grietje—Hantice—Feb. 19.
Wit: Mathys Valentine.

BOGERT, Jacob and Marytje—Hendrik—May 28.
Wit: Jacob Ja. and Aaltje Zobriske.

VAN BLERKOM, Pieter H. and Jannitje—Harmanus—June 9.
Wit: Hannes J. and Lena Ackerman.

1779
HOPPE, Andries G. and Tryntje—Hendrik—Dec. 12.
Wit: Gerrit H. and Antje Hoppe.

1782
STOERM, Staats—Hendrik—Jan. 11.
Wit: Hendrik.

1784
HOPPE, Pieter—Hendrik—May 16.
Wit: Hendrik Dremes and wife.

TERHUNE, Jan—Harmen—July 11.
Wit: Harmen Lutkins and wife.

STORM, Staats ————————

1785

BOGERT, Jacob—Hendrik—Apr. 10.
    Wit: Jacob Bogert and wife Maria.
ZABRISKIE, Hendrik I. and Polly—Hendrikus—Aug. 14.
    Wit: Wyntje I. Zabriske.

1786

VERVELEN, Gideon and Maria—Hendrik, b. Dec. 1, 1785—Jan. 29.
    Wit: Cornelis and Catrina Eckerson.

1787

SLOT, Isaac and Lea—Helena, b. July 28—Aug. 26.
    Wit: Christiaan J. and Maria Zabriskie.
TRAPHAGE, Jonathan H. and Polly—Hendrik—Sep. 16.
    Wit: Hendrik and Grietje Traphage.

1788

TRAPHAGE, Jonathan and Catriena—Hendrik—Jan. 1.
    Wit: Hendrik and Grietje Traphage.
JERSEY, Pieter and Annaatje—Hendrik, b. Mar. 4—Apr. 20.
    Wit: Jan and Grietje Servent.
VAN BLERCOM, David and Maria—Harman—June 22.
GERRITSEN, Johannis and Maria—Hessel, b. July 11—July 27.
    Wit: Abraham and Catriena Cadmus.
GERRITSON, Johannis H. and Maria—Hessel, b. July 13—Aug. 10.
    Wit: Hessel and Sara Gerritson.

1789

Bos, Dirk and Antje—Hendrik—Apr. 29.
ZABRISKE, Jan J. and Hendrikje—Hendrikje, b. Apr. 20—June 7.
    Wit: Gerrit and Abigail Van Rype.
ZABRISKE, Abraham and Maria—Hendrik, b. July 28—Aug. 9.

1790

SHARP, Morris and Elisabeth—Hester—Dec. 12.

1791

SMITH, Gerrit and Hette—Hette, b. Jan. 4—Jan. 30.
    Wit: Hendrik and Hette Frerikse.
PULESVELT, Petrus and Nense—Hendrik, b. June 25—July 24.
    Wit: Hendrik and Cornelia Pulesvelt.
DATIE, John and Polly—Hannah, b. Aug. 1—Aug. 21.
    Wit: Abraham and Hannah Datie.

1792

BOUMAN, Michael and Maria—Hermanus—Feb. 26.
    Wit: Hermanus and Maria Kerlogh.
POULUSSE, John and Klaasje—Hendrik, b. Jan. 7—Feb. 26.
    Wit: Hendrik and Jacomyntje Hoppe.
GOETSCHIUS, Piatus and Catriena—Hester—Apr. 10.
HOPPE, Gerrit J. and Maria—Hendrik, b. Aug. 20—Sep. 16.
    Wit: Hendrik and Jannetje Terhuen.
ECKERSON, Nikolaes and Maria—Hendrik, b. Oct. 18—Nov. 11.
    Wit: Hendrik and Maria Oldis.

1793

SICKELSEN, Jacobus and Maria—Henricus—Mar. 10.

1794
WESTERVELT, Albert and Margrietje—Hendrik, b. May 19—June 22.
MESSEKER, Helmegh and Fytje—Hendrik, b. May 24—June 22.
VANHOORN, Pieter and Rachel Van Gelder—Hettie, b. Mar. 15—June 22.

1795
TERHUEN, Hendrik and Rachel—Hendrikje, b. Mar. 27—Apr. 19.
Wit: Gerrit and Abigail Van Rype.
MESSEKER, Lodewyk and Sara—Hendrik—Oct. 18.
Wit: Edward and Abigail Earle.
BOSCH, Samuel and Lena—Hendrik, b. Sep. 22—Dec. 25.

1796
ROTAN, Abraham and Maria—Hendrik, b. Oct. 25—Dec. 25.
Wit: Hendrik and Jannitje Terhuen.

1797
Bos, Reinhart and Elisabeth—Hendrik, b. May 21—June 4.
Wit: Isaak and Maria Vrerikse.
ZABRISKA, Cornelius and Maria—Hendrik, b. Nov. 5—Nov. 26.
Wit: Hendrik and Maria Zabriske.
ACKERMAN, Abraham and Salome—Hendrik, b. Nov. 28—Dec. 24.

1798
ZABRISKE, Jan J. and Margrietje—Hendrikje, b. Dec. 23, 1797—Feb. 5.
Wit: Gerrit and Abigail Van Rype.
LUTKENS, Stephen and Rachel—Harmen, b. Feb. 13—Mar. 4.
CHRISTOPHER, John and Aaltje—Hendrik, b. Feb. 23—Mar. 4.

1800
VAN RYPEN, Frederik and Maria—Harmen, b. May 24—June 29.
Wit: Harmen and Maria Van Rypen.

1801
ACKERMAN, Jacobus and Lea—Henderik, b. Mar. 17—Apr. 19.
Wit: Hendrik and Aaltje Hopper.
VAN IMBURGH, Henry and Polly—Henry, b. July 13—July 28.
CONKLIN, Lewis and Rebeckah—Hannah, b. Nov. 21—Dec. 27.

1802
VAN VOORHEESEN, Nicasie and Beeltje—Hendrik, b. Jan. 2—Jan. 31.

1803
TERHUNE, Albert and Rachel—Hendrik, b. Feb. 13—Mar. 27.
HARRIS, Isaac and Annatje—Hendrik, b. Mar. 20—Apr. 27.
Wit: Neesje Harris.
BARTOLF, Stephanus and Jannetje—Henry, b. May 28, 1801—June 20.
BLAUVELT, Arie and Jacomyntje—Hendrik, b. June 22—July 24.

1805
HOPPER, Hendrik and Jacomyntje—Hendrik, b. Dec. 29, 1804—Jan. 27.
HARING, Garrit and Maria—Hetty, b. Jan. 23—Feb. 17.
SMITH, Henry and Rachel—Hetty, b. June 1—June 23.
COLE, Adriaan and Elisabeth—Harmen, b. July 2—Aug. 3.
Wit: Antje Cole.

1806

ROMEN, Peter and Louisa—Hendrik, b. Dec. 17, 1805—Sep. 7.
ACKERMAN, Gerrit A. and Geertje—Hendrik, b. Nov. 13—Dec. 14.

1808

HOPPER, John and Maretje—Hendrik, b. Dec. 13, 1807—Jan. 1.
VALENTYNE, Abraham and Maria—Hendrik, b. Mar. 5—May 15.
BOS, Lodewyck and Lena—Hendrik, b. July 5—Aug. 7.
TYCE, Henry and Maria—Hendrik, b. Jan. 31—Sep. 18.
ACKERMAN, Albert and Elisabeth—Hester, b. Oct. 3—Oct. 23.

1809

STORM, Jacob and Leah—Hendrik, b. Oct. 24, 1808—Jan. 1.
ESLER, Andrew and Rachel—Hendrik, b. Dec. 15, 1808—Jan. 22.
DEBAUN, John and Aaltje—Hetty, b, Mar. 18—Apr. 3.
HERRES, Jacob and Hester—Hendrik, b. July 24—Aug. 27.

1810

VANDERBEEK, Paulus and Annaatje—Harmen, b. Mar. 17—Apr. 22.

1811

DEMAREST, Albert and Annatje—Hendrik, b. Dec. 5, 1810—Feb. 10.
GOETSCHIUS, Henry and Selly—Hermanus, b. Mar. 18—Apr. 14.

1812

DAY, William and Jenna—Harriet, b. Mar. 8—May 9.
SNYDER, Adam and Caty—Henry, b. July 7—July 10.

1813

CONCLE, Isaac and Jane—Henry, b. Jan. 20—Feb. 21.
FREEMAN, Francis and Mary—Hassel, b. Dec. 28, 1812—Feb. 28.
SNYDER, Richard and Ally—Henry, b. Mar. 9—Apr. 18.
TURSE, Lawrence and Jane—Hannah, b. May 1—May 30.

1814

HOPPER, Andrew H. and Maria—Henry, b. Jan. 16—Feb. 13.
ZABRISKIE, Jacob A. and Anny—Hannah, b. Aug. 27—Dec. 10.

1815

BANTA, Garrit D. and Harriet—Henry, b. Oct. 13—Nov. 3.
VANDERBEEK, John H. and Anne—Harman, b. Oct. 4—Nov. 5.

1816

LYDACKER, John G. and Caty—Henry Hopper, b. June 28—Mar. 3 (*sic*).
WESTERVELT, Luke and Polly—Hetty Van Dien, b. Feb. 20—Apr. 7.
ZABRISKIE, Henry H. and Sally—Henry, b. July 18—Aug. 11.

1817

TAYLOR, John and Agnes—Hannah, b. May 6—July 13.
DEMAREST, James J. and Anny—Henry, b. June 2—July 20.
ACKERMAN, John A. and Polly—Henry, b. Aug. 29—Sep. 21.

1818

VAN EMBURGH, John and Polly—Henry, b. Jan. 25—Feb. 22.

1818
VANDERBEEK, James and Peggy—Hannah, b. Mar. 17—Apr. 26.

HOPPER, Albert G. and Polly—Henry, b. July 30—Sep. 20.

ACKERMAN, David D. and Effy—Hannah, b. May 5—May 30.

1819
HOPPER, Andrew P. and Anne—Henry, b. Aug. 8—Sep. 5.

1820
ZABRISKIE, Andrew J. and Polly—Hester Jane, b. May 29—June 25.

ACKERSON, John and Mary—Hannah, b. Aug. 17—Sep. 17.

1826
VANDERBEEK, Andrew and Polly—Henrietta, b. Oct. 15—Dec. 10.

1827
VANDERBEEK, Jerry and Hannah—Hannah, b. Jan. 11—Feb. 11.

HOPPER, Andrew P. and Anne—Hellen, b. Oct. 29—Dec. 2.

VAN BUSKIRK, Albert and Dolly—Hannah, b. Nov. 25—Dec. 30.

1828
HUTCHISON, Pardon and Tyna—Henry, b. Jan. 3—Feb. 17.

EARLE, Jacob and Maria—Hannah, b. Apr. 25—May 25.

BREVOORT, Garrit and Maria—Henry, b. May 1—May 26.

TERHUNE, Henry and Maria—Henry, b. May 2—June 1.

VANDERBEEK, Jurry C. and Eliza—Hannah, b. Sep. 17—Oct. 19.

1829
HOPPER, Garrit A. and Sophia—Hannah, b. Jan. 11—Feb. 7.

1830
VAN RYPER, Harmen F. and Caty—Hannah, b. Feb. 1—Feb. 20.

VAN WINKLE, John and Caty—Hannah Jane, b. June 26—Sep. 5.

STORMS, Cornelius and Sally—Henry, b. Nov. 21—Dec. 26.

1831
VANDERBEEK, Jurry and Hannah—Henry, b. Mar. 24—Apr. 24.

HOPPER, John An. and Ellen—Hannah, b. July 22—Sep. 11.

1832
BRICKLE, George and Ally—Hiram, b. Oct. 23—Nov. 25.

1833
VANDIEN, John H. and Hannah—Harman, b. Dec. 25, 1832—Mar. 24.

ZABRISKIE, Cornelius J. and Jane—Henry Lewer (?) b. July 3—Oct. 24.

1837
SNYDER, James and Charity—Henry, b. June 2—July 8.

1840
HOPPER, George D. and Rachel—Henry Garison, b. July 28—Dec. 13.

1841
ACKERMAN, Garrit D. and Eliza—Hannah Jane, b. Aug. 28—Oct. 17.

1844
BANTA, Henry H. Jr. and Ann—Henry Schuyler, b. Sep. 16—Nov. 10.

1847
WESTERVELT, John P. and Sally P.—Henry, b. Feb. 8—Apr. 10.

1853
DE VOUW, Eliza Jane, Widow—Harman, b. Dec. 28, 1852—Jan. 25.
1822
OBLENUS, Peter and Martha—Hester Ann, b. Mar. 11—Apr. 7.
1823
VANDERBEEK, Jurry C. and Elizabeth—Hannah, b. Dec. 7, 1822—Jan. 11.
WESTERVELT, Peter A. and Martha—Henry, b. Apr. 17—May 3.
VANDIEN, Casparus and Mary—Henry Hennion, b. Mar. 6—May 3.
SNYDER, George T. and Charity—Hannah, b. Mar. 26—May 4.
HOVER, Benjamin and Jemima—Hannah, b. June 27—July 26.
VANDERBEEK, Hermanus and Jane—Henry, b. Oct. 26—Nov. 14.
HOPPER, Jacob H. and Caty—Henry, b. Nov. 13—Dec. 14.

1824
SMITH, Harmen P. and Jane—Harmen, b. Dec. 1, 1823—Jan. 25.
1825
HOPPER, Cornelius A. and Betsy—Hester Ann, b. Mar. 7—Apr. 9.
VAN EMBURGH, Albert and Hannah—Henry, b. Sep. 25—Nov. 12.
1826
VAN EMBURGH, Henry H. and Peggy—Henry, b. Feb. 14—Mar. 19.
VAN HOUTEN, Abraham and Abigail—Hetty Duchas, b. Feb. 7—Apr. 30.
Row, Peter Jr. and Jane—Henry, b. June 1—July 23.
STORMS, Coenradus and Abby—Henry, b. Sep. 7—Oct. 15.
1827
ACKERMAN, Abraham I. and Peggy—Henry Terhune, b. Dec. 14, 1826
—Jan. 14.
1830
TERHUNE, Henry Z. and Maria—Helen Jane, b. Feb. 1—Mar. 7.
ZABRISKIE, Henry A. and Patty—Henry, b. Nov. 1—Dec. 5.
1831
ACKERMAN, Peter D. and Hester—Hannah, b. Jan. 14—Mar. 20.
1833
LYDACKER, David G. and Susan—Hester Maria, b. Mar. 4—May 19.
1838
TOURSE, Garrit and Maria—Hannah Jane, b. July 30—Sep. 10.
1840
TERHUNE, Casparus and Getty—Hannah Jane, b. July 12—Sep. 6.
1841
BANTA, Thomas Jr. and Ally—Hannah, b. Feb. 13—Mar. 21.
LEIGHTON, John and Margaret—Henrietta, b. Jan. 6, 1835—Mar. 28.
ACKERMAN, John—Hannah Jane, b. Sep. 29—Oct. 24.
1845
ACKERMAN, Abraham J. and Caty—Hannah Jane, b. Apr. 28—June 8.
1849
LOWE, Klaas and Jannetje Depui—Henry, b. Nov. 15, 1848—Feb. 1.

1851

ZABRISKIE, Guilliam J. and Lavina—Hannah Margaret—Jan. 26.

"I" and "J"

1770

BANTA, Wiert C. and Elisabeth—Jan—July 29.
    Wit: Jan C. Banta; Annatje Banta.

MACDANEL, Cornelis—Jan, b. Sept. 4—Oct. 8.

VAN HOUTE, Isaac and Maria—Jacobus—Nov. 4.
    Wit: Jacobus and Mettie Post.

————and————Junici—Dec. 2.
    Wit: Cobus and Jannitje V. Voorhese.

V. BLERKOM, David and Lisabeth—Jacobus—Dec. 25.
    Wit: Albert and Gerrebrecht V. Blerkom.

1771

ALYEE, Isaac and Annaatje—Jacob, b. Jan. 17—Feb. 3.
    Wit: Jacob T. and Jannitje Eckerson.

RITE, Willem and Aaltje—Jan—Feb. 24.
    Wit: Jan and Styntje Ackerman.

VANORDER, Jan and Jannitje—Jan—Feb. 24.
    Wit: Abram J. and Santje Vanderbeek.

TERHUYN, Abram and Marytje—Jacob—Mar. 17.
    Wit: Hendrik J. and Marytje Zabriskie.

BLAUVELT, Cobus and Jannitje—Johannes, b. Mar. 2—Apr. 1.
    Wit: Johannis and Rachel Blauvelt.

ACKERMAN, Gerrit and Rachel—Jacobus—June 9.
    Wit: Jacobus and Jannitje V. Voorhese.

DUMAREE, Benjamin and Lidea—Jannitje—June 23.
    Wit: Pieter B. and Jannitje Dumaree.

PEEK, David and Sarah—Jacobus, b. June 18—July 21.
    Wit: Jacobus and Willempje Peek.

KOM, Johannis V[an] B[lar] and Rebecka—Johannis, b. July 9—July 21.
    Wit: Johannis and Marytje V[an] B[lar] Kom.

MOURUSSE, Jacobus and Lena—Isaac, b. July 24—Aug. 11.
    Wit: Isaac and Marytje Mourusse.

ZABRISKIE, Jacob J. and Aaltje—Jacob—Sept. 1.
    Wit: Dirk and Lea Terhuyn.

ACKERMAN, Cornelis and Lisabeth—Johannis—Sept. 15.
    Wit: Petrus and Maria Ackerman.

VANBOSKERCK, Jan J. and Hester—Johannis, b. May 30—Oct. 2.
    Wit: Hannes and Grietje Brevoort.

PIETERSE, Niklaas and Maria—Jan—Nov. 3.
    Wit: Willem Pieterse.

ACKERMAN, Hannes J. and Lena—Jannitje—Dec. 1.
    Wit: Cobus and Jannitje V. Voorhese.

RYKE, Hendrik and Crestina—Jannitje—Dec. 26.
    Wit: David P. Dumaree.

ECKERSON, Phlip—Jacob—Dec. 29.

1772

GARDINIER, Jan and Jacomyntje—Jacob—Feb. 16.
    Wit: Jacob and Rachel Banta.

ZABRISKIE, Hendrik J. and Willempje—Jacob—July 5.
　　Wit: Jacob H. and Wyntje Zabriskie.
HOPPE, Abram and Antje—Jacob—Aug. 16.
　　Wit: Johannes A. Terhuyn; Marytje Zabriskie.
HOPPE, Gerrit J. and Marytje—Jan—Aug. 16.
　　Wit: Jan and Elisabeth Hoppe.
BANTA, Cornelis A. and Maria—Joseph, b. Aug. 15—Sept. 27.
　　Wit: Isaac and Annatje Alyee.
COCKROW, Niklaas and Pietertje—Josie—Nov. 8.
　　Wit: Pieter and Lena Van Zeyl.
ZABRISKE, Albert J. and Geesje—Jacob—Dec. 6.
　　Wit: Jacob J. and Jannitje Zabriske.
ACKERMAN, Arie and Maria—Johannis, b. Dec. 3—Dec. 6.
　　Wit: Hannes A. and Jacomyntje Ackerman.

1773

ACKERMAN, David A. and Jacomyntje—Isaac—Jan. 3.
　　Wit: Isaac and Saartje Storm.
OOLDES, Hendrik and Marytje—Johannes—May 30.
　　Wit: Jan J. and Aaltje Hoppe.
ZABRISKIE, Jacob H. and Wyntje—Jannitje—June 27.
　　Wit: David and Jannitje Dumaree.
VAN ORDER, Jan P. and Jannitje—Jannitje—Aug. 22.
　　Wit: Willem Smith; Jannitje V. Blerkom.
MILTENBERRI, Luwis and Lisabeth—Joannes—Nov. 7.
　　Wit: Petrus and Antje Van Blerkom.
PERRI, Daniel and Jannitje—Isaac—Dec. 18.
　　Wit: Isaac and Grietje Perri.

1774

MESSEKER, Abram and Rachel—Johannis—Jan. 16.
　　Wit: David D. and Lisabeth Ackerman.
VAN WINKEL, Paulus and Emitje—Jacob—Jan. 23.
　　Wit: Jacob J. and Jannitje Zabriskie.
STORM, Isaac and Saartje—Jacob—Jan. 23.
　　Wit: Jacob and Jannitje Storm.
TRAPHAGE, Hendrik and Claartje—John—Mar. 20.
　　Wit: Jan J. and Aaltje Hoppe.
TRAPHAGE, Jonathan and Catriena—Jacobus, b. Feb. 7—Mar. 27.
　　Wit: Jacobus and Jannitje Van Gelder.
ZABRISKIE, Christiaan J. and Maria—Jacob—Apr. 24.
　　Wit: Jacob C. Zabriske.
JERSEY, Peter and Annatje—Jannitje, b. May 6—May 29.
　　Wit: Abram J. and Ginne Post.
MOURUSSE, Mourus and Tryntje—Jacob, b. Mar. 26—June 28.
　　Wit: Jacob and Trnytje Mourusse.
VANDERHOEF, Dirk and Catriena—Jacob, b. Feb. 13—June 28.
MICKLER, Hannes and Margrietje—Margrietje and Johannis—Aug. 21.
　　Wit: For Johannis, Hannes and Rebecca Van Blerkom.
TOIRS, Niklaas and Lisabeth—Jacob, b. Sep. 19—Oct. 30.
　　Wit: Jacob and Saartje Hoppe.

1775

VAN BLERKOM, Isaac and Sara—Isaac—Jan. 29.
Wit: Hannes and Rebecka Van Blerkom.

DEGROOT, Jacobus—Jacobus—Feb. 2.
Wit: Johannis and Marytje Moore.

ACKERMAN, David A. and Jacomyntje—Jacob—Feb. 19.
Wit: Jan. and Marytje Eckerson.

HOPPE, Albert and Rachel—Jacob—Mar. 12.
Wit: John and Antje Vanimburgh.

ZABRISKE, Abram A. and Maria—John—Apr. 2.
Wit: Jan A. Terhuyn and Geertje J. Zabriskie.

DUBAEN, Joost and Grietje—Jacob, b. Mar. 21—Apr. 9.
Wit: Jacob and Marytje Dubaen.

MABIE, Jan and Lea—Jannitje, b. July 2—Apr. 9.
Wit: Pieter and Jannitje Mabie.

MYER, Hannes C. and Sara—Jannitje, b. June 27—July 9.
Wit: Isaac and Jannitje Post.

TERHUYN, Steven and Jannitje—Jan—Aug. 27.
Wit: Jan D. and Marytje Terhuyn.

HOPPE, Andries A. and Lisabeth—Jannitje—Nov. 15.
Wit: Abram H. and Antje Hoppe.

1776

HERMERSTOND, James—James—Jan. 7.

POST, Isaac and Jannitje—Jannitje—Mar. 10.

JURRY, Fredrik and Marter—Jones, b. Dec. 9, 1775—Mar. 31.

PERRY, Daniel and Jannitje—Jannitje, b. Mar. 15—Apr. 7.
Wit: Cobus and Annaatje Perry.

HOPPE, Gerrit J. and Marytje—Jacob—Apr. 14.
Wit: Jacob H. and Wyntje Zabriske.

DAVIS, Niklaas and Maria—Johannis—May 6.
Wit: Pieter and Lena Van Zeyl.

BROWER, Widow Antje—Jacobus—June 16.
Wit: Abram J. and Santje Vanderbeek.

DAVIS, Niklaas—Johannis—July 24.
Wit: Hermanus and Saaartje Van Zeyl.

———, ——— and ——— —Johannis—July 24.
Wit: Harme and Antje Lutkens.

1780

BOGERT, Cobus J. and Cornelia—Jannitje—Mar. 12.

VAN ALE, Cornelis and Susanna—Johannis—May 13.

HOPPE, Abram and Antje—Jacob—Sep. 17.

1782

VAN DALSE, Hendrik—John—Jan. 6.
Wit: Jan Van Dalse.

WESTERVELT, John and Antje—Johannis, b. Dec. 21, 1781—Jan. 14.

VAN BLERKOM, Abram—Jannitje—Jan.
Wit: David Van Blerkom and wife.

ECKERSON, Edward—Jenny, b. Feb. 8—Feb. 17.
    Wit: Jacob Eckerson and wife.
BOGERT, Casparus and Jannitje—Jenny, b. Feb. 11—Feb. 17.
BREVOORT, Samuel—Johannis, b. Feb. 25.
    Wit: Johannis and Grietje Brevoort.
VERVELE, Gideon and Maria—Jannitje, b. Sep. 8—Oct. 13.
    Wit: Cobus and Tittie Pilesvelt.
BLAUVELT, Pieter—Jannitje, b. May 17—June 6.
    Wit: Barend Verseur and wife.
ALJEE, Abram and Jacomyntje—Jonathan, b. Dec. 4, 1781—Feb. 3.

1783 (?)

ACKERMAN, David G.—Jan—July 20.
    Wit: Jan Terhuen and wife Trintie.

1783

GERRITSE, Hannis and Maria—Johannis—Feb. 2.
RATAN, Jacobus and Willempje—Jan—June 4.
    Wit: Jan and Lea Zabriskie.
DAVIDS, Claas—Isaac—June 28.
    Wit: Isaac Kiep and wife.
ZABRISKIE, Abram and Maria—Jelletje—Aug. 24.
    Wit: Albert Zabriskie and wife.

1784 (?)

SESIE (or Lesie), Pieter—Isaac—Mar. 7.

1784

HOPPE, Gerrit—Jacomyntje—Feb. 11.
    Wit: Jan Boskerk and wife.
BANTA, Jacob—Jan—May 30.
    Wit: Jan Smith and wife.
DEMAREE, Samuel—Jacobus—Aug. 22.
    Wit: Jacobus Perry and wife.
TERHUNE, Albert and Aaltje—Jacob—Aug. 22.
    Wit: Jacob Zabriske and wife.
BOS, Dirk and Antje—Jan—Dec. 4.
    Wit: Jan and Jantje Vanderbeek.

1785

LESIE, Johannis—Isaac—Mar. 20.
WESTERVELT, Jan and Rachel—Jacob—May 1.
    Wit: Arie Westervelt and wife Geertje.
SPIER, David and Margrietje—John—July 3.
    Wit: Pieter and Aaltje Van Order.
BOGERT, Steven and Maria—Jacobus and Petrus, b. July 8—July 24.
    Wit: Petrus and Cathalyntje Westervelt: Jacobus and Cornelia
        Bogert.
MAYBE, John and Leah—Johannis, b. June 28—July 24.
JERSEY, Pieter and Annatje—Jacob—Sep. 11.
    Wit: Jacob and Anna Holstead.
ECKERSON, Thomas and Cornelia—Jannitje, b. Oct. 2.
    Wit: Jacob Eckerson.

Post, Jacob and Sara—Jacob—Nov. 13.

Woertendyk, Reinier and Annatje—Jannitje, b. Nov. 26—Dec. 25.
Wit: Reinier and Jannitje Woertendyk.

Van Vlerkom, Peter and Jannitje—Jannitje, b. Nov. 24—Dec. 25.

1786

Hoppe, Gerrit Wm. and Grietje—Jonathan—Jan. 15.
Wit: Jan A. and Maria Hoppe.

Ackerman, Arie and Christina—Johannis, b. Jan. 18—Feb. 26.
Wit: Gerrit I. and Maria Hoppe.

Yurrie, Frederik and Jacomyntje—Jacobus, b. Sep. 1, 1783—Feb. 26.

1784

Van Blercom, Pieter and Christina—Jannitje, b. Nov. 4—Dec. 5.

1786

Waard, Pieter and Nancy—Jenneke, b. Apr. 1—Apr. 2.

Vande Beek, Johannis and Abigail—Jacob, b. Mar. 11—Apr. 2.
Wit: Jacob Vander Beek and wife.

Van Rype, Johannis and Geertje—John, b. Apr. 19—May 21.
Wit: Harme and Maria Van Rype.

Haring, Jan and Jannitje—Isaac, b. Apr. 20—June (?) Jan. (?) 4.
Wit: Jan and Elisabeth Haring.

Syoert, Isaac and Grietje—John, b. Apr. 23—June 4.
Wit: Abraham and Maria Zabriske.

Banner, James and Geesje—John De, b. May 28—July 2.
Wit: Jan, David and Angonietje Eckerson.

Rotan, Johannis and Jannitje—Johannis, b. July 10—July 23.

1787

Debow, Johannis and Margrietje—Jacomyntje, b. July 25, 1786—Jan. 12.
Wit: Jonathan and Catriena Traaphage.

Messeker, Lodewyk and Sara—Johannis—Apr. 15.
Wit: Hermanus and Elisabeth Van Zeyl.

Conklin, Lewis and Elisabeth—John, b. Apr. 7—May 20.
Wit: John and Catriena Conklin.

Zabriskie, Albert J. and Metje—Jacob, b. May 3—May 27.
Wit: Jacob A. and Sara Hoppe.

Ackerman, Abraham and Elisabeth—John—July 8.
Wit: John and Elisabeth Pulisvelt.

Eckerson, Jacob and Annaatje—Jan, July 26—Aug. 5.

Debaen, Andreas and Jannitje—Jacobus, b. July 25—Aug. 5.
Wit: Jacobus and Antje Debaen.

Miller, George and Hannah—Joost, b. July 15—Aug. 19.
Wit: Paulus and Doortie Vanderbeek.

Rotan, Daniel and Jannitje—Johannis, b. Aug. 9—Aug. 26.
Wit: John and Jannitje Rotan.

Eckerson, Thomas and Annaatje—John—Sep. 16.

Van Boskerk, Jan and Sara—Johannis, b. Aug. 12—Sep. 16.
Wit: Gerrit and Maria Hoppe.

More, John and Maria—Joseph—Sep. 16.

VAN DIEN, Albert and Polly—Johannis, b. Sep. 15—Oct. 7.
Wit: Jan and Molly Van Boskerk.

BERKHOF, Hendrik and Maria—Johannis—Dec. 30.

1788

POST, Johannis and Sara—Jacobus—Feb. 3.

ACKERMAN, David D. and Jannitje—Jannitje, b. Mar. 6—Mar. 23.
Wit: Jurrie and Maria Vanderbeek.

GOETSCHIUS, Joseph and Jannitje—Johannis Hendrikus—Apr. 20.

HOPPE, Nicasie and Maria—Jan, b. Mar. 19—Apr. 20.
Wit: Andreas and Elisabeth Hoppe.

HOPPE, Hendrik H. and Jacomyntje—Jan, b. May 31—June 22.
Wit: Rebecka Nagel.

BOGERT, Stephen and Fyke—Jacobus, b. June 23—Aug. 3.
Wit: Jacobus and Annaatje Aljee.

VAN VOORHESEN, Jan and Tryntje—Jacobus, b. July 13—Aug. 10.
Wit: Jacobus and Cornelia Bogert.

POOST, Abraham and Jannitje—Jannitje, b. Aug. 12—Aug. 31.

TERYEUR, Abraham and Elisabeth—Jacob, b. Sep. 11—Sep. 28.
Wit: Jacob and Marytje Debaen.

TAYLOR, William and Phebe—John, b. July 11—Oct. 19.

JANSE, Johannis and Fytje—Johannis, b. Nov. 18—Dec. 21.
Wit: Cornelius and Aaltje Haring.

1789

BERTOLF, Petrus and Angonietje—Jacobus, b. Oct. 18, 1788—Mar. 1.

ACKERMAN, Jacobus G. and Rachel—Jacob, b. Apr. 28—May 10.

ECKERSON, Cornelius and Catriena—Johannis, b. Mar. 30—June 7.
Wit: Johannis and Rachel Koning.

HARRIS, John and Grietje—Johannis, b. July 25—Aug. 9.
Wit: Johannis and Polly Gerritson.

FESYUOR, Jan W. and Wyntje—Johannis, b. Sep. 11—Nov. 1.
Wit: Jan and Lea Mebie.

1790

MUYSENER, Petrus and Peggy—Jacobus, b. Nov. 29, 1789—Jan. 24.
Wit: Jacobus and Lena Muysinger.

STRAAT, Jan and Susanna—John, b. Jan. 15—Jan. 31.
Wit: Jan and Maria Ryer.

RYER, Ryer and Maria—Jacobus, b. Feb. 26—Mar. 15.
Wit: Jacobus and Sara Woertendyck.

TERHUNE, Abraham and Soecke—Jacob, b. Mar. 2—Mar. 15.
Wit: Jacobus and Willempje Ratan.

BOGERT, Albert J. and Maria—Jacob—Jan. 31.
Wit: Jan J. Zabriskie; Jannitje Bogert.

BERDAN, Reinier and Geertje—Jan. b. July 22—Aug. 15.
Wit: Jan and Hendrikje Berdan.

ACKERMAN, Abraham and Salome—Johannis, b. Oct. 8—Dec. 12.

CERELLACH, John and Lena—John, b. Aug. 6—Dec. 12.
Wit: Battius and Grietje Schoenmaker.

1791

DEMAREST, Samuel C. and Catriena—Johannis, b. Dec. 25, 1790—Jan. 23.
    Wit: Johannis and Elisabeth Ackerman.

MEBE, Isaac and Sara—Isaac, b. Jan. 10—Jan. 30.

GOETSCHIUS, Jan and Annaatje—Jacob, b. Dec. 30, 1790—Jan. 30.

YOUMENS, John and Elisabeth—John, b. Dec. 8, 1790—Jan. 30.

DEE, Salomon and Sally Dey—Jacob, b. Jan. 6—Feb. 16.

FERGUSON, Samuel and Jenny—Jannetje, b. Feb. 26—Apr. 17.

VANDERBEEK, Jacob and Annaatje—Jacobus, b. Mar. 26—Apr. 17.
    Wit: Hendrik and Maria Frederikse.

ECKERSON, Nicholaas and Maria—Johannis, b. May 12—June 12.
    Wit: Jan and Maria Eckerson.

LOZIER, John and Margrietje—Jannitje, b. Mar. 28—June 12.

WORTENDYK, Reinier and Annaatje—Johannis, b. Mar. 26—June 13.
    Wit: Johannis and Maragrietje Fersyeur.

VANEMBURGH, Hendrik and Maria—John, b. June 28—July 17.
    Wit: John and Lea Vanemburgh.

VALENTYNE, David and Rachel—Jacob, b. July 1—July 17.
    Wit: Jacob and Liesje Valentyne.

CROUTER, Johannis and Maragrietje—Jacob and Aaltje, b. June 20—
    July 24.
    Wit: Jacob and Elisabeth Crouter.

VAN VLERKOM, Johannis and Elisabeth—Johannis, b. July 16—Aug. 14.
    Wit: Johannis and Rebecka V. Vlerkom.

SLOT, Isaac and Lea—Jacob, b. Sep. 13—Oct. 23.

1792

THOMSON, Samuel and Jemima—Jacobus, b. Jan. 13—Feb. 26.

POST, Jacobus and Rachel—John—Feb. 26.

ACKERMAN, Arie and Christina—Jacomyntje—Feb. 26.

CLENDENNY, Walter and Osseltje—John—Apr. 10.

ACKERMAN, Johannis and Annatje—John, b. Mar. 18—Apr. 10.

HOPPE, Gerrit J. and Elisabeth—Jan, b. Mar. 3—Apr. 10.
    Wit: Jan J. and Catriena Hoppe.

STORM, John and Maria—Isaac—Apr. 10.

VAN BLERKOM, John and Sara—Jannitje—Apr. 10.

TERHUNE, Abraham and Soecke—John, b. June 13—June 16.
    Wit: Johannis and Abigael Vanderbeek.

JERSE, John and Maria—John, b. May 29—June 16.

CARLOGH, Nicolaas and Maria—Jacobus, b. Aug. 24—Sep. 30.
    Wit: Jacobus and Sara Wannemaker.

FESHEUR, Abraham and Elisabeth—John, b. Sep. 18—Sep. 30.
    Wit: Jaan and Aaltje Debaan.

QUACKENBOS, Barend and Catriena—Johannis, b. Mar. 5—Mar. 24.

HOPPE, Hendrik G. and Rachel—Jacob—Mar. 24.
    Wit: Jacob J. and Wyntje Zabriske.

1793

DEBAAN, Andrias and Jannitje—Jacob, b. Dec. 4, 1792—Mar. 3.
    Wit: Joost and Margrietje Debaan.

ECKERSON, Thomas and Cornelia—John, b. Nov. 21, 1792—Feb. 17.
  Wit: John and Lena Eckerson.
DODS, James and Mary—Jacobus, b. Dec. 1—Feb. 17.
  Wit: Abraham and Hannah Dator.
VAN WERT, Abraham and Ester—John—May 19.
  Wit: John and Lea Van Wert.
BLAUVELT, Johannis and Metje—Johannis, b. May 14—June 9.
  Wit: Jan and Maria Eckerson.
BLAUVELT, Daniel and Jannetje—John, b. Mar. 3—June 9.
  Wit: John and Sara Van Vlerkom.
VOS, John and Jannitje—Jacobus, b. June 2—June 23.
  Wit: Paulus and Grietje V. d. Beek.
DEMAREST, Catrina—Jannitje, b. May 9—June 30.
  Wit: Andries and Jannetje Debaen.
MCCALL, John and Geertrui—Jannetje, b. Mar. 3—July 7.
RYKER, Johannis and Jannetje—Jannetje, b. June 15—Aug. 4.
  Wit: Albert and Jannetje Van Voorhesen.
DURIE, Pieter and Osseltje—Jan, b. June 19—July 28.
  Wit: Jan and Rachel Durie.
RIDDENAAR, Coenraad and Elisabeth—John, b. July 31—Aug. 25.
BACKER, Jacob and Grietje—Jacob, b. June 14—Aug. 25.
BERDAN, Johannis and Maria—John, b. Aug. 30—Sep. 15.
LYDECKER, Gerrit and Martyntje—John, b. Oct. 10—Oct. 27.
CAMPBELL, John and Tietje—John, b. Nov. 13—Dec. 1.
                        1794
VAN SCHYVEN, William and Saartje—Johannis—Jan. 1.
  Wit: Johannes and Jannetje Dremus.
DEBAAN, Jan and Aaltje—Jannitje, b. Feb. 10—Mar. 16.
  Wit: Reinier Woertendyk; Jannitje Woertendyk.
ACKERMAN, Gerrit and Geertje—John, b. Apr. 10—May 4.
  Wit: Hendrik and Jannetje Terhuen.
STRAAT, John and Soecke—Jacobus, b. Apr. 8—May 4.
  Wit: Jacobus and Sara Wannemaker.
DEGROOT, Jacobus and Maria—Jacobus, b. Mar. 12—May 4.
ZABRISKIE, Albert and Lea—John, b. Apr. 20—May 4.
  Wit: Cornelia Zabriskie.
EARLE, Edward and Abigail—John, b. Apr. 15—May —.
  Wit: Gerrit and Jannitje Ackerman.
VAN VLERCOM, John and Sara—Isaac, b. May 17—June 22.
TEBOW, Peter and Susanna Te Bouw—Johannis, b. May 4—June 22.
HARING, David and Tryntje—Joost, b. May 17—July 6.
  Wit: Joost and Tryntje Mebie.
FORGESON, Samuel and Jenny—Johannis, b. May 7—July 20.
  Wit: Maria Myer.
VANORDEN, John and Tryntje—John, b. June 6—June 29.
BANTA, Hendrik and Maria—Jacob, b. Aug. 9—Aug. 31.
  Wit: Jacob and Jannitje Stagg.
VAN HOUTEN, Jacobus and Elisabeth Berry—Jacobus, b. Apr. 3, 1793—
      Aug. 31.

VANDERBEEK, Coenradus and Annatje—Jurry, b. June 19—Aug. 10.
Wit: Jurry and Maria Vanderbeek.
HOPPE, Gerrit J. and Elisabeth—John, b. Sep. 6—Sep. 28.
Wit: Jan and Trientje Hoppe.
ECKERSON, Thomas and Susanna—Jacobus, b. Aug. 15—Sep. 21.
Wit: Jacobus and Sara Demarest.
HOPPE, Nicasie and Maria—Jacob, b. Sep. 17—Oct. 5.
Wit: Albert and Aaltje Terhune.
ACKERMAN, Daniel and Cathalyntje—Jannitje, b. Sep. 13—Oct. 5.
Wit: David and Jannitje Ackerman.
COOL, Abraham and Annatje—Isaac, b. Sep. 13—Oct. 5.
Wit: Isaac and Jannetje Cool.
POST, Jacob and Sara—John, b. Sep. 25—Oct. 19.
VAN DIEN, Albert and Maria—Jan Van Boskerk, b. Sep. 9—Oct. 26.
Wit: Jan and Geesje Van Boskerk.
TERHUNE, Abraham and Soecke—Jacob, b. Oct. 21—Nov. 16.
Wit: Jacobus and Willempje Ratan.

1795
BROWER, Petrus and Rachel—Johannis, b. Jan. 27—Feb. 12.
Wit: Johannis and Abigael V. D. Beek.
BLAUVELT, Isaack and Elisabeth—Jacobus, b. Jan. 18—Mar. 8.
VAN ALEN, Jan and Angonietje—Jacobus, b. Feb. 17—Mar. 29.
Wit: Jacobus and Cornelia Bogert.
HOPPE, Petrus and Elisabeth—Jonathan, b. Feb. 24—Apr. 6.
CHRISTOPHER, John and Aaltje—Jenny—Apr. 6.
ROMYN, Roelof—John, b. Mar. 28—May 24.
DEBAAN, Jacob and Osseltje—Jacob, b. May 2—May 17.
DERIST, Leashon and Elisabeth—Jacob, b. May 14—June 21.
V. D. BEEK, Harman and Antje—Jannetje, b. Aug. 28—Sep. 20.
VAN VOORHESEN, Jan and Tryntje—John, b. Oct. 2—Oct. 18.
SMITH, Abbott and Susanna—Jacobus, b. July 24—Oct. 25.
Wit: Jacobus and Catriena Smith.
DEE, Salomon and Sally—Isaak, b. Sep. 25—Oct. 27.
WOERTENDYK, Albert and Maragrietje—Jannitje, b. Nov. 10—Nov. 26.
Wit: Reinier and Jannitje Woertendyk.
CROUTER, Jacob and Maria—Jacobus, b. Nov. 30—Dec. 20.
Wit: Jacobus Crouter.
1796
FESYEUR, Cornelius and Jannetje—Jannitje, b. Dec. 15, 1795—Jan. 24.
Wit: Daniel and Jannitje Perry.
WATSON, Pieter and Maragrietje—John, b. Jan. 11—Feb. 7.
Wit: John and Maria Peeck.
DEGROOT, Jacobus and Maria—John, b. Feb. 23—Mar. 20.
DECKER, Cornelis and Nancy—John, b. Dec. 10, 1795—Apr. 3.
VANDIEN, Herman and Aaltje—Jan, b. July 15—Aug. 7.
Wit: Jan and Lea Zabriskie.
ROTAN, Jan and Jannitje—Jannitje, b. May 30—July 17.
HALDEROM, William and Catriena—Johannis, b. June 3—July 3.

CERELLAGH, Johannis and Leentje—Jure, b. Aug. 22—Sep. 25.
 Wit: Jure and Sara Cerallagh.
BOGERT, John and Maragrietje—Jannitje, b. Nov. 27—Dec. 25.
 Wit: David and Jannitje Ackerman.

1797

VAN WERT, Isaak and Elisabeth—John, b. Feb. 10—Mar. 19.
 Wit: Matheus and Wyntje Barboro.
ECKER, Paulus and Maria—John, b. Feb. 7—Mar. 19.
ZABRISKE, Jacob J. and Wyntje—Jannitje, b. Mar. 4—Mar. 19.
 Wit: Jacob and Jannitje Zabriske.
DURJEE, David and Geertje—Jannitje, b. July 23—Aug. 20.
DEBAAN, Carel and Sara—Jannitje, b. Nov. 6—Dec. 24.

1798

BOS, Lodewyk and Leentje—John, b. Jan. 22—Feb. 11.
 Wit: John and Maria Ryer.
DURIE, Samuel and Catriena—Jannitje, b. Feb. 25—Apr. 1.
 Wit: Andries and Jannitje Debaan.
HEMMION, Nicholaas and Lena—Johannis, b. Oct. 23, 1797—May 29.
WRIGHT, John and Abigail—Jannitje, b. Mar. 21—May 29.
TERHUNE, Albert and Lea—Isaac, b. June 13—June 20.
 Wit: Pieter and Jacomyntje Stor.
ACKERMAN, Gerrit and Geertje—Jannitje, b. May 24—June 20.
 Wit: Abraham and Maria Ratan.
SMIT, Jacobus and Catriena—Jannitje, b. Aug. 14—Aug. 26.
 Wit: Daniel and Jannitje Perry.
VAN HOORN, John and Elisabeth—John—Aug. 26.
DEGROOT, Jacobus and Maria—John, b. July 22—Aug. 26.
ZABRISKA, Albert and Aaltje—John, b. July 5—Sep. 9.
VANDERBEEK, Coenradus and Annatje—Jurie—Oct. 14.
TERHUNE, David and Catriena—Jannetje, b. Nov. 19—Dec. 9.
 Wit: John and Antje Terhune.
LOZIER, Abraham and Annaatje—Jannetje, b. Sep. 15—Dec. 9.

1799

MOURESEN, Pieter and Grietje—Jacob, b. Nov. 12, 1798—Jan. 6.
BROUWER, John and Trientje—John, b. Dec. 3, 1798—Jan. 6.
 Wit: John and Maria Jersey.
RATAN, Abraham and Wyntje—Jacobus, b. Dec. 14, 1798—Jan. 6.
 Wit: Jacobus and Cornelia Bogert.
WESTERVELT, Albert and Maria—Joseph—Mar. 24.
DEMAREST, Syme and Maria—Johannis, b. Jan. 25—Mar. 24.
VALENTYNE, David and Rachel—John, b. Feb. 10—Apr. 14.
 Wit: John Eckert and Rachel Valentine.
SHERWOOD, Isaak and Anna—Isaak, b. June 10—July 21.
VAN ORDEN, John and Tryntje—Jannetje, b. Sep. 9—Oct. 6.
BLAUVELT, Daniel and Annatje—Jannetje, b. Sep. 8—Oct. 6.
 Wit: Cornelius and Jannetje Blauvelt.

Post, Jose and Aaltje—John, b. Aug. 3—Oct. 6.
Wit: John and Catriena Storm.
See, John and Polly—John, b. Sep. 20—Oct. 13.
Doremus, Jacobus and Polly—Johannis, b. Dec. 2—Dec. 18.

1800

Van Houten, John and Antje—Isaak, b. Dec. 17, 1799—Jan. 5.
Scisco, William and Elisabeth—John, b. Jan. 17—Feb. 23.
Thompson, James—an adult—Apr. 13.
Dods, Thomas and Rachel—Jacobus, b. Mar. 19—Apr. 6.
Wit: James and Maria Dods.
Blauvelt, Isaak and Sara—Jacobus, b. May 24—June 29.
Wit: Jacobus and Rachel Blauvelt.
Bogert, Cornelius and Catrina—Johannis, b. Aug. 7—Aug. 31.
Wit: Johannis and Maria Gerritson.
Goetsius, Piatus and Catriena—John, b. Sep. 3—Sep. 21.
Van Rypen, Cornelius and Elisabeth—John, b. Sep. 6—Oct. 2.
Ackerman, Abraham and Sarah—Jacomyntje, b. Oct. 5—Nov. 2.
Thew, James and Sarah—John, b. Oct. 9—Nov. 9.
Wortendyk, Cornelius—Johannis, b. Oct. 26—Nov. 9.
Wit: Maria Wortendyk.
Degroot, Jacobus and Maria—Jannetje, b. Oct. 24—Nov. 30.
Stuart, Adolph—Jacobus, b. Oct. 17—Dec. 28.
Wit: Jacobus and Jannetje Demarest.

1801

Eckerson, Thomas and Susanna—John, b. Dec. 28, 1800—Jan. 18.
Wit: John and Geertje Eckerson.
Taylor, Aaron and Jannetje—Aima, b. Dec. 16, 1797; and Jonathan,
b. Sept. 22, 1800; both bapt. Feb. 22.
Debow, Johannis and Grietje—Johannis, b. Oct. 25, 1800—Feb. 22.
Doremus, Andreas and Ebbe—John, b. Mar. 3—Mar. 22.
Wit: Jacobus and Polly Duremus.
Zabriskie, Jacob and Leah—John, b. Feb. 26—Mar. 29.
Dobbs, Thomas and Eva—Jacob, Feb. 28—Apr. 12.
Maybe, Peter and Jannetje—Jannetje, b. Mar. 3—Apr. 19.
Wit: William and Jannetje Maybe.
Lutkins, Stephen and Rachel—John, b. Apr. 1—Apr. 26.
Perry, Daniel and Sarah—Jannetje—June 7.
Wit: Daniel and Jannetje Perry.
Mouresen, Petrus and Margrietje—John, b. June 27—July 25.
Debaan, Petrus and Jacomyntje—Jacob, b. June 15—Aug. 2.
Wit: Jacob and Raachel Debaun.
Vanderbeek, Cornelius and Hilletje—Jacob, b. July 28—Aug. 9.
Post, Abraham and Elisabeth—Jacob, b. Aug. 18—Sep. 13.
Wit: Jacob and Sarah Post.
Zabriskie, John and Margrietje—Johannis, b. Aug. 28—Sep. 20.
Sisco, William and Elisabeth—Isaac, b. Oct. 16—Nov. 22.
Lezier, John C. and Margeret—John, b. Aug. 22, 1800—Jan. 17.

1802

STULTZ, Henry and Margaret—Jacob, b. Dec. 17, 1801—Jan. 31.
POST, Peter P. and Jannetje—Jan, b. Feb. 12—Mar. 14.
   Wit: Jan and Fytje Haring.
ECKER, Cornelius and Margrietje—Jacobus, b. Feb. 22—Apr. 4.
ECKERSON, Thomas and Polly—Jacob, b. Mar. 19—Apr. 18.
   Wit: Jacob and Sarah Post.
THOMSON, James and Sarah—Jannetje, b. Mar. 27—Apr. 18.
LUTKINS, Harmen and Elisabeth—John, b. Aug. 29—Oct. 10.
   Wit: Margrietje Bogert.
PERRY, Peter and Margaret—John, b. Sep. 26—Oct. 17.
WILLS, Thomas and Rachel—Joseph, b. Oct. 3—Oct. 24.
DEY, Solomon and Habby(?)—John, b. Oct. 16—Nov. 14.
CUYPER, Gerrit and Charity—Joost, b. Oct. 21—Nov. 21.
MABY, Peter and Ginny—John, b. Nov. 12—Dec. 25.
DEMAREST, Albert and Annatje—John, b. Dec. 4—Dec. 25.
HOPPER, Hendrik and Charity—Jacob, b. Dec. 7—Dec. 26.

1803

TERHUNE, Albert and Maretje—Jacobus, b. Jan. 24—Mar. 13.
BARR, David and Maria—John, b. Mar. 2—Apr. 3.
   Wit: John and Margaret Tolman.
WESTERVELT, Pieter and Martyntje—Jacobus, b. July 13—Aug. 7.
HOPPER, Andries and Sally—John, b. Aug. 6, 1802—Sep. 11.
VAN ALEN, John and Angonietje—John, b. Sep. 11—Oct. 9.

1804

HOPPER, Andries and Antje—John, b. Jan. 24—Feb. 16.
TERHUNE, Albert and Martina—John, b. Mar. 9—Apr. 2.
ACKERMAN, David D. and Metje—John, b. Apr. 24—May 20.
TERHUNE, Albert and Leah—Jacomyntje, b. June 12—July 1.
DELAMATER, Abraham and Sarah—Isaac, b. July 17—Aug. 9.
TOLMAN, Jacob and Sarah—Jacob, b. Aug. 23—Sep. 9.
   Wit: Jacob and Sarah Post.
CROUTER, Jacobus and Margrietje—Joseph, b. Oct. 8—Nov. 4.
ZABRISKIE, Jacob J. and Leah—Jacob, b. Dec. 8—Dec. 26.
   Wit: Jacob and Catriena Berdan.

1805

ACKERMAN, Lawrence and Hetty—John, b. Jan. 11—Jan. 27.
BANTA, Thomas and Elizabeth—John, b. Jan. 29—Feb. 24.
TOERS, Abraham and Rachel—John, b. Mar. 19—Apr. 28.
VAN RIPEN, Frederik and Mary—John, b. Mar. 30—May 5.
CONKLIN, Isaak and Jannetje—Isaak, b. Sep. 21—Sep. 22.
FORSHUR, Cornelius and Maria—John, b. Aug. 23—Sep. 29.
   Wit: John and Wyntje Forshur.
BLAUVELT, Abraham and Metje—Jacobus, b. Aug. 6—Oct. 6.
DEGROOT, James and Annatje—James, b. Oct. 27—Dec. 8.
CONKLIN, Lewis and Leah—John, b. Nov. 21—Dec. 15.

1806

WESTERVELT, Lucas and Maria—John, b. Dec. 24, 1805—Jan. 19.

SNYDER, Gerrit and Catriena—Jacobus, b. Jan. 13—Feb. 2.
  Wit: Jacobus and Rachel Blauvelt.

VALENTINE, John and Elizabeth—Jacob, Mar. 6—May 18.

HARING, Abraham and Margrietje—Joseph, b. May 22—June 22.

HOPPER, Andrias and Antje—John, b. Aug. 28—Sep. 21.

HOPPER, Hendrik and Charity—John, b. Aug. 21—Sep. 21.

TALMAN, John I. and Geertje—John, b. Sep. 6—Sep. 17.

POST, Abraham and Elisabeth—Jacob, b. Oct. 15—Nov. 12.

1807

HOPPER, Andries and Sally—Jacob, b. Dec. 2, 1804—Jan. 4.

DOREMUS, Andrew and Abby—Jannetje, b. Mar. 19—May 3.

HARING, Petrus and Elisabeth—John, b. June 1—July 19.

ECKERSON, David and Maria—Joseph, b. Sep. 20—Oct. 18.

1808

QUACKENBUSH, John and Maria—John, b. Dec. 27, 1807—Jan. 24.

CAMPBELL, Abraham and Margrietje—John, b. Jan. 28—Feb. 21.

YEOMANS, John and Caty—John, b. Mar. 12—June 26.

FETTER, Guilbert and Maria—John William—July 31.

TALLMAN, Jacob and Sally—John, b. Aug. 16—Sep. 18.

RYER, John and Polly—Jacob Demarest, b. Aug. 21—Sep. 18.

TAYLOR, Samuel and Sarah—John, b. Mar. 29—Aug. —.

GOETSCHIUS, Hendrik and Sally—John, b. Oct. 10—Oct. 30.

1809

VANIMBURG, Hendrik and Maria—Joris, b. Dec. 7, 1808—Jan. 15.

CHRISTOPHEL, Joseph and Eefje—John, b. Oct. 13, 1808—Jan. 15.

VANDERBEEK, Dirk and Margrietje—John, b. Dec. 6, 1808—Jan. 29.

DOREMUS, Jacobus and Polly—Jost, b. Feb. 16—Apr. 30.

ROSEGRANT, Eliah and Cornelia—John, b. June 9—July 30.

WESTERVELT, John J. and Hetty—John, b. July 12—Aug. 13.

VANDERBEEK, Jacob and Sally—Jannetje, b. July 3—Aug. 20.

ACKERMAN, Gerrit and Jannetje—Jannetje, b. Aug. 2—Aug. 27.

VANBOSKERK, John and Elisabeth—John, b. Aug. 13—Oct. 1.

LUTKINS, Herman and Elisabeth—Jacobus, b. Sep. 8—Oct. 22.

VAN BLERCOM, Isaac and Elisabeth—John, b. Sep. 13—Oct. 22.

POST, Jacob and Maria—Jacob, b. Nov. 6—Dec. 10.

POST, Alexander and Nietje—John, b. Nov. 26—Dec. 21.

1810

TERHUNE, Herman and Rachel—John, b. Jan. 11—Feb. 18.

HARRES, Isaac and Annatje—John, b. Feb. 9—Mar. 18.

BOGERT, Petrus and Elisabeth—Jacob, b. Mar. 28—Apr. 22.

VANDERBEEK, Coenradus and Annatje—Jannetje—Jan. 7.

VANDERBEEK, Dirk and Maragrietje—Johannes, b. Mar. 27—May 13.

CAMPBELL, William and Jannetje—Jannetje, b. Feb. 27—May 6.

VANBLERCOM, Daniel and Dirkje—John, b. Mar. 26—May 27.
VANDIEN, Casparus and Maria—John Bogert, b. Apr. 11—May 31.
D'EBAUN, David and Lena—Jacob, b. May 12—June 3.
DEMAREST, Jacobus and Lea—Johannis, b. June 24—July 19.
RYER, Michael R. and Tryntje—John, b. July 16—Oct. 11.
TERHUNE, Richard and Annatje—Jacob, b. Aug. 16—Oct. 28.
VANHOUTEN, Jacob and Elisabeth—John, b. Sep. 5—Nov. 25.
JURRY, Johannis and Jannetje—John, b. Oct. 23—Dec. 2.
QUACKINBUSH, Teunis and Maria—John, b. Oct. 25—Dec. 2.

1811

VANBLARCOM, Gerrit and Maria—Jannetje, b. Jan. 25—Feb. 24.
POST, Peter and Hannah—John, b. Mar. 4—May 19.
MARKS, Hendrik and Anny—John, b. July 27—Aug. ———.
ECKERSON, David and Maria—Jannetje, b. July 4—Aug. ———.
PULIS, Peter and Nancy—Jannetje, b. July 8—Nov. 3.

1812

ZABRISKE, Abraham and Susanna—Jacob, b. Mar. 23—May 10.
BREWER, Charles and Rachel—John, b. June 22—Aug. 9.
CLEARWATER, Fredrik and Hester—John Hopper, b. Oct. 29—Nov. 22.
COPER, Gerrit and Charity—James Miller, b. Nov. 10—Dec. 6.
CHRISTOPHER, Joseph and Eve—Jacob, b. Aug. 8—Sep. 17.
VAN SAUN, Jacob and Polly—Jacob, b. Sep. 7—Oct. 22.
ELTINGE, Wilhelmus and Jane—Jan Van Winkle, b. Oct. 1—Nov. 26.

1816

BLAUVELT, Abraham and Maria—Isaac, b. Dec. 23, 1815—Jan. 21.
BOGART, Cornelius and Jane—Josiah Cardner, b. Jan. 12—Mar. 3.

1817

VANDERBEEK, Paul and Hannah—John, b. Mar. 30—May 4.
CARLOUGH, Jeremiah and Elisabeth—Jacob, b. June 12—June 29.
RYERS, Barend and Sarah—John, b. Aug. 27—Sep. 21.
TERHUNE, Abraham Ab. and Polly—Jemima, b. Aug. 16—Sep. 21.
HOPPER, Henry P. and Elisabeth—Isaac, b. Sep. 1—Oct. 5.
ZABRISKIE, Jacob I. and Jane—John, b. Sep. 7—Oct. 12.

1818

BOGART, John S. and Margaret—Jane, b. July 29—Aug. 18.
BOGART, James S. and Sally—John Westervelt, b. Nov. 16—Dec. 26.

1819

WESTERVELT, Peter A. and Caty—James, b. Jan. 14—Feb. 8.
TAYLOR, John and Agness—John Zabriskie, b. Jan. 7—Feb. 21.
ZABRISKIE, Henry J. and Betsy—Jacob, b. June 7—June 27.
CARLOUGH, Jerimah and Betsy—Jerimah, b. Sep. 22—Oct. 3.
VAN RODEN, William and Tyna—Jemimah, b. Sep. 17—Dec. 12.

1820

SNYDER, Garrit and Catharina—Isaac, b. Apr. 13—May 14.
VANDIEN, Garret C. and St.—John, b. May 15—June 25.

1821
Turse, Lawrence and Hannah—Jacob Young, b. July 6—Oct. 7.

1822
Blauvelt, John I. and Sarah—Isaac, b. Oct. 12—Dec. 1.

1823
Wortendyke, Abraham and Catharina—Isaac, b. Oct. 2—Nov. 2.

1824
Pake, Martin and Betsy—John, b. Sep. 5—Oct. 3.
Zabriskie, Cornelius J. and Jane—John Hopper, b. Aug. 12—Oct. 3.
Demarest, James J. and Anna—John Vanemburgh, b. Oct. 16—Nov. 28.
Row, Peter, Jr. and Jane—John, b. Oct. 8—Nov. 28.

1825
Ackerman, Peter D. and Hester—Isaac, b. Oct. 14—Nov. 12.

1826
Vanderbeek, James and Peggy—James, b. Dec. 18, 1825—Feb. 19.
Banta, Garret D. and Harriet—Jacob Terhune, b. Jan. 29—Feb. 19.

1748
Dugrau, Jan and Lena—Janneke—Nov. 20.
  Wit: Anthony and Polly Van Blerkom.

1749
Terhuyn, David and Sara—Jan—Jan. 22.
  Wit: Cornelis and Lisabeth Bongaert.
Ackerman, Albert and Rachel—Jannitje—Apr. 23.
  Wit: Albert H. and Thelletje Zabriske.
Storm, Staets and Susan—Isaak—May 28.
  Wit: David and Marytje Hammon.
Dubaen, Jacob and Marytje—Jacobus—Aug. 15.
  Wit: Jacobus and Catryna Dubaen.
Zobriske, Albert Hen. and Thelletje—Jacob—Dec. 31.
  Wit: Jacob H. Zobriske; Lea Terhuyn, wife of Derrik.

1750
Ryer, Jan and Susanna—Jan, b. Feb. 12, 1750.
  Wit: Pieter and Rachel Mabe.
Hoppe, Willem and Antje—Jan—Mar. 20.
  Wit: Jan and Lisabeth Hoppe.
Van Blerkom, Jan G. and Vrouwtje—Jan—May 24.
  Wit: Jan and Lisabeth Hoppe.
Van Rype, Frederik and Antje—Johannis—Aug. 3.
  Wit: Hannis and Saartje Van Rype.
Banta, Abram and Annatje—Jakomyntje—Sep. 10.
  Wit: Thomas and Matje Ekker.
Van Voorhees, Cobus and Jannitje—Jacobus—Nov. 11.
  Wit: Gerrit D. and Lena Ackerman.
Bongaert, Cornelis and Lisabeth—Joost—Dec. 23.
  Wit: Albert J. Zabriske and Cornelia Bongaert.

1751

STORM, Abram and Aaltje—Johannis—Jan. 20.
Wit: Hannes and Lisabeth Ackerman.

ACKERMAN, Gerrit D. and Lena—Jannetje—May 12.
Wit: Jacobus and Jannitje Van Voorhees.

VAN BLERKOM, Hannes and Marytje—Johannis, b. July 7.
Wit: Abram and Rachel Van Gelder.

VANHOUTEN, Helmach—Janneke—Sep. 15.
Wit: Helmach D. and Antje Vanhoute.

——, —— and —— —Johannis—Oct. 6.
Wit: Pieter and Margrietje Dubouw.

1752

AMERMAN, Jan and Eva—Jacobus—Jan. 5.
Wit: Teunis and Cathalyntje Spier.

DUBAEN, Jacob and Marytje—Joost—May 17.
Wit: Ryer and Abigael Debouw.

MOORE, Jeremias and Lisabeth—Jannitje—June 21.
Wit: Andries Debouw.

BROUWER, Uldrick J. and Aaltje—Isaak—Aug. 9.
Wit: Isaac and Rachel Brouwer.

DUGRAU, Abel and Maaike—Jannitje, b. Sep. 14.
Wit: Hermanus and Jenneke Dugrau.

MYER, Abram and Catrientje—Jacob—Oct. 29.
Wit: Samuel and Marytje Brovoort.

HOPPE, Albert and Rachel—Jonathan—Oct. 29.
Wit: Hannes and Annatje Alyee.

1753

HOPPE, Willem and Antje—Jannitje—Jan. 21.
Wit: Hannes and Marytje Ryerse.

RUTAN, Abram and Saartje—Johannis—Jan. 28.
Wit: Arie and Lena Coerte.

ACKERMAN, Gerrit D. and Lena—Johannis—June 3.
Wit: Louwrens D. and Rachel Ackerman.

ACKERMAN, David D. and Annatje—Jannetje—July 1.
Wit: Hendrik and Cornelia Storm.

TERHUYN, Albert A. and Elisabeth—Johannis—July 1.
Wit: Cornelis and Rachel Duremes.

KROM, Hendrik and Grietje—Isaak—Dec. 2.
Wit: Isaak and Lena Conklin.

1754

BOOGERT, Albert and Machteld—Jacobus—Jan. 13.
Wit: Jacobus and Elsje Boogert.

BANTA, Jan H. and Grietje—Jan and Angonietje (twins)—July 28.
Wit: Jan J. and Wyntje Deryie; Jan B. and Maria Westervelt.

SLODT, Steven and Marietje—Johannis—Oct. 24.
Wit: Sam and Angonietje Sidman.

VANDER BEEK, Paulus and Annatje—Jannatje—Sep. 29.
Wit: Abram Ari and Lena Ackerman.

ZOBROWISKE, Steven and Tryntje—Jannetje—Dec. 8.
Wit: Jan J. and Aaltje Zobrowiske.

1755

VEEDER, Hermanus and Antje—Jacob—Jan. 1.
Wit: Hendrik C. and Maria Zobriske.

VANDERBEEK, Paulus I. and Rachel—Jannetje—Mar. 9.
Wit: Andries and Jannetje Dubouw.

BANTA, Jacob W. and Lena—Jan—Sep. 21.
Wit: Johannis H. and Lena Ackerman.

BALDEN, Steven and Antje—Joost—Sep. 28.
Wit: Joost and Carstyntje Zobriske.

1756

SYOURT, Willem and Trientje—Isaak—Apr. 25.
Wit: Roelof and Tryntje Westervelt.

DEBAEN, Petrus and Maria—Jacob, b. June 14—July 8.
Wit: David I. and Margrietje Demarest.

KOOL, Jacob and Rachel—Isaak, b. July 14—Sep. 5.
Wit: Lucas and Jannetje Kierstede.

VAN BLERKOM, Isaak and Saartje—Jannetje—Nov. 7.
Wit: Andries and Jannetje Debow.

ZABRISKE, Jacob and I. and Aaltje—Jan.—Dec. 25.
Wit: Jan and Aaltje Zabriske.

1757

VONCK, Pieter and Marytje—Jan, b. Jan. 15—Feb. —.
Wit: Hannes and Vrouwtje Van Schyven.

VANDERBEEK, Abram and Susanna—Jacob, b. July 26—Aug. —.
Wit: Femmetje Vanderbeek.

HOPPE, Hendrik and Wyntje—Jan.—Oct. 22.
Wit: Jan and Marietje Huysman.

1758

VANDERBEEK, Paulus and Rachel—Jacob—Jan. 14.
Wit: Isaak and Annatje Vanderbeek.

BANTA, Jan J. and Sara—Johannis—Feb. 5.
Wit: Sieba J. and Dievertje Banta.

MARCELESSE, Johannis and Belitje—Jacobus—Feb. 26.

DEY, Teunis and Hesther—Johannis, b. Apr. 16—May 14.
Wit: Isaak Schuyler and Antje Dey.

VAN RYPE, Simeon and Margriet—Jurrien—July 28.
Wit: Abram and Lea Cadmus.

WESTERVELT, Casparus and Martyntje—Johannis, b. July 26—Aug. 13.
Wit: Petrus and Cathalyntje Westervelt.

SLOT, Steven and Marytje—Isaak—Aug. 20.
Wit: Isack and Lisabeth Van Deuse.

DUBAEN, Jacob and Marytje—Johannis—Oct. 22.
Wit: Ned. and Antje Parrelman.

JENKENS, John and Jacomyntje—Jacobus, b. Sep. 26—Nov. 12.
Wit: Lambert and Lybe Laroi.

ACKERMAN, Willem and Grietje—Johannis—Nov. 12.
Wit: Johannes and Lisabeth Ackerman.

BOGERT, Lucas and Rachel—Jacobus—Nov. 19.
Wit: Cobus and Elsje Bogert.

1759

BALDWIN, Antje—Joost—Apr. 9.
Wit: Silvester and Machtel Earl.

VAN ZEYL, Hannes J.—Jakomyntje—May 24.
Wit: Hannes Van Zeyl and Lena Baremole.

RYERSE, Dirk and Lena—Jannetje—June 10.

VAN ZEYL, Hannes A. and Catriena—Johannis—July 1.
Wit: Hannes and Marytje Van Blerkom.

ALYEE, Isaak and Naatje—Joseph, b. June 27—July 22.
Wit: David and Rachel Eckerse.

RYERSE, Hannes F. and Marytje—Joris, b. July 3—Aug. 12.
Wit: Willem and Antje Hoppe.

LIVEASY, Robert and Annatje—Jacob—Nov. 10.
Wit: Roelof and Tryntje Westervelt.

VAN SCHYVE, Hannis and Vrouwtje—Jan—Dec. 2.
Wit: Niclaas and Samme Dumare.

VAN BLERCOM, Isaac and Sara—Johannis—Dec. 10.
Wit: Johannis and Marytje Van Blercom.

1760

VANHOREN, Lucas and Margrietje—Johannis—Feb. 17.
Wit: Gerrit and Catharina Blauvelt.

HOPPE, Abram and Rebecka—Jannetje—Mar. 22.
Wit: Hendrik A. and Wyntje Hoppe.

WESTERVELT, Casparus J. and Martyntje—Johannis, b. Apr. 10—Mar. 22.
Wit: Johannis and Eefje Westervelt.

ZABRISKE, Albert Jan and Geesje—Jan—May 8.
Wit: Jan Ja. and Aaltje Zabriske.

BENSEN, Matheus and Marytje—Hannes—Sep. 28.
Wit: Jan and Margrietje Berdan.

ZABRISKIE, Andries J. and Corstyntje—Jan—Sep. 28.
Wit: Jan and Aaltje Zobriske.

¹FOCHI, Pieter and Maria—Jan—Nov. 16.
Wit: Jan and Catharina Fochi.

1761

VAN ES, Syme and Lisabeth—Jacob—Jan. 25.
Wit: Lisabeth and Abram Betolf.

HOPPE, Jan and Lisabeth—Jacob and Niklaas (twins)—Jan. 25.
Wit: Jan and Vrouwtje Van Blerkom; Gerrit and Cornelia Kip.

ZABRISKE, Andries and Lisabeth—Jannetje—Jan. 1.
Wit: Albert H. and Thelletje Zabriske.

RYERSE, Dirk F. and Betje—Johannis—Feb. 21.
Wit: Hannes Van Winkel.

HOPPE, Gerrit H. and Antje—Hendrik—Mar. 29.
Wit: Hendrik I. and Trintje Hoppe.

ACKERMAN, Willem and Grietje—Jacobus—Mar. 29.
Wit: Jacobus and Jannetje V. Voorhees.

STORM, Abram and Aaltje—Isaak, b. Apr. 17—May 10.
Wit: Isaac and Annatje Alyee.

---

¹Probably a corruption of Verseur.

BANTA, Jan H. and Grietje—Jacob—Nov. 1.
Wit: Jacob H. and Lena Banta.

HOPPE, Gerrit I. and Elsje—Jan—Dec. 6.
Wit: Jan and Geertje Hoppe.

V. DERBEEK, Abram C. and Saartje—Hannes—Dec. 20.
Wit: Hannes A. and Jacomyntje Ackerman.

1762

*TRAPHAGEN, Jonathan (or Hendrik) and Claartje—Jonathan—Jan. 1.
Wit: Willem Traphage and Rachel H. Hoppe.

HOPPE, Jan J. and Geertje—Jan—Jan. 24.
Wit: Jan A. and Lisabeth Hoppe.

BERDAN, Jan A. and Margrietje—Japick—Feb. 14.
Wit: Petrus and Jannetje Van Zeyl.

MABY, Hannes and Femmitje—Jacob, b. Mar. 28—May 2.
Wit: Abram and Brechje Dubaen.

CONKLIN, Isaak and Lena—Isaak—Oct. 17.
Wit: Samuel and Grietje Demare.

VANBLERKOM, Isaac and Sara—Johannis—Dec. 19.
Wit: Johannis and Marytje Vanblerkom.

1763

TERHUYN, Dirk and Lea—John—Oct. 9.
Wit: Jan A. and Lisabeth Hoppe.

†VOCHIE, Barend and Francyntje—Jannetje—Nov. 1.
Wit: Gerrit and Jannetje Blauvelt.

1764

ECKERSEN, Dirk—Jan—Jan. 29.
Wit: N. Springstien.

VAN ORDER, Jan and Jannitje—Johannis—Jan. 29.
Wit: Hannes and Trientje Van Zeyl.

DEPUU, Abram and Rachel—Johannis, b. Feb. 6—Mar. 18.
Wit: Johannis C. and Catriena Blauvelt.

ACKERMAN, Gerrit D. and Lena—Jacobus—Apr. 15.
Wit: Roelof and Tryntje Westervelt.

ACKERMAN, Hannes I. and Lena—Jacobus—Apr. 15.
Wit: Jacobus and Jannetje V. Voorhees.

SERVENT, Jacob and Trientje—Jacob—Apr. 15.
Wit: Jacob and Marytje Bogert.

SIDMAN, Samuel and Angonietje—John—Apr. 15.
Wit: Gerrit J. and Elsje Hoppe.

BERTOLF, Johannis and Wybrecht—Johannis, b. May 19—June 10.
Wit: Cobus H. and Lisabeth Bertolf.

VESIEUR, Willem and Lisabeth—Jan—June 7.
Wit: Jan and Catriena Veseur.

ACKERMAN, David J. and Nietje—Johannis—July 8.
Wit: Hannes and Lena Ackerman.

---

*The name *Jonathan* had been crossed out in the original and *Hendrik* put in its place, in a different handwriting.

†Probably a corruption of **Verseur.**

BONGAERT, Steven and Rachel—Jan—Sep. 16.
 Wit: Cobus and Cornelia Bongaert.
PERHEMEUS, Theodorus and Margrietje—Jacob, b. Sep. 14—Oct. 14.
STEGG, Isaac and Lena—Jacob—Oct. 28.
 Wit: David and Antje Banta.
TURNEUR, Jacobus and Grietje—Jacomyntje, b. Oct. 7—Nov. 4.
PARLEMAN, Jacobus—Jacobus, b. Dec. 9—Dec. 20.
 Wit: Andries and Jannitje Debouw.

1765

RYER, John and Susanna—Jannetje, b. Feb. 28—Mar. 31.
 Wit: Rynier and Jannetje Wortendyk.
PILESFELT, Hendrik and Cornelia—Johannis, b. Mar. 24—Apr. 14.
 Wit: Cobus and Tietje Pielesfelt.
ACKERMAN, Jan and Styntje—Johannis, b. Apr. 4—Apr. 28.
 Wit: Dom. B. and Lisabeth V. d. Linde.
ZABRISKE, Hendrik C. and Maria—Maria—Aug. 21.
 Wit: Andries and Lisabeth Zabriske.
BROUWER, Abram—Jannetje—Aug. 21.
 Wit: Andries and Jannetje Debouw.
PILESFELT, Jacobus and Tittie—Johannis—Nov. 3.
 Wit: Garrit and Tryntje Blauvelt.

1766

HOPPE, Albert and Rachel—Isaac—Jan. 12.
 Wit: Jan J. and Geertje Hoppe.
ACKERMAN, Gerrit J. and Rachel—Johannes—Mar. 16.
 Wit: Hannes and Lena Ackerman.
BLAUVELT, David and Rachel—Johannes, b. Apr. 19—May 10.
 Wit: Hannes and Catriena Blauvelt.
VANBLERKOM, David and Gerritje—Jan—June 1.
 Wit: Rachel Van Blerkom.
ZABRISKE, Jacob J. and Jannetje—Jan—Sep. 14.
 Wit: Andries and Tiena Zobriske.
STEGG, Isaac and Lena—Isaac—Sep. 21.
 Wit: Gerrit J. and Rachel Ackerman.
McDANNEL, Cornelis and Catriena—Jacob—Sep. 7.
 Wit: Jacob Eckerson.
VAN BLERKOM, David and Elisabeth—Jacomyntje—Dec. 18.
 Wit: David A. and Jacomyntje Ackerman.

1767

DUBAEN, Jacob and Rachel—Jacob, Rachel, b. Jan. 26—Feb. 15.
 Wit: Jacob B. and Sara Coel; Abram and Brechje Dubaen.
HOPPE, Andries A. and Lisabeth—Jacob—Mar. 22.
 Wit: Jacob and Saartje Hoppe.
LEVISIE, Paulus and Elisabeth—Jan—Mar. 29.
 Wit: Jan and Jannitje Vanderbeek.
WARD, Samuel and Abigael—Jones—Mar. 29.
 Wit: Pieter H. and Jannitje Vanblerkom.

BANTA, Cornelis A. and Maria—Joseph, b. Aug. 15—Sep. 6.
Wit: Isaac and Annatje Alyee.
VAN BLERKOM, David and Lisabeth—Jannetje—Sep. 27.
Wit: Pieter Maybe, Jr., and wife.

1768

LUTKENS, Pieter and Annatje—Jan—Feb. 21.
Wit: Jan and Belitje Doremus.
PILESVELT, Andries and Cornelia—Johannes, b. Jan. 26—Mar. 6.
Wit: Hannes and Tryntje Winter.
COCKROW, Niklaas and Pietertje—Jannetje—Mar. 13.
Wit: Jacob and Marytje Bogert.
HUNTER, Robert and Mollie—Jannetje—Mar. 27.
Wit: Jacobus and Titie Pilesvelt.
ACKERMAN, David D. and Jannetje—Jannetje—Mar. 27.
Wit: Jurjen and Marytje V. derbeek.
DUBAEN, Jacob and Marytje—Jacob—May 15.
Wit: Jan and Grietje Straet.
ACKERMAN, Gerrit J. and Rachel—Johannes—Aug. 28.
Wit: Johannes J. and Lena Ackerman.
TRAPHAGE, Hendrik and Claartje—Jacobus—Aug. 28.
Wit: Jan H. and Fytje Hoppe .
ALYEE, Isaac and Annatje—Jan, b. June 3—Aug. 28.
Wit: Jan and Grietje Banta.
BLAUVELT, Gerrit and Annatje—Jannetje, b. Aug. 2—Sep. 19.
Wit: Christiaan and Jannetje Blauvelt.
ACKERMAN, Johannis and Lena—Johannis—Oct. 23.
Wit: Abram J. and Brechje Ackerman.
ZOBRISKE, Andries J. and Carstina—Jan—Dec. 19.
Wit: Jan and Aaltje Zobriske.
TOIRS, Lourens and Lisabeth—Jan—Dec. 25.
Wit: Jan and Styntje Ackerman.

1769

PARRELMAN, Han Jurry and Maria—Isaac—Sep. 10.
Wit: Maurits Mourusse and Annatje Debow.
ACKERMAN, Arie and Marytje—Johannes, b. Apr. 26—May 20.
Wit: Hannes A. and Jacomyntje Ackerman.

1837

TERHUNE, Henry and Maria—John Nichousis, b. Dec. 20, 1837(?)—Feb.
25, 1837(?).

1842

BANTA, Henry H. and Ann—Jane Maria, b. Sep. 5—Oct. 23.

1803

DURYEA, David and Geertje—Joannes, b. May 9—May 29.
HOPPER, Jacob and Sophiah—John, b. June 25—July 10.
Wit: John and Jacomyntje Zabriskie.
MABYE, William and Aaltje—John, b. Dec. 7—Dec. 28.

1807

TAYLOR, Samuel and Sarah—John, b. Mar. 29—May 17.

QUACKENBUSH, Teunis and Mary—Jannetje, b. May 4—May 31.

HOPPER, Jacob and Geesje—Jane, b. June 18—Sep. 27.

TERHUNE, Albert and Rachel—John, b Sep. 17—Oct. 11.

HARRIS, Isaac and Annatje—Jacob, b. Sep. 11—Oct. 25.
    Wit: Jacob and Rachel Van Saan.

1808

ZABRISKIE, John and Jannetje—John, b. Mar. 29—Apr. 18.

1809

ACKERMAN, David and Metje—Isaak, b. Apr. 7—May 7.

GERRETSEN, Hessel and Maria—John, b. Apr. 25—May 22.

1810

CAMPBELL, Abraham and Maragrietje—Jacobus, b. Jan. 28—Feb. 25.
    Wit: Sara Demarest.

VAN SAAN, Jacob and Maria—Jacob, b. Feb. 23—Apr. 1.

GERRETSON, Albert and Jacomyntje—John, b. Nov. 25—Dec. 9.

1811

STAAG, Isaac and Maria—John, b. Feb. 22—Mar. 17.

VAN WINCEL, Robert and Tryna—John, b. Feb. 6—Apr. 14.

TERHUNE, Albert and Rachel—Jacob, b. June 23—July 21.
    Wit: Elisabeth Bogert.

BUSH, John and Maria—John, b. Sep. 16—Nov. 10.

ZABRISKIE, Jacob and Antje—Jacob, b. Dec. 1—Dec. 26.

1812

DAY, William and Jenne—Julian, b. Sep. 3, 1809—Mar. 8.

1813

TERHUNE, Peter and Helena—John Richard, b. Jan. 31—Mar. 7.

VANDERBEEK, Paul and Hannah(?)—James, b. Apr. 4—Apr. 25.

VANDERBEEK, James and Margaret—Jacob, b. July 15—Aug. 29.

1814

ACKERMAN, John and Polly—John, b. June 20—July 24.

VAN ORDER, David and Ally—James, b. Aug. 7—Aug. 28.

FREELAND, Tunis and Margaret—John, b. Aug. 28—Oct. 2.

VANDERBEEK, Abraham and Letty—Jacob, b. Oct. 4—Oct. 20.

VAN SAUN, Cornelius and Rachel—Jacob, b. Oct. 7—Nov. 6.

1815

CLEARWATER, Frederik and Hetty—Joseph, b. July 10, 1814—Feb. 12.

YELVERTON, Anthony and Rachel—John Hopper, b. Mar. 18—June 25.

SNYDER, George and Maria—John, b. May 28—June 25.

SNYDER, Garrit and Catharina—John, b. June 10—July 2.

WESTERVELT, Peter A. and Martha—John, b. July 21—Aug. 20.

HOPPER, John H. and Mary—John, b. Oct. 21—Nov. 26.

QUACKENBUSH, John I. and Suse—Jacob, b. Oct. 31—Dec. 25.

GARRITSON, Jacob I. and Rachel—John, b. Dec. 1—Dec. 30.

1816

Post, Andrew and Syntje—John Andrew Ackerman, b. Feb. 20—Mar. 17.

Bush, Lodewyk and Lenah—Jannetje, b. Apr. 16—May 12.

Van Horn, Daniel and Pietertje (?)—Jemima, b. Sep. 21—Oct. 6.

Zabriskie, Andrew I. and Polly—John, b. Oct. 22—Nov. 17.

Westervelt, Peter A. and Caty—John, b. Dec. 7—Dec. 15.

1817

Van Dien, Garrit H. and Anne—John Zabriskie, b. Apr. 21—May 25.

Banta, Garrit D. and Harriet—John, b. Nov. 22—Dec. 13.

1818

Quackenbush, John I. and Susan—John, b. Feb. 1—Mar. 8.

Berdan, John, Jr. and Sally—John Degrau, b. Feb. 14—Mar. 29.

Westervelt, Casparus and Maria—John, b. Aug. 30—Oct. 5.

Maby, Abraham and Sechy—Jane, b. July 30—Oct. 5.

Van Winkle, David and Bridget—John, b. Sep. 17—Nov. 1.

Vandien, Garrit and Jane—John Buskirk, b. Sep. 12—Nov. 15.

1819

Ward, James and Ann—John, b. Feb. 28—Apr. 18.

Zabriskie, Andrew and Polly—John, b. Mar. 21—Apr. 18.

Vanderbeek, Paul P. and Hannah—John, b. Nov. 19—Dec. 25.

1820

Zabriskie, Casper and Caty—John, b. Sep. 12—Oct. 15.

Hover, Benjamin and Jemima—Joseph, b. Nov. 17—Dec. 3.

1821

Vanderbeek, Hermanus and Jane—Jacob, b. May 26—July 29.

Zabriskie, John A. and Betsy—James, b. Aug. 22—Sep. 8.

Hopper, Albert G. and Polly—John Cooper, b. Sep. 26—Oct. 21.

Demarest, James J. and Anne—Jacob Brown, b. Sep. 22—Nov. 4.

1822

Terhune, Hannah—John Ackerman, b. Oct. 22, 1821—Jan. 12.

Zabriskie, Andrew J. and Polly—John, b. Apr. 28—May 26.

Van Blarcom, Peter, Jr. and Hannah—John, b. Mar. 16—May 26.

Berdan, John, Jr. and Sally—John Degray, b. July 19—Aug. 18.

Van Imburgh, Henry H. and Peggy—Jacob Demarest, b. July 12—Aug. 4.

Zabriskie, Henry A. and Patty—John, b. Aug. 3—Sep. 1.

Zabriskie, Pieter A. and Anne—James, b. Oct. 6—Nov. 17.

1823

Van Saun, Jacob, Jr. and Polly—John, b. May 23—June 29.

Roll, John and Isabella—James, b. July 8—Aug. 9.

Vanderbeek, James and Peggy—John, b. Sep. 1—Oct. 5.

Zabriskie, John H. and Maria—Jacob, b. Oct. 6—Oct. 20.

1824

VANDERBEEK, Jurry and Elisabeth—John, b. Feb. 16—Mar. 21.
MYRES, John and Betsey—Jane Kip, b. Feb. 17—Apr. 4.
ZABRISKIE, John A. and Betsey—Jacob, b. June 5—July 3.
BLAUVELT, John I. and Sarah—Jacob, b. Sep. 13—Oct. 17.

1825

HOPPER, Garrit A. and Sophia—Jane, b. Mar. 15—Apr. 24.
LUTKINS, John S. and Maria—Jacob, b. July 23—Aug. 7.
SNYDER, Richard and Ally—John, b. Apr. 13—Sep. 4.

1826

VAN NORDEN, David and Ally—John, b. Feb. 3—Mar. 5.
ZABRISKIE, Abraham A. and Jane—John, b. July 27—Aug. 19.
ROMINE, John D. and Maria—Jane, b. July 1—Aug. 19.
OBLENIS, Peter and Elisabeth—John Henry, b. Aug. 2—Sep. 3.
VANDIEN, Garrit and Jane—John Voorhis, b. Sep. 9—Nov. 12.

1827

VANDERBEEK, Jeremiah C. and Elisabeth—John, b. Sep. 4, 1826—Jan. 1.
VAN WINKLE, Cornelius J. and Caty—John Henry, b. Feb. 11—Mar. 25.
VAN BLARCOM, Henry and Caty—John Henry, b. Aug. 27—Sep. 23.
HOPPER, Jacob H. and Caty—John, b. Aug. 24—Oct. 21.
KING, Esra A. and Margaret—Jacob, b. May 1—Nov. 18.

1828

HENCOCK, William and Polly—John Anthony, b. Feb. 1—Mar. 2.
VOORHIS, John and Rachel—John Quackinbush, b. Feb. 15—Mar. 16.
VAM EMBURGH, Henry H. and Peggy—James, b. Mar. 3—May 11.
ZABRISKIE, Cornelius J. and Jane—Jacob, b. June 2—July 27.

1829

VANDERBEEK, Andrew and Polly—Jacob Stagg, b. Nov. 1, 1828—June 21.
ACKERMAN, Abraham and Peggy—John, b. May 18—June 21.
HARRIS, Henry and Hannah—Isaac, b. June 19—Aug. 22.
BLAUVELT, James and Hannah—Isaac, b. July 17—Aug. 23.

1830

WESTERVELT, Peter A. and Mathilda—James Bogert, b. Mar. 12—Apr. 25.
ACKERMAN, John G. and Maria—Jane, b. June 16—July 25.
CARLOUGH, Abraham and Maria—Jeremiah, b. July 18—Sep. 5.

1831

ZABRISKIE, Peter A. and Anne—John, b. Feb. 4—Mar. 6.
ZABRISKIE, John J. and Sally—Jane, b. Mar. 8—Apr. 9.
DOREMUS, Ralph and Peggy—Jacob Conklin, b. Apr. 10, 1830—Apr. 9. [?]
SNYDER, George and Charity—Jane, b. Apr. 20—May 15.
EARLE, Jacob and Maria—John, b. June 4—July 3.
HALL, William and Jane—James, b. July 17—Aug. 28.
VANDERBEEK, Andrew and Polly—Jacob Stagg, b. July 26—Oct. 1.

1832

ACKERMAN, Abraham J. and Levina—John Henry, b. Jan. 16—Mar. 25.
TERHUNE, Abraham A. and Catharina—Jasper, b. Feb. 5—Mar. 25.
SNYDER, James and Charity—Jacob Spier, b. Mar. 18—Apr. 22.
MOURUS, John D. and Eliza—John Andrew, b. Apr. 3—May 13.
HENCOCK, William and Mary—Jacob, b. Apr. 18—May 20.

1833

HOPPER, John An. and Ellen—John Andrew, b. Nov. 17, 1832—Feb. 24.
JERALOMAN, James and Mary—James Varick, b. May 21—July 27.
ZABRISKIE, Gilliam and Tina—Jacob, b. Aug. 18—Sep. 22.

1834

ACKERMAN, Peter D. and Hester—Jemima, b. Oct. 9, 1833—Feb. 22.
BLAUVELT, James, Jr. and Hannah—Jacob, b. Dec. 23, 1833—Mar. 2.
VANDIEN, Richard A. and Ally—John, b. Apr. 13—June 8.
VANDERBEEK, Jerry C. and Ann—Jacob Zabriskie, b. Apr. 23—June 22.
ZABRISKIE, Henry A. and Patty—Jemima, b. July 21—Aug. 3.
CAMPBELL, Samuel and Betsy—Jacob Andrew Jackson, b. June6—Nov.2.

1835

BALDWIN, Richard and Caty Ann—Joseph, b. Dec. 10, 1834—Feb. 8.
BANTA, Aaron and Betsey—John, b. Feb. 4—Mar. 29.
ZABRISKIE, Peter A. and Anne—Jacob, b. Mar. 4—Apr. 18.
ACKERMAN, Abr. J. and Lavina—Jane, b. July 2—Aug. 16.

1836

ZABRISKIE, John J. and Sally—John, b. Sep. 9—Nov. 13.

1838

VAN VOORHIS, William and Maria—John, b. Nov. 13, 1837—Feb. 4.
ACKERMAN, Ralph D. and Hetty—John, b. Dec. 31, 1837—Feb. 4.
BOGART, Albert and Jane—John, b. Nov. 1, 1837—Apr. 22.
BLAUVELT, James, Jr. and Hannah—James, b. May 5—July 1.
VAN SAUN, John J. and Elsje—Isaac, b. July 30—Sep. 2.
ACKERMAN, John and Jane—Jacob, b. Aug. 23—Oct. 14.
ACKERMAN, Albert and Dorcas—Jane, b. Aug. 28—Oct. 14.

1839

KING, Ezra A. and Margaret—James Henry, b. Sep. 1, 1838—Feb. 17.
BANTA, Thomas T. and Ellen—Jacob, b. Jan. 18—Mar. 3.
HORSBROOK, Augustus and Jane—Joseph, b. May 12—May 20.
BUSH, Benjamin and Margaret—John Henry, b. May 20—July 28.
VANDERBEEK, William and Mary Jane—James, b. May 26—July 7.
BOGART, Stephen J. and Catharina—John Westervelt, b. Sept. 3—Oct. 13.

1840

ZABRISKIE, John T. and Ann—John, b. Jan. 12—Feb. 23.
VAN SAUN, Lucas I. and Jane—Isaac, b. Nov. 15, 1839—Jan. 9.

1841

MOWERSON, Abraham and Rachel—John Jacob, b. Apr. 30—Aug. 14.

1842

BREVOORT, Garrit and Maria—Jacob Zabriskie, b. Jan. 23, 1832—Jan. 18.
ACKERMAN, David A. and Mary Ann—John Jacob, b. Mar. 6—Apr. 23.

1843

WESTERVELT, John P. and Sally—John Bogert, b. Jan. 30—Mar. 19.
JOHNSON, Joel M. and Hannah—John Edsall, b. Feb. 2—Mar. 12.
HASBROCK, Augustus and Jane—James Hartenburgh, b. Sep. 22—Nov. 5.

1844

ACKERMAN, Garrit D. and Eliza—Jemima Jane, b. Nov. 16, 1843—Feb. 11.
JOHNSON, Joel M. and Hannah—Joel Munson, b. Dec. 18, 1843—Feb. 11.
WESTERVELT, John C. and Leah—Jasper, b. June 10—Aug. 3.
CARLOUGH, Abraham and Maria—Jeremiah, b. Mar. 15—Aug. 31.

1845

THE SAME—John Jacob, b. Feb. 17—June 22.
BOGART, John C. and Jannette—John Augustus, b. May 25—July 27.
ZABRISKIE, Stephen I. (or T.) (?) and Jane—John Jacob, b. June 27—
Aug. 31.

1846

ZABRISKIE, Garrit H. and Rachel Ann—John, b. June 19—Aug. 2.
ZABRISKIE, Andrew C. and Sarah Margaret—John Henry, b. July 5—
Aug. 30.
TERHUNE, Peter and Maria—John, b. Aug. 4—Nov. 15.

1847

VAN BLARCOM, Jacob Z. and Maria—John Henry, b. Apr. 5—Aug. 26.
ZABRISKIE, Abraham J. and Mary—John Jacob, b. June 22—Sep. 5.
GAUDENERE, Henry and Maria—James Larance, b. Aug. 24—Oct. 16.

1848

BANTA, John G. and Sarah Ann—John Henry, b. Mar. 7, 1847—June 2.
———, Henry and Margaret Ann—Jemima Jane, b. Nov. 19, 1847—
Jan. 22.
BOGART, Josiah Gardner and Peggy—Isaac, b. Jan. 9—May 13.

1849

HARMUTMAN, Peter and Geertrui Venniceman(?)—Job, b. Dec. 5, 1848
—July 8.

1850

BERDAN, Cornelius Z. and Margaret—John, b. Aug. 19—Sep. 29.

1851

WESTERVELT, John P. and Sally—Jemima, b. July 7, 1850—Jan. 12.
ACKERSON, Cornelius J. and Ann—John—Feb. 3.
ZABRISKIE, Thomas B. and Catharine—Jane Elizabeth, b. Nov. 26, 1850—
Feb. 23.
DEVOE, Harman and Eliza Jane—John Quackenbush, b. Apr. 10—May 11.
MOWERSON, Abraham and Rachel—James Williams, b. Mar. 24—June 1.
ACKERMAN, Peter P. and Eliza—John Demarest, b. July 20—Oct. 11.
BOGART, Albert D. and Leany—John Henry, b. July 17—Nov. 30.
ZABRISKIE, Garrit H. and Rachel Ann—Jemima, b. May 27—Aug. 13.

"K"

1815

DEMAREST, James J. and Anne—Kazia, b. Sep. 2—Oct. 22.

1821

HOPPER, Andrew P. and Anne—Kazia, b. Feb. 3—Feb. 25.

"L"

1749

ACKERMAN, Gerrit D. and Lena—Lisabeth—Aug. 27.
Wit: Pieter and Lisabeth Post.

1750

ACKERMAN, Abram I. and Hester—Lisabeth—Mar. 20.
Wit: Hannes and Lisabeth Ackerman.

VAN BLERKOM, Pieter and Susanna—Lisabeth—Apr. 15.
Wit: Gerrit and Elsje Hoppe.

SEDMAN, Samme and Angonietje—Lisabeth—Nov. 11.
Wit: Isaak I. and Lisabeth Van Deuse.

1752

JURRIKSE, Harme and Jannetje—Lisabeth—Mar. 8.
Wit: Samuel and Rebecka Bos.

TOERS, Hannes and Geertje—Lea—Feb. 9.
Wit: Abram C. Ackerman and Francyntje Toers.

ZABRISKE, Jacob C. and Lena—Lea—July 29.
Wit: Andries C. and Lisabeth Zabriske.

1754

PYPER, David—Lodewyk—Jan.——
Wit: Hannes and Vrouwtje Van Schyve.

SYOURT, Joost and Lidea—Lewis—Nov. 25.
Wit: Lewis and Hatty Conklin.

1755

EARL, Sylvester and Machtel—Lisabeth—Aug. 17.
Wit: Albert J. and Geertje Zobriskie.

BANTA, Abram and Annatje—Lea—Sep. 14.
Wit: Jan and Grietje Banta.

MEYER, Hannes M. and Lea—Lena—Nov. 4.
Wit: Adolf and Lena Meyer.

ACKERMAN, Hannes H. and Lena—Lisabeth—Nov. 16.
Wit: Hannes and Lisabeth Ackerman.

1756

BERRY, Philip—Lena—Jan. 5.
Wit: Simeon and Lisabeth Van Winkel.

MACELESE, Ceel and Elisabeth—Janneke, b. Oct. 18—Nov. 7.
Wit: Pieter and Janneke Macelese.

DEMAREST, Cornelis and Marytje—Lisabeth—Nov. 7.
Wit: Hannes and Lisabeth Ackerman.

1759

DEVENPOORT, Omphre and Willemina—Lea—Jan. 31.
Wit: Leendert and Lea Kool.

V. BLERKOM, Hermanus and Aaltje—Lena—Apr. 14.
Wit: Hannes H. and Lena Ackerman.

1761

SLOT, Steven and Marritje—Lisabeth—Jan. 25.
Wit: Isaak and Lisabeth Van Deuse.

VAN ZEYL, Hans and Catharina—Lena, b. Jan. 27—Feb. 1.
Wit: Hendrik Ryke and Lena Baremole.

TOERS, Louwrens and Lisabeth—Lena—July 5.
Wit: Hannes and Lena Van Houte.

1762

BOGERT, Cornelis and Lisabeth—Lisabeth—Mar. 8.
Wit: Klaas and Rachel Zobriske.

1763

LAROI, Hannes and Margrietje—Lena, b. Mar. 20—Apr. 17.
Wit: Gerrit and Lena Ackerman.

HEATON, Richard and Maria—Lisabeth, b. Apr. 14—May 7.
Wit: Samuel P. and Lena Dumare.

1765

VANHOREN, Cornelis C. and Geesje—Lisabeth, b. Oct. 10—Nov. 10.
Wit: Cornelis and Lisabeth Vanhoren.

1766

JURLIE (or Surlie), James and Marytje—Lourens—Mar. 30.
Wit: Teunis and Grietje Helm.

VANDIEN, Thomas and Polly—Lisabeth—Mar. 23.
Wit: Cornelis and Lisabeth Bogert.

DUBAEN, Jacob and Marytje—Lisabeth—June 1.
Wit: Dirk and Lisabeth Vanhoren.

1767

KROM, Teunis and Catriena—Lisabeth, b. Feb. 22—Apr. 19.
Wit: Cornelis and Catrina Macdannel.

1769

MICKLER, Hans and Grietje—Lisabeth—Feb. 5.
Wit: Pieter and Lisabeth Swin.

POST, Hannes and Trientje—Lisabeth—Dec. 3.
Wit: Cobus and Metje Post.

1770

DERYIE, Jan P. and Jannitje—Lisabeth—Feb. 4.
Wit: Hannes and Lisabeth Blauvelt.

COCKROW, Niklaas and Pietertje—Lisabeth—Mar. 25.
Wit: Nates and Lisabeth Steger.

V. BLERKOM, David J. and Geritje—Lisabeth—Sep. 20.
Wit: Lucas and Lisabeth Vanblerkom.

ZOBRISKE, Jacob H. and Wyntje—Lisabeth—Dec. 2.
Wit: Albert and Lisabeth Terhuyn.

1771

ACKERMAN, Albert G. and Antje—Lena—June 23.

Wit: Gerrit and Lena Ackerman.
DUMAREE, Cornelis I. and Grietje—Lea—Aug. 4.
DAVIS, Niklaes and Marytje—Lisabeth—Aug. 25.
Wit: Hannes J. and Rebecka Van Blerkom.
ZABRISKIE, Christiaan J. and Marytje—Maria—Apr. 15.
Wit: Steve and Titje Terhune.

1773
BROUWER, Abram D. and Antje—Lea—June 20.
Wit: Jan W. and Lea Van Voorhese.

1774
HOPPE, Hendrik J. and Aaltje—Lisabeth—May 8.
Wit: Jan and Lisabeth Hoppe.
TRAPHAGE, Hendrik—Marytje—May 29.
Wit: Jurry and Marytje Vanderbeek.
SWIN, Pieter and Elisabeth—Marytje—May 29.
Wit: Jan and Jannetje Van Orden.

1776
V. DERBEEK, Hannes and Ebbie—Lea—Jan. 28.
Wit: Hendrik and Polly Terhune.
BANTA, Angenietje—Lisabeth Bogert, b. Apr. 17—May 12.
Wit: Jan and Grietje Banta; Hendrik and Grietje Banta.

1778
ZOBRISKE, Abram A. and Marytje—Lisabeth—Sep. 13.
Wit: Albert A. and Betje Terhuyn.

1779
WESTERVELT, Johannes and Antje—Lucas, b. May 28—July 25.
Wit: Cornelis L. and Lisabeth Bogert.
VALENTINE, Jacob and Grietje—Lisabeth—Sep. 19.

1780
BOGERT, Casparus and Jannetje—Lisabeth—May 15.
Wit: Belkje Bogert.

1783
V. HOOREN, Daniel—Lisabeth—Feb. 20.

1784
VANDEBEEK, Johannis—Lea—Apr. 25.
Wit: Hendrik Hoppe and wife.
ACKERMAN, David—Lea—Apr. 25.
LAZIER, Abram—Lisabeth—Aug. 22.

1785
HOPPE, Gerrit—Elisabeth—Apr. 10.
Wit: Hendrik Hoppe and wife.
HOPPE, Andries and Tryntje—Lea—May 1.
Wit: Hendrik and Rachel Terhune.
BAMPER, Jacob and Antje—Lodewyk Marcelis—May 16.
Wit: John and Anne Barberrier.
EARLE, Edward and Abigail—Lena—Oct. 23.
Wit: Abraham and Margrietje Rotan.

1786

BANTA, Hendrik and Maria—Lena, b. May 3—May 21.
    Wit: Jacob Stagg and Sara Bogert.
ACKERMAN, Johannis and Elisabeth—Lena, b. May 19—June 26.
    Wit: Lena Ackerman.

1788

TOERS, Arie and Rachel—Louwrens, b. June 2—June 29.

1789

VAN VOORHEESEN, Abraham and Angonietje—Lea, b. Sep. 10—Oct. 25.
    Wit: Jan and Lea Van Voorheesen.

1792

MESSEKER, Lodewyk and Sara—Lodewyk, b. Jan. 29—Feb. 26.
JENKINS, Lambert and Annatje—Lena, b. Feb. 15—Apr. 10.

1793

PERRY, John and Charity—Lidea, b. Sep. 8—Oct. 13.

1794

ACKERMAN, Marmeduck and Lena—Lena, b. Aug. 6—Aug. 31.
STOR, Jacob and Geesje—Lea, b. Aug. 4—Sep. 14.
    Wit: Gerrit Post and Anna Van Rype.

1795

TERHUUN, Hendrik and Tryntje—Lea, b. Feb. 22—Mar. 15.
    Wit: Jan and Lea Van Imburg.
COERTEN, John and Catrina—Lena, b. Apr. 15—May 17.
    Wit: Leuwer (Lewis?) and Lena Winter.

1796

TERHUNE, Andrias and Antje—Lea, b. Feb. 2—Feb. 7.
    Wit: Johannis and Abigail Vanderbeek.

1797

MEBE, Abraham and Maria—Lea, b. Jan. 13—Mar. 19.
ECKERSON, Gerrit and Annaatje—Lea, b. Nov. 1—Nov. 26.

1798

HALDEROM, William and Catriena—Lena, b. Feb. 28—Apr. 1.
    Wit: Niclaas and Lena Halderom.
TERHUNE, Abraham and Soeke—Lea, b. June 24—Aug. 26.
    Wit: Hendrik and Aaltje Hopper.
MESSEKER, Lodewyk and Sara—Lena—Dec. 9.

1799

ECKER, Abraham and Tryntje—Lea, b. Mar. 22—Apr. 14.
MEBE, Pieter and Jannetje—Lea, b. Apr. 30—July 7.
TOERS, Jacob and Aaltje—Lourens, b. Oct. 6—Nov. 3.

1800

HOPPER, Hendrik and Charrette—Lewis, b. July 10—July 27.

1801

WORTENDYCK, John and Elisabeth—Metje, b. Jan. 23—Mar. 1.
    Wit: John and Metje Van Blarcom.
DURIE, Peter and Osseltje—Leah, b. Mar. 23—Apr. 19.

1802
Tours, Abraham and Rachel—Lawrence, b. July 21—Nov. 21.
1805
Storm, Abraham and Susanna—Leah, b. Jan. 27—Feb. 24.
Eckerson, Thomas and Susannah——Leah, b. Aug. 8—Sep. 6.
1809
Zabriskie, Jacob H. and Antje—Lence Willempje, b. Aug. 13—Sep. 1.
Cuyper, Gerrit and Geertje—Lena, b. Nov. 16—Dec. 17.
1810
Zabriske, Abraham and Susanna—Lea, b. Oct. 9—Nov. 25.
1814
Welber, Henry and Elisabeth—Laura, b. Mar. 24—July 24.
Zabriskie, John A. and Jane—Lavina, Nov. 24—Dec. 25.
1818
Vanderbeek, Harmanus and Jane—Lydia, b. Aug. 11—Sep. 6.
1819
Earl, Gerrit E. and Sally—Lewis, b. Feb. 25—June 13.
Snyder, John A. and Helon—Lewis, b. Sep. 6—Oct. 3.
Tinkey, Garret and Anna—Ledyan, b. Feb. 21—Apr. 22.
1820
Christopher, Joseph and Effy—Levina, b. Aug. 15—Sep. 30.
1823
Van Emburgh, John H. and Polly—Levinah Zabriskie, b. Apr. 17—
   May 18.
1825
Post, John and Caty—Leah, b. Nov. 18—Dec. 11.
1826
Snyder, George T. and Charity—Lawrance, b. Dec. 31, 1825—Feb. 5.
1827
Terhune, Henry I. and Sally—Letitia, b. Nov. 21, 1826—Feb. 11.
Lutkins, John S. and Maria—Levina, b. Jan. 21—Mar. 25.
1830
Zabriskie, Jacob and Eliza—Leah Alettah, b. Aug. 20—Oct. 3.
1832
Post, Elisabeth, wife of James Post—Letty Maria, b. Jan. 16—Apr. 22.
1833
Van Orden, Adam and Rosamon—Letty Jane, b. July 16—Aug. 10.
1842
Van Saun, John I. and Elsje—Levina, b. Apr. 7—May 15.
1846
Banta, Cornelius and Catharina—Lydia, b. Nov. 28, 1845—June 7.
Banta, Henry, Jr. and Ann—Lavina, b. Mar. 17—June 7.

"M"

1749
Van Deuse, Isaak and Lisabeth—Maria— Aug. 13.
   Wit: Cobus and Rebecka Laroe.

WANNEMAKER, Hendrik and Lisabeth—Margrietje—Sep. 17.
Wit: Coenraad and Margriet Vredriks.

1751

RUTAN, Daniel D. and Susan—Marytje—June 14.
Wit: Hannes and Francyntje Brikker.

ODEL, Benjamin and Nelli—Maria—Aug. 25.
Wit: Isaac and Lena Conkling.

MYER, Hannes and Lena—Marytje—Aug. 25.
Wit: Samuel and Marytje Bravoo.

ZABRISKE, Jacob I. and Aaltje—Maria—Feb. 10.
Wit: Albertus and Anna Maria Terhuyn.

———, ——— and ——— —Marytje—Sept. 29.
Wit: Bille and Maragrietje Ginckins.

HOPPE, Gerrit and Elsje—Marytje—Oct. 20.
Wit: Abram and Marytje Lasier.

1752

VAN ZEYL, Peter and Lena—Marytje and Lena (twins)—Jan. 5.
Wit: Hendrik and Marytje Messeker; Isack and Lena Conkling.

TERHUYN, Albert A. and Lisabeth—Maria—Jan. 26.
Wit: Albertus and Anna Maria Terhuyn.

TERHUYN, Dirk A. and Lea—Maria—Sep. 24.
Wit: The same as above.

WANNEMAKER, Pieter D. and Marytje—Margrieta—Sep. 24.
Wit: Adolf Schyoert and Margrieta Schyoert.

1753

ALYEE, Cobus and Annatje—Margrieta—Mar. 4.
Wit: Pieter and Margrieta Alyee.

ZABRISKE, Albert C. and Aaltje—Marytje—Oct. 1.
Wit: Jacob C. and Lena Zabriske.

BANTA, Jacob and Lena—Maria—Dec. 23.
Wit: Cornelis and Lidea Myer.

1754

STORM, Abram and Aaltje—Maria—Jan. 13.
Wit: Cornelis and Marytje Demarest.

GRAU, Hermanus D. and Jannike—Geertrui—Apr. 14.
Wit: Joris and Antje Stegg.

BROUWER, Uldrick and Aaltje—Marytje—Apr. 14.
Wit: Hannes and Jacomyntje Ackerman.

ZOBRISKE, Jacob H. and Wyntje—Marytje—Apr. 15.
Wit: Albertus and Marytje Terhuyn.

HOPPE, Albert and Rachel—Margrietje—Oct. 13.
Wit: Stefanus and Santje Terhuyn.

PARLMAN, Ned D. and Antje—Margriet—Nov. 25.
Wit: Steve and Maritje Slot.

1755

HOPPE, Willem and Antje—Maria, b. Apr. 29—May 11.
Wit: Jacob Jan Zobriske and Marytje Hoppe.

BONGAERT, Cornelis and Lisabeth—Martyntje—June 15.
Wit: Abram and Martyntje Haring.

V. BLERKOM, Hermanus and Aaltje—Margrietje—Oct. 12.
Wit: Louwrens Ackerman and Grietje Van Voorhees.
MEYER, Marcus and Willemyntje—Maria—Nov. 16.

1756

ACKERMAN, Johannis Ar. and Jacomyntje—Marytje—Feb. 1.
Wit: Jurry and Marytje Vanderbeek.
BONGAERT, Albert C. and Sara C.—Maria, b. Jan. 17—Feb. 15.
Wit: Abram A. and Marytje Haring.
SIDMAN, Samuel and Angonietje—Marytje, b. Feb. 4—Mar. 7.
Wit: Benjamin and Wybrech Demare.
ZABRISKE, Hendrik and Maria—Martyntje—May 30.
Wit: Abram and Martyntje Haring.
ACKERMAN, Albert and Rachel—Metje—Dec. 25.
Wit: Abram G. Ackerman and Lena Van Winkel.

1757

ECKER, Thomas and Marytje—Maria, b. Jan. 9—Jan. 16.
Wit: Cornelis and Matje Demarest.

1759

TOERS, Lourens and Lisabeth—Marytje—Jan. 21.
Wit: Niklaas and Mettie Volk.
PECKER, Jacob and Elisabeth—Maria—May 20.
Wit: Hannes and Marytje Vanblerkom.
MOURESE, Dirk and Rachel—Marytje—May 3.
Wit: Pieter and Marytje Mourese.
LODEWYK, Hendrik and Rosina—Maria—Sep. 9.
Wit: Christiaen and Maria Caef.
RYERSE, Joris F. and Maria—Marte—Sep. 23.
Wit: Marte F. and Antje Ryerse.
TERHUYN, Abram and Marytje—Maria—Dec. 20.
Wit: Jacob I. and Aaltje Zabriske.

1760

ALYEE, Albert and Maria—Maria, b. Feb. 20—Mar. 9.
Wit: Isack and Annatje Alyee.
MABE, Pieter, Jr. and Jannitje—Myndert, b. Feb. 19—Mar. 29.
Wit: Myndert and Lena Hogenkamp.

1763

JENKINS, Willem and Margriet—Maria, b. Jan. 20—Feb. 29.
Wit: Jacob and Marytje Kogh.
HOPPE, Willem and Antje—Magdalena, b. Apr. 2—Apr. 27.
Wit: Abram and Rebecka Hoppe.

1764

ZABRISKE, Jacob J. and Jannitje—Marytje—Apr. 15.
Wit: Hannes and Marytje Brevoort.
MYER, Hannes C. and Saartje—Maria—Apr. 15.
Wit: Thomas and Marytje Eckersen.

1765

HUYLER, Cornelia—Margrietje—Jan. 13.
Wit: Jan and Grietje Banta.

PIELISFELT, Willem and Lisabeth—Maria, b. Mar. 15—Apr. 14.
Wit: Christiaan and Marytje Pilesfelt.

BRUYN, Coenraad and Antje—Marytje, b. May 7—May 26.
Wit: Abram and Marytje Ackerman.

1762

ZOBRISKE, Hendrik C. and Maria—Margrietje—Mar. 20.
Wit: Isaak and Margrietje Blance.

SCHOEMAKER, Lodewyk and Catryn—Anna Margriet—June 27.
Wit: Dirk Wannemaker and Margriet Milrien.

ECKERSEN, Dirk and Maria—Maritje—Sep. 5.
Wit: Cobus and Ariaantje Springstien.

VAN SCHYVE, Hans and Vrouwtje—Maria—Dec. 19.
Wit: Joseph and Maria Fits.

1763

V. DER VOORT, David and Brechje—Maria, b. Feb. 27—June 12.

1765

VESEUR, Barend and Sientje—Maria—Dec. 28.
Wit: Pieter and Maria Vosuer.

1766

TERHUYN, Abram and Marytje—Maria—Mar. 16.
Wit: Jacob J. and Aaltje Zobriske.

*WENDYK, Reinier and Jannitje—Maria, b. Mar. 25—Apr. 6.
Wit: Pieter and Maria Veseur.

WESTERVELT, Johannis and Antje—Maria—July 13.
Wit: Abram and Marytje Terhuyn.

HOGENKAMP, Jan and Elisabeth—Myndert, b. Aug. 29—Sep. 21.
Wit: Myndert and Helena Hogenkamp.

V. D. BEEK, Paulus and Rachel—Marytje—Sep. 14.
Wit: Jacob and Marytje Ryerson.

RYERSE, Ryer J. and Lisabeth—Maria—Sep. 14.
Wit: Cathalyntje and Johannis R. Ryerse.

DOBS, Willem and Rachel—Maria—Sep. 14.
Wit: Willem and Maria Rutan.

1767

ECKERSEN, David and Angonietje—Maria—Feb. 25.
Wit: Thomas and Maria Eckersen.

PILESFELT, Hendrik and Cornelia—Maria—Mar. 22.

SLOT, Steven and Marietje—Marytje—June 7.
Wit: Christiaan and Marietje Van Deuse.

ODEL, Hendrik and Marytje—Marytje—Sep. 27.
Wit: Joseph and Ariaantje Wessels.

MYER, Cornelis M. and Ariaantje—Mettie—Nov. 5.
Wit: Niklaas and Mettie Volk.

HELM, Samuel and Tryntje—Marte—Dec. 6.

---

*Probably Wortendyk.

1768

PIELESFELT, Coenraad and Eva—Margrietje, b. Jan. 2—Mar. 6.
Wit: Jan and Grietje Huyler.

PARRELMAN, Cobus and Antje—Margrieta—June 5.
Wit: Samuel and Rebecka Bos.

1769

HOPPE, Albert and Rachel—Marytje—Jan. 29.
Wit: Abram and Marytje Ackerman.

VAN BLERKOM, David J. and Lisabeth—Marytje—Jan 29.
Wit: Abram and Maritje Maebie.

PIETERSE, Niklaas and Maria—Maria, b. Jan. 21—Feb. 19.
Wit: Jacob and Lena Myer.

BONGAART, Andries and Trientje—Maria—Feb. 19.
Wit: Samuel and Lea Terhuyn.

BANTA, Cornelis A. and Maria—Maria—Dec. 31.
Wit: Isaak and Annatje Alyee.

1770

BANTA, Samuel and Elisabeth—Maria, b. Jan. 23—Feb. 18.
Wit: Thomas and Maria Eckerson.

DUBAEN, Jacob and Marytje—Margrietje—July 29.
Wit: Samuel and Rebecka Bos.

DOBS, William and Rachel—Maria—Dec. 30.
Wit: Willem and Vroutje Rutan.

1771

LAROI, Hannes and Grietje—Maria—Jan. 13.
Wit: Albert W. and Marytje Van Voorheese.

HOPPE, Andries A. and Lisabeth—Micle—Feb. 24.
Wit: Micle and Saartje Post.

POST, Pieter P. and Neesje—Metje—Mar. 17.
Wit: Cobus C. and Mettie Post.

WALDEROM, Barend and Lena—Margrietje, b. Feb. 15—Apr. 1.
Wit: Abram and Grietje Blauvelt.

VERSEUR, Barend and Francyntje—Magdalena—Apr. 28.
Wit: Hannes and Magdalena Verseur.

VANDERBEEK, Jurry and Marytje—Maria—May 19.
Wit: Hannes A. and Jacomyntje Ackerman.

TRAPHAGE, Jonathan and Catriena—Maria, b. May 10—June 2.
Wit: Jacob and Maria Cogh.

WOERTENDYK, Frederik and Majere—Majere, b. June 26—July 21.

ECKERSEN, Jan and Marytje—Mettie—Sep. 1.
Wit: Cornelis and Ariaantje Myer.

VANHOREN, Hannes B. and Rachel—Margrietje, b. Aug. 20—Sep. 15.
Wit: Gerrit and Grietje Gerritse.

BANTA, Jacob A. and Rachel—Maria, b. Nov. 3—Dec. 1.
Wit: Cornelis and Maria Smit.

1772

MYER, Cornelis M. and Ariaantje—Marte—Jan. 5.
Wit: Marte J. and Lisabeth Myer.

TRAPHAGE, Hendrick and Willemyntje—Mettie—Mar. 8.
Wit: Dirk and Cornelia Dykman.

ECKERSON, Thomas T. and Cornelias—Maria—Aug. 23.
Wit: Thomas and Maria Eckerson.

POURHEMIUS, Johannis and Maria—Margrietje—Sep. 13.
Wit: Theodore and Margrietje Pourhemius.

BOGERT, Cobus and Cornelia—Marytje—Dec. 25.
Wit: Hendrik and Marytje Oldes.

1773

DUMAREE, Cornelis J.—Maria, b. Feb. 15—Mar. 21.
Wit: Thomas Eckerson.

LAROI, Jacobus S. and Annatje—Marietje—Nov. 7.
Wit: Gerrit A. and Margriet Gerritse.

VAN RYPE, Harme and Maria—Maria—Dec. 25.
Wit: Cobus and Annatje Perry.

1774

ZOBRISKE, Hendrik I. and Willempje—Magdalena—Feb. 6.
Wit: Cornelis C. and Lena Bogert.

ACKERMAN, David D. and Jannitje—Margrietje—July 10.
Wit: Abram D. and Margrietje Ackerman.

BLAUVELT, Christiaen and Cathalyntje—Margrietje—Aug. 7.
Wit: Willem and Grietje Halderom.

1775

GUTSIUS, Jan—Maria—Jan. 7.
Wit: Adam Beatie and wife.

ECKERSEN, Jan and Marytje—Maria, b. Jan. 3—Jan. 22.
Wit: Coenradus and Maria Storm.

ACKERMAN, Arie and Marytje—Margrietje, b. July 2—Aug. 20.
Wit: Willem and Margrietje Halderom.

BANTA, Jan C. and Annatje—Maria, b. Aug. 8—Sep. 17.
Wit: Richard and Maria Eathen.

WANNEMAKER, Dirk—Maria—Sep. 17.
Wit: Coenraad C. and Marytje Wannemaker.

DEY, Isaac and Syntje—Maria—Dec. 3.

1776

RUTAN, Jacob W. and Grietje—Maria—Jan. 28.
Wit: Niklaas and Marietje Pieterse.

1778

HOPPE, Jan J. and Jannitje—Maria—May 5.
Wit: Abram A. and Femmitje Boskerck.

1776

RUTAN, David W. and Aaltje—Maria, b. July 11—July 28.
Wit: Willem and Rachel Dobs.

V. BLERKOM, David J. and Gerritje—Martynus—Aug. 25.
Wit: Jan and Lisabeth Fliereboom.

1778

BAMPER, Jacob and Antje—Margrieta Helena, b. Oct. 17—Nov. 14.
Wit: Abram and Helena Brasher.

POST, Jacob and Saartje—Maria—Nov. 15.

1779

ACKERMAN, Hannes G. and Lisabeth—Maria—Apr. 5.
Wit: Harme and Maria Van Rype.
HARRISON, James and Mary—Margrit—Apr. 5.

1780

SLOT, Isaac and Lea—Maritje—Sep. 24.
Wit: Steven and Marietje Slot.

1781

DEMAREE, Thomas and Lena—Maria, b. July 20—Aug. 19.
ECKER, Cornelis—Maria—Nov. 6.
Wit: Isaak and Jacomyntje Blauvelt.
TERHUYN, Albert and Aaltje—Maria, b. June 3—June 12.
Wit: Abram and Marytje Terhuyn.

1782

HOPPE, Jan W. and Annatje—Marytje Martyntje, b. Jan 7, 1781—Feb. 10.
HOPPE, Jan and Maria—Maria—May 11.
VANDIEN, Thomas and Pollie—Maria—Dec. 20.
Wit: Jan Zabriskie.

1783

VAN BLERCOM, Johannis—Maria—Feb. 16.
HOPPE, Hendrik—Metje—Mar. 14.
Wit: Hendrik Terhune and wife.

1784

————, ———— and ———— —Maria—May 30.
BROUWER, Jacob—Maria—June 27.
STORM, Isaac—Metje—June 27.
Wit: Jac Ecker and wife.
LOZIER, Jan—Mary—Aug. 8.
KOOL, Abram—Grietje—Sep. 5.
VAN HOUTEN, Petrus and Marritje Onderdonck—Maria—Sep. 19.
Wit: Petrus and Maritje Van Houten.
DOREMES, David and Lea—Margrietje, b. Sep. 2—Dec. 2.
Wit: Johannis and Grietje Prevoo.

1785

HOPPER, Gerrit A. and Cathalyntje—Marytje—Mar. 6.
WOERTENDYK, Vrerik—Mary (?)—May 1.
Wit: Cornelis Smit and wife.
HALDRUM, Hendrik—Maria—May 1.
HOPPEN, Gerrit and Antje—Maria—May 5.
MYER, Jacob and Abigail—Maria, b. Aug. 17—Sep. 25.
Wit: Hendrik and Maria Riddenaar.

1786

WILSON, Albert and Maria—Maria—Feb. 26.
Wit: Gerrit Jinkens and Elisabeth Stagg.
SERVENT, Jan and Margrietje—Martha, b. Feb. 21—Apr. 9.
Wit: Johannis and Rebecka Fesyeur.
BLAUVELT, Daniel and Jannetje—Maria, b. Mar. 8—Apr. 16.

1789

BENSEN, Albert and Jannetje—Matheus, b. Jan. 28—Feb. 8.
Wit: John and Maritje Van Vlercom.

VRERICKSON, Isaak and Maria—Maria, b. Jan. 7—Feb. 8.
Wit: Joseph Horn.

POST, Jacobus and Rachel—Metje, b. Jan. 2—Mar. 1.

DEMAREST, Samuel and Catriena—Maria, b. Feb. 9—Mar. 1.
Wit: Harmen and Maria Van Rypen.

ECKERSON, Petrus and Annatje—Maragrietje—Apr. 5.
Wit: Johannis and Maragrietje Crouter.

DEMAREST, Daniel and Maria—Maria, b. Feb. 15—June 7.

ACKERMAN, Gerrit G. and Jannetje—Maria, b. July 12—Aug. 9.
Wit: Petrus and Elisabeth Poelisfelt.

1790

STEEL, Matheus and Elisabeth—Maria—Jan. 24.
Wit: Albert and Jannetje Benson.

HOPPE, Jan A. and Maria—Martyntje—Aug. 15.
Wit: Gerrit A. and Cathalyntje Hoppe.

BOGERT, Stephen and Sophia—Maria—Aug. 15.
Wit: Albert J. and Maria Bogert.

VAN RYPEN, Frederik and Maria—Maria, b. June 6—Aug. 3.
Wit: Harmen and Maria Van Rypen.

POST, John and Annatje—Maria, b. Nov. 13—Dec. 19.
Wit: Richard Davids and Maria Post.

1791

ACKERMAN, Gerrit and Geertje—Maria, b. Jan. 29—Feb. 24.
Wit: Andries and Maria Hoppe.

SNYDER, Thomas and Maria—Maria, b. Mar. 2—Apr. 3.

ACKERMAN, Abraham and Elisabeth—Magdalena, b. Apr. 9—June 22.
Wit: Gerrit G. and Jannetje Ackerman.

DETE, Abraham and Hannah—Maragrietje, b. July 1—July —.

VAN WERT, Abraham and Esther—Martha, b. Feb. 12—Oct.—.
Wit: Isaak Van Wert and Betsey Schoemaker.

1792

VALENTYN, Wiert and Metje—Margrietje, b. Feb. 6—Feb. —.
Wit: Hendrik Valentyn and Ariaantje Myer.

EARL, John and Rachel—Myntje, b. Mar. 1—Apr. —.
Wit: Gerrit A. and Cathalyntje Hoppe.

SARVENT, Jacob and Annatje—Maria and Catriena (twins)—May 31.
Wit: Lourens and Maria Van Boskerk; Teunis and Catriena Krom.

WOERTENDYK, Jacobus and Sara—Maria, b. May 29—May 31.
Wit: Ryer and Maria Ryerse.

TEYSEN, Hendrik and Maria—Maragrietje, b. May 16—May 31.
Wit: Abraham Teysen.

STAULS, Charles and Jannetje—Margrieta, b. Aug. 9.

BANTA, Jacob and Hester—Margrietje—Oct. 21.

BOGERT, Petrus P. and Margrietje—Maria, b. Jan. 25.
Wit: Petrus and Maria Bogert.

BLAUVELT, Isaak, Jr. and Sara—Maria—Jan. 13.

1831
ACKERMAN, David D. and Effy—Martha Maria, b. Dec. 31, 1830—Mar. 20.

1832
ACKERMAN, Albert A. and Dorcas—Martha, b. May 6—June 24.

1833
ACKERMAN, Aaron J. and Elisabeth—Maria Louisa, b. Nov. 22, 1832—Mar. 31.

ZABRISKIE, John J. and Maria—Mary, b. July 9—Aug. 18.

1834
KING, Esra A. and Margaret—Margaret Ann, b. Feb. 17—Apr. 26.

ACKERMAN, Garrit D. and Eliza—Mary Elisabeth, b. Oct. 3—Nov. 9.

ZABRISKIE, Casparus and Catharina—Mary Martana, b. Oct. 23—Dec. 11.

1835
PAKE, Martin and Elisabeth—Maria Elizabeth, b. Mar. 19—May 10.

ACKERMAN, Abraham J. and Caty—Mathilda, b. May 11—June 14.

HOPPER, Henry A. and Margaret Ann—Maria Ann, b. July 28—Aug. 30.

HAMMON, Thomas and Patty—Mary Elisabeth, b. Oct. 5—Nov. 1.

KING, Ezra A. and Elisabeth—Mary Elizabeth, b. Oct. 11—Dec. 13.

1837
GARDNER, Josiah and Peggy—Maria Jane, b. Mar. 11—May 14.

1840
HAMMOND, Thomas and Patty—Martha Esther, b. Feb. 22—June 7.

BLAUVELT, James, Jr., and Hannah—Mary Elisabeth, b. Feb. 28—June 7.

RATHBONE, John C. and Eliza—Martha, b. Sep. 26—Oct. 21.

ACKERMAN, Abraham J. and Peggy—Margaret Esther, b. Sep. 26—Nov. 8.

1841
JERALEMAN, James N. and Mary—Mary, b. Apr. 7—May 16.

1842
ZABRISKIE, Stephen T. and Jane—Margaret Jane, b. Sep. 29—Nov. 6.

1845
ZABRISKIE, Guilliam J. and Levina—Mary Zetesa, b. Dec. 11, 1844—Jan. 12.

WESSELS, Wessel and Catharina—Mary Bogart, b. Jan. 15—Sep. 21.

1847
PERRY, Daniel and Sally—Margaret Catharina, b. Mar. 13—Sep. 12.

ZABRISKIE, John C. and Eliza Maria—Maria Jane, b. Aug. 24—Oct. 24.

1848
ACKERMAN, David R. and Maria—Maria Debaun, b. Aug. 28—Sep. 24.

1843
QUACKENBUSH, Abraham and Sally Ann—Margaret Ann, b. June 14—Sep. 16.

ZABRISKE, Garrit H. and Rachel Ann—Martha, b. Oct. 26—Dec. 10.

1848

ACKERMAN, Abraham J. and Catharine—Mary Catharine, b. Feb. 4—
Aug. 27.

1849

PERRY, Daniel D. and Sarah—Margaret Catharine, b. Mar. 13, 1837—
July 22.

1786

V. BLERKOM, David and Polly—Maria—June 18.
Wit: Jan and Maria Eckerson.

SMITH, Petrus and Jannetje—Maria, b. July 14—Aug. 13.
Wit: Jan and Elisabeth Smith.

OSBORN, James and Maria—Margrietje, b. Sep. 1—Oct. 1.

HOPPE, Hendrik and Aaltje—Marytje, b. Sep. 14—Oct. 1.
Wit: Jan and Maria Zabriske.

DATER, John and Polly—Margrietje, b. Oct. 18—Nov. 12.
Wit: Lodewyk Bush; Margrietje Shulters.

BANTA, Hendrik and Margrieta—Margrietje, b. Oct. 20—Dec. 3.
Wit: Jan and Elisabeth Banta.

1787

FERSYEUR, Abraham and Elisabeth—Magdalena, b. Feb. 3—Mar. 4.
Wit: Johannis and Rebecka Fersyeur.

ALYEE, Samuel and Catriena—Maria—Feb. 11.

WANNEMAKER, Pieter and Hester—Maria—Apr. 9.
Wit: Maria Wannemaker.

TERHUNE, Abraham O. and Sukie—Maria, b. June 27—July 15.
Wit: Thomas and Polly Van Boskerk.

SMYTH, Jacobus and Catriena—Maria, b. July 14—Aug. 1.
Wit: Petrus and Jannetje Smith.

TERHEUN, Hendrik and Rachel—Marytje, b. Aug. 2—Aug. 19.
Wit: Stephen and Geertje Hoppe.

JENKINS, Gerrit and Elisabeth—Margrietje, b. July 28—Aug. 26.

VAN HORN, Daniel and Annatje—Metje, b. Aug. 8—Sep. 9.

BERVOORT, Samuel and Martyntje—Maria, b. Aug. 26—Sep. 27.

FREDERIKS, John and Maria—Maria—Oct. 28.
Wit: Jacob and Maria Conklin.

RYERS, Ryer and Maria—Michael, b. Oct. 20—Nov. 11.

1788

SIDMAN, Samuel and Jannetje—Maria—Jan. 13.
Wit: William and Maria Vos.

DEMAREST, David and Margrietje—Maria—Feb. 3.

VANDERBEEK, Jan and Aaltje—Maria, b. Jan. 19—Feb. 24.
Wit: Jan and Angonietje Westervelt; Abraham and Sara Vanderbeek.

VANBLERKOM, Pieter and Christina—Maritje—Apr. 20.
Wit: Jan and Maritje Vanblerkom.

WATSENS, Pieter and Maragrietje—Maria, b. Oct. 11—Nov. 2.
Wit: Hendrik and Maria Bos.

HOPPER, Abraham and Geertje—Marietje, b. Oct. 26—Nov. 9.
Wit: Jan and Marietje Zabriskie.

1789

CHAPPLE, Thomas and Maria—Maria—Jan. 25.
Wit: Abraham and Elisabeth Hopper.
FISHER, Rynder and Polly—Maria, b. Dec. 11, 1788—Feb. 8.
Wit: David and Liesje Fisher.

1793

SHURTE, Adolph and Elisabeth—Margrietje, b. Mar. 3, 1792-Feb. 24.
ACKERMAN, Abraham and Salome—Maria, b. Feb. 16—Mar. 10.
Wit: Jan A. and Maria Hoppe.
KNEGT, Coenraad and Grietje—Martienus, b. Nov. 13, 1792—Mar. 10.
PERRY, Johannis and Dirkje—Maria, b. Dec. 30, 1792—Apr. 14.
Wit: Isaak and Maria Haaring.
MUYSINGER, Coenraad and Catriena—Margrietje—May 19.
Wit: John Muysinger; Margrietje Backer.
DEMAREST, Leah—Margrietje.
Wit: Cornelius and Elisabeth Demarest.
DURIE, Jan and Rachel—Maria, b. Aug. 25—Sep. 22.
Wit: Jacobus and Maria Bogert.
DECKER, William and Aaltje—Margrietje, b. Sep. 16—Oct. 27.
DAYTOR, Adam and Syntje—Maragrietje, b. Oct. 6—Nov. 17.

1794

VRERIKSE, Abraham and Elisabeth—Maragrietje, b. Dec. 7, 1793—Jan. 1.
VALENTYN, Hendrik and Maria—Maria, b. Feb. 11—Mar. 24.
Wit: Felter Swin; Maria Valentyn.
VANDIEN, Dirk and Geertje—Maria—Apr. 20.
Wit: Joost and Maria Bogert.
SCHOERTES, Adolph and Elisabeth—Metje, b. Apr. 16—May 4.
Wit: Pieter and Metje Woertendyk.
HOPPE, Abraham and Geertje—Maria, b. May 31—July 20.
WOERTENDYK, Jan and Elisabeth—Marjeree, b. June 22—July 20.
Wit: Jacobus and Marjeree Anderson.
HORN, Joseph and Ebby—Maria, b. Mar. 31—July 27.
DILL, George and Dortie Gable—Maria, b. July 1—July 27.
VAN WERT, William and Esther—Martha, b. Jan. 3—Aug. 10.
Wit: William Vanwert; Esther Odem.
DEMAREST, Simon and Maria—Maatje, b. Jan. 15, 1791—Aug. 24.
VALENTYN, Wiert and Metje—Maria, b. Aug. 6—Aug. 24.
DECKER, Cornelis and Lea—Margrietje, b. Sep. 10—Sep. 28.
BERBERO, Casparus and Maria—Maragrietje—Nov. 30.
Wit: Matheus and Maragrietje Berbero.

1795

ECKERSON, Nicholas and Maria—Maria, b. Dec. 10, 1794—Feb. 1.
Wit: Jacob and Maria Eckerson.
TERHUNE, Albert and Rachel—Marten, b. Feb. 9—Mar. 8.
Wit: Hendrik and Maria Terhune.
PULISFELT, Pieter and Elisabeth—Maria, b. Mar. 25—Apr. 19.
SHARP, Morris and Elisabeth—Matheus, b. Feb. 22—Apr. 28.

PIETERSON, Thomas and Sally—Maria, b. May 23—June 21.
Wit: Nicholaas and Maria Pieterson.
V. D. BEEK, Arie and Lena—Maria, b. June 5—July 12.
DEMAREST, Cornelis and Maria—Margrietje, b. Aug. 19—Oct. 18.
GOETSCHIUS, Nathan and Maria—Matheus, b. July 8—Aug. 16.
ECKERSON, Edward and Hetty—Maria, b. Oct. 8—Nov. 8.
Wit: Laurens and Maria Van Boskerk.
ACKERMAN, Johannis and Sara—Maria, b. Oct. 2—Nov. 1.
Wit: Petrus and Maria Ackerman.

1796

BANTA, Jacob and Hester—Margrietje, b. Jan. 1—Jan 24.
MEBE, Pieter and Jannetje—Maria, b. Jan. 5—Jan. 24.
Wit: Abraham and Maria Mebe.
WESTERVELT, Albert and Maria—Martyntje, b. Jan. 12—Feb. 28.
DEBAAN, Petrus and Maria—Maria, b. Feb. 20—Mar. 20.
CUYPER, Gerrit and Geertje—Margrietje, b. July 26—Aug. 7.
WOERTENDYK, Cornelius and Sophia—Marietje, b. May 15—July 3.
VANBLERKOM, John and Elisabeth—Margrietje, b. Oct. 31—Dec. 25.

1797

DEMAREST, Simon and Cornelia—Maria, b. Jan. 16—Feb. 19.
RIDDENAAR, Coenrad and Elizabeth—Margrietje, b. Nov. 17, 1796—Jan. 2.
Wit: Pieter and Margrietje Watson.
HOPPE, Isaac and Rachel—Martyntje, b. Mar. 18—Apr. 16.
Wit: Gerrit and Cathalyntje Hoppe.
TERHUEN, Abraham and Tryntje—Maria, b. Mar. 31—Apr. 23.
POWEL, John and Klaasje—Maria, b. Apr. 8—June 4.
SNYDER, Thomas and Maria—Margrietje, b. July 8—Aug. 20.

1798

DEBAAN, Andrias and Jannetje—Maria, b. Jan. 4—Feb. 11.
DEMAREST, Simon and Maria—Maria, b. Jan. 20—Feb. 11.
LABACH, Lena—Maretje Yeomans, b. Oct. 2, 1797—Feb. 11.
VAN DIEN, Albert and Maria—Maria, b. Jan. 31—Mar. 4.
DETOR, Adam and Rosina—Matheus, b. Mar. 2—Apr. 1.
Wit: Matheus and Grietje Berbero.
ACKERMAN, Abraham and Sara—Metje, b. Feb. 28—Apr. 15.
Wit: David D. and Sara Ackerman.
BOGERT, Cornelis and Catriena—Maria, b. Apr. 22—May 29.
WOERTENDYK, Reinier and Annaatje—Marlena, b. Apr. 8—June 3.
MESSEKER, Dirk and Leentje—Maria, b. Feb. 24—June 17.
DECKER, Cornelius and Lea—Maria, b. May 23—June 17.
Wit: Johannes and Maria Myer.

1799

ECKERSON, Thomas and Susanna—Maragrietje, b. Dec. 8, 1798—Jan. 6.
DEMAREST, Nikolaas and Maria—Maragrietje, b. Sep. 27, 1798—Jan. 16.
SMITH, Jores and Geertje—Maragrietje, b. June 1—July 17.
STORM, Hendrik and Margrietje—Maria, b. June 24—July 14.
Wit: Coenradus and Maria Storm.

HOPPE, Isaac and Rachel—Maria, b. June 25—July 14.

DOUGHTY, Robert and Mary—Margrieta, b. Mar. 11—Sep. 1.

GUY, John and Sally—Maria, b. Oct. 23—Dec. 15.

VALENTINE, Hendrik and Maria—Margretje, b. Oct. 17—Dec. 22.
Wit: Coenraad and Margrietje Knegt.

1800

ZABRISKIE, Jacob and Elisabeth—Margretha, b. Dec. 29, 1799—Jan. 23.
Wit: Gilliam and Margrietje Terhune.

HOPPER, Andrew and Sara—Margrietje, b. Jan. 26—Mar. 30.

ZABRISKIE, Abraham J. and Susanna—Maria, b. Mar. 17—Apr. 13.

VALENTINE, John and Elisabeth—Margrietje, b. Feb. 6—May 4.
Wit: Coenraad and Margrietje Knegt.

DEBAAN, Albert and Maatje—Margrietje, b. July 1—July 13.
Wit: Joost and Margrietje Debaan.

BLAUVELT, Cornelius and Jannetje—Maria, b. Sep. 2—Sept. 28.
Wit: Abraham and Maria Blauvelt.

HOPPER, Garet and Maria—Maria, b. Nov. 14—Nov. 30.

YEOMENS, John and Trientje—Margrietje, b. Oct. 22—Nov. 30.

1801

PAULUS, Peter and Nancy—Margrietje, b. Dec. 9, 1800—Jan. 5.

DEMAREST, Jacob and Geesje—Margaret, b. Apr. 12—May 10.
Wit: Dirk and Margaret Ackerman.

VANDERBEEK, Jacob and Annatje—Maria, b. July 19—Aug. 9.

1802

POLHEMUS, Theodorus and Elisabeth—Maria, b. Dec. 27, 1801—Jan. 17.

ZABRISKIE, Nicholas and Wyntje—Maria, b. Mar. 9—Mar. 28.
Wit: John and Myntje Zabriskie.

ACKERMAN, Gerrit A. and Jannetje—Margrietje, b. May 3—May 30.
Wit: Abr. and Margrietje Rotan.

ELTINGE, Wilhelmus and Jane—Maria Blandina, b. Aug. 2—Aug. 29.

ZABRISKIE, Jacob J. and Wyntje—Maria, b. Sep. 1—Oct. 10.

1803

DEMAREST, Simon and Maria—Maria, b. Mar. 15—May 30.

ACKERSON, James and Sarah—Mytian(?), b. Sep. 5, 1801—June 19.

TAYLOR, Aaron and Jannetje—Mary, Dec. 1, 1802—June 19.

COCH, Albert and Margrietje—Marytyntje, b. June 14—July 3.

SHURTE, Adolph and Aaltje—Margrietje, b. May 27—July 10.

QUACKENBUSH, Jacob and Maria—Margrietje, b. Aug. 27—Sep. 22.
Wit: Margrietje Quackenbush.

TERHUNE, John and Antje—Maria Eliza, b. Nov. 4—Dec. 3.

1804

LYDECKER, Garret and Maria—Martyntje, b. Dec. 28, 1803—Feb. 5.
Wit: William and Elisabeth Clerk.

VANDERBEEK, Coenradus and Annatje—Maria, b. Apr. 11, 1803—Apr. 8.

ACKERMAN, Daniel and Cathalyntje—Margrietje, b. May 11—July 1.

WATSON, Peter and Margrietje—Margrietje, b. Sep. 28—Oct. 28.
ECKERSON, Peter and Margrietje—Maria, b. Oct. 23—Nov. 18.
   Wit: Thomas and Maria Eckerson.

1805

ECKERSON, Thomas and Susannah—Maria, b. Dec. 23, 1804—Jan. 20.
VANWART, Hendrik and Annatje—Martha, b. Dec. 9, 1804—Feb. 24.
DURIE, David and Geertje—Sarah Martyntje, b. Mar. 2—Apr. 14.
   Wit: Martyntje Traphagen.
VANRYPEN, Cornelius and Elisabeth—Maria, b. May 29—Aug. 4.
VANDERBEEK, Cornelius and Hilletje—Maria, b. July 23—Sep. 8.

1806

BREVOORT, Hendrik and Maria—Martyntje, b. Mar. 21—Apr. 5.
GOETSIUS, Hendrik and Sara—Maria, b. Apr. 20—May 11.
PULIS, Pieter and Nancy—Marytje, b. June 10—July 13.
ZABRISKIE, Cornelius and Maria—Mary Martina, b. Aug. 21—Sep. 21.
DEBAUN, Jacob and Osseltje—Maria, b. Sep. 28—Oct. 12.
WESTERVELT, Peter A. and Caty—Margaret, b. Oct. 4—Dec. 7.
ZABRISKIE, Jacob C. and Elisabeth—Maria, b. Nov. 24—Dec. 23.

1807

CUYPER, Gerrit and Geertrui—Maria and Elisabeth—Jan 9.
DEMAREST, Albert and Annatje—Maria, b. Jan. 9—Feb. 8.
ACKERMAN, David and Metje—Metje, b. Mar. 12—Apr. 12.
TERHUNE, Harmen and Rachel—Matje, b. Apr. 19—May 17.
SMITH, Cornelius A. and Jannetje—Marytje, b. May 17—June 21.
OSBURN, Matthew and Aaltje—Margrietje, b. Apr. 30—July 19.
YURRY, John and Elisabeth—Martha, b. Sep. 9—Oct. 4.
BOGERT, Petrus and Elisabeth—Maria, b. Oct. 28—Dec. 6.
   Wit: Stephen and Maria Bogert.

1808

FORSHEA, Abraham and Elisabeth—Magdalena, b. Dec. 24, 1807—Feb. 21.
HALDROM, William and Catriena—Marytje, b. Feb. 28—Mar. 20.
CONKLIN, Louis and Lena—Maria—July 31.
TERHUNE, John and Polly—Mary Ann, b. July 16—Aug. 21.
PETERSON, Nicholas and Magdalen—Maria, b. Aug. 29—Sep. 18.
HOPPER, Andries and Antje—Maritje, b. Sep. 23—Oct. 16.
HOPPER, Hendrik and Charity—Mary Ann, b. Nov. 28—Dec. 26.

1809

ZABRISKE, Gerrit and Martyntje—Maragrietje, b. Jan. 4—Jan. 29.
   Wit: Albert and Maragrietje Westervelt.

1808

DEMAREST, Albert and Annatje—Margrietje, b. Dec. 2—Dec. 25.

1809

VAN BLERCOM, John and Annatje—Maria, b. June 28—July 16.
VAN RYPEN, Cornelius and Elisabeth—Maria, b. May 2—Aug. 24.

1810

BARDAN, John and Maria—Maria Catriena, b. Dec. 28, 1809—Feb. 11.

POST, Abraham and Geesje—Maria, b. Dec. 11, 1809—Feb. 4.

SNYDER, Adam and Caty—Myntje, b. Jan. 21—Mar. 18.

ECKERSON, David and Grietje—Maria, b. May 21—June 11.

BOSH, Lodewyk and Leentje—Maria, b. May 26—July 1.

CONKLIN, Lewis and Lena—Maretje, b. July 28—Aug. 9.

WALDEROM, Barend and Martyntje—Mary Ann, b. Sep. 9—Oct. 7.

JURRY, John and Elisabeth—Margaret, b. Aug. 24—Sep. 30.

LEYDECKER, Albert G. and Jannetje—Martyntje, b. Sep. 23—Oct. 21.

1811

ZABRISKIE, Cornelius and Polly—Mathilda Bogert, b. Dec. 10, 1810—Jan. 20.

ZABRISKIE, Jacob and Geesje—Martha, b. Jan. 12—Mar. 17.

HOPPER, Andrew and Polly—Myntje, b. Feb. 22—Mar. 31.

BANTA, Jacob H. and Maragrietje—Margrietje, b. July 2—Aug. —.

SMITH, Pieter and Lena—Maragrietje, b. Mar. 5, 1810—Nov. 18.

1812

HOPPER, Hendrik and Elisabeth—Maria, b. May 23—June 21.

HOPPER, Andrew P. and Anne—Polly, b. Aug. 22(?)—Aug. 22.

ZABRISKIE, Garrit and Jane—Maria, b. Aug. 20—Sep. 27.

CHRISTOPHER, Jacob and Geesje—Mary, b. Nov. 24—Dec. 27.

1813

BANTA, Henry W. and Jane—Marjarat, b. Dec. 14, 1812—Jan. 17.

GARRISON, Jacob and Rachel—Maria, b. Mar. 29—Apr. 25.

CROUTER, Cornelius and Agnes—Maria, b. Sep. 8—Oct. 10.

1814

SNYDER, Richard and Ally—Maria, b. Oct. 3—Oct. 30.

HOPPER, Albert H. and Mary—Maria, b. Oct. 3—Dec. 11.

1815

GARRISON, Peter and Margaret—Maria, b. Jan. 19—Mar. 12.

ZABRISKIE, Henry and Matje—Maria, b. May 29—July 2.

1816

ACKERMAN, David D. and Matje—Maria, b. Apr. 12—May 19.

VAN SAUN, Cornelius and Rachel—Margaret, b. Aug. 16—Sep. 22.

EARL, Garrit and Sally—Mary Ann, b. Aug. 27—Oct. 13.

QUACKENBUSH, Samuel and Polly—Martin, b. Dec. 2—Dec. 14.

1817

ZABRISKIE, Henry A. and Patty—Maria, b. Jan. 24—Feb. 23.

BUSH, John I. and Maria—Margaret, b. Feb. 16—May 11.

1818

BERDEN, Richard and Willemine—Mary Van Dien, b. Oct. 3—Nov. 1.

HOPPER, John H. and Mary—Mary Ann, b. Oct. 23—Nov. 15.

1819

VAN DIEN, Casparus—Maria, b. Dec. 14, 1818—Apr. 13.

GARRISON, Albert and Jemima—Mary Ann, b. June 14—July 25.

SNYDER, George T. and Charity—Mary, b. Aug. 31—Sep. 19.

GARRISON, Peter I. and Margaret—Margaret, b. Aug. 8—Oct. 2.

1820

BERDAN, John, Jr. and Sally—Mary, b. Mar. 21—Apr. 30.

DOREMUS, George, Jr. and Harriet—Margaret, b. Nov. 2—Dec. 3.

VAN EMBURGH, John H. and Polly—Maria, b. Nov. 25—Dec. 17.

1821

VAN RIPER, Harmen and Caty—Maria, b. Jan. 28—Feb. 26.

VAN EMBURGH, Albert and Hannah—Margaret, b. Aug. 2—Sep. 3.

1823

MYRES, John C. and Levina—Maria Jane, b. Nov. 6, 1822—Jan. 26.

ZABRISKIE, Abraham C. and Maria—Maria, b. Apr. 30—June 2.

HENCOCK, William and Polly—Mary, b. Oct. 5—Nov. 2.

VANDERBEEK, Abraham J. and Litty—Mary, b. Nov. 28—Dec. 28.

1824

STORMS, Cornelius and Sally—Margaret, b. Mar. 17—Apr. 4.

BAMPER, Gerrit H. and Polly—Margaret Ann Zabriskie, b. Apr. 26—July 25.

VAN EMBURGH, Henry H. and Peggy—Maria, b. Aug. 9—Sep. 5.

LEYDECKER, John C. and Catharina—Mathilda, b. Oct. 28—Nov. 14.

1825

QUACKENBUSH, John J. and Susan—Maria, b. Apr. 2—May 8.

SNYDER, John and Ellen—Mary, b. June 14—July 24.

TURSE, Samuel and Rachel—Maria, b. Sep. 15—Nov. 12.

HOPPER, Jacob H. and Caty—Maria, b. Oct. 23—Nov. 27.

KOUGH, Casparus and Tyna—Maria, b. Feb. 5—Mar. 27.

1826

ACKERMAN, Albert and Dorcas—Margaret Rutan, b. Mar. 12—Apr. 2.

BUTLER, Thomas C. and Jane Ann—Martha Sara, b. May 15—July 9.

ZABRISKIE, John A. C. and Betsy—Margariet, b. June 21—July 23.

ZABRISKIE, Peter A. and Anna—Maria, b. Sep. 15—Oct. 29.

1827

HOVER, Benjamin and Jemima—Margaret, b. Jan. 14—Feb. 11.

HOPPER, David G. and Tyna—Maria Jemima, b. May 25—June 17.

BLAUVELT, James, Jr. and Hannah—Maria Elizabeth, b. May 24—July 1.

ACKERMAN, Andrew G. and Caty—Maria, b. Aug. 12—Sep. 9.

BENSON, Cornelius and Maria—Maria Jane, b. Sep. 7—Oct. 21.

ACKERMAN, John G. and Maria—Mary Tettor, b. Sep. 17—Oct. 12.

SNYDER, George T. and Charity—Margaret, b. Sep. 17—Oct. 26.

1829

VAN BLARCOM, Henry and Mary—Mariam, b. Dec. 5, 1828—Jan. 11.

ZABRISKIE, John I. H. and Maria—Margaret, b. Dec. 25, 1828—Jan. 25.

ACKERMAN, Peter D. and Hester—Martha, b. Feb. 16—Apr. 5.
GARRISON, John H. and Anne—Maria Zabriskie, b. Mar. 18—Apr. 19.
ACKERMAN, John G. and Maria—Martha, b. Apr. 3—May 6.
1816
KIP, Ralph R. and Jane—Margaret, b. Dec. 1, 1815—Jan. 7.
1836
BOGART, John C. and Jannetje—Maria Catharina, b. May 17—July 3.
ACKERMAN, Gerrit D. and Eliza—Martha Ann, b. Sep. 3—Oct. 24.
1840
MYERS, John M. and Rachel—Marten, b. Jan. 4—Mar. 16.
1841
WESTERVELT, John P. and Sally—Mathilda, b. May 29—July 4.
1842
ACKERMAN, Abraham J. and Caty—Margaret Elizabeth, b. May 27—July 17.
1843
HOPPER, George D. and Rachel—Maria Jemima, b. Feb. 8—Apr. 16.
1844
QUACKINBUSH, David and Anne—Maria Ann, b. Sep. 10, 1843—Feb. 11.
1845
PERRY, Daniel and Sally—Maria Cooper, b. Apr. 8—June 22.
1846
BOGERT, Josiah Gardener and Margaret—Mathilda Elisabeth, b. Aug. 25, 1845—Jan. 4.
BERDAN, Reinier J. and Catharina—Mary Ann, b. July 13—Sep. 20.
1848
DATOR, Abraham and Maria—Mary Catherina, b. July 19—Sep. 16.
1850
BOGART, Albert and Martha—Maria Catharina—Sep. 21.

"N"
1755
HOPPE, Jan A. and Lisabeth—Nicasie, b. May 15—June 15.
  Wit: Gerrit H. and Cornelia Kip.
1759
ZABRISKE, Hendrik C. and Maria—Neesje—Jan. 21.
  Wit: Hannes and Maritje Vanhoren.
WANNEMAKER, Willem and Catrientje—Niklaas—June 24.
  Wit: Coenraad and Marytje Wannemaker.
WESSELS, Joseph and Ariaantje—Niklaas, b. July 7—July 27.
  Wit: Benjamin and Nancy Ooldes.
1763
WESSELS, Joseph and Ariaantje—Nellie, b. Oct. 21—Nov. 4.
  Wit: Jan and Styntje Ackerman.
1766
ZABRISKIE, Jan and Marytje—Niklaas—Dec. 18.
  Wit: Niklaas and Rachel Zabriskie.

1769
ECKERSEN, Jan and Marytje—Niklaas—Sep. 10.
  Wit: Niklaas and Matje Volk.

1771
ESSILI, Jan and Lisabeth—Nellie—Oct. 20.
  Wit: Isaac and Lena Stagg.

1772
ZABRISKIE, Benjamin and Annatje—Niklaas—May 17.
  Wit: Niklaas and Rachel Zabriskie.

1776
STORM, Isaak and Sara—Niklaas—May 5.
  Wit: Niklaas and Metje Volk.

1778
NELSON, John and Lisabeth—Nikolaas, b. July 30—Aug. 11.

1781
BROUWER, Jacob and Tryntje—Nikolaas—Nov. 11.
  Wit: Albert T. and Mettie Zabriskie.

1786
PIETERSON, Nikolaas and Maria—Nikolaas, b. Oct. 4—Oct. 22.
  Wit: Nikolaas and Elisabeth Halderom.

1793
VAN ALEN, Gerrit and Geertje—Neesjen, b. Dec. 9, 1792—May 12.
CERRELLACH, John and Leentje—Nikolaas, b. Sep. 15—Oct. 20.
  Wit: Coenraad Backer; Betje Cerrellach.

1795
HOPPE, Gerrit and Maria—Nicasie, b. Jan. 16—Feb. 15.
  Wit: Nicasie and Maria Hoppe.

1800
PIETERSON, John and Lise Barbera—Nikolaas, b. Feb. 17—Mar. 19.
  Wit: Nicolaas and Maria Pieterson.

1803
ECKERSON, John and Geertje—Nikolaas, b. Nov. 1—Nov. 27.
  Wit: Nikolaas and Lenah Halderom.

1804
MATANGE, Isaac and Trientje—Nikolaas—Sep. 6.
  Wit: Rachel Guy.
CUYPER, Garret and Geertje—Nikolaas, b. Oct. 15—Nov. 22.

1805
JERSEY, Peter and Maria—Naatje, b. Feb. 8—Mar. 3.

1806
HALDEROM, William and Catriena—Nicholas, b. Jan. 19—Feb. 9.
  Wit: Nicholas and Magdalen Halderom.

1809
DURYEA, John I. and Leitje(?)—Nancy, b. Jan. 9—Jan. 15.

1820

HARRIS, Isaac and Hannah—Nancy, b. Sep. 26—Nov. 20.

1821

HENCOCK, William and Polly—Nancy, b. Mar. 7—Apr. 8.

1827

ACKERMAN, John J. and Maria—Nikolaas Brinkerhoff, b. Apr. 8—May 27.

ACKERMAN, Henry A. and Betsy—Nikolaas Hopper, b. Sep. 17—Oct. 21.

"O"

1759

DEVENPOORT, Nathaniel and Grietje—Omphre—Jan. 31.
  Wit: Omphre & Lisabeth Devenpoort.

1768

MILLER, James and Mary Devenpoort—Omphre—May 25.

1774

SMITH, Abram and Catriena—Omphre, b. Feb. 17—June 28.

1800

VAN VOORHEES, Nicausie and Belitje—Osseltje, b. Dec. 9, 1799(?)—Jan. 8.
  Wit: Dirk & Osseltje Brinkerhoff.

1801

VANDERBEEK, Coenradus and Annatje—Osseltje, b. Nov. 28, 1800(?)—Mar. 8.

"P"

1749

EISTERLI, Marte and Gouda—Pieter—May 2.
  Wit: Ryer & Abigael Debouw.

1751

DUBAAN, Jacob and Marytje—Pieter—Mar. 3.
  Wit: Andries & Jannitje Dubouw.

ACKERMAN, Albert and Rachel—Pryntje—Jan. 20.
  Wit: Frederik & Saartje Cadmus.

1753

ECKER, Thomas and Marytje—Petrus, b. Apr. 26.
  Wit: Jacob & Rachel De Marest.

DERYIE,, Daniel and Vrouwtje—Petrus—Oct. 14.
  Wit: Jan Deryee.

WANNEMAKER, Hermanus and Susan—Pieter, b. Oct. 1—Oct. 28.
  Wit: Pieter & Claartje Wannemaker.

1754

DUBAEN, Jacob and Marytje—Petrus—Mar. 24.
  Wit: Samuel & Rebecka Bos.

VAN BLERCOM, Hannes and Marytje—Petrus—Mar. 30.
  Wit: Jacobus W. Van Voorhees; Santje A. Rutan.

DEY, Teunis and Esther—Philip, b. July 10—Aug. 4.
  Wit: Philip & Anna Schuyler.
ALYEE, Isaac and Annatje—Petrus, b. Sep. 29—Sep. 29.
  Wit: Hannes & Annatje Alyee.

1755

VAN BLERKOM, Pieter and Susanna—Petrus—Jan. 26.
  Wit: Albert S. & Saartje Terhuyn.
DEBOW, Ryer and Abigael—Pieter—Aug. 3.
  Wit: Pieter & Maragriet Debouw.

1756

ACKERMAN, Abram J. and Hester—Petrus, b. May 11—May 30.
  Wit: Jan P. & Willempje Demarest.
DEMAREST, Samuel and Lea—Petrus—June 27.
  Wit: Pieter D. Demarest.
RIDDENAAR, Hendrik and Grietje—Petrus—June 27.
  Wit: Adolf & Lena Myer.

1757

VAN ZEYL, Egbert and Willempje—Pieter—Oct. 22.
  Wit: Pieter & Margriet Dubouw.

1758

REP, Johan Cor. and Lisabeth—Petrus—June 25.
  Wit: Pieter & Marytje Vonck.

1759

DEMAREST, Petrus S. and Maria—Petrus, b. May 2—May 20.
  Wit: Petrus D. & Sara Demarest.

1760

DEY, Teunis and Esther—Petrus, b. Mar. 1—Mar. 30.
  Wit: Pieter P. Schuyler and Maria Dey.
ACKERMAN, Niklaes and Maria—Petrus—May 27.
  Wit: Petrus S. Dumare and Vrouwtje Westervelt.

1761

DUREMES, Hendrik and Grietje—Pryntje, b. Aug. 4—Aug. 30.
  Wit: Thomas Duremes and Geertje Van Winkel.
PECKER, Jacob—Philippus—Dec. 20.
  Wit: Philippus Hofman.

1763

VESEUR, Hannes and Lena—Pieter, b. July 12—Aug. 30.
  Wit: Pieter & Maria Veseur.
BROUWER, Abram D. and Antje—Petrus—Aug. 30.
  Wit: Hendrik & Lena Vanblerkom.

1765

VANHOREN, Dirk B. and Lisabeth—Pieter, b. Apr. 8—Apr. 28.
  Wit: Andries & Jannitje Debow.

1766

JONG, Hendrik and Annatje—Phebe—Apr. 6.

1768

PULISFELT, Hendrik and Cornelia—Petrus, b. Oct. 19—Nov. 13.
Wit: Pieter Pilesfelt.

1769

V. DERBEEK, Paulus and Rachel—Paulus—Jan. 29.
Wit: Jacob & Jannitje Brouwer.

BOGERT, Petrus and Maria—Petrus, b. Oct. 22—Nov. 12.
Wit: Petrus & Maria Ackerman.

1771

MAYBE, Jan and Lea—Petrus—Jan 20.
Wit: Pieter Maybe, Jr. & wife.

VAN BLERKOM, Pieter H. and Jannitje—Petrus—Feb. 24.
Wit: Abram & Lisabeth Van Blerkom.

PERRY, Daniel and Jannitje—Pieter & Maria, b. Sep. 24—Oct. 13.
Wit: Pieter & Lisabeth Perry; Pieter & Maria Verseur.

POST, Pieter A. and Geertje—Petrus, b. Nov. 7—Dec. 15.
Wit: Roelof Jacobusse, Grietje Post.

1772

VANBLERKOM, David J. and Gerritje—Petrus—Jan. 26.
Wit: Pieter & Jannitje Maybe.

ECKERSON, David and Angonietje—Paulus—Mar. 15.
Wit: Paulus C. & Annatje Vanderbeek.

1773

ECKERSEN, Thomas T. and Cornelia—Petrus, b. Oct. 9—Nov. 7.
Wit: Petrus & Maria Dubaan.

1774

WESTERVELT, Casparus and Rachel—Petrus, b. Aug. 17—Sep. 4.
Wit: Pieter J. & Annatje Dumaree.

VANBOSKERK, Abram A. and Femmitje—Paulus, b. Mar. 19—Apr. 9.
Wit: Paulus J. & Rachel Vanderbeek.

V. BLERKOM, Johannis and Rebecka—Petrus, b. Jan. 19—Feb. 4.
Wit: Petrus & Antje Van Blerkom.

1776

MESSEKER, Abram and Rachel—Petrus—Mar. 10.
Wit: Petrus & Antje Van Blerkom.

VANBLERKOM, David H. and Polly—Petrus—May 26.
Wit: Petrus P. & Lena H. Van Blerkom.

JERSEY, Pieter and Annatje——Annatje—Aug. 25.
Wit: Hendrik & Geertrui Servent.

1779

ACKERMAN, David A. and Jacomyntje—Pieter—Dec. 12.
Wit: David & Rachel Hoppe.

1780

DE PYSTER, Abraham and Carstina—Peter Rosevelt—Nov. 19.

1779

WESTERVELT, Abraham and Antje—Petrus, b. Aug. 14—Sep. 14.

1781

VAN ZILE, Albert and Rachel—Petrus—Feb. 25.
Wit: Petrus & Jannetje Van Sile.

1782

HENDRIK, Pieter—Pieter—June 25.

1786

POST, Abraham and Jannetje—Petrus, b. Mar. 11—May 21.
VAN SYL, Hermanus and Elisabeth—Polly, b. May 17—June 18.
Wit: Pieter & Susanna Debouw.
TAYLOR, William and Phebe—Phebe, b. Apr. 1—Oct. 1.

1787

VANDER BEEK, Arie and Lena—Paulus, b. Sep. 25—Nov. 11.
Wit: Paulus & Annatje Vanderbeek.

1788

FISBAG, Stephen and Catriena—Petrus, b. Oct. 23—Nov. 9.
Wit: Petrus Muysinger and Sientje Vos.
PERRY, John and Charity—Polly—Nov. 16.
Wit: Hendrik & Peggy Valentyn.

1789

BOVENHUYSEN, Nikolaas and Grietje—Pieter—Jan. 11.
Wit: Hendrik & Sally Poelisfelt.
V. ZEYL, Hermanus and Elisabeth—Pieter, b. Jan. 11—Feb. 1.
Wit: Robert McCall and Betsy Conklin.
DATEY, Abraham and Hannah—Polly, b. Feb. 8—Mar. 22.
Wit: Andrias & Catriena Hopper.
POST, Johannis and Catriena—Pieter—July 5.
Wit: Casparus & Maria Cogh.

1790

DEMAREST, David and Margrietje—Petrus, b. Aug. 22, 1789—Jan. 31.
Wit: Jacob & Annatje Eckerson.
POST, Pieter and Rachel—Petrus—Dec. 19.

1791

BRUYN, Marten and Annatje—Pieter Post, b. Oct. 11, 1790—Jan. 1.
Row, Pieter and Elisabeth—Petrus, b. July 16—Aug. 14.
Wit: Pieter & Maria Pulisvelt.
Bos, Samuel and Lena—Pieter, b. July 30—Sep. 11.
Wit: William & Annaatje Van Voorheesen.
VANDERBEEK, Paulus and Margrietje—Paulus, b. Sep. 21—Nov. 16.

1792

DEBOW, Johannis and Margrietje—Pieter, b. Jan. 16—Feb. 26.
Wit: Pieter & Rachel Vanhorn.
BOSCH, Lodewyk and Lena—Pieter, b. Feb. 25—June 16.
Wit: Dirk & Antje Bosch.
ACKERMAN, Gerrit G. and Jannetje—Petrus, b. Sep. 13—Sep. 16.
Wit: Pieter & Maria Pulisvelt.
DEI, Solomon and Sally—Polly—Sep. 30.

1793

FRERIKSE, Hendrik and Grietje—Pieter, b. Jan. 28—Mar. 10.
WOERTENDYK, Reinier and Annatje—Petrus, b. Jan. 8—Mar. 31.
PULISFELT, Petrus and Nanny—Pieter, b. Feb. 15—Apr. 14.
GERRITSEN, Johannis and Maria—Pieter, b. Oct. 1—Oct. 27.

1794

SISCO, Willem and Elisabeth—Polly, b. Dec. 13, 1793—Jan. 19.
  Wit: Richard & Santje De Groot.
BOGERT, Albert J. and Maria—Pieter—Mar. 24.
  Wit: Eva Bogert.
Bos, Lodewyk and Leentje—Pieter, b. May 22—June 29.
  Wit: Dirk & Antje Bos.
JOHNSON, Hugh and Rachel—Pieter, b. July 11—July 27.
Bos, Pieter and Phrone—Pieter, b. July 10.
  Wit: Reinhart & Elisabeth Bos.
VAN BLERKOM, Johannis and Elisabeth—Petrus—Aug. 31.
  Wit: Petrus & Maria Van Blerkom.
PECKER, Coenraad and Klaartje—Pieter, b. Sep. 3—Sep. 28.
BROUWER, Jan and Catriena—Pieter, b. Oct. 12—Nov. 9.
Row, Philip and Maria—Petrus, b. Sep. 29—Nov. 23.
  Wit: Albert & Rachel Van Zeyl.

1795

VAN ZYL, Hermanus and Elisabeth—Polly, b. Jan. 1—Mar. 29.
  Wit: Thomas & Geertje Myer.
VANHOUTEN, John and Margrietje—Paulus—Apr. 19.
  Wit: John & Elisabeth Stagge.
V. ZEYL, Abraham and Rachel—Petrus, b. Nov. 8—Dec. 13.

1797

WOERTENDYK, Pieter and Metje—Pieter, b. June 15—July 9.
DEMAREST, Jacob and Geesje—Pieter, b. July 3—Aug. 20.
  Wit: Pieter & Antje Hoppe.
DURIE, Pieter and Osseltje—Pieter, b. Nov. 24—Dec. 24.

1798

DEMAREST, Albert and Annatje—Pieter, b. Aug. 5—Aug. 26.
WESTERVELT, Daniel and Elisabeth—Petrus, b. Oct. 27—Dec. 9.

1799

DEBAAN, Petrus and Ebbe—Pieter, b. June 10—July 7.
DEMAREST, Gileaam and Maatje—Petrus, b. June 9—Aug. 4.
PERRY, Peter and Margrietje—Peter, b. June 16—July 13.

1800

DEMAREST, Guileaam and Maatje—Petrus, b. Oct. 12—Nov. 16.

1801

ACKER, John and Elisabeth—Polly, b. June 18, 1800—Feb. 22.
ECKERSON, Paulus and Maria—Petrus, b. Mar. 4—Mar. 22.
  Wit: Petrus & Maria Debaun.

ZABRISKIE, Albert and Aaltje—Peter, b. Oct. 30—Nov. 15.
HOPPER, Andries and Antje—Peter, b. Nov. 6—Nov. 26.
  Wit: Peter & Antje Hopper.
1802
VANDERBEEK, Aurie and Lena—Paulus, b. Feb. 11—Mar. 14.
ACKERMAN, David and Metje—Peter, b. Apr. 2—May 2.
GUY, John and Sally—Philip, b. Nov. 1—Nov. 14.
BLAUVELT, Isaac and Saartje—Phebe, b. Oct. 24—Nov. 21.
ECKERSON, Peter and Margaret—Peter, b. Nov. — —Nov. 28.
TICE, John—Peter, b. Oct. 31—Dec. 12.
1803
DEBAUN, Albert and Maatje (or Maritje)—Peter, b. Jan. 24—Feb. 17.
1804
BERTULF, Stephen and Jannitje—Pieter Post, b. Nov. 24, 1803—Jan. 8.
VAN IMBURGH, Hendrik and Maria—Peter, b. Feb. 11—Mar. 2.
FOLLY, William and Antje—Peter, b. Apr. 19, 1803(?)—Apr. 19.
MABEE, Peter and Jannetje—Peter, b. Oct. 8—Nov. 4.
1805
TERHUNE, Albert and Rachel—Paulus, b. Dec. 11, 1804—Jan. 13.
FORSHUR, Abraham and Elisabeth—Peter, b. Jan. 25—Feb. 20.
HOPPER, Jacob and Sophia—Peter, b. May 25—June 23.
DEBAUN, Peter and Abigail—Peter, b. Aug. 15—Sep. 22.
HOPPER, Henry and Elisabeth—Peter, b. Nov. 2—Dec. 1.
1806
MESSECRE, Lodewyk and Saartje—Peter, b. Dec. 14, 1805—Jan. 19.
SMITH, George and Geertje—Peter, b. Dec. 11, 1805—Jan. 26.
WATSON, Peter and Margaret—Petrus, b. Mar. 27—Apr. 27.
JERSEY, Peter and Maria—Peter, b. July 27—Aug. 10.
VOSS, Henry and Margaret—Petrus, b. Nov. 1—Nov. 30.
BOGERT, John and Jacomyntje—Petrus Bogert, b. Apr. 14—May 24.
1807
DEMAREST, Jacob and Geesje—Pieter, b. Aug. 15—Aug. 30.
WESTERVELT, Hendrik and Aaltje—Pieter, b. Sep. 21—Oct. 11.
  Wit: Jacob & Maragrytje Cole.
1808
SMITH, Edward and Anny—Pieter, b. Dec. 21, 1807—Feb. 14.
FELTER, Alexander and Caty—Peter, b. Jan. 27—Apr. 29.
DEGROOT, James S. and Naatje—Peter, b. May 15—Sep. 18.
HOPPER, Andries A. and Paggy—Patty, b. Oct. 19—Nov. 27.
1809
VAN RYPEN, Frederik G. and Mary—Peter, b. Dec. 5, 1808—Jan. 22.
STORM, Henderik and Margrietje—Peggy, b. May 7—June 4.
  Wit: Cornelius & Maragrietje Halderom.
STORM, John and Aaltje—Peggy, b. May 7—June 4.
JERSEY, Abraham and Annatje—Peter, b. Oct. 19—Nov. 12.
POST, Johannis and Elisabeth—Peter, b. July 19—Sep. 30.

1811

BOGERT, John S. and Margaret—Peggy Westervelt, b. Dec. 21, 1810—Jan. 6.

1813

HOPPER, John and Mary—Peter, b. May 7—May 27.
CHRISTOPHER, Joseph and Efy—Peter, b. Mar. 24—May 30.

1814

VAN EMBURGH, Henry and Polly—Polly, b. Sep. 16—Oct. 30.

1815

VANDERBEEK, Paul and Hannah—Paulus, b. Mar. 12—Apr. 23.
TERHUNE, Albert and Rachel—Pheby, b. Nov. 12—Dec. 25.

1817

DEGRAFF, Henry and Letty—Peggy, b. Dec. 22, 1816—Mar. 16.
BOGERT, Peter and Elisabeth—Phebe Ann, b. Feb. 24—Mar. 30.
MOWERSON, Jacob and Mary—Patty, b. May 7—June 29.
HOPPER, Andrew C. and Anne—Polly, b. Oct. 15—Nov. 9.
WARD, James and Anne—Peter, b. Nov. 2—Dec. 28.

1819

VAN EMBURGH, Albert H. and Hannah—Polly, b. Dec. 13, 1818—Jan. 24.
KOUGH, Casparus and Tyna—Peggy, b. Mar. 20—May 2.

1820

VANDERBEEK, Abraham C. and Elisabeth—Peggy, b. Apr. 10—Apr. 30.
HOPPER, Nicholas and Whiby—Polly, b. Nov. 22—Dec. 17.

1821

TERHUNE, Martin and Caty—Patty, b. May 25—June 17.
ACKERMAN, John and Bridget—Polly, b. Sep. 2—Oct. 7.

1822

ACKERMAN, David D. and Agnes—Peter, b. Mar. 14—Apr. 7.
SNYDER, Garrit and Catharina—Polly, b. Nov. 6—Dec. 1.

1823

TERHUNE, Marten and Caty—Peter Blauvelt, b. Feb. 25—Mar. 23.
SNYDER, Richard and Ally—Peggy, b. Jan. 20—June 1.

1825

TERHUNE, Henry Z. and Maria—Peter, b. Dec. 17, 1824—Jan. 8.
EVERSON, Benjamin and Sally—Peter, b. Oct. 27—Nov. 27.

1828

VANDERBEECK, James and Peggy—Peter, b. Mar. 18—May 11.
VANDERBEECK, John C. and Peggy—Peter Christie, b. Dec. 17, 1827—May 18.

1832

BLAUVELT, James, Jr. and Hannah—Phebe, b. Feb. 5—Apr. 15.

1835

VAN WAGENER, Garrit and Jemima—Peter Henry, b. Sep. 24—Nov. 1.

1837

ZABRISKIE, Gulliaam and Tina—Peter, b. Dec. 24, 1836—Feb. 18.

ACKERMAN, Peter D. and Hester—Phebe, b. Mar. 28—June 25.

1838

HELMS, Daniel and Catharine—Peter, b. May 28—July 22.

1843

QUACKENBUSH, Abraham and Sally Ann—Peter, b. Aug. 14—Sep. 16.

"R"

1750

JURRIKSE, Cobus and Rachel—Rachel—Feb. 17.
Wit: Hannes D. & Rachel Ackerman.

DUBOW, Ryer and Abigael—Rebecka—July 10.
Wit: Samuel & Rebecka Bos.

1751

ZABRISKE, Steven and Tryntje—Rachel—Mar. 17.
Wit: Albert & Rachel Hoppe.

RYERSE, Marten and Antje—Rachel—June 14.
Wit: Hannes & Rachel Van Rype.

1752

RYER, Jan and Susanna—Ryer—Mar. 8.
Wit: Frederik & Antje Van Rype.

VAN ZEYL, Petrus and Jannitje—Rachel—May 7.
Wit: Hannes A. & Triena Van Zeyl.

1753

HOPPE, Gerrit Jan and Elsje—Rachel—July 29.
Wit: Albert & Rachel Hoppe.

1755

STORM, Abram and Aaltje—Rachel—Nov. 16.
Wit: Hannes & Rachel Storm.

VAN BLERKOM, Lucas and Lisabeth—Ryer—Dec. 26.
Wit: Hannes Ar. & Jakomyntje Ackerman.

1756

HOPPE, Gerrit A. and Hendrika—Rachel, b. May 20—May 30.
Wit: Jacob & Rachel Banta.

1758

HOPPE, Andries and Marytje—Rachel—Jan. 15.
Wit: Steven & Tryntje Zabriske.

1759

KOOL, Hannes and Catriena—Rachel—Jan. 31.
Wit: Jacob & Lea Devenpoort.

WOERTENDYK, Rynier and Jannitje—Rynier—Apr. 9.
Wit: Fredrik & Sara Woertendyk.

HOPPE, Jan J. and Geertje—Rachel—Oct. 21.
Wit: Hendrik J. & Catrintje Hoppe.

1761

HOPPE, Albert and Rachel—Rachel—Mar. 23.
Wit: Pieter & Antje Ackerman.

BOGERT, Lucas and Rachel—Rachel—May 10.
Wit: Pieter A. & Rachel Vanhoute.
DOREMES, Cornelis H.—Rachel, b. Oct. 29—Dec. 6.
Wit: Hendrik & Eegje Deremes.

1762
WOERTENDYK, Frederik and Sara—Reinier, b. May 11—May 30.
Wit: Reinier & Jannitje Woertendyk.

1763
WESTERVELT, Johannes and Antje—Roelof—Oct. 16.
Wit: Roelof & Tryntje Westervelt.
VANDERBEEK, Paulus J. and Rachel—Rachel—Oct. 16.
Wit: Jan & Jannitje Vanderbeek.

1764
VAN GELDER, Jonathan and Marietje—Rachel, b. Apr. 22—May 13.
Wit: Abram & Rachel Van Gelder.

1765
ZABRISKE, Jacob J. and Aaltje—Rachel—Jan. 13.
Wit: Steven & Tryntje Zabriske.
ZABRISKE, Jacob H. and Wyntje—Rachel—July 21.
Wit: Niklaas & Rachel Zabriske.

1766
COCKROW, Niklaas and Pietertje—Rachel—Feb. 9.
Wit: Hendrik & Lena Van Blerkom.

1767
ECKERSON, Jacob and Lea—Rachel—Jan. 4.
Wit: Cornelis & Rachel Eckerson.
ACKERMAN, Albert and Rachel—Rachel—May 3.
Wit: Abram & Marytje Ackerman.

1769
VANBLERKOM, Isaac and Sara—Rachel—Feb. 5.
Wit: Paulus & Rachel Vanderbeek.

1770
TAELMAN, Theunis and Margrietje—Rebecka, b. May 5—May 27 .
ALYEE, Abram and Jacomyntje—Rachel—Dec. 9.
Wit: Albert & Rachel Hoppe.

1771
VANDERBEEK, Abram J. and Santje—Rachel—Jan. 3.
Wit: Hendrik C. & Fytje Banta.
ACKERMAN, David A. and Jacomyntje—Rachel—Mar. 17.
Wit: Gerrit J. & Rachel Ackerman.
STRAAT, Dirk and Rebecka—Rebecka—Apr. 1.
Wit: Jan Straet.
VAN VOORHEESE, Nicasie and Jannitje—Rachel—Apr. 28.
Wit: Albert & Rachel Ackerman.
MYER, Hannes C. and Sara—Rachel—June 30.
BOGERT, Jacob J. and Grietje—Rachel—July 21.
Wit: Jan & Rachel Bogert.
MYER, Cornelis and Ariaantje—Richard—July 21.

1772

ACKERMAN, Petrus and Maria—Rachel—Feb. 16.
   Wit: Pieter & Rachel Bogert.
HOPPE, Gerrit H. and Antje—Rachel—Oct. 18.
   Wit: Steven & Geesje Bogert.

1773

VAN GELDER, Cobus and Jannitje—Rachel, b. Jan. 18—Jan. 24.
   Wit: Jonathan Van Gelder.
VAN BLERKOM, Hannes J. and Rebecka—Ryer—Feb. 21.
   Wit: Ryer Debow.

1775

ZABRISKE, Jacob Ja. and Jannitje—Rachel—Jan. 22.
   Wit: Jacob & Aaltje Zabriske.

1773

BOGERT, Steven and Geesje—Rachel— Aug. 1.
   Wit: Garrit G. & Rachel Gerritse.
VANDERBEEK, Hannes and Abigael—Rachel—Sep. 5.
   Wit: Paulus J. & Rachel Vanderbeek.

1774

Bos, Samuel, Jr. and Lena—Rebecka—Feb. 6.
   Wit: Samuel & Rebecka Bos.
DOBBS, Willem and Rachel—Rachel—Mar. 20.
   Wit: John & Lea Maybe.

1775

VANHOREN, Hannes B. and Rachel—Rachel—Feb. 19.
   Wit: Dirk & Lisabeth Vanhoren.
TRAPHAGE, Jonathan and Trientje—Rachel, b. Dec. 11—Dec. 31.

1777

WESTERVELT, Abraham and Antje—Roelof, b. Apr. 12—Apr. 30.
   Wit: Johannis & Antje Westervelt.

1780

HOPPE, Jan A. and Marytje—Rachel, b. Nov. 1—Nov. 19.
   Wit: Petrus & Rachel Hoppe.

1784

DEBOUW, Pieter—Reinier, b. May 7—June 17.
   Wit: Andries Debouw & wife.
GUTSIUS, Piatus—Rachel—May 16.
   Wit: ——— & Rachel Westervelt.

1786

LUTKE, Harmen and Antje—Rachel, b. Mar. 1—Mar. 19.
   Wit: Hendrik G. & Rachel Hoppe.
HOPPE, Petrus and Elisabeth—Rachel, b. June 27—July 9.
   Wit: Abraham & Maria Hoppe.

1787

WOERTENDYK, Cornelis and Sophia—Reinier, b. Aug. 21—Sep. 16.
   Wit: Reinier & Jannetje Woertendyk.

1788

BRICKMAN, Lodewyk and Marytje—Reinhart—Jan. 21.
   Wit: Pieter & Catriena Swin.
ACKERMAN, John J. and Elsje—Rachel—Jan. 22.

V. D. BEEK, Jacob and Annaatje—Rachel—Aug. 17.
Wit: Paulus & Doortje V. d. Beek.
LABACH, Jan and Maragrietje—Rachel—Nov. 30.
JACOBUSSE, Roelof and Lydia—Rachel—Dec. 7.
Wit: Abraham & Jannetje Vanderbeek.

1789
TAYLOR, Jonas and Ariaantje—Rachel, b. Jan. 21—Mar. 1.

1790
WOERTENDYK, Jacobus and ,Sara—Rachel, b. Jan. 2—Jan. 24.
Wit: Jan & Rachel Durie.
HOPPER, Gerrit A. and Cathalyntje—Rachel—Jan. 31.
Wit: Isaac & Rachel Hopper.
HOPPE, John and Maria—Rachel—Oct. 17.
Wit: Jacobus & Ariaantje Beem.

1791
WILSON, Albert and Maria—Rachel, b. Aug. 16—Sep. 11.
WOERTENDYK, Albert and Maragrietje—Reinier, b. Sep. 21—Oct. 16.
Wit: Reinier & Jannetje Woertendyk.

1793
VANDERBEEK, Coenradus and Annatje—Rebecka, b. Oct. 2, 1791 (?)—
Feb. 10.
Wit: Samuel & Rebecka Demarest.
HOPPE, Isaac and Rachel—Rachel, b. Mar. 12—Apr. 7.
QUACKENBOS, Leendert and Jannitje—Rensje, b. Mar. 6—Mar. 31.
Wit: Abraham Quackenbos.
ACKERMAN, Johannis and Maria—Rachel, b. Apr. 27—May 19.
Wit: Garrit & Rachel Ackerman.
WOERTENDYK, Jacob—Reinier—Sep. 8.
Wit: Reinier & Jannetje Woertendyk.
WESTERVELT, Roelof and Rachel—Rachel, b. Sep. 15—Oct. 13.
RIDGWAY, John and Peggy—Rachel, b. Sep. 30—Oct. 27.
Wit: Isaac & Catriena Stagg.

1794
VAN VOORHESEN, Abraham and Jannetje Beem—Rachel, b. May 14.
RUTAN, Daniel and Jannitje—Rachel, b. Sep. 7—Sep. 28.
Wit: Hendrik & Rachel Swin.
BANTA, Abram and ,Catriena—Rachel, b. July 21—Nov. 2.
Wit: Jacob & Rachel Banta.
HOPPE, Abraham and Elisabeth—Rachel, b. Oct. 12—Nov. 9.
Wit: Isaac & Rachel Hoppe.
DEMAREST, Symon and Cornelia—Rebecka, b. Nov. 13—Nov. 30.
Wit: Joost & Polly Van Boskerk.

1795
BOGERT, Jan and Margrietje—Rachel, b. Feb. 23—Mar. 15.
Wit: Steven & Maria Bogert.
TYSEN, Pieter and Maria—Rachel, b. Feb. 21—Apr. 19.
MEKRAAF, Martin and Christina—Rachel, b. Nov. 3, 1794—Aug. 23.

1796

WRIGHT, John and Abigael—Rachel, b. July 11—Aug. 7.

DEMAREST, Symon and Maria—Rachel, b. Nov. 23—Dec. 25.

1797

DEMAREST, Albert and Annatje—Rachel, b. Dec. 25, 1796—Jan. 22.
    Wit: John & Rachel Durie.

CERELLACH, George and Jannitje—Robert, b. Sep. 20, 1796—Apr. 17.

BERBERO, Casparus and Maria—Rachel, b. Mar. 20—Apr. 17.
    Wit: John & Rachel Hicks.

ECKERSON, Edward and Catriena—Rachel and Sarah (twins), b. Oct.
    4—Nov. 26.
    Wit: Jacob, Catriena, Petrus & Maria Eckerson.

1800

ANDERSON, Jacobus and Margary—Rebecka, b. Sep. 14, 1799—Apr. 14.

DEMAREST, Symon and Maria—Rachel, b. May 9—July 13.
    Wit: Corynus & Rachel Remsen.

WOERTENDYK, Rynier and Annatje—Rachel, b. Aug. 16—Sep. 7.

1801

BARTOLF, Samuel and Eltje (?)—Rachel, b. Sep. 5, 1800—Feb. 22.

ZABRISKIE, Abraham and Susanna—Rachel, b. June 18—July 12.

1802

DEMAREST, Simon and Maria—Rachel, b. Dec. 15, 1801—Jan. 21.

VAN SCHYVEN, William and Saartje—Rachel, b. Feb. 5—Mar. 21.
    Wit: Thomas & Rachel Dodds.

1803

POST, John and Elisabeth—Rachel, b. Sep. 18—Oct. 2.

BUSH, Reinard and Elisabeth—Reinard, b. Sep. 27—Oct. 31.

1804

FORSHUR, Cornelis and Maria—Rachel, b. Jan 9—Jan 29.

WESTERVELT, Lucas and Maria—Rachel, b. Mar. 12—Apr. 1.

SMITH, James and Caty—Rachel, b. Apr. 3—May 13.

JURRY, John and Elisabeth—Rachel, b. Sep. 4—Oct. 7.

LYDECKER, Gerrit and Maria—Richard, b. Nov. 22—Dec. 15.

1805

FOSTER, Henry and Ann—Rachel, b. Oct. 2, 1803—Dec. 17.

PAUL, John and Claasje—Rebecka, b. Mar. 8—Apr. 17.

1806

POST, Abram and Geesje—Rachel, b. May 19—June 15.

PETERSON, Nicholas and Magdalen—Rytje, b. May 25—June 15.

VANIMBURGH, Hendrik and Maria—Ralph Westervelt, b. June 24—July 20.

1807

COOK, Francis and Rachel—Rachel, Dec. 5, 1806—Jan. 18.

RYER, John R. and Polly—Reier, b. Mar. 6, 1806—Mar. 5.

BUSH, Peter and Grietje—Richard, b. Oct. 13—Nov. 1.

1808

SNYDER, Gerrit and Catriena—Rachel, b. Feb. 15—Mar. 13.
  Wit: Andreas & Rachel Snyder.
VALENTINE, John and Elisabeth—Rachel, b. June 3—Aug. 7.
TERHUNE, Richard and Anna— (?) —Mar. 23.
POLHEMES, John and Caty—Rebecka, b. June 19—Oct. 30.
QUACKINBUSH, Jacob and Maria—Rachel, b. Nov. 18—Dec. 26.
SMITH, Henry and Rachel—Rachel, b. Dec. 8—Dec. 25.

1809

HOPPER, Gerrit and Polly—Rachel, b. Oct. 5—Nov. 5.
WESTERVELT, Pieter and Martyntje—Rachel, b. Oct. 27—Nov. 26.

1810

WOERTENDYK, Cornelius and Annatje—Rachel, b. Mar. 5—Apr. 22.
OSBURN, Matthew and Aaltje—Rebeckah, b. Feb. 26—May 6.

1811

ACKERMAN, John and Polly—Rachel, b. June 5—July 1.
DEBAUN, John P. and Polly—Rachel, b. Aug. 12—Sep. 8.

1813

MACLAIN, William and Dorothy—Rachel, b. Feb. 25—Mar. 21.

1814

ACKERMAN, David D. and Aggy—Ralph, b. Mar. 24—Apr. 17.
WESTERVELT, Peter A. and Caty—Ralph, b. Oct. 4—Nov. 6.

1815

RETAN, Abraham D. and Lydia—Rachel, b. Jan. 10—Mar. 27.

1816

SNYDER, Adam and Caty—Rachel, b. Jan. 22—Mar. 17.
COUGH, Jasper, Jr. and Tyne—Rachel, b. Apr. 9—May 19.
ZABRISKIE, Jacob H. and Anne—Rachel Ann, b. Aug. 28—Oct. 6.

1818

SNYDER, John A. and Lina—Rachel, b. Feb. 14—Mar. 8.
VANDERBEEK, John H. and Anne—Richard, b. Mar. 19—Apr. 26.
VAN SAUN, Jacob and Polly—Rachel, b. July 9—Aug. 23.
VAN SAUN, Cornelius and Rachel—Rachel, b. Sep. 26—Nov. 1.

1819

ZABRISKIE, Henry and Patty—Rachel, b. Apr. 2—May 2.
POST, John and Caty—Rachel, b. Nov. 30—Dec. 25.

1820

CLEARWATER, Frederick and Hetty—Rachel, b. Nov. 3, 1819—Feb. 6.

1821

SNYDER, Richard and Ally—Rachel, b. Feb. 23—Apr. 8.
VAN NORDEN, David and Ally—Rachel, b. Apr. 2—May 6.
BANTA, Garrit D. and Harriet—Rachel Ann, b. Aug. 23—Sep. 8.
TOURSE, Lawrence and Jane—Rachel, b. Sep. 12—Oct. 7.
MYRES, John and Elisabeth—Richard, b. Oct. 16—Dec. 16.

1822
QUACKENBUSH, John and Susan—Rachel, b. Oct. 29—Dec. 1.
1823
VANDIEN, Gerrit C. and Sophia—Richard, b. Dec. 19, 1822—Jan. 26.
ZABRISKIE, Casparus J. and Caty—Robert Post, b. June 13—July 13.
LUTKINS, John S. and Maria—Rachel Ann, b. Sep. 21—Oct. 5.
1827
ACKERMAN, Peter D. and Hester—Rachel, b. Dec. 31, 1826—Feb. 11.
SNYDER, Richard and Ally—Richard, b. Aug. 23—Nov. 18.
1829
SMITH, John, Jr. and Patty—Rachel Ann, b. Mar. 3—May 16.
1830
BUSH, John, Jr. and Anne—Rachel, b. Dec. 24, 1829—Apr. 12.
ZABRISKIE, Casparus J. and Caty—Rachel Catharine, b. Oct. 10—Nov. 21.
1831
ZABRISKIE, Stephen J. and Jane—Rachel Ann, b. Mar. 10—Apr. 3.
HAMMON, Thomas and Patty—Rachel Ann, b. Mar. 11—Apr. 10.
HOPPER, Jacob H. and Caty—Rachel Ann, b. Apr. 19—May 29.
SNIDER, Richard and Ally—Richard—Nov. 13.
1832
CARLOUGH, John and Maria—Rachel Jane, b. July 26—Aug. 18.
VANDERBEEK, Jeremiah C.—Richard, b. July 19—Aug. 18.
1834
VANDERBEEK, James and Peggy—Rachel, b. Oct. 15, 1833—Jan. 1.
SNYDER, James and Charity—Rachel Ann, b. Nov. 6—Dec. 11.
1835
TERHUNE, Abraham A. and Caty—Rachel Ellen, b. Nov. 23, 1834—Jan. 18.
ACKERMAN, Abraham A. and Dorcas—Rachel, b. Apr. 17—May 24.
1837
CARLOUGH, Abraham and Maria—Rachel Catharine, b. Feb. 28—May 21.
1838
VAN ORDEN, Adam and Roseaman—Rachel Ann, b. Dec. 23, 1837—Jan. 6.
TERHUNE, Henry P. and Maria—Richard, b. Jan. 25—Mar. 25.
1839
ACKERMAN, Garrit D. and Eliza—Rachel Catharine, b. June 1—July 7.
1840
BLAUVELT, James, Jr. and Hannah—Rachel Margaret, b. Feb. 28—June 7.
GARDNER, Josiah and Peggy—Rachel Catharine, b. July 15—Aug. 23.
1843
QUACKENBUSH, David and Ann—Rachel Jane, b. Jan. 21, 1842—Mar. 12.
HOPPER, Henry A. and Margaret Ann—Rachel Laticia, b. May 28—July 9.
1845
HORSBROOK, Augustus and Jane—Richard Oliver, b. Apr. 2—Aug. 3.

1847
CARLOUGH, Abraham and Maria—Rachel, b. Oct. 25, 1846—May 11.
1849
BOGERT, Albert C. and Jane—Rachel Catharine, b. Nov. 26, 1848—Feb. 25.
"S"
1748
STORM, Hendrik and Cornelia—Staats—Nov. 13.
Wit: Staats & Susannah Storm.
1749
VAN WINKEL, Hannes S. and Janneke—Simeon and Janneke (twins)—
Dec. 24.
Wit: Jacob, Vrouwtje, & Jannike Van Winkel; Dirk Ryerse.
1752
VAN WINKEL, Jacob and Vrouwtje—Simeon—Apr. 19.
Wit: Albert & Rachel Ackerman.
1755
RYER, John and Sunna—Sara—Jan. 12.
Wit: Frederik & Sara Woertendyk.
DERYIE, Jan D. and Jannitje—Samuel—Nov. 16.
Wit: Cornelis & Maria Smit.
STORM, Hendrik and Cornelia—Staats—Dec. 14.
Wit: Staats & Susanna Storm.
1756
OOLDES, Benjamin and Nellie—Sara—May 9.
Wit: Josie & Ariaantje Wessels.
GALLEWE, John and Lea—Isaak—June —.
Wit: Steven & Marritje Slot.
VAN RYPE, Fredrik and Saartje—Simeon, b. July 18—Aug. 15.
Wit: Albert & Rachel Ackerman.
1757
ACKERMAN, Hannes A. and Jakomyntje—Sara—Sep. 4.
Wit: David A. & Sara Ackerman.
WALDEROM, Hannes and Wyntje—Samme Bense, b. Aug. 28—Sep. 4.
Wit: Samme Bense and Lisabeth Lydecker.
1758
HOPPE, Gerrit A. and Hendrikje—Steven—Oct. 22.
Wit: David & Sara Terhuyn.
1759
DEY, Dirk and Sara—Sara—June 24.
Wit: Jacob & Vrouwtje Van Winkel.
1760
Bos, Samuel and Rebecka—Saartje—June 8.
Wit: David D. & Saartje Ackerman.
1761
VAN BLERKOM, Gerrit and Hillegont—Samuel—Feb. 22.
Wit: Lourens Ackerman; Jannetje V (an) Blerkom.
WESSELLS, Joseph and Ariaantje—Sara—July 5.
Wit: Albert & Rachel Ackerman.

1762

Ryer, John and Soike—Susannah—Feb. 14.
Wit: Isaak & Lisabeth Post.
Helm, Samuel and Catrientje—Samuel, b. Mar. 1—Mar. 20.

1763

Bogert, Jacob and Marytje—Steven—July 24.
Wit: Steve & Tryntje Zabriske.
Storm, Hendrik and Cornelia—Susannah—Oct. 2.
Wit: Abram & Saartje V. derbeek.

1764

Woertendyk, Fredrik and Macere—Sara, b. June 5—June 24.
Wit: Jan P. & Jannitje Deryie.

1765

Post, Isaac and Jannetje—Sara—Nov. 10.
Wit: Abram & Sara Post.

1766

Woertendyk, Frederik and Majeri—Susannah, b. Aug. 8—Aug. 31.
Wit: John & Susannah Ryer.

1767

Alyee, Jacobus and Annatje—Saphira (?) Saffya or Saffyee (?)—Jan. 25.
Ekkerson, Jan and Maria—Susanna—Apr. 12.
Wit: Jacob & Maria Ekkerson.

1768

Fisher, Joost—Saartje—Mar. 6.
Hoppe, Andries A. and Lisabeth—Saartje, b. Apr. 7—May 5.
Wit: Abram & Saartje Post.
Zabriskie, Hendrik C. and Maria—Sara—June 26.
Wit: David & Sara Terhune.
Lutkins, Harme H. and Antje—Steven—Oct. 23.
Wit: Christiaan A. & Rachel Zabriskie.

1769

Ackerman, David (H.?) and Myntje—Sara—Mar. 19.
Wit: Abram W. & Grietje Rutan.

1770

Toirs, Lourens and Elisabeth—Sara—Nov. 4.
Wit: Fredrik & Saartje Cadmus.

1771

Post, Hannes A. and Trientje—Susannah—Apr. 21.
Wit: Guliaam & Susannah Dumaree.

1772

Post, Abram, Jr. and Jannitje—Saartje—Dec. 6.
Wit: Abram & Saartje Post.

1773

Kogh, Casper and Lidia—Steven, b. June 3—June 6.
Wit: Jan J. & Lea Zabriske.

1774
DEVENPOORT, Leendert and Mary—Sara, b. Feb. 7, 1773—June 28.
ACKERMAN, Cornelis and Elisabeth—Lawrence—Aug. 28.
  Wit: David J. & Antje Ackerman.
Bos, Pieter and Annatje—Samuel—Sep. 17.
  Wit: Samuel S. & Lena Bos.

1754
VOLK, Nikolaas and Metje—Sara—Sep. 8.
  Wit: B. & Nellie Odel.
    (Is also to be found under the letter C.)

1775
WOERTENDYK, Frederik and Sara—Jan. 29.
  Wit: Frederik & Majeri Woertendyk.
RUTAN, Johannis A. and Elisabeth—Saartje, b. Sep. 25—Dec. 14.
  Wit: Jacobus & Willempje Rutan.

1776
BENSEN, Matheus and Marytje—Samuel—Jan. 28.
VESEUR, Hannes and Lena—Samuel, b. Jan. 29—Mar. 31.
  Wit: Samuel & Lisabeth Banta.
ZABRISKE, Albert J. and Geesje—Steven—Mar. 31.
  Wit: Steven Zabriskie.
QUACKINBOS, Pieter and Grietje—Susannah, b. June 15—July 7.
  Wit: Willem & Santje Pieterse.

1779
MOUNT, Richard and Rachel—Susannah—Dec. 12.

1781
TERHUYN, Steven and Jannitje—Steven, b. Aug. 28—Oct. 7.
  Wit: Christiaan & Martyntje Zobriske.

1782
BOES, Sam—Sam—Sep. 17.
STORM, Coenradus— ? —Dec. 2.
  Wit: Jacob Eckerse & wife.

1784
HOPPER, Jacob—Sara—Apr. 11.
POST, Abraham—Sannie—Apr. 11.
GEERITSE, Johannis—Sara—Sep. 5.

1785
HOPPE, Jan and Maria—Sally, b. June 5—Sep. 5.
  Wit: Sallie Cuyper.
RYER, Jan and Maria—Sukee—Sep. 25.
  Wit: Sukie Demarest.

1786
ACKERMAN, Johannis and Annaatje—Sara, b. June 6—June 18.
  Wit: Gerrit & Elisabeth Ackerman.
Bos, Jacobus and Aaltje—Samuel, b. May 16—July 2.
  Wit: Samuel & Lena Bos.
BEMPER, Jacob and Antje—Sara Brower—July 17.

Bos, Samuel and Lena—Sara, b. July 18—Aug. —.
  Wit: John & Sara Beem.
Tyson, John and Annatje—Saartje, b. Sep. 3—Oct. 1.
  Wit: Harmen & Trientje Retan.

1787

Valentyn, Wiert and Metje—Sara, b. May 28—June 17.
  Wit: Cornelis & Ariaantje Myer.
Van Dien, Andreas and Sara—Sara—Sep. 9.
Dee, Isaac and Francyntje—Susannah—Sep. 16.
Terhuun, Stephen and Jannetje—Sara—Sep. 30.
  Wit: Pieter & Antje Demarest.
Straat, Jan and Sukie—Sukie, b. Oct. 24—Nov. 11.
Banta, Samuel and Elisabeth—Samuel, b. Nov. 26—Dec. 9.
  Wit: Abraham & Dievertje Banta.
Eckerson, Edward and Catriena—Susannah, b. Dec. 15—Dec. 30.

1788

Post, Jan J. and Annatje—Sara, b. Mar. 4—Apr. 20.
  Wit: Jan & Nancy Post.
Jacobusse, Roelof and Lydia—Susannah and Sara—Dec. 7.
  Wit: Abraham & Jannetje Vanderbeek.
Westervelt, Jan and Angonietje—Sara, b. June 6—July 5.
Vandien, Albert and Maria—Sara, b. Aug. 9—Aug. 30.
  Wit: Harman & Aaltje Vandien.
Hoppe, Andrias and Catriena—Stephen, b. May 21—Aug. 30.
  Wit: Stephen & Geertje Hjoppe.

1790

Banta, Hendrik and Maria—Sietsje, b. Aug. 11—Aug. 15.
  Wit: Cornelis & Sietsje Bogert.
Eckerson, Thomas and Susannah—Sara, b. Apr. 4—May 2.
  Wit: Jacobus & Sara Demarest.

1791

Debow, Petrus and Susannah—Sara, b. Dec. 27, 1790—Jan. 30.
Terhune, John and Catriena—Steven, b. Feb. 1—Feb. 24.
  Wit: Steven Lutken and Lea Blauvelt.
Durjee, Jan and Rachel—Sara, b. Apr. 2—Apr. 25.
  Wit: Jacobus & Sara Woertendyk.
Perry, John and Charity—Sally, b. Mar. 26—Apr. 25.
Benner, Jeams and Geesje—Samuel, b. Apr. 17—May 29.
Rotan, Jan and Rachel—Sara, b. Sep. 10—Oct. 9.
  Wit: Abraham & Maria Rotan.
Post, Johannis and Catriena—Samuel b, Aug. 22—Oct. 9.
  Wit: Jacob & Maria Kogh.

1792

Van Zeyl, Hermanus and Elisabeth—Susannah—Feb. 26.
  Wit: Pieter & Susannah Debow.
Vanhorn, David and Sara—Sara—Nov. 11.

1794

RATAN, John and Rachel—Susannah, b. Nov. 28, 1793 (?)—Jan. 2.
    Wit: Abraham & Susannah V. d. Beek.
RATAN, Abraham and Maria—Sara, b. Apr. 20—May 4.
    Wit: Jacobus & Willempje Ratan.
DEBOUW, John and Margrietje Aljee—Syntje, b. Apr. 4—May 4.
BERTOLF, Jacobus and Metje Post—Sally, b. Dec. 24—May 4.
ZABRISKE, Albert and Metje—Simeon, b. Sep. 20—Oct. 26.
STORM, Isaac and Elisabeth—Saartje, b. July 29—Oct. 1.

1795

McCALL, Alexander and Rachel—Sara, b. Nov. 23, 1794—Feb. 1.
    Wit: John & Sara Van Blerkom.
POST, Pieter and Rachel—Sara, b. June 10—June 28.
MYER, Thomas and Geertje—Sara, b. Sep. 21—Oct. 18.

1796

DURIE, Samuel and Catriena—Sara, b. Dec. 13, 1795—Jan. 1.
    Wit: Thomas & Sara Pieterson.
SISCO, Willem and Elisabeth—Semme, b. Dec. 7, 1795—Jan. 24.

1797

DEBAAN, Jacob and Osseltje—Samuel, b. Jan. 25—Feb. 19.
    Wit: Samuel & Rebecka Demarest.
TERHUNE, John S. and Antje—Stephen, b. May 4—May 21.
POTTER, John and Maria—Samuel, b. June 20—July 3.
TERHUNE, Jan and Eva—Sara, b. June 27—Aug. 20.
    Wit: Christiaan & Maria Zabriskie.
REYER, Reyer and Maria—Soecke, b. Sep. 5—Oct. 1.
VANDERBEEK, Arie and Lena—Sara, b. Oct. 18—Nov. 26.

1798

REYER, John and Maria—Syntje, b. Apr. 27—June 3.
    Wit: Barend & Francyntje Fesyeur.
STORM, Staats and Maragrietje—Susannah, b. May 15—June 3.
DEMAREST, David and Geesje—Samuel, b. Apr. 8—Oct. 14.
    Wit: Samuel & Rebecka Demarest.

1799

BERDAN, John I. and Mary—Stephen, b. Nov. 28—Dec. 20.

1800

DEMAREST, Albert and Annatje—Samuel, b. Oct. 1—Oct. 26.
    Wit: Samuel & Catriena Durie.

1801

WILSON, Polly—Sarah, b. Nov. 3, 1800—Jan. 18.
ZABRISKIE, Albert and Metje—Stephen, b. Jan. 13—Feb. 8.
    Wit: Wyntje Zabriskie.
HEDDE, Eseyes and Elisabeth—Sally, b. June 5—July 21.
RYER, John and Maria—Sarah, b. June 5—July 21.

RUTAN, Abraham and Lydia—Susannah, b. June 16—July 24.
    Wit: Abraham & Susannah Vanderbeek.
LUTKENS, Hendrik and Eva—Stephen, b. July 16—Aug. 9.
MASSACRE, Lodewyk and Sarah—Sarah, b. Sep. 1—Nov. 1.

1802

ZABRISKIE, Jacob and Elisabeth—Stephen Terhune, b. Dec. 14, 1801—Jan. 17.
    Wit: Jacob & Maria Terhune.
BOGERT, Jan and Margrietje—Stephen, b. May 10—May 30.
    Wit: Stephen & Maria Bogert.
WORTENDYK, Cornelius and Annatje—Sophia, b. Aug. 26—Oct. 3.
HARING, Jacob and Femmetje—Stephanas Goetsius, b. Nov. 3—Nov. 21.
DEMAREST, Benjamin and Susannah—Samuel, b. Aug. 20—Dec. 12.
    Wit: Samuel & Rebeckah Demarest.
SCISCO, William and Elisabeth—Susannah, b. Oct. 2—Nov. 27.

1803

DEMAREST, Daniel and Maria—Sarah, b. Aug. 19—Dec. 3.

1804

ECKERSON, Edward and Hetty—Sally, b. Jan. 25—Feb. 12.
HOPPER, Garret and Mary—Stephen, b. May 5—May 21.
DEY, Jacobus and Peggy—Sally, b. June 24—Aug. 8.
MASSACRE, John and Phebe—Sally, b. Oct. 1—Nov. 25.

1805

TERHUNE, David and Catriena—Sarah, b. July 1—July 28.
SCISCO, William and Elisabeth—Solomon, b. Sep. 2—Oct. 13.
BERVORT, John and Jannetje—Samuel, b. Sep. 19—Oct. 20.
SMITH, Edward and Anne—Susannah, b. Oct. 9—Nov. 17.
GARDENIER, Jacob and Maria—Sarah, b. Oct. 16—Dec. 1.

1806

TERHUNE, Albert I. and Martyntje—Stephen, b. Feb. 9—Mar. 9.
    Wit: Stephen & Rachel Lutkens.
HOPPER, Michiel and Jannetje—Saartje, b. Mar. 9—Mar. 16.
DEGROOT, Jacobus and Maria—Susannah, b. Nov. 14, 1805—Sep. 14.

1807

LESHON, David (?) and Elisabeth—Solomon, b. Mar. 27—May 31.
ROSEGRANT, Simeon and Sarah—Simeon, b. Feb. 12—Sep. 27.
WORTENDYK, Cornelius and Annatje—Sally, b. Sep. 8—Nov. 8.
HARING, Abraham and Maragrietje—Sarah, b. Apr. 14—May 15.

1808

DEMAREST, Jacobus and Lea—Samuel, b. Aug. 19—Oct. 16.

1809

ECKERSON, Jacob and Leah—Sarah, b. Feb. 4—Feb. 26.
WORTENDYK, Frederik and Cornelia—Sarah, b. Feb. 12—Mar. 12.
    Wit: Garret & Sarah Hogenkamp.

1809
ECKERSON, Garret and Annatje—Trientje, b. July 20—Mar. 12.
COLE, Cornelius and Marie—Thomas, b. Apr. 16—May 1.

1811
MABEY, Abraham and Sichey—Sally, b. Apr. 7—May 19.
LUTKENS, Harmen and Elisabeth—Stephen, b. June 27—July 11.
POLHEMUS, John and Caty—Theodorus, b. May 20—Aug. 11.
HOPPER, Albert and Maria—Samuel, b. Aug. 4—Sep. 1.
BREVOTE, Hendrik and Polly—Samuel & Rachel, b. Dec. 9, 1810(?)—Jan. 29.
    Wit: Rachel Vanbush.

1812
WESTERVELT, John J. and Hatty—Sally—Jan. 1.
WESTERVELT, Deter and Caty—Samuel—Aug. 9.

1813
BOGERT, James S. and Sarah—Stephen J., b. Apr. 3—May 9.

1814
DAY, William and Jenny—Sally, b. Sep. 14.
YELVERTON, Anthony and Rachel—Sarah, b. Aug. 4—Sep. 4.

1819
CHRISTOPHER, Jacob and Kaziah—Stephen, b. Jan. 7—Feb. 7.
GARRITSON, Jacob I. and Rachel—Stephen, b. Sep. 16—Oct. 17.

1821
RYERS, Barney and Sarah—Sarah Jane, b. Feb. 8—Mar. 25.
BOGERT, Peter S. and Betsy—Stephen, b. Mar. 27—Apr. 22.
ZABRISKIE, Christian J. and Hannah—Simon Demarest, b. Apr. 7—June 3.

1823
SNYDER, John A. and Helen—Sally, b. Apr. 18—May 18.
VANDIEN, Garrit and Jane—Sarah, b. June 29—July 26.
TERHUNE, Richard and Hannah—Susan, b. Sep. 23—Nov. 14.

1824
VANDIEN, Garrit and Jane—Sally, b. Aug. 20—Sep. 20.

1825
BLAUVELT, James I. and Hannah—Sarah Ann, b. Feb. 5—Mar. 6.

1826
HOPPER, Andrew H. and Polly—Sarah Margaret, b. Aug. 16—Sep. 17.
TAYLOR, John S. and Mary—Sarah Jane, b. Nov. 19—Dec. 23.

1827
BERDAN, John, Jr. and Sarah—Sarah Catharine, b. May 4—June 17.

1828
HOPPER, Henry G. and Margaret—Sarah, b. June 13—July 6.

1829
VOORHIS, Michael and Jane—Susan Ann, b. Apr. 20—June 21.

1830

QUACKINBUSH, John J. and Susan—Sarah Ann, b. Feb. 29—Apr. 4.

1831

VANDIEN, Richard A. and Ally—Sarah, b. Oct. 23, 1830—Jan. 2.

1832

ZABRISKIE, Christian J. and Hannah—Simon, b. Mar. 30.
   Wit: Christian & Elisabeth Zabriskie.

1834

BOATY, George and Rachel—Sarah Elisabeth, b. Sep. 21, 1832—Feb. 1.

POST, Maria—Sally Ann, b. Mar. 20—May 17.

ZABRISKIE, John A. and Sally—Sarah Jane, b. Aug. 26—Dec. 7.

1835

OBLENUS, Peter and Elsje—Sarah Elisabeth, b. Oct. 9, 1834—Jan. 11.

1836

JERALEMAN, James N. and Mary—Stephen Berdan, b. Nov. 2, 1835—
   Mar. 26.

VANDERBEEK, Jurry C. and Ann—Sarah Elisabeth, b. Nov. 10—Dec. 25.

1838

KING, Ezra A. and Margaret—Sarah Catharine, b. Sep. 10, 1837—Mar. 11.

CROWTER, Peter—Stephen, b. Sep. 22, 1835—May 19.

CROWTER, Peter—Samuel, b. Jan. 27—May 19.

ZABRISKIE, Casparus J. and Caty—Sophia, b. June 20—Sep. 2.

1839

VAN DIEN, Cornelius G. and Susan—Sophia Catharine, b. Jan. 24—
   Mar. 17.

1840

QUACKENBUSH, David and Ann—Susan Amelie, b. May 25—Sep. 20.

1841

VAN DIEN, Cornelius G. and Susan—Sophia Elisabeth, b. Jan. 24—
   Mar. 28.

1842

HORSBROOK, Augustin and Jane—Stephen, b. Jan. 28—Apr. 3.

SNYDER, Isaac and Mary Ann—Sarah Catharine, b. Feb. 25—Apr. 10.

1843

BANTA, Cornelius and Catharine—Sarah, b. Jan. 15—May 14.

1845

HOPPER, George D. and Rachel—Sarah Augusta, b. May 7—Aug. 24.

1846

TERHUNE, Casparus and Getty—Stephen, b. Mar. 19—May 24.

1847

FURDON, Abraham and Louisa—Stephen, b. Apr. 10—Aug. 22.

BERDAN, Cornelius Z. and Margaret—Sarah Elisabeth, b. Oct. 19—Dec. 25.

ACKERMAN, Mary Ann—Sarah Elisabeth, b. Mar. 13—May 28.

VAN SAUN, John I. and Elsje—Sarah, b. June 7—July 22.

1849

LEAVY, William and Leah Ann—Samuel Banta, b. Jan. 31—Apr. 7.
PERRY, Daniel D. and Sarah—Sarah Margaret, b. May 16—July 22.

"T"

1750

BOGERT, Lucas and Doritie—Tryntje—Nov. 11.
Wit: Steven & Tryntje Zabriskie.

1752

HOPPE, Hendrik and Trientje—Trientje—Apr. 19.
Wit: Albert & Rachel Hoppe.

1755

IESTERLI, Marte and Gouda—Thomas—Dec. 14.
Wit: Benjamin & Neeltje Oldes.

1756

ECKENSEN, Jacob and Susannah Maria—Thomas, b. May 3—May 30.
Wit: Thomas & Maria Eckesen.
TOIRS, Lourens and Lisabeth—Thomas—Aug. 8.
Wit: Dirk & Saartje Dey.

1760

ECKESEN, Jan and Lena—Thomas, b. May 26—June 14.
Wit: Thomas & Maria Eckesen.

1761

BERTOLF, Hannes and Wybrecht—Trientje—June 14.
Wit: Willem & Antje Hoppe.

1762

MYER, Hannes C. and Sara—Thomas, b. Mar. 13—Apr. 13.
Wit: Thomas & Maria Eckersen.
ECKERSEN, David and Angonietje—Thomas, b. June 27—July 18.
Wit: Thomas & Marytje Eckersen.
ECKERSEN, David and Angonietje—Thomas—Sep. 5, 1762 (?).
Wit: Thomas & Marytje Eckerson.
TOERS, Lourens and Lisabeth—Thomas—Oct. 17.
Wit: Dirk D. Dey & wife.

1764

VAN ORDER, Andries and Lisabeth—Tryntje—Feb. 5.
Wit: Samuel & Trientje Helm.
BOGERT, Cobus and Cornelia—Tryntje—Apr. 23.
Wit: Roelof & Tryntje Westervelt.

1766

ECKERSON, Jacob T. and Jannetje—Thomas, b. Aug. 14—Aug. 31.
Wit: Thomas & Maria Eckersen.

1767

BONGAERT, Steven and Rachel—Trientje—Feb. 15.
Wit: Gerrit H. & Antje Hoppe.

1768

RIDDENAER, Hendrik and Grietje—Tryntje—Jan. 3.
  Wit: Hendrik & Marytje Oldes.
RUTAN, Daniel and Santje—Tryntje—Mar. 27.
  Wit: Johannis A. & Trientje Post.
DEY, Teunis and Hester—Teunis, b. Aug. 19—Sep. 18.
  Wit: Ariaantje V. de Linde.

1767

MILLIDGE, Thomas and Sarah—Thomas—Nov. 28.

1770

WESTERVELT, Casparus and Wyntje—Trientje—Jan. 14.
VAN GIESE, Isaac R. and Pryntje—Thomas—Jan. 20.
COGH, Casper and Lidea—Trientje—Sep. 30.
  Wit: Jacob J. & Jannitje Zabriskie.
GERRITSE, Pieter H. and Effie—Trientje—Aug. 4.
  Wit: Hans & Trientje Demodt.

1771

VAN IMBURGH, John and Antie—Tryntje—Nov. 24.
  Wit: Cobus J. & Cornelia Bogert.

1772

STEGG, Isaac and Lena—Thomas, b. Dec. 13, 1771—Jan. 5.
  Wit: Abram & Marytje Ackerman.
BANTA, Samuel and Elisabeth—Thomas, b. Aug. 27.
  Wit: Thomas & Maria Eckersen.

1773

VANDIEN, Thomas and Polly—Trientje—Nov. 28.
  Wit: Daniel & Vrouwtje Duryie.
PIETERSE, Niklaas—Thomas, b. Jan. 11—Nov. 28.
  Wit: Barend & Syntje Veseur.

1775

ECKERSON, Thomas T. and Cornelia—Thomas, b. Apr. 1—May 14.
  Wit: Jacob & Jannitje Eckerson.
DOBS, William and Rachel—Trientje, b. Sep. 6—Oct. 22.
  Wit: Andries & Trientje Holderom.

1776

POST, Abram and Jannetje—Trientje, b. Feb. 15—Mar. 31.
  Wit: Jacob & Saartje Post.

1779

OLDES, Hendrik and Marytje—Tryntje—Apr. 5.
  Wit: Roelof Westervelt; Cornelia Bogert.
DEPYSTER, Abraham and Styntje—Steven Baldwin—Apr. 11.
  Wit: Antje Baldwin.

1780

VAN BLERKOM, David and Polly—Trientje—Sep. 17.

1781

WESTERVELT, Abraham and Antje—Trientje, b. Aug. 8—Sep. 16.
Wit: Jacobus Bogert and daughter Trientje.

ECKERSON, Edward and Catriena—Thomas, b. Mar. 14—Apr. 9.
Wit: Thomas & Cornelia Eckerson.

TAYLOR, Stephen and Elisabeth—Teunis, b. May 4—Oct. 1.

1788

BERTOLF, Hendrik and Margrietje—Tryntje—Feb. 3.

WESTERVELT, Albert and Margrietje—Tryntje—May 4.
Wit: Jacobus & Cornelia Bogert.

FRERIKSE, Hendrik and Maria—Tryntje—Sep. 28.

BENNER, James and Geesje—Thomas, b. Sep. 12—Oct. 19.
Wit: John & Martina Eckerson.

ROTAN, Jan and Jannetje—Tryntje, b. Nov. 13—Oct. 19.
Wit: Gerrit & Tryntje Blauvelt.

1789

BANTA, Hendrik and Margrietje—Teunis, b. Mar. 25—May 10.
Wit: Teunis & Sara Demarest.

1791

HOPPE, Isaac and Rachel—Teunis, b. Jan. 6—Feb. 6.
Wit: Teunis & Margrietje Cuyper.

1792

STAGGE, John and Elisabeth—Thomas, b. Oct. 8—Nov. 11.
Wit: Thomas & Esther Stagge.

1793

DEBAAN, Jan and Wyntje—Tryntje, b. Sep. 16—Sep. 29.
Wit: Jan T. Banta.

1794

VAN BOSKERK, Pieter and Sally—Thomas—Mar. 30.

PAULUSSE, John and Klaasje—Teunis, b. Apr. 15—May —.

1795

JANSEN, Abraham and Elisabeth—Tietje, b. Dec. 10, 1794—Jan. 4.
Wit: Jacobus & Tietje Poelisvelt.

BANTA, John and Cornelia—Tryntje, b. Oct. 21—Nov. 8.
Wit: John & Wyntje Debaen.

WILLS, Thomas and Rachel—Thomas, b. Oct. 28—Nov. 15.
Wit: David Marines; Dirkje Ackerman.

1796

BLAUVELT, Joseph and Maria—Trientje, b. Feb. 14—Mar. 27.

1797

GARDNER, Thomas and Aaltje—Thomas, b. Jan. 10—Feb. 19.

VAN AULEN, John and Angonietje—Trientje, b. Feb. 22—Mar. 19.

HOPPER, Gerrit and Maria—Trientje—Sep. 3.
Wit: Jacobus & Trientje Clerck.

1798

BOGERT, Jan and Margrietje—Trientje, b. Nov. 19—Dec. 9.

1799

MEBE, Abraham and Maria—Trientje, b. Nov. 11, 1798—Jan. 6.

ACKERMAN, Abraham and Maragrietje—Trientje, b. Mar. 15—Apr. 14.
Wit: Petrus & Trientje Ackerman.

CAMPBELL, William and Jannetje—Tietje, b. July 14—July 28.
Wit: John & Tietje Campbell.

1800

VANDIEN, Casparus and Polly—Thomas, b. Dec. 29, 1799—Mar. 2.
Wit: Dirk & Antje Vandien.

ECKERSON, Peter and Margrietje—Thomas, b. Aug. 20—Sep. 7.
Wit: Thomas & Cornelia Eckerson.

VANDERBEEK, Paulus and Margrietje—Tyne, b. Sep. 3—Sep. 21.

SORLIE, Lourens and Elisabeth—Trientje, b. Sep. 16—Nov. 30.
Wit: John & Trientje Terhune.

1801

TERHUNE, Abraham and Susannah—Trientje, b. Jan. 28—Mar. 22.

HARING, David and Tryntje—Tryntje, b. Apr. 5—Apr. 26.
Wit: Hendrik & Annatje Van Weert.

SNYDER, Thomas and Maria—Trientje, b. Apr. 5—Apr. 26.

1802

HOPPER, Hendrik D. and Esther—Tyna, b. Jan. 10—Feb. 14.

DEMAREST, Barend and Susannah—Trientje, b. July 10—Aug. 1.
Wit: Samuel & Catriena Deryea.

HOPPER, Michael and Ginny—Tetje, b. Oct. 25—Nov. 24.
Wit: John & Tetje Campbell.

PULIS, Pieter and Nancy—Trientje, b. Nov. 6—Nov. 28.

TERHUNE, Albert and Antje—Thomas, b. Nov. 5—Dec. 5.

1803

HOPPER, Henry and Annatje—Thomas, b. Mar. 29—Apr. 24.

VANDERVOORT, Cornelius and Maria—Thomas, b. Apr. 27, 1802—June 19.

DEBOW, Andries and Tyne—Tyne, b. Sep. 3, 1801—June 20.

1804

VANDIEN, Cornelius and Jenny— ——jne, b. July 28—Sep. 2.

TERHUNE, Harmen and Rachel—Trientje, b. Nov. 28—Dec. 19.

1806

BUSH, Lodewyk and Magdalen—Trientje, b. Feb. 6—Mar. 16.

CROUTER, James and Margaret—Trientje, b. Aug. 15—Sep. 14.

1807

WORTENDYK, Jacob and Elisabeth—Titje, b. Mar. 16—Apr. 19.

CONKLIN, Isaak and Jannetje—Theodorus, b. July 19—Aug. 30.
Wit: Theodorus Polhemus.

FORSHUR, David and Maria—Trientje, b. Sep. 29—Oct. 18.
Wit: William & Catriena Halderom.

1808

HOPPER, Michael and Jannetje—Trientje, b. Oct. 10—Oct. 23.

ECKERSON, Thomas and Polly—Thomas, b. Sep. 27—Nov. 6.

TERHUNE, Albert G. and Martyntje—Trientje, b. Mar. 13—Apr. 16.

ECKERSON, Carl and Angonietje—Thomas, b. June 1—June 25.

STOR, Abraham P. and Antje—Tyne, b. Sep. 25—Oct. 22.

1811

BLANCH, Thomas and Elisabeth—Thomas Elias, b. Nov. 12, —— —Jan. 20

PETERSON, Nicholas and Lena—Thomas, b. Feb. 25—Mar. 24.

VAN RYPEN, Frederik and Maria—Thomas, b. Aug. 2—Sep. 22.

1812

VAN EMBURGH, Hendrik and Polly—Trientje, b. Jan. 31—Mar. 5.

HOPPER, Garret H. and Polly—Thomas, b. Feb. 29—Mar. 30.

RATAN, Abraham and Lydea—Trientje, b. Feb. 5—May 17.

1815

ZABRISKIE, Andrew I. and Polly—Thomas, b. Dec. 31, 1814—Jan. 1.
  Wit: Hester Van Buskirk.

SNYDER, George T. and Charity—Thomas, b. Dec. 28, 1814—Feb. 5.

HOPPER, Albert G. and Polly—Tyna, b. July 10—Aug. 18.

1816

SNYDER, Richard and Ally—Thomas, b. Feb. 24—Apr. 7.

1817

ZABRISKIE, Andrew J. and Polly—Thomas Buskirk, b. Sep. 13—Oct. 5.

1819

MYERS, John and Betsy—Thomas, b. Dec. 23, 1818—Feb. 7.

McGRAFF, Andrew and Catharine—Tyna, b. Aug. 5, 1818—Sep. 19.

1820

MYRES, John and Betsy—Tyna, b. Nov. 24—Dec. 31.

1821

VANDIEN, Casparus and Polly—Thomas, b. Mar. 21—July 29.

1824

BANTA, Garrit D. and Harriet—Thomas, b. Dec. 25, 1823—Jan. 10.

1825

BRICKELL, George and Letty—Thomas, b. Sep. 1—Oct. 2.

1826

ZABRISKIE, Stephen J. and Jane—Thomas Buskirk, b. Nov. 15—Dec. 23.

1827

COOPER, Cornelius T. and Maria—Thomas, b. Feb. 12—Mar. 11.

1829

VANDERBEEK, Paul P. and Hannah—Tyna, b. Oct. 11, 1828—Jan. 23.

1834

ACKERMAN, John J. and Jane—Theodorus, b. Oct. 5—Nov. 2.

1835
VANDERBEEK, Jerry C. and Ann—Thomas, b. Aug. 26—Oct. 4.

"V"

1763
DUMARE, Petrus S. and Feytje—Vroutje—Oct. 16.
    Wit: David S. & Jennie Dumare.

1771
GERRITSE, Gerrebrand and Leentje—Vroutje—Jan. 1.
    Wit: Jacob & Vroutje Van Winkel.

1782
VAN RYPE, Gerrit—Vredrik, b. Mar. 8—Apr. 7.
    Wit: Harme Van Rype, Jr. & wife.

1793
DEMAREST, Daniel and Maria—Vroutje, b. July 1—Oct. 20.

1795
DEMAREST, Symen and Maria—Vroutje, b. Dec. 10, 1794 (?)—Jan. 11.
    Wit: Frederik & Vroutje Woertendyk.

"W"

1751
BOGERT, Cornelis J. and Lena—Willemtie—Jan. 1.
    Wit: Albert & Mechtel Bogerd.
MORE, Jeremiah and Lisabeth—Wilms—Apr. 7.
    Wit: Hannes & Marytje Van Blerkom.

1753
VAN VOORHEES, Jan and Lea—Willem—Dec. 30.
    Wit: Hannes & Marytje Van Blerkom.

1756
VAN SCHYVEN, Hannes and Vroutje—Willem—May 9.
    Wit: Albert & Rachel Ackerman.

1757
BANTA, Jacob W. and Lena—Wiert—Aug. 4.
    Wit: Wiert & Geertrui Banta.

1758
SYOURT, Willem and Trientje—Willem—Oct. 22.
    Wit: Arie & Lisabeth Laroi.

1759
ZABRISKE, Jacob J. and Aaltje—Wyntje—June 10.
    Wit: Jacob H. & Wyntje Zabriske.

1761
MILLS, Thomas and Maaike—Willem—Mar. 29.
    Wit: Jurry & Marietje Westervelt.

1762
LANE, Henry and Betsie—Willem Henry—Aug. 1.
    Wit: Gerrit & Elsje Hoppe.

1765
TERHUYN, Dirk and Lea—Wyntje—Nov. 10.
    Wit: Jacob H. & Wyntje Zabriskie.

1766

BONGAERT, Lucas and Rachel—Willempje—Mar. 2.
Wit: Cobus & Willempje Rutan.

1767

ZABRISKE, Jacob H. and Wyntje—Wyntje—Mar. 22.
Wit: Hendrik & Wyntje Hoppe.

BOGGS, Thomas and Trientje—Willem—Dec. 23.

1768

TERHUYN, Abram A. and Marytje—Wyntje—Mar. 6.
Wit: Albert A. & Betje Terhuyn.

ZABRISKE, Jacob H. and Wyntje—Wyntje—Nov. 6.
Wit: Hendrik & Wyntje Hoppe.

1789

DOBBS, William and Rachel—Walterus—May 15.
Wit: Abram W. & Grietje Rutan.

1770

HOPPE, Jan W. and Annatje—Willem, b. Jan. 26—Apr. 15.
Wit: Willem & Antje Hoppe.

1771

BOGERT, Cornelis A. and Sietsje—Willempje—Aug. 4.
Wit: Albert R. & Willempje Romyne.

1772

HOMS, Jan, Jr. and Debra—Wyntje—June 28.
Wit: Wyntje Homs.

1773

VERSIEUR, Hannes and Lena—Willem, b. Feb. 15—Mar. 21.
Wit: Willem & Lisabeth Versieur.

VAN BLARCOM, Isaac and Sara—Willem—May 16.
Wit: Douglas & Geesje Carns.

ACKERMAN, Abram and Marytje—Wyntje—Sep. 23.
Wit: Jan J. & Aaltje Hoppe.

LAROI, Hannes and Grietje—Willem—Oct. 10.
Wit: Willem & Margriet Jenkins.

1774

CLEA, Christiaan and Maria—Wilhelm, b. Dec. 4, 1773—June 28.

HOPPE, Abram H. and Antje—Wyntje—July 10.
Wit: Abram & Marytje Ackerman.

1778

HOPPE, Abram H. and Antje—Wyntje—Nov. 1.
Wit: Abram & Marytje Ackerman.

1781

BERTOLF, Crynus and Susanna—Wybrecht, b. May 16—June 3.
Wit: Samuel & Trientje Bertolf.

SHURTE, Isaak and Margriet—Willem—Apr. 7.
Wit: Albert & Trientje Zabriske.

1782

DE PEYSTER, Abram—Willem Abram—Sep. 5.

1785

ACKERMAN, Abram G.—Willem—Apr. 10.
 Wit: Jacobus Ackerman; Lea Dods.
VANHORN, Jacobus and Lea—William, b. Aug. 1—Oct. 2.

1786

TANNING, or TANNARY, Pieter—William—Feb. 26.
DEE, Salomon and Sally—William, b. Aug. 14—Oct. 1.
 Wit: John & Maria More.

1787

BELL, William and Rachel—William Swan, b. Dec. 27, 1786—Jan. 28.
VALENTYN, Jacob and Elisabeth—William, b. Dec. 26.
 Wit: Wiert & Metje Valentyn.
HARING, Cornelis A. and Antje—Willem, b. Feb. 27—Mar. 25.
HOPPE, Gerrit W. and Margrietje—William, b. Nov. 15—Dec. 25.
 Wit: Andreas W. & Maria Hoppe.

1788

POST, Frederik and Annatje—Wyntje, b. Sep. 5—Dec. 21.
 Wit: John & Wyntje Fesyeur.

1789

V. D. BEEK, Johannis and Abigail—Wyntje, b. Feb. 14—Mar. 8.
 Wit: Thomas & Maria Van Boskerk.
HOPPE, Hendrik and Aaltje—Wyntje, b. Mar. 16—Apr. 4.
 Wit: Johannis & Abigail Vanderbeek.

1790

CAIRNS, David and Elisabeth—William—Mar. 14.

1791

ZABRISKA, Hendrik and Maria—Wyntje—Sep. 29.
 Wit: Jan & Elisabeth Zabriska.

1792

PULISFELT, Coenraad and Elisabeth—William, b. Oct. 3—Nov. 11.
 Wit: Abraham & Catriena Pulisfelt.

1793

POST, Pieter and Rachel—Wyntje, b. Dec. 4, 1792—Feb. 10.
ROUW, Phillip and Maria—William, b. Feb. 22—Mar. 10.
BOSCH, Samuel and Lena—Wybrech, b. July 30—Aug. 18.
 Wit: Thomas & Esther Stagg.
FESYEUR, Cornelius and Jannetje—William, b. Aug. 11—Sep. 8.
 Wit: David & Polly Fesyeur.

1794

VALENTYN, David and Rachel—William, b. Mar. 3—Apr. 20.
 Wit: William Eckhart and Maria Valentyn.
VAN ZYL, Abraham and Rachel—William, b. Mar. 30—Apr. 20.
 Wit: Johannis Van Zyl and Syntje Ackerman.
WINTER, Lewis and Lena—William, b. June 23—Sep. 14.
GOETSCHIUS, Piatus and Catriena—William, b. Sep. 21—Oct. 19.
 Wit: Garret & Geertje Ackerman.
FESYEUR, David and Maria—William, b. Nov. 3—Nov. 16.

1795

WINTER, John and Hendrikje—William, b. Apr. 30—June 14.
Wit: Cornelis & Hattie Degrauw.

FRERIKSE, Hendrik and Margrietje—William, b. Aug. 20—Oct. 18.
Wit: William & Sally Pecker.

1797

DEREST, Lieshon and Elisabeth—Willem and Christina (twins), b. Mar.
24—Apr. 17.
Wit: Salomon & Sally Dee.

FERGUSON, Samuel and Jannetje—William, b. Aug. 16—Nov. 26.

1798

CUYPER, Geerit and Geertrui—Willemyntje, b. Oct. 27—Dec. 9.

ROTAN, Abraham and Lydia—Willempje, b. Nov. 8—Dec. 9.
Wit: Willempje Rotan.

1800

ECKERSON, Cornelius and Catriena—William, b. May 7, 1799—Mar. 30.

WRIGHT, Albert and Annatje—William, b. Apr. 16—May 18.

1801

WRIGHT, John and Abigail—William, b. Feb. 9—June 21.

TERHUNE, Albert and Leah—Wyntje, b. June 23—July 21.
Wit: Henry & Aaltje Hopper.

CAMPBELL, William and Jannitje—William, b. Oct. 16—Nov. 22.

MORE, John and Jennie—William, b. Oct. 31—Nov. 22.

1802

JURRY, John and Elisabeth—William, b. Feb. 14—Mar. 7.

1804

HIDDEN, Elisabeth—William, b. Aug. 6, 1803—Feb. 26.

WILLIAMS, John and Annatje—William, b. July 4—Sep. 6.

1805

ZABRISKIE, Jacob H. and Antje—William, b. Jan. 6—Jan. 27.

CAMPBELL, William and Jannetje—William, b. Feb. 11—Mar. 6.

DUREST, Lison and Elisabeth—William, b. Jan. 5—Mar. 17.

1806

FORSHUER, Abram and Elisabeth—William, b. Oct. 29—Dec. 18.

1807

POST, John and Elisabeth—Wyntje, b. Oct. 17—Nov. 15.

1811

THOMPSON, James and Sarah—John, b. Feb. 16—May 19.

1827

BOGERT, William and Betsy—William, b. Oct. 29, 1826—Jan. 28.

1833

BOGART, John C. and Jennet—William Pell, b. Feb. 5—Mar. 24.

1834

ZABRISKIE, Cornelius J. and Jane—William, b. July 2—Aug. 31.

HORSBROOK, Augustus and Jane—Wilhelmus Eltinge, b. July 2—Sep. 28.

1840

TERHUNE, Henry Z. and Maria—William, b. Aug. 10—Oct. 18.

1841

ZABRISKIE, John T. and Anne—William, b. Mar. 22—May 16.

1819

BANTA, John W. and Maria—Wiert, b. Oct. 7,—Nov. 14.

1820

VANDERBEEK, James J. and Peggy—William, b. July 11—Aug. 20.

VAN DALSON, John and Jane—William, b. Aug. 23—Sep. 17.

1822

Row, Peter, Jr. and Jane—William, b. Dec. 10, 1821—Mar. 10.

1824

CLEARWATER, Frederik and Hatty—William Rathbone, b. May 30—July 3.

1843

PERRY, Daniel D. and Sally—William Henry, b. June 6—Aug. 13.

ℐℰ ℐℰ ℐℰ ℐℰ

LIST OF MEMBERS, 1799

List of Members found by Rev. Wilhelmus Eltinge, at the time of his family-visitation through the Congregation of Paramus about May 1, 1799.

JACOB ZABRISKIE and wife Jannetje.
HARMEN LUTKENS and wife Antje.
ALBERT ZABRISKIE and wife Metje.
ANTJE ZABRISKIE, widow of Jacob.
WYNTJE ZABRISKIE.
GARRET HOPPER.
JOHN I. ZABRISKIE and wife Leah.
JOST BOGERT and wife Maria.
CHRISTIAN ZABRISKIE and wife Maria.
ANDRIES ZABRISKIE and wife Maria.
CHRISTIAN A. ZABRISKIE and wife Maria.
JOHANNIS H. GARRISON and wife Maria.
CASPARIS BOGERT and wife Jannitje.
MARIA ZABRISKIE, widow of Hendrick.
JANNITJE NAGEL, widow of Barend.
JACOB ZABRISKIE and wife Helena.
LIDEA KOGH, wife of Casparus.
SUSANNA VAN BERCUM, widow of Peter.
JANNETJE TERHUNE, widow of Stephen.
WYNTJE ZABRISKIE, widow of Jacob H.
ALBERT I. ZABRISKIE and wife Maria.
ABRAHAM ZABRISKIE and wife Maria.
HENDRICK ZABRISKIE.
ABRAHAM WESTERVELT and wife Antje.
JOHANNIS WESTERVELT and wife Annatje.
GARRET ACKERMAN and wife Rachel.
ELSHE HOPPER, widow of Garret.
SAMUEL BANTA and wife Elisabeth.
PETRUS DEMAREST and wife Maatje.
ABRAHAM HOPPER and wife Antje.
GARRET I. HOPPER and wife Maria.
MARIA TERHUNE, wife of Abraham.
STEPHEN BOGERT and wife Maria.
ABRAHAM RUTAN and Margrietje.
ALBERT A. TERHUNE and wife Aaltje.
HENRY A. TERHUNE and wife Rachel.

DAVID G. ACKERMAN and wife Aaltje.
CORNELIUS VAN DIEN.
HILLEGOND VAN DER BEEK.
JOHANNIS VAN DER BEEK and wife Abigail.
PETER HOPPER and wife Annatje.
JOHN R. BERDAN and wife Hendrickie.
JACOMYNTJE ACKERMAN, widow of David.
ABRAHAM QUACKENBUSH.
THEODORUS POLHEMUS and wife Elisabeth.
JACOBUS B. DEMAREST and wife Jannitje.
HENDRICK STORM and wife Cornelia.
CASPARUS WESTERVELT and wife Rachel.
CORNELIUS DEMAREST and wife Maria.
LAWRANCE TOERS and wife Elisabeth.
MARIA VAN DER BEEK, widow of Jusia (or Juria).
ANNATJE VAN DER BEEK, widow of Paulus.
JACOBUS BOGERT and wife Cornelia.
JOHN PULISFELT and wife Elisabeth.
ANTIE ACKERMAN, wife of Albert I.
BENJAMIN ZABRISKIE and wife Annatje.
DANIEL WESTERVELT and wife Elisabeth.
JACOB BANTA and wife Hester.
JOHN BANTA and wife Vrouwtje.
JOHN ZABRISKIE and wife Jacomyntje.
HENDRICK BANTA.
CHRISTIAN BLAUVELT and wife Cathalyntje.
EDWARD ECKERSON and wife Caty.
WILLEMPIE RUTAN, widow of Jacobus.
HENDRICK H. STORM and wife Aaltje.
JOHANNES G. ACKERMAN and wife Elisabeth.
GARRIT VAN RYPER and wife Abigail.
CORNELIUS WORTENDIKE and wife Sophia.
RYNA (?) WORTENDIKE.
BAREND FERSHUIR and wife Francintje.
CATHARINA FERSHUIR, wife of ———.
NICHOLAS HULDROM and wife Helena.
NICHOLAS PETERSON and wife Maria.
ANDRIES HOPPER and wife Elisabeth.
HENDRICK HOPPER and wife Aaltje.
ABRAHAM I. HOPPER and Geertie.
ELISA'TH HOPPER, widow of John.
NICAUSIE HOPPER and wife Maria.
STEPHEN HOPPER and wife Geertie.
ANDRIES DE BAUN and wife Jannitje.

HARMAN VAN RYPEN and wife Maria.

JOHN G. ACKERMAN and wife Maria.

GEERTIE VAN BLERCOM, wife of David.

DAVID ACKERMAN, JR., and wife Jannitje.

ABRAHAM DEBAUN and wife Leah.

JOHN QUACKINBUSH and wife Annatie.

JOHN JANSEN and wife Sophia.

THOMAS D. ECKERSEN and wife Susanna.

DAVID ECKERSEN and wife Angenitie.

THOMAS I. ECKERSEN and wife Maria.

JACOB ECKERSEN and wife Annatie.

MARIA LABACH.

THOMAS ECKERSON and wife Cornelia.

LEAH TERHUNE, widow of Dirk.

ALBERT TERHUNE and wife Elisabeth.

JOHN TERHUNE and wife Catharina.

HENRY TERHUNE and wife Jannitje.

DAVID ACKERMAN and wife Antje.

DAVID HOPPER and wife Rachel.

GRAVESTONE RECORDS FROM PARAMUS
REFORMED DUTCH CHURCH YARD

COPIED OCTOBER 12, 1931

The rows are here numbered from east to west, and the stones in each row read from south to north. "Intermediate rows" are short rows interspersed at irregular intervals between the longer rows, and occur mostly in the oldest part of the yard. In this oldest section are a large number of "home-made" markers roughly shaped and, in many instances, bearing crudely cut initials, monograms, or otherwise abbreviated inscriptions. These latter have been interpreted as closely as modern type will permit. Those without identifying marks are here designated "rough markers." On some of the older stones the capital "I" occurs with a cross mark through the middle. This letter was frequently employed by the Dutch as an equivalent to the English "J," as well as "I," and where occurring in the following records has been set in italics, thus: *I*. In the following arrangement surnames have been placed first. Inscriptions quoted in full are preceded where possible by the surname. Where the surname is obscure a dash is used. The sign / separates the lines of the original inscriptions.

About twenty years ago the late Everett L. Zabriskie of Ridgewood copied most of the stones in this yard. This copy, made available to the public through the kindness of Mrs. Zabriskie, has been of assistance in compiling this record, especially in the case of the following stones now illegible or missing, Nos. 20, 37, 45, 171, 367, 369, 398, 400 and 510. At the time of making his copy Mr. Zabriskie noted that the inscriptions were gone from five stones, and that 124 field stones had no inscriptions.

Row 1

1. Ackerman, Alley Terhune, wife of David, d. May 23, 1837, aged 82.1.10.
2. Ackerman, David, d. July 8, 1831, aged 87.2.0.
3. Oblenis, Martha Mode Ackerman, wife of Peter, d. Sept. 20, 1831, in 29th year.
4. Ackerman, Garret I., b. July 14, 1777, d. Jan. 19, 1852, aged 74.6.5.
5. Ackerman, Maria Post, wife of Garret I., d. Nov. 7, 1839, aged 59 years.
6. Banta, Jacob, d. Aug. 28, 1831, aged 69.10.21.
7. Banta, Jan. I., b. July 5, 1754, d. Sept. 11, 1807, aged 53.2.6.
8. Banta, Hester Hopper, wife of Jacob, d. March 3, 1843, aged 71.8.12.
9. Ackerman, Garret, d. Nov. 23, 1808, aged 72.2.24.
10. Ackerman. Anny Van Horn, "the wifie of D. AM. departed life 13 of Decmber 1813 aged 79 years and 5 month".
11. Ackerman, Thomas D., d. Jan. 1, 1806, aged 0.2.23.

12. Ackerman, Abram J., b. March 8, 1793, d. Oct. 24, 1807, aged 14.7.16.
13. Demarest, Cornelius, d. June 11, 1813, aged 91.3.23.
14. Demarest, Maria Ackerman, wife of Cornelius, d. Sept. 18, 1803, aged 81.7.0.
15. Rall, Ursula Vanderbeck, wife of John, d. Sept. 2, 1828, aged 27.9.4; also their daughter Hannah Jane, d. Dec. 13 (or 18), 1832, aged 7.7.14.
16. Vanderbeek. Anno / 1790 / den 15 Desember / is geboren Angnietye / Vanderbeek en sy is / gestorven October / 18 in het yaar 1793.
17. Vanderbeek. *I* H Y / 1794 y 19 / IS GB *I*VDB / EN *I*S GS *I* 1793 / MEY 3.
18. Zabriskie. Anno 1793 / Augustus 23 / is R Z / gestorven.

Row 2

19. Storms, Conradus, d. Oct. 13, 1844, aged 94.6.17; also Mary Storms, aged 23.2.26.
20. [Storms, Maria Ackerman, wife of Coenrades, d. Dec. 22, 1818, aged 72 years.]   Face of stone split off and inscription entirely gone, 1931; supplied from copy by E. L. Z.
21. Rutan, Abraham, d. March 15, 1822, aged 82.11.23.
22. Rutan, Margaret Rutan, wife of Abraham, d. June 7, 1825, aged 84.5.22.
23. Ackerman, Garret G., d. Jan. 28, 1826, aged 70.0.13.
24. ———. Inscription split off, 1931.
25. Ackerman, Johannes, d. Oct. 4, 1828, aged 75.4.1.
26. Ackerman, John G., d. Aug. 13, 1829, aged 60.11.27.
27. Ackerman, Maria, wife of John G., d. Dec. 1, 1857, aged 85.1.15.
28. Zabreski. 1777 / den 28 Agustus is / Steven A. Zabreski / overleden.
29. ———. Rough marker.
30. B———. 1784 / S B / March 24.
31. ———. Rough marker.
32. ———. 88 11 VAN / APRIL 1782.
33. Ackerman. 1771 (?) 20 Aug (?) / is Jannitye Acker / man overleden. (Stone broken through first line of inscription).
34. Demarest ?. C S D M R. (Cornelius Demarest ?)
35. Banta, Charity Mariah, daughter of Dr. Garret, d. Oct. 21, 1827, aged 0.7.14.
36. Terhune, Harriot, d. Oct. 5, 1793, aged 3.10.0.
37. [Ackerman, John and Henry, sons of John; John d. Sept. 29, 1819, aged 5.3.9; Henry d. Oct. 3, 1819, aged 2.1.4]   Face of stone split off and inscription entirely gone, 1931; supplied from copy by E. L. Z.
38. Ackerman, Annetta, wife of James W., d. Feb. 27, 1851, aged 80.3.0.
39. Ackerman, James W., d. June 27, 1829, aged 68.3.0.
40. Demarest, John, d. Feb. 3, 1830, aged 39.13.

Row 3

41. ———. Inscription split off, 1931.
42. Westervelt. 1809 / July de 8se is overle / den / Daniel Westervelt / geboren de 16d Octo / ber 1759 oudt zynde /49 yaer 8 maenden / en 22 dagen.

43. Westervelt, Cattelyntye Haring, wife of Peter, b. May 3, 1732, d. Feb. 29, 1820, aged 87.9.29.
44. Westervelt, Peter, b. April 4, 1732, d. May 2, 1819, aged 87.0.29.
45. Westervelt, Agnes, daughter of ――――, d. Oct. 8, [1823], aged 3.[6].26. (Stone broken, 1931, figures in brackets from copy by E. L. Z.
46. Westervelt, Sarah Elizabeth, daughter of Peter and Matilda, d. March 30, aged 0.3.1. (No year given).
47. Westervelt, Adeline Smith, wife of Henry, d. Dec. 4, 1809, aged 36.3.18.
48. Westervelt, Daniel, son of Henry and Adeline, d. Feb. 18, 1832, aged 22.6.15.
49. Earle, Edward, d. Feb. 14, 1832, aged 83 years.
50. Earle, Abigail, d. Oct. 22, 1832, aged 70.10.18.
51. Earle, John, d. Oct. 22, 1834, aged 40.6.7.
52. H――――. Anna 1778 / is M H Overleden / April de 8.
53. ――――. Rough marker.
54. Storm ?. 16 I 1761 / A S T O M / S T B 23 D / 1777.
55. Storm ?. A S / 2 D V MEI / 1793.
56. Zabriska. Anno 1798 Den 21 Dag / Iuni is Overleden / Albert I. Zabriska.

Row 4 (Intermediate)

57 and 58. Two rough markers.
59. H――――. 1777 / D H + H.
60 to 65. Six rough markers.
66. Ackerman. Bregye / Ackerman / is overleden / den 3 dag Octr. / 1792.
67. Banta. 1794 / Octr. 30 is / Maregrietye Banta / Overleden Out 2 / Jaer en 9 Dagen.

Row 5

68. Durie, Charity Westervelt, wife of David, d. Aug. 23, 1832, aged 56.6.11.
69. Westervelt, Caspares, d. Nov. 15, 1810, in 76th year. (D. A. R. Marker).
70. Westervelt, Rachel Zabriskie, wife of Casparus, d. Dec. 14, 1829, aged 83.5.16.
71. Triphagen, Martinte Westervelt, wife of William, d. May 10, 1831, aged 67.0.29.
72. Banta, Maria, daughter of Jacob M. (or H.), d. Sept. 11, 1838, aged 20.0.11.
73. Westervelt, John C., b. April 10, 1760, d. Feb. 23, 1839, aged 78.10.13.
74. Westervelt, Agnes Van Derbeck, wife of John C., d. Sept. 16, 1840, aged 75.0.1.
75. Westervelt, Matilda, wife of Peter A., d. Feb. 13, 1843, aged 50.2.4.
76. Westervelt, Peter A., d. Sept. 15, 1878, aged 82.0.26.
77. ――――. Rough marker.
78. Hoppe. 1777 / den 22 Siptember is / Elizabeth A. Hoppe / Overleden.
79. ――――. Rough marker.

80. H——. AO / 1777 AG 12 / is *I* H̄ overleden.
81. H——. 1777 / den 1 Agustus / is Elisabeth / hoppe overleden.
82. ——. Rough marker.
83. Z——. Anno / 1791 / September / Den 19 is / N Z / gestorven.
84. Van Dien, Marie Bogert, wife of Thomas, d. March 24, 1793, aged 48.4.0.
85. Zabriskie. 1793 den 12 / Augustus is / Jan A. Zabriskie / overleden.

Row 6

86. Storms. Storms, Caty Ann, daughter of Coenradous and Hetty, d. Sept. 26, 1832, aged 3.4.26.
87. Ackerman, Alley, daughter of Albert, d. Aug. 9, 1810, aged 4.2.17.
88. H——. 1764, H. H.
89. ——. Rough marker.
90. M——. 1767 / *I* 9 A M.
91. ——. Rough marker.
92. S——. A S 1777.
93. Zabriske. 1785 / Sip 1 (or 7) is Merÿa / Zabriske Overlede.
94. Zabriske. 1787 / den 14 Mey / is lisabeth / Zabriske over.
95. Van Der Beek. Ano 1785 / 29 Septem / A V D B.
96. Zabriske. 1788 / den 4 November / is Geesÿe Zabris / ke Overleden.
97. ——. Rough marker.
98. Van D——. Anno 1793 / Septem is / gestorven / T V D.

Row 7

99. Hopper. 1819 / yune de 9d is overleden / Elisabeth Ackerman / Huysvrouw van de Over / ledene Andreas J. Hopper / Geboren de 10d maart 1750 / out 69 yaren 2 Maenden / en 30 Dagen.
100. Ackerman, David G., son of Garret D., d. Sept. 27, 1823, aged 20 years.
101. Ackerman, Charity, wife of Garret D., d. Aug. 3, 1848, aged 72.10.29.
102. Ackerman, Garret D., d. June 26, 1860, aged 85.9.26.
103. Ackerman, Margaret Holdrum, wife of Abraham P., d. Nov. 30, 1849, aged 69.8.5.
104. Ackerman, Abraham P., d. May 20, 1827, aged 49.9.0.
105. Ackerman, Peter, d. March 21, 1830, aged 73.10.0.
106. Ackerman, Catharine Perry, wife of Peter, d. March 25, 1842, in 89th year.
107 to 109. ——. Three rough markers.

Row 8 (Intermediate)

110 to 116. ——. Seven rough markers.
117. H——. Ano 1778 / My DE 24 / IS L (or C) H in / D. H. O. S. P.
118 and 119. ——. Two rough markers.
120. S——. Actober / 12 S S 1785.

121. V——. N. V. / IOHNUARY / 12 1786.
122. Van B——. I V B / 1793.
123. M——. 1788 / 12 Fabruary / C M. (The M possibly V N).

Row 9

124. Ackerman. 1797 / IOHN + A / CKERMAN + OV.
125 and 126. ——. Two rough markers.
127. Ackerman, Henry P., son of Peter P. and Ellen, d. Nov. 13, 1855, aged 24.3.27.
128. Ackerman, Hester Storms, daughter of Peter P. and Ellen, d. Dec. 17, 1846, aged 10 months.
129. Banta, Jacob G., d. June 4, 1862, aged 54 years; Williampe Ackerman, his wife, d. Aug. 14, 1844, aged 29.7.9.
130. Westervelt, Hannah Ackerman, wife of Peter A., d. May 14, 1845, aged 44.4.6.
131. Westervelt, Elizabeth Ackerman, wife of Peter A., d. July 15, 1881, aged 79.3.8.
132. Ackerman, John Henry, son of William and Catharine, d. April 13, 1852, aged 2.8.15.
133. Ackerman, Peter A., d. March 5, 1864, aged 58.9.8.
134 to 137. ——. Four rough markers.
138. V——. M V 15 M I 1790.

Row 10 (Intermediate)

139. H——. 1760 / H. H R H. (Probably two individuals).
140. Ackerman. 1791 / den 25 ÿuly / Abraham I / Ackerman ove / overleden.
141. H——. 1760 / A H.
142. Terhune, Rachel Hopper, wife of Henry A., d. Sept. 29, 1830, aged 74.4.9.
143. H——. H. T. H.
144. Hopper. het 25 Juny 1768 / maregrit van bussen / het wiyf van / gerret hopper 31 out.
145. Hoppe. 16 IUNE / 1772 / LEA HOPPE.
146. Hopper. Anno 1780 / Gerrit Hopper / is in den Heer / ont slaapen / den 24 v. Aprel.
147. ——. Rough marker.
148. Hoppe. 1786 April 15 / is Gerrit Hoppe / Overleden.
149. Hoppe. 1786 den 4 / November is / Jan Hoppe over.
150. Hoppe. 1787 / den 2 Februari / is derrick hoppe / overleden.
151. Z——. Anno / 1791 / Augustus / De 10 is / M Z / gestorven.
152. Zabriskie, John, d. March 16, 1820, aged 78.5.24.

Row 11

153. Zabriskie, Mary, d. Sept. 23, 1826, aged 24.6.14.
154. Zabriskie, Nicklas, d. May 24, 1823, aged 56.6.2.
155. Zabriskie, Lavinia, wife of Nicholas J., d. Dec. 10, 1834, aged 66.9.8.
156. Zabriskie, John, son of Nicholas and Lavinia, d. Jan. 12, 1801, aged 4.1.27.
157 to 168. ——. Twelve rough markers.

Row 12

169. Vanderbeek ?. 1796 S 21 / P V D B.
170. ——. Rough marker.
171. [Vanderbeek, Sarah Ackerman, wife of Abraham, d Jan. 26, 1827, aged 87.7.7.] Supplied from copy by E. Z.; stone not found, 1931.
172. Van Derbeak, Abraham, b. July 17, 1732, d. April 26, 1817, aged 84.9.0.
173. Van Derbeck, John, d. Dec. 27, 1830, aged 69.1.4.
174. to 179. ——. Six rough markers.
180. ——. 1760 / I A M. (Possibly an Ackerman stone. See No. 10 and No. 217 where Ackerman is abbreviated to AM.)
181 and 182. ——. Two rough markers.
183. Van H——. *I* N V H / 1760 (or 1766).
184 and 185. ——. Two rough markers.
186. ——. 1776 / A H.
187. ——. Rough marker.
188. A——. M A.
189. ——. Rough marker.
190. Van B——. A V B 2 / A P R / 1789.
191. ——. Rough marker.
192. Z——. H. Z., June 6, 1789.
193. ——. Rough marker.
194. Z——. C (or L) Z, Aug. 30, 1795.

Row 13

195. ——. Rough marker.
196. Van Der Beek. ANNO + 1718 / DEN + 17 VAN MEY / IS + GEBOREN + POULIS + VAN DER BEEK / EN HY IS OVERLEDEN / IN HET YAAR + 1795 / DEN + 10 + MAART.
197. Vander Beek. ANNO 1730 DEN + 6 D + APRIL IS / GEBOREN + YURRI + VANDER / BEEK + EN HY IS + OVLEDEN / NOVEMBER DEN 7 + D 1794.
198. Stevens, Polly Ackerman, wife of Abraham, d. Feb. 8, 1816, aged 22.11.23.
199. Zabriskie, Maria Jane, daughter of John and Sally, d. June 28, 1831, aged 0.3.20.
200. Ackerman, Jane, daughter of Abram and Lavinia, b. June 2, 1825, d. Aug. 26, 1835.
201. Ackerman, Abraham, d. Sept. 19, 1844, aged 32.0.4.
202. Westervelt, Henry, son of John P. and Sarah, d. Aug. 17, 1848, aged 1.6.9.
203. Westervelt, Albert P, d. July 30, 1845, aged 79.3.0.
204. Westervelt, Elizabeth, widow of Albert P., d. July 2, 1863, aged 87.2.15.
205. Westervelt, Albert P., Jr., d. May 14, 1858, aged 31.9.14. (Verse shows he left wife and child.)
206 to 213. Eight rough markers.
214. Stek. 1778 / DEN + 4 + MERT / IS Lena Stek + / overleden.
215. Ackerman. ANNO 1781 / DEN 5 DAG VAN / MERTH *IS* OVER / LEEDEN MARIA / ACKERMAN.
216. ——. 1787 / MAY 29 / RACHEL P. HO / OVARLADEEN.
217. Ackerman. ANNO 1788 D[EN   ] / DAG IANUARE I[S] / ANTIE ACKERMAN / DEN DOCHTER VAN / A. A. M.

218. Ackerman. ANNO 1789 / DEN.25.DAG.OC / TOBER.IS.ABRA / HAM.G. ACKERMAN / OVERLEEDEN.
219. Van Buskirk, Wynte, wife of John, b. Aug. 26, 1773, d. Jan. 24, 1799.

Row 14 (Intermediate)

220 to 226. ———. Seven rough markers.
227. Van Buskirk ?. Anno 1776 / DEN 2 DAG A / GUST IS *IN.D.H.* / S.P.A.*I*.V. BK.
228 to 232. ———. Five rough markers.
233. Chapman, John Warren, son of Dr. George Warren and Christiana, d. Nov. 11, 1790, aged 0.11.26.
234 and 235. ———. Two rough markers.
236. Westervelt, John S., d. Dec. 29, 1801, aged 23 days.
237. ———. Rough marker.

Row 15

238. Van Dien, Elizabeth, daughter of Richard and Eleanor, d. Sept. 27, 1832, aged 4.7.15.
239. Fox, Jane Bogert, wife of John, d. July 12, 1835, aged 68.2.4.
240. Ackerman, Sarah Jane Zabriskie, wife of William M. K., d. Oct. 28, 1852, aged 18.2.2.
241. Zabriskie, John, son of John and Sally, d. Sept. 4, 1838, aged 1.11.25.
242. Zabriskie, John I., d. Aug. 20, 1839, aged 31.4.22; Sarah Stevens, his wife, d. Nov. 16, 1869, aged 56.5.0; their daughter Maria Jane, d. June 28, 1831, aged 0.3.20. (All on one monument).
243 to 253. ———. Eleven rough markers.
254. Ackerman ?. 1764 / I A M.
255. H———. AO 1765 SEP 4 / A T H.
256. H———. [AN]NO 1768 NO / VEM 15 / A T H.
257 and 258. ———. Two rough markers.

Row 16 (Intermediate)

259 to 263. ———. Five rough markers.
264. H———. *I I H*, DYED / FEBRUARY 19 [   ] / G *I* H DYED APRIL / THE 10 ANNA DOMNI 1789. Stone broken as indicated by brackets. Evidently two inscriptions.
265. Oldis. BENJAMIN / OLDIS BORN 1710 / AND DIED NOVEMBER / 11 1791.
266. ———. Rough marker.
267. H———. Anno 1795 / September / 14 is / A T H / gestorven.
268. ———. Rough marker.
269. Terhune, Albert, d. Nov. 18, 1806, aged 51.1.20.

Row 17 (First behind church)

270. Westervelt, John I, d. Aug. 8, 1857, aged 74.7.19.
271. Westervelt, Hester Van Dien, wife of John I., d. Aug. 28, 1841, aged 51.5.21.
272. Zabriskie, Sarah Van Dien, wife of Abraham H., d. Feb. 5, 1852, aged 64.5.25.
273. Van Dien, Richard A., d. April 7, 1838, aged 41.7.29.
274. Blauvelt, Peter, d. Jan. 24, 1831, aged 39.9.28.

275. Van Dien, Caspaures Demarest, son of Garret and Jane, d. Aug. 21, 1828, aged 12.10.29.
276. (Van Dien). Sally, d. July 30, 1828, aged 3.0.19; also Jane Voorhies, d. July 31, 1828, aged 1.10.—. (Probably daughters of Garret and Jane Van Dien).
277. Banta, Garret V. D., son of Jacob T. and Rachel, d. July 21, 1828, aged 15 months.
278. Banta, Rachel Van Dien, wife of Jacob T., d. Nov. 29, 1840, aged 32.8.14.
279. Van Dien, Sarah, daughter of Garret and Jane, d. Sept. 4, 1823, aged 0.2.5.
280. Van Dien, Richard, son of John B. and Elizabeth, d. Aug. 31, 1846, aged 1.6.23.
281. Van Dien, Margaret, daughter of John B. and Elizabeth, d. Nov. 11, 1847, aged 0.8.18.
282. ———. Rough marker.
283. Van H——?. *I* N V H / DEN 5 August / DE *IAR* 1783. (First line might be *I* V V H or *I* W H; second line might be DE 15 August).
284 to 292. ———. Nine rough markers.
293. Ackerman ?. AN 1706 / S A M. (The date plainly 1706, but so far antedates the church as to seem impossible).
294 to 296. ———. Three rough markers.
297. B——. A 1774 / G T B / T VA B. (The middle character of the third line might be VA, UA, WA or W).
298 and 299. ———. Two rough markers.
300. Hoppir, Garret I. G., b. April 7, 1798, d. Jan. 14, 1801, aged 3.9.7; also Mariah I. Hopper, b. Feb. 17, 1798, d. Jan. 13, 1801, aged 3.10.27.
301. Hopper, Andrew I., b. Feb. 25, 1770, d. June 12, 1802, aged 32.3.16.
302. ———. Rough marker.

Row 18 (Intermediate)

303 to 306. ———. Four rough markers.

Row 19

307. Vanderbeek, Mary Van Bussum, wife of Jacob A., d. Nov. 13, 1822, aged 68.6.1.
308. Vanderbeek, Jacob A., b. July 26, 1757, d. Feb. 13, 1842, aged 84.6.18.
309. Banta, Jacob T., d. March 25, 1857, aged 50.0.9.
310. Banta, Jacob J., son of Jacob T. and Rachel, d. Aug. 12, 1848, aged 19.1.26.
311. Van Dien, Elizabeth Doremus, wife of John B., d. July 1, 1850, aged 28.4.22.
312. Van Dien, Garret, d. Nov. 7, 1853, aged 68.0.16.
313. Van Dien, Jane Demarest, wife of Garret, d. Aug. 16, 1876, aged 86.7.24.
314. H——. 1777 / A H OVER / August / 25.
315. H——. C *I* H / 19 Juny 1770. (The *I* enclosed in the C).
316. H——. *I* + H dyed / IN IANUARY THE 31 ANNO / DOMNI 1788.
317. (Ter Huyn ?). Anno 1776 / 11 September / died *I* T H.
318. Ter Huyn. Ano 1772 / Maert 14 / Ana Maria ter / Huÿn.
319. Ter Huyn. Ano / 1773 / Mÿ 23 / Allbartus T H / A T H.

320. ———. Rough marker.
321. R———. ANNO / 1770 / H R 56 o. ❦ (The final letter probably stands for "oudt").
322. B———. 1775 / R T B / JUNE 9 D.
323. B———. 1795 / A T B/ SEPTEMBER 14.
324. Hopper, Chatrine, consort of John I., d. Dec. 27, 1818, aged 52.6.16.
325 to 329. ———. Five rough markers.

Row 20

330. Naugle, Barnet J., d. Feb. 25, 1866, aged 87 years.
331. Naugle, Maria Westervelt, late wife of Bernard, d. Aug. 20, 1839, aged 75.11.23.
332. Ackerman, Sarah Cooper, widow of Ab. I., d. Oct. 16, 1857, aged 90.11.1.
333. Ackerman, Abraham I., d. Nov. 22, 1843, aged 80.1.12.
334. Hopper, Mary Hopper, wife of John A., b. Nov. 17, 1760, d. Aug. 9, 1844, aged 83.8.22.
335. Hopper, John A., b. March 17, 1745, d. Feb. 3, 1824, aged 78.10.17.
336 Zabriskie, Mary Van Dien, wife of Cornelius, d. Oct. 27, 1846, aged 65.10.12.
337. Terhune, Ellen Zabriskie, wife of Abraham, Jr., d. April 30, 1830, aged 25.3.25.
338. Terhune, Abraham, Jr., d. July 14, 1853, aged 51.7.29.
339. Berdan, John Degraw, son of John and Sarah, b. Feb. 14, 1818, d. Aug. 5, 1819, aged 1.5.25.
340. Zabriskie, Cornelius, d. Oct. 1, 1861, aged 85.2.27.
341. Vanderbeak, Coenraudes, d. Sept. 21, 1823, aged 69.7.4.
342. Joralemon, Stephen B., son of James W. and Mary, d. Oct. 31, 1840, aged 1.11.10.
343. Vanderbeak, Hannah Demarest, wife of Coonraudes, d. June 1, 1855, aged 83.11.19.
344. ———. Rough marker.
345. W———. an 1778 / is A W OUL / d 24 my / Jni. (The meaning of the last three letters is obscure).
346 to 351. ———. Six rough markers.
352. Swan, William, d. Feb. 16, 1773, aged 31 years.
353 to 356. ———. Four rough markers.
357. A———. G A / 1773.
358. Van der Beek ?. 1781 den / 30 AG. is / M V D B.
359 to 362. ———. Four rough markers.
363. Hopper, Elezabeth, d. Aug. 4, 1807.

Row 21

364. Zabriskie, Eliza Garrison, daughter of Garret A. and Catie, b. Feb. 12, 1817. d. July 27, 1888.
365. Zabriskie, Caty Westervelt, wife of Garret A., d. March 14, 1877, aged 88.11.3.
366. Zabriskie, Garret A. L., d. Nov. 28, 1853, aged 70.8.0.
367. [Zabriskie, Martha Ann, d. Dec. 19, 1838, aged 24.6.26]. Inscription split off, 1931; supplied from copy by E. L. Z.
368. Zabriskie, Elletta Maria, daughter of Garret A. and Caty, d. Dec. 20, 1827, aged 2.2.26.
369. [Van Emburgh, Polly, daughter of Albert, d. Oct. 16, 1823, aged 4.10.3]. Stone broken off and missing 1931; inscription supplied from copy by E. L. Z.

370. Zabriskie, Benjamin, d. Nov. 12, 1824, aged 79.8.4.
371. Zabriskie, Hannah Hopper, wife of Benjamin, d. May 1, 1822, aged 78.6.3.
372. Ackerman, John A., d. July 24, 1855, aged 64.9.16.
373. Ackerman, Bridget, wife of John A., d. Sept. 10, 1864, aged 72.4.26.
374. B——. I X B / Died 9 of March / 1799 was born / the 3 of March / 1737 old stile / aged nearly 62 years. (The X probably not meant for an initial).
375. ——. Rough marker.
376. W——. T W / IANY 26 / 1777.
377. W——. R W / died June 19 1795 / Aged 80 y 1 M 12 D.
378. Ackerman. 1781 den 8 / April is Gerrit / Ackerman overl.
379. Ackerman. In / memory / van Albert Ackerman is / overleden den 19 dag van / October in het yaar onsens / Heeren 1801 oudt synde / 76 yaaren 1 maandt ende 15 / dagen.
380. E——. M E / 1797.
381 and 382. ——. Two rough markers.
383. Banta, Rachel Brevoort, wife of Abraham T., b. Dec. 9, 1811, d. July 25, 1848, aged 36.7.16.
384. Baldwin, Maria Hopper, late wife of Thomas, d. Jan. 19, 1866, aged 80.11.6.
385. Brevoort, Samuel H., d. Oct. 26, 1841, aged 29.10.14.
386. Hopper, Catharine Cooper, wife of Garret A., d. April 12, 1850, aged 87.1.18.
387. Hopper, Garret A., d. Dec. 18, 1830, aged 75.10.20.
388. Hutchinson, Mary Matilda, daughter of Pardon and Matilda, d. July 18, 1835, aged 1.3.20.
389. Hutchinson, Eliza M., daughter of Pardon and Matilda, d. Jan. 8, 1843, aged 1.8.17.
390. Hutchinson, Pardon, d. June 20, 1852, aged 48.8.16; Matilda Brevoort, his wife, d. June 19, 1879, aged 78.4.0.
391. Hopper, Ellen Winters, wife of Samuel, d. March 21, 1843, aged 27.2.14; also their infant, d. April 12, 1843, aged 0.1.1.
392. Hopper, Albert G., d. Sept. 3, 1855, aged 73.0.3.
393. Hopper, Mary Brevoort, wife of Albert G., d. Dec. 4, 1871, aged 84.3.8.
394. Ackerman, Maria I., b. March 17, 1779, d. Feb. 26, 1801, aged 21.11.9.
395. ——. Rough marker.

Row 22

396. Zabriskie, Albert, d. Dec. 8, 1838, aged 85.7.25.
397. Zabriskie, Martha, wife of Albert, d. Sept. 9, 1833, aged 76.9.2.
398. [Terhune, Clarence, d. Feb. 11, 1825, aged 37.6.12]. Stone broken off and missing, 1931; inscription supplied from copy by E. L. Z.
399. Gurdnear, Polly Ryer, wife of Henry, d. Oct. 10, 1852, aged 35.5.13. (Verse indicates husband and children living).
400. [Turse, Aaron, killed by a wagon wheel, Jan. 20, ——, aged 61 years]. Inscription split off, 1931; supplied from copy by E. L. Z.
401. Van Emburgh, Henry H., d. April 15, 1870, aged 68.9.2.
402. Van Emburgh, Margaret Demarest, wife of Henry H., d. Oct. 16, 1831, aged 30.6.4. (Verse indicates several minor children living).

403. Van Emburgh, Jane Carlock, wife of Henry H., d. Aug. 20, 1852, aged 36.6.23.
404. Van Emburgh, John, d. Aug. 17, 1803, aged 66.10.0.
405. Ackerman. In Memory / van Ragel huysvrow / van Albert Ackerman / overleden den 10d dag / van June in het yaar / onsen Heeren 1807 / oudt synde 80 yaaren / 2 maande en 19 dagen.
406. Mitchell, Elizabeth, d. April 16, 1802, aged 57.0.5.
407. ———. Rough marker.
408. Brower, Elizabeth Hopper, wife of Abraham, d. March 1, 1809, aged 37.9.16.
409. H———. *I* H / 1777.
410 to 413. ———. Four rough markers.
414. Codmus, Abraham, d. March 15, 1801.
415. ———. Rough marker.

Row 23

416. Archbold, John M., d. Oct. 20, 1827, aged 66.3.5.
417. Ackerman, Margaret E., d. March 14, 1854, aged 0.5.25.
418. Ackerman, Abraham H., d. Aug. 15, 1850, aged 0.1.15.
419. Ackerman, Henry A., son of Abraham and Peggy, b. Dec. 14, 1826, d. March 16, 1836, aged 9.3.2.
420. Garrison, Jemima Ackerman, wife of Albert, d. June 14 (or 11), 1822, aged 30.5.1.
421. Ackerman, Christiana Cooper, wife of Aaron I., d. Oct. 31, 1833. aged 68.6.10.
422. Ackerman, Aaron I., b. Oct. 18, 1808, d. July 27, 1834, aged 25.9.9.
423. Van Vorst, Mary Jane, daughter of Henry J. and Harriet, d. Feb. 15, 1858, aged 5.9.8.
424 to 428. ———. Five rough markers.
429. Van B———. 1779 / H V B.
430 and 431. ———. Two rough markers.
432. Collins, Iohn, d. Oct. 26, 1800, aged 45 years.
433. ———. Rough marker.
434. H———. L T H / Nov. 24, 1807.
435. Cadmus. Al / hier / leght Begraven het / Lichaam van Catharina / Gerritse de weduwe van / Abraham Cadmus is / Overleden de 17d January 1803 / Oudt Zynde 40 yar 9 / Manden en 18 Dagen.
436. Cadmus. Al / Hier / Leght Begraven het / Lichaam van / Abraham Cadmus / is overleden 15de Maert / 1801 en is Geboren 27te November 1760 out / zynde 40 yaar / 5 Maanden en 18 dagen.

Row 24

437. Van Dien, Margaret, wife of Cornelius, d. Dec. 4, 1832, aged 81.3.15.
438. Van Dien, Richard C., d. July 11, 1825, aged 40.5.15.
439. Van Dien, Cornelius, d. March 8, 1829, aged 83.1.19.
440. Van Dien, Sophia Catharine, daughter of Cornelius and Susan, d. March 30, 1840, aged 1.2.6.
441. Mersan, Mary Magdalen, daughter of Michael and Jane, d. Sept. 3, 1802, aged 6.6.0.
442. ———. Rough marker.

443. Van Derbeek, Abigail Terhune, wife of Jon. P., d. Aug. 25, 1800, aged 49 years.
444. Van Derbeek, Paul I., d. Sept. 24, 1800, in 19th year.
445. Van Derbeek, John P., d. June 9, 1828, aged 76.11.10.
446. Conklin, John L., d. Feb. 22, 1847, aged 42.3.0.
447. Conklin, Lewis L., d. Jan. 17, 1828, aged 56.6.27.
448. Conklin, Ellen, d. June 7, 1857, aged 73.0.28. "Our Mother".
449. Conklin, Rebeckah, wife of Luis, b. June 2, 1783, d. Feb. 29, 1804, aged 20.8.27.
450. Conklin, Hannah, d. Nov. 23, 1801, aged 8.10.1; also Mariah Conklin, d. July 6, 1808, aged 2.3.18. (Parents not given).
451. Van Allen, James, son of John, d. Aug. 1, 1818, aged 21.5.15.
452. Bogert, Cornelia, wife of Jacobus, d. Nov. 23, 1815, aged 77.0.13.
453. Van Allen, Catharine, daughter of John, d. March 1, 1815, aged 18.0.7.
454. Van Allen, Agness Bogert, wife of John P., d. Jan. 19, 1844, aged 67.7.4.
455. ———. Rough marker.
456. Bogert, Jacobus, d. Aug. 3, 1814, aged 81.3.21.
457. R———. 1808 / Aug. 23 / C V R adS*I*.
458. ———. Rough marker.
459. Banta, Cornelius, son of Henry, d. July 23, 1812, aged 8.9.18.

Row 25

460. ———. Rough marker.
461. Van Gelder, Catherine, wife of Jonathan, d. Sept. 4, 1818, aged 79.11.2.
462. Van Derbeek, Maria, daughter of Jacob P., d. June 7, 1808, aged 6.10.19.
463. R———. S R.
464. Oldis, Garret, b. July 17, 1754, d. Feb. 25, 1830, aged 75.7.8.
465. H———. 1774 / APRIL DE 7 / D. T. H.
466. Oldis, Rebeckah Hoogland, wife of Garret Oldis, d. Nov. 13, 1813, aged 55.5.9.
467. ———. Rough marker.
468. Horn, Jacob, d. Feb. 6, 1813, aged 49.8.4. (Verse indicates widow and child).
469. Durea, Hannah, wife of John, b. Jan. 17, 1772, d. June 23, 1800, in 28th year.

Row 26

470. Bogert, Cornelius I., d. Aug. 25, 1832, aged 59.8.18.
471. Bogert, Jane Post, b. April 21, 1781, d. Oct. 1854. (Day of month not given).
472. Watson, Sarah, d. Feb. 7, 1829, in 71st year.
473. H———. 1796 m 6 / T P H.
474. Van Horn, Sally, daughter of Daniel and Rachel, d. March 29, 1830 aged 14.11.4.
475. Hopper, Isaac A., d. Feb. 21, 1819, aged 54.1.25.
476. Hopper, Rachel Cooper, wife of Isaac A., d. Sept. 22, 1832, aged 65.9.0.
477. Terhune, "an infant girl" of Abraham and Caty, d. Jan. 26, 1819, aged 11 days.

Row 27

478. Lydecker, Martinche Haring, wife of Garret A. "Lyd," b. April
     7, 1767, d. Nov. 6, 1799, aged 32.7.0.
479. Lydecker, Garret A., b. April 15, 1763, d. Oct. 27, 1824, aged 61.6.12.
480. Lydecker, Mary Van Riper, wife of Garret A., b. July 12, 1773, d.
     April A D 1807, aged 33.10.8.
480-a. Lydecker, Evelina Amelia, daughter of David and Susan, d. Oct.
     3, 1840, aged 0.10.25.
481. Spear, Jacob H., d. Feb. 25, 1826, aged 24.0.20.
482. Spear, Henry, Jr., d. March 3, 1843, aged 66.11.0.
483. Spear, Martha, wife of Henry, Jr., d. Jan. 13, 1860, aged 88 years.
484. Blauvelt, Isaac, d. Oct. "54th", 1806, aged 71.6.11.
485. Blauvelt, Geertye, widow of Isaac, d. 1824, aged 83 years.
486. Blauvelt, Isaac, Jr., d. June 19, 1813, aged 52.7.11.
487. Van Dien, Mary Kough, wife of Caspaures, d. Feb. 5, 1819, aged
     38.3.12.
488. Hopper, Andrew A., b. April 2, 1761, d. Oct. 15, 1799, aged 38.7.13.

Row 28 (Intermediate)

489. Kough, Caspar, son of Caspar, Jr., and Tyny, d. Dec. 24, 1821,
     aged 7.10.15.
490. Kough, Lydia Terhune, daughter of Caspar, Jr., and Tyny, d.
     Sept. 12, 1830, aged 0.9.4.
491. Zabriskie, Garret, d. July 3, 1854, aged 85.10.9.
492. Zabriskie, Maria Westervelt, wife of Garret, d. March 25, 1846,
     aged 79.8.20.
493. Zabriskie, Albert G., d. Feb. 19, 1815, aged 23.3.9; also Garret, son
     of Albert G. and Catty Zabriskie, d. March 31, 1815, aged
     0.5.16.
494. Rutan, Henry, son of John H. and Elizabeth, d. July 1, 1856, aged
     3.3.0.
495. Hopper, b. June 14, 1805, d. July "2th" 1805.
496. Hopper, Abraham, d. April 6, 1801, aged 51.11.24.
497. Hopper, Anny, d. Oct. 21, 1803, aged 53.9.0.
498. Vanderbeak, Altye, wife of John, d. Sept. 5, 1799, in 32nd year.

Row 29

499. Zabriskie, Hannah Merseiles, wife of Garret, d. June 11, 1838,
     aged 82.2.3.
500. Bowne, John, d. Oct. 28, 1819, aged 18.9.3.
501. Post, William Jacob, son of John and Hannah, d. Dec. 23, 1854,
     aged 0.1.10.
502. Van Derbeek, John, d. July 17, 1818, aged 1.3.17.

Row 30

503. Bogert, John Westervelt, son of James S., d. Aug. 14, 1828, aged
     9.8.29.
504. Pake, Catharine Ann Hopper, wife of John, d. May 10, 1847, aged
     21.0.17.
505. Hopper, Mary Ann, wife of John A., d. March 25, 1829, aged
     22.3.14.
506. Winters, Charles Augusta, son of William and Charity A., d. May
     12, 1848, aged 2.7.5.

507. Winters, Ann S., daughter of William and Charity A., d. June 20, 1846, aged 0.10.28.
508. T——. L. J. T.
509. ——. Rough marker.
510. [Vanderbeek, children of Jeremiah and Elizabeth: John, d. Sept. 16, 1826, aged 2.7.0; Hannah, d. Sept. 18, 1826, aged 3.9.11; Frederick, d. Sept. 18, 1826, aged 1.1.23]. Stone broken off and missing, 1931; supplied from copy by E. L. Z.
511. Vanderbeek, children of Jeremiah and Elizabeth: John, d. Aug. 23, 1831, aged 4.8.19; Frederick, d. Aug. 29, 1831, aged 1.0.18.
512. Vanderbeek, Elizabeth Ackerman, wife of Jeremiah, d. July 19, 1832, aged 35.5.19.
513. Vanderbeek, Jeremiah, d. Dec. 31, 1836, aged 38.3.22.
514. Delamarter, Hannah Van Ryper, wife of Isaac, d. July 20, 1828, aged 20.5.1.
515. Van Riper, Frederick, d. Jan. 25, 1834, aged 65.5.26.
516. Van Riper, Maria Vanderbeek, d. March 9, 1861, aged 89.10.8.
517. Van Riper, "Infant son" of Abraham and Anna, d. March 8, 1852, aged 14 days.
518. Valleau-Rathbone Monument, "Erected by John V. Rathbone, in loving memory of his ancestors—1896":
Valleau, Elleanor, b. in New York Cty May 11, 1759, d. in New York City Aug., 1842, a Resident of New Jersey for many years.
Rathbone, Capt. Wait, b. in the Town of Stoning, Conn., Aug. 18, 1744, d. at the home of his son, William P. Rathbone, in Franklin Township, Bergen Co. Nov. 14, 1832.
Rathbone, Mary Brown, wife of Capt. Wait, b. in Stoning, Conn., Jan. 11, 1749, d. at her son's home in Bergen Co., Oct. 1834.

Row 31

519. Doty, Rachel, wife of Aaron, d. Jan. 14, 1832, aged 24.1.28; also Jacob L., son of Aaron and Rachel Doty, d. Aug. 18, 1832, aged 0.6.15.
520. Quackenbush, Maria, wife of Jacob, d. July 6, 1835, aged 61.10.12.
521. Quackenbush, Jacob, d. Dec. 13, 1828, aged 62.1.13.
522. Quackenbush, Susan Rutan, wife of John J., b. Nov. 28, 1793, d. Oct. 23, 1888, aged 94.10.26.
523. Quackenbush, John J., d. June 15, 1849, aged 52.10.0.
524. Snyder, Catharine, d. Feb. 8, 1858, aged 68. 1.15.
525. Snyder, Garret, d. April 9, 1848, aged 63.4.8.
526. Terheun, Henry, d. Jan. 6, 1826, aged 62.11.8.
527. Snyder, Andrew, son of Garret and Caty, d. Aug. 25, 1828, aged 18.0.27.
528. Gero, Rachel, wife of Benjamin, daughter of Garret and Caty Snyder, d. Sept. 2, 1829, aged 21.6.18.
529. Snyder, Garret, son of Garret and Caty, d. Nov. 27, 1829, aged 12.0.7.
530. Cooper, Hannah, wife of Thomas, d. Sept. 16, 1849, aged 69.5.20.
531. Terhune, Helena Zebriskie, wife of Peter I., d. March 13, 1852, aged 78.1.22.
532. Terhune, Peter I., d. Jan. 11, 1855, aged 83.11.1.

Row 32

533. Vanderbeek, Hannah, daughter of Yurre and Hannah, d. Sept. 13, 1832, aged 5.8.2.
534. Vanderbeek, John, son of George and Hannah, b. July 9, 1836, d. Jan. 6, 1837, aged 0.5.27.
535. Vanderbeek, Hannah, daughter of George and Hannah, b. March 12, 1834, d. April 21, 1843, aged 9.1.9.
536. Vanderbeek, George, b. Oct. 6, 1766, d. Feb. 6, 1842, aged 76.4.0.
537. Vanderbeek, Hannah Young, wife of George, d. March 30, 1882, aged 81.2.27.
538. Banta, Richard, d. Jan. 13, 1833, aged 4.9.7.
539. Bogert, Mariah Westervelt, wife of Stephen, b. May 18, 1749, d. March 16, 1831 (or 1834), aged 84.9.29.
540. Blauvelt, Jemima, wife of Aaron, d. April 15, 1838, aged 59.9.0.
541. Blauvelt, Aaron, d. Nov. 20, 1836, aged 59.5.6.
542. Baker, Jacob Denis, son of Jacob and Maria, d. Oct. 26, 1838, aged 8.10.26.
543. Baker, Mary Helms, wife of Jacob, d. Oct. 14, 1838, aged 45.4.14.
544. Baker, Hannah Ellen, daughter of Jacob and Maria, d. Feb. 28, 1835, aged 13.9.1.
545. Baker, Agness Shedden, daughter of Jacob and Mary, d. July 14, 1830, aged 1.5.12.

Row 33

546. Carlock, Cornelus Smith, son of Jeremiah and Eliza, d. April 19, 1849, aged 4.2.12.
547. Hopper, Mary, d. April 29, 1849, aged 94 years.
548. Hopper, Garrit, d. Jan. 19, 1829, aged 80.8.17.
549. Van Dien, Cornelias G., d. April 30, 1841, aged 70.1.0.
     Van Dien, Garrit, son of Cornelias G. and Jane, d. Feb. 27, 1828, aged 5.3.21.
550. Blauvelt, Joseph, d. May 18, 1830, aged 33.8.3.
551. Westervelt, Margaret Zabriskie, wife of Albert R., d. Jan. 18, 1832, aged 72 years.
552. Westervelt, Albert R., d. June 19, 1846, aged 83.3.11.
553. Zabriskie, John Abr., d. March 2, 1832, aged 42.9.29.
554. Zabriskie, Rebecca, d. Jan. 10, 1863, aged 69.2.8.

Row 34

555. Carlock, Eliza Post, wife of Jeremiah, d. Dec. 21, 1864, aged 44.10.7. (Verse indicates husband and children living).
556. Ackerson, Mary, wife of Thomas, b. Oct. 4, 1778, d. Dec. 26, 1841 aged 65.2.22.
557. Ackerson, Thomas, b. April 1, 1775, d. March 10, 1844, aged 68.11.9.
558. Carlock, infant of Abraham and Maria, d. Aug. 21, 1840, aged 9 hours.
559. Carlock, Abraham, son of Abraham and Maria, d. Aug. 7, 1839, aged 12 days.
560. Carlock, Rachael Catharine, daughter of Abraham and Maria, d. Oct. 29, 1837, aged 0.8.3.
561. Carlock, Abraham, son of Abraham and Maria, d. Sept. 11, 1838, aged 0.5.2.

562. Carlock, Jeremiah, son of Abraham and Maria, d. Sept. 2, 1839, aged 9.1.14.
563. Carlock, Eleanor Lavinia, daughter of Jacob and Maria, d. March 12, 1844, aged 6 months.
564. Carlock, Henry, d. April 14, 1844, aged 40.1.13.
565. Call, Jacob, d. March 6, 1836, aged 24.5.28.
566. Call, Deborah, wife of John A., d. Oct. 11, 1848, aged 61.1.11.

Row 35

567. Van Nostrand, John, d. Jan. 7, 1849, aged 66.4.16.
568. Van Nostrand, Anna, wife of John, d. Nov. 12, 1844, aged 63.3.15.
569. Bogart, Hester Tebow, wife of John, d. Oct. 16, 1847, aged 64 years.
570. Lozier, Mary, d. Oct. 28, 1853, aged 91 years.
571. Carlock, Eliza Lozier, wife of Jeremiah, d. Nov. 5, 1853, aged 68 years.
572. Carlock, Jeremiah, d. Sept. 8, 1847, aged 73 years.
573. Mabie, Ellen M., wife of Aaron, d. Jan. 10, 1847, aged 23.0.4.

Row 36

574. Terhune, Henry S., d. March 23, 1853, aged 83.4.2.
575. Terhune, Tiney, wife of Henry S., d. Feb. 3, 1844, aged 72.2.24.
576. Terhune, Abraham A., d. June 13, 1850, aged 76.2.12.
577. Terhune, Catharine Westervelt, wife of Abraham A., d. May 1, 1854, aged 72.8.23.
578. Terhune, George Demarest, son of Abraham A. and Catharine, d. Sept. 27, 1851, aged 0.5.22.

Row 37

579 and 579-a. Two rough markers.
580. Zabriskie, Jacob H., d. Nov. 2, 1844, aged 72.4.4.
581. Zabriskie, Anne Hopper, wife of Jacob H., d. Nov. 15, 1863, **aged** 89.7.0.
582. Crouter, Stephen, b. Oct. 30, 1784, d. April 6, 1846, aged 61.5.6.
583. Crouter, Elizabeth Blauvelt, wife of Stephen, b. June 1, 1788, d. Oct. 5, 1846, aged 58.4.4.

Row 38

584. Zabriskie, John Jacob, son of Jacob and Elizabeth, d. Feb. 1, 1853, aged 2.9.29.
585. Zabriskie, Elizabeth, daughter of George W. and Eliza, d. Jan. 7, 1846, aged 9.5.7.
586. Zabriskie, Thomas, son of George W. and Eliza, d. May 12, 1847, aged 1.3.13.
587. Zabriskie, Elizabeth, daughter of George W. and Eliza, d. July 20, 1849, aged 1.7.26.
588. Zabriskie, Sarah, wife of Jacob, d. Jan. 22, 1848, aged 49.5.0.
589. Blauvelt, Jacob, d. Aug. 19, 1848, aged 23.11.6.
590. Van Houghten, John, b. Jan. 30, 1763, d. May 2, 1848, aged 85.3.3.
591. Van Houten, Margaret, wife of John, d. Dec. 10, 1853, aged 82.1.26.
592. Storms, Henry C., d. Aug. 12, 1853, aged 76.2.6.
593. Storms, Margaret, wife of Henry C., d. May 20, 1867, aged 84.7.14
594. Banner, Betsy, wife of James, d. April 14, 1852, aged 62.1.13.
595. Banner, James, d. April 6, 1852, aged 57.9.3.

Row 39

596. Vanderbeek, Rachel Jane, daughter of James W. and Margaret Ann, d. Aug. 5. 1862, aged 0.7.11.
597. Vanderbeek, Margaret Fox, wife of Paul, d. June 27, 1859, aged 88.4.14.
598. Vanderbeek, Paul, d. Dec. 11, 1844, aged 75.11.10.
599. ————. Rough marker.
600. Terhune, Garret, son of Stephen G. and Maria, d. May 28, 1852, aged 1.3.13.
601. Terhune, Martha, daughter of Stephen G. and Maria, d. May 11, 1851, aged 3.3.27.
602. Zabriskie, Hannah Maria, daughter of Jacob L. H. and Sarah Jane, d. Sept. 9, 1849, aged 5.3.12.
603. Zabriskie, Margaret Ann, daughter of Jacob L. H. and Sarah Jane, d. June 2, 1847, aged 0.7.23.
604. Cooper, Thomas, d. Oct. 21, 1849, aged 81.0.21.
605. Carlock, Cornelius Smith, d. Sept. 19, 1839, aged 18.1.22.
606. Hopper, Albert, d. Sept. 30, 1841, aged 43.6.4.
607. Blauvelt, Hannah Zabriskie, wife of James, d. May 3, 1842, aged 36 years; also their son Matthew M., d. aged 7 months (no date).
608. Blauvelt, Maria Elizabeth, daughter of James and Hannah Blauvelt, Junr., d. Jan. 29, 1838, aged 10.8.5.
609. Hopper, Nicholas G., d. May 13, 1854, aged 59.3.27.
610. Hopper, Wiby Voorhis, wife of Nicholas G., d. March 25, 1879, aged 78.0.21.
611. Hopper, Eliza Jane, daughter of Nicholas G. and Wiby, d. May 11, 1839, aged 1.8.3.
612. Storms, Cornelius, d. April 12, 1839, aged 38.8.14; also Henry, son of Cornelius and Sarah Storms, d. Feb. 17, 1837, aged 6.2.27.

Row 40

613. Van Derbeek, Rebecca E., daughter of John P. and Hannah, d. Nov. 11, 1853, aged 3.3.28.
614. Zabriskie, Martha Ann, daughter of Jacob L. H. and Sarah Jane, d. March 23, 1852, aged 4.0.17.

❧ ❧ ❧ ❧

INDEX

Numbers refer to pages, except in the gravestone entries, in which the number—always preceeded by the number sign (‡)—refers to the numbered item in the gravestone list, pages 146———.

For convenience all different spelling of the same surname are grouped under one spelling, but cross references are given where the name differs so as not to be readily recognizable.

Where a name appears more than once on the same page the number of times it appears is given in parentheses after the page number.

The following abbreviations are used in this index:

    c.==child.
    f.==father.
    gs.==gravestone.   (Number refers to item, not to page).
    m.==mother.
    mem.==member.
    w.—witness or sponsor.

"A"

AAL, Adam, *w.* 3.
ACKER, Doritje, *c.* 38.
    Elisabeth, *m.* 38, 115.
    John, *f.* 38, 115.
    Polly, *c.* 115.
ACKERMAN, ———, *gs.* ‡293.
    A., *gs.* ‡217.
    Aaltje, *m.* 10, 14, 41, 42, 49; *c.* 8, 15, 18 (2), 19; *w.* 4, 10, 13, 15; *mem.* 144.
    Aaron I., *gs.* ‡421, ‡422: J. *f.* 101.
    Aart Cuyper, *c.* 12.
    Abigael, *c.* 5.
    Abram, *f.* 6, 48, 139; *c.* 6; *w.* 3, 8, 9, 96, 97, 119, 134, 139 (2); *gs.* ‡200: A., *w.* 5, 6: Ari, *w.* 78: C., *w.* 89: D., *w.* 9, 98: G., *f.* 140; *w.* 95: I., *f.* 89; *gs.* ‡332: J., *f.* 87, 112; *w.* 6, 7, 34, 57, 83; *gs.* ‡12.
    Abraham, *f.* 14, 22, 33, 38, 59, 67, 68, 73, 86, 100, 103, 104, 136; *c.* 3, 5, 12, 13, 14 (2), 18 (2), 19 (2), 20 (2); *gs.* ‡140, ‡201, ‡419: A., *f.* 124: D., *f.* 20, 33 (2), 39, 44: G., *gs.* ‡218: H., *f.* 45; *gs.* ‡418: I., *f.* 21, 62; *gs.* ‡333: J., *f.* 24, 62, 87, 101 (2), 102, 109: P., *gs.* ‡103, ‡104: Rutan, *c.* 22: U., *f.* 21.
    Adoline, *c.* 22.
    Agnes, Agenes, Aggy, *m.* 33, 117, 123; *c.* 21.
    Albert, *f.* 18, 19, 40, 48, 60, 77, 87, 95, 108, 111, 119; *c.* 4, 6, 10, 14, 21; *w.* 6, 10, 47, 48, 119, 125 (3), 138; *gs.* ‡87, ‡379, ‡405: A., *f.* 44, 45, 101: G., *f.* 49, 90: I., *mem.* 144.
    Alley, *gs.* ‡87: Terhune, *gs.* ‡1.
    Andreas, *c.* 16, 17.
    Andrew, *f.* 54; *c.* 22: G., *f.* 33, 108: Hopper, *c.* 21.
    Angenietje, *c.* 15; *w.* 40.
    Ann Maria, *c.* 21.
    Annet, *c.* 21.
    Annatje, Annatie, Annaatje, *m.* 3, 4, 13, 14, 15, 18, 19, 36, 48, 69, 78, 127; *c.* 4, 13, 14, 15; *w.* 3, 6, 9, 13.
    Annetta, *gs.* ‡38.
    Anny Van Horn, *gs.* ‡10.
    Antje, Antie, *m.* 49, 55, 90; *c.* 6 (2), 11, 16, 19; *w.* 2, 4, 9, 10 (2), 13, 35, 36, 118, 127; *gs.* ‡217; *mem.* 144, 145.
    Ariaantje, *w.* 5.
    Arie, 12, 64, 67, 69, 83, 98; *c.* 3, 5, 15; *w.* 5, 50.
    Aron, *c.* 19.

Betsy, Betje, *m.* 2, 20, 111.
Brechje, Brechtje, Bregye, *w.* 6, 7, 57, 83 ; *gs.* ‡66.
Bridget, *m.* 19, 39, 44, 117 ; *gs.* ‡373 : Westervelt, *c.* 24.
Carstyntje, *w.* 26.
Cathalyntje, *m.* 15, 38, 39, 71, 105 ; *w.* 37.
Catharine, Catarine, Catharina, Catriena, *m.* 33, 54, 102 ; *c.* 29, 30,
    31 ; *gs.* ‡132 : Ann, *c.* 33 ; Maria, *c.* 33 ; Mathilda, *c.* 34 : Perry,
    gs. ‡106.
Caty, *m.* 21, 33, 62, 101, 108, 109 : Ann, *c.* 32.
Charity, *c.* 33 ; *gs.* ‡101 : Ann, *c.* 33.
Christina, Christiana, *m.* 12, 67, 69 ; *w.* 50 : Cooper, *gs.* ‡421.
Cobus, *f.* 1.
Cornelia, *c.* 29.
Cornelis, Cornelius, *f.* 63, 127 ; *c.* 29, 30, 33 ; *w.* 9, 41 : Henry, *c.* 33.
    D., *gs.* ‡10.
Daniel, *f.* 15, 16, 38, 39, 71, 105 ; *c.* 34, 35, 39 (2) ; *w.* 24, 37.
David, Davidt, *f.* 3, 12, 14, 30, 36, 37, 39, 41, 42. 53, 84, 91, 106, 116 ;
    c. 35 (3), 36 (2), 37, 38 (3), 39 (3) ; *w.* 3, 12, 13, 15 (2), 34.
    37, 71, 72 ; *as.,* ‡1, ‡2 ; *mem.* 144, 145 ; Jr., *mem.* 145 : A., *f.* 6,
    35, 64, 65, 88, 113, 119 ; *w.* 82, 125 : D., *f.* 3, 4, 8, 32, 33, 35, 41,
    48, 49, 61, 68, 74, 78, 83, 98, 101, 107, 117, 123 ; *w.* 6, 14, 64,
    104, 125 : G., *f.* 10, 49, 66 ; *w.* 13 ; *gs.* ‡100 ; *mem.* 144 : H., *f.*
    126 ; *w.* 4, 10 : Henry, *c.* 40 : J., *f.* 6, 81 ; *w.* 9, 10, 35, 36 (2),
    40, 127 : R., *f.* 101.
Dirk, *w.* 105.
Dirkje, *m.* 1 ; *w.* 135.
Dorcas, *m.* 22, 40, 44, 45, 87, 101, 108, 124.
Doritje, *c.* 38.
Effy, *m.* 32, 39, 61, 101.
Elisabeth, Elizabeth, *m.* 13, 14, 18, 19, 29, 52, 60, 67, 92, 100, 101,
    127 ; *c.* 40 (2), 41 (2), 42, 43 (2), 44, 45 (2) ; *w.* 18, 37, 41, 69,
    127 ; *gs.* ‡99, ‡131, ‡512 ; *mem.* 144 : Ann. *c.* 44.
Eliza, *m.* 22, 46, 54, 61, 88 (2), 101, 109, 124 ; *c.* 44.
Ellen, *gs.* ‡127 : Jemima, *c.* 46 : Maria, *c.* 45.
Elsje, *m.* 120 ; *c.* 41.
Garret, Garrit, Gerrit, *f.* 15, 16, 17, 18, 19, 38, 43, 48, 53, 63, 70,
    72, 75, 100 ; *c.* 48 (3), 49 (3), 52, 53 (2), 54 (2) ; *w.* 37, 50, 70,
    90 (2), 121, 127, 140 ; *gs.* ‡9, ‡378 ; *mem.* 143 : A., *f.* 22, 60, 105 :
    An., *f.* 34 : D., *f.* 5 (2), 22, 54, 61, 78 (2), 81, 88, 89, 101, 109,
    124 ; *w.* 4, 49, 77 ; *gs.* ‡100, ‡101, ‡102 : G., *f.* 100, 114 ; *w.* 51,
    100 ; *gs.* ‡23 : I., *gs.* ‡4, ‡5 : J., *f.* 41, 82, 83 ; *w.* 82, 119.
Geertje, *m.* 15, 16, 17, 19, 38, 53, 60, 70, 72, 100 ; *c.* 52 ; *w.* 140.
Gerardus, *c.* 51.
Grietje, *m.* 6, 35, 40, 49, 79, 80 ; *c.* 48, 49 ; *w.* 34, 40.
Hannah, *c.* 61, 62 ; *gs.* ‡130 : Jane, *c.* 61, 62 (2).
Hannes, *f.* 5 ; *w.* 3, 78, 81, 82, 89 (3), 94 : A., *f.* 125 ; *w.* 64, 81, 83,
    97 : Ar., *w.* 118 : D., *w.* 10, 118 : G., *f.* 99 : H., *f.* 89 ; *w.* 5, 90 : I.,
    f. 40, 81 : J., *f.* 63.
Hans A., *w.* 4.
Hendrik, Henderick, *c.* 55, 59 (2), 60 ; *w.* 56.
Henry, *f.* 20 ; *c.* 60 ; *gs.* ‡37 : A., *f.* 111 ; *gs.* ‡419 : P., *gs.* ‡127 :
    Terhune, *c.* 62.
Hester, *m.* 21, 30, 31, 43, 62, 77, 87, 89, 109, 112, 118, 124 ; *c.* 60 ; *w.*
    34 : Storms, *gs.* ‡128.
Hetty, *m.* 74, 87.
I., *gs.* ‡180, ‡254.
Isaac, Isaak, *c.* 64, 77, 84.
Jacob, *c.* 65, 68, 87.
Jacobus, *f.* 14, 19, 29, 59 ; *c.* 63, 80, 81 (2) ; *w.* 14, 140 : G., *f.* 14, 51,
    68 ; *w.* 42.
Jacomyntje. Jacomyn, Jakomyntje, *m.* 5, 35, 64, 65, 95, 113, 119, 125 ;
    c. 69, 73 ; *w.* 3, 4, 12, 64, 81, 82, 83, 94, 97, 118 ; *mem.* 144.
James W., *gs.* ‡38, ‡39.
Jan, *f.* 4, 11, 82 ; *c.* 66 ; *w.* 5, 26, 63, 83, 109.
Jane, *m.* 45, 87, 137 ; *c.* 86, 87 (2) ; *w.* 30 ; *gs.* ‡200.
Jannetje, Jannitje, Jannitie, Jannitye, *m.* 8, 12, 18, 35, 36, 68, 75,
    83, 98, 100, 105, 114 ; *c.* 63, 71, 68, 72, 75, 77, 78 (2), 83 ; *w.* 1,
    37, 70, 71, 72, 100 ; *gs.* ‡33 ; *mem.* 145.
Jemima (see Jacomyntje), *c.* 87 ; *gs.* ‡420 : Jane, *c.* 88.
Johannes, Johannis, Jannes, *f.* 2, 13, 15 (2), 29, 69, 83, 92, 104, 121,
    127 ; *m.* 1 ; *c.* 63, 64, 67, 68, 78, 79, 81, 82 (2), 83 (3) ; *w.* 13,
    42, 49, 69, 79 ; *gs.* ‡25 : Ar., *f.* 95 : D., *f.* 36 : G., *mem.* 144 : H.,
    w. 79 : J., *w.* 7, 57, 83.
John. *f.* 13, 18, 19, 39, 44, 52 (2), 62, 84, 87, 117, 123 ; *c.* 67, 69, 70,
    74 (2), 84, 86, 87 ; *gs.* ‡37, ‡124 : A., *f.* 18, 19, 39, 60 ; *gs.* ‡372,

Cobus, *f.* 94; *w.* 40.
David, *c.* 35 (2).
Elsie, *c.* 40.
Hannes, *f.* 40; *w.* 78, 112.
Hendrick, *f.* 17; *c.* 56.
Isaac, Isaak, *f.* 35 (2), 48, 63, 80, 83, 112; *w.* 64, 80 83, 95, 97.
Jacob, *c.* 63.
Jacobus, *f.* 126; *w.* 68.
Jacomyntje, *m.* 66, 119; *w.* 4.
Jan, *c.* 83.
Jonathan, *c.* 66.
Joseph, *c.* 80.
Maria, *m.* 7, 8, 95 (2); *c.* 102.
Margrietje, Margrieta, *m.* 129; *c.* 48, 94; *w.* 48, 94.
Naatje, *m.* 80.
Pieter, Petrus, *c.* 112; *w.* 48, 94.
Rachel, *c.* 119.
Saphira, Saffyee, Saffya, *c.* 126 (3).
Samuel, *f.* 102.
Sara, *m.* 17.
AMERMAN, AMELMAN, Eva, *m.* 78; *w.* 8.
Jacobus, *c.* 78.
Ja. *f.* 78; *w.* 3.
ANDERSON, Jacobus, *f.* 122; *w.* 103.
Margary, Marjeree, *m.* 122; *w.* 103.
Rebecka, *c.* 122.
ARCHBOLD, John M., *gs.* ‡416.
ARIAANSE, Gerrit, *w.* 50.
ASLEY, David, *c.* 36.
Elisabeth, *m.* 36.
John, *f.* 36.
AUSBON, Catriena, *c.* 29.
David, *c.* 29; *w.* 29.
John, *f.* 29.
Martyntje, *m.* 29.
AYCRIGG, Benjamin, *c.* 23.
John, *f.* 23.
Rachel, *m.* 23.

"B"

BAARMOEL, BAREMOLE, BEERMOOR, Hendrikus, *c.* 2.
Johannis, *c.* 1.
Lena, *w.* 80, 90.
Lieven, *f.* 1, 2.
Rachel, *m.* 1, 2.
BAKER, BACKER, Agnes Shedden, *gs.* ‡545.
Coenraad, *w.* 110.
Grietje, *m.* 70.
Hannah Ellen, *gs.* ‡544.
Jacob, *f.* 70; *c.* 70; *gs.* ‡542, ‡543, ‡544, ‡545: Denis, *gs.* ‡542.
Maria, *gs.* ‡542, ‡544, ‡545.
Margrietje, *w.* 103.
Mary Helms, *gs.* ‡543.
BALDWIN, BAELDIN, BALDEN, BALLDIN, Antje, *m.* 25, 27, 79, 80; *w.* 27, 134.
Carstina, *c.* 25.
Catharina, *m.* 40.
Caty Ann, *m.* 87.
Christina, *c.* 27, 31.
David, *f.* 40; *c.* 40.
Elisabeth, *m.* 31.
Joseph, *c.* 87.
Joost, *c.* 79, 80.
Maria Hopper, *gs.* ‡384.
Richard, *f.* 87.
Steven, *f.* 25, 27, 79.
Thomas, *f.* 31; *gs.* ‡384.
BAMPER, BEMPER, Antje, *m.* 91, 98, 127.
Gerrit H., *f.* 108.
Jacob, *f.* 91, 98, 127.
Lodewyk Marcelis, *c.* 91.
Margaret Ann Zabriskie, *c.* 108.
Margrieta Helena, *c.* 98.
Sara Brower, *c.* 127.

Thomas, *f.* 16, 24, 49, 74; *c.* 134, 137; *w.* 7, 16 : Jr., *f.* 21, 22, **34**, 62 :
    T., *f.* 87 : W., *f.* 41.
Tryntje, *m.* 51; *c.* 135; *w.* 25.
Vrouwtje, *mem.* 144.
Wiert, *c.* 138, 142; *w.* 138; C., *f.* 63.
Williampe Ackerman, *gs.* ‡129.
BARBERRIER, BARBORO—see Berbero.
BARDAN—see Berdan.
BARR, David, *f.* 43, 74.
Elisabeth, *c.* 43.
John, *c.* 74.
Maria, Mary, *m.* 43, 74.
BARTOLF—see Bertolf.
BAYARD, BEYERD, Adam, *c.* 15.
Betsey, *w.* 42.
David, *f.* 15 ; *w.* 42.
Grietje, *m.* 15.
BEATY, BEATIE, BOATY, Adam, *w.* 98.
George, *f.* 54, 132 : Albert, *c.* 54.
Rachel, *m.* 54, 132.
Sarah Elisabeth, *c.* 132.
BEEM, Ariaantje, *w.* 121.
Jacobus, *w.* 121.
Jannetje, *m.* 121.
John, *w.* 128.
Sara, *w.* 128.
BEER, Antje, *w.* 56.
Hendrik, *w.* 41, 56.
BEERMOOR—see Baarmoel.
BELL, BEL, Anne, *m.* 32, 53.
Bellie, *f.* 50.
Charity Ann, *c.* 32.
Elsje Earl, *c.* 41.
Garrit, Gerrit, *c.* 53 : I. H., *f.* 32, 53 : Jan Hoppe, *c.* 50.
Gerard De Peyster, *c.* 50.
Rachel, *m.* 41, 50 (2), 140.
William, *f.* 41, 140 : M., *f.* 50 : Swan, *c.* 140.
BENNER—see Banner.
BENNET, Abbe, *m.* 45.
Elisabeth, *c.* 45.
Samuel, *f.* 45.
BENSON, BENSE, BENSEN, Albert, *f.* 100; *w.* 100.
Cornelius, *f.* 108.
Eva, *w.* 34.
Gerrit, *w.* 34.
Hannes, *c.* 80.
Jannetje, *m.* 100; *w.* 100.
Maria, *m.* 108 : Jane, *c.* 108.
Marytje, *m.* 80, 127.
Matheus, *f.* 80, 127; *c.* 100.
Samuel, Samme, *c.* 127; *w.* 125.
BERBERO, BERBERIE, BARBORO, BARBERRIER, Anne, *w.* 91.
Casparus, *f.* 103, 122; *w.* 42.
Grietje, *w.* 104.
John, *w.* 91.
Maria, *m.* 103, 122.
Maragrietje, *c.* 103 ; *w.* 103.
Matheus, *w.* 72, 103, 104.
Rachel, *c.* 122.
Wyntje, *w.* 72.
BERDAN, BARDAN, Antje, *w.* 4.
Catharina, Catriena, *m.* 109 ; *w.* 74.
Cornelius, *c.* 32 : Z., *f.* 88, 132.
Dirk, *c.* 36, 37.
Geertje, *m.* 68.
Hendrikje, Hendrickie, Hendrika, *w.* 56, 68 ; *mem.* 144.
Hankee, *w.* 36.
Jacob, *w.* 74 : D., *f.* 36.
Jan, *c.* 68 ; *w.* 36, 68, 80 : A., *f.* 81 : R., *w.* 56.
Japick, *c.* 81.
Johannis, *f.* 37, 70.
John, *f.* 107 ; *c.* 70, 88 ; *gs.* ‡339 : Jr., 32, 85 (2), 108, 131 : Degraw,
    c. 85 (2) ; *gs.* ‡339 : I., *f.* 129 : R., *mem.* 144.
Margaret, Margrietje, *m.* 81, 88, 132 ; *w.* 80.
Maria, *m.* 37, 70, 107 : Catriena, *c.* 107.

Hendrik, *c.* 59.
Isaac, Isaak, *f.* 53, 71, 73, 116 ; *c.* 76, 77, 86 ; *w.* 52, 99 ; *gs.* ‡484, ‡485 : Jr., *f.* 100 ; *gs.* ‡486.
Jacob, *c.* 86, 87 ; *gs.* ‡589.
Jacobus, *c.* 71 73, 74 ; *w.* 73, 75.
Jacomyntje, *m.* 30, 59 ; *w.* 99.
James, *f.* 21, 86 ; *c.* 87 ; *gs.* ‡607, ‡608 : Jr., *f.* 87 (2), 101, 108, 117, 124 : I., *f.* 131.
Jannetje, Jannitje, *m.* 63, 70, 99, 105 ; *c.* 66, 72, 83 ; *w.* 72, 81, 83.
Jemima, *gs.* ‡540.
Johannes, Johannis, *f.* 35, 70 ; *c.* 63, 70, 82 ; *w.* 35, 63 : C., *w.* 81.
John, *c.* 70 : I., *f.* 77, 86.
Joseph, *f.* 135 ; *w.* 29 ; *gs.* ‡550.
Lea, *w.* 128.
Lisbeth, Lisabeth, *w.* 6, 90.
Margrietje, *m.* 13 ; *c.* 98.
Maria, *m.* 36, 76, 135 ; *c.* 99, 100, 105 ; *w.* 12, 13, 105 : Elisabeth, *c.* 101, 108 ; *gs.* ‡608.
Matthew M., *gs.* ‡607.
Metje, *m.* 70, 74.
Peter, Pieter, *f.* 66 ; *gs.* ‡274.
Phebe, *c.* 116, 117.
Rachel, *m.* 27, 82 ; *w.* 35, 63, 73, 75 : Margaret, *c.* 124.
Sara, Sarah, Saartje, *m.* 53, 73, 77, 86, 100, 116 : Ann, *c.* 131.
Tryntje, *c.* 135 ; *w.* 36, 82, 135.
BOGERT, BOGART, BOGAERT, BOGERD, BOOGERT, BONGAART, BONGAERT, BONGERT, Aaltje, *m.* 31 ; *c.* 9, 13 ; *w.* 15.
Abram, Abraham, *c.* 7, 14.
Agness, *gs.* ‡454.
Albert, *f.* 14, 22 (2), 31, 45, 78, 87, 109 ; *c.* 22 ; *w.* 8, 138 : C., *f.* 95, 125 : D., *f.* 88 : I., *f.* 13 : J., *f.* 68, 115 ; *w.* 27, 100 : James, *c.* 22 : Zabriskie, *c.* 20.
Aletta, *c.* 22.
Andries, Andreas, *f.* 9, 97 ; *c.* 9, 15.
Angonietje, *c.* 9, 10.
Annatje, *c.* 6 ; *w.* 27.
Antje, *c.* 3, 5 (2), 7 ; *w.* 1, 5, 10, 25.
Belkje, *w.* 91.
Betsy, *m.* 131, 141.
Carstyna, *c.* 2.
Casparus, *f.* 15, 28, 66, 91 ; *c.* 25 ; *mem.* 143.
Catharine, Catharina, Catriena, Catrina, *m.* 73, 87, 104 ; *c.* 32.
Christiana, *c.* 33.
Cobus, *f.* 5, 98, 133 ; *w.* 3, 5, 6, 79, 82 : J., *f.* 10, 65 ; *w.* 134.
Cornelia, *m.* 5, 10, 26, 65, 98, 133 ; *c.* 26, 31 ; *w.* 5, 6, 29, 35, 66, 68, 71, 72, 77, 82, 134 (2), 135 ; *gs.* ‡452 ; *mem.* 144.
Cornelis Cornelius, *f.* 2, 20, 73, 76, 77, 90, 94, 104 ; *c.* 27, 28 ; *w.* 15, 27, 31, 37, 77, 90, 98, 128 : A., *f.* 139 : I., *gs.* ‡470 : J., *f.* 138 : James, *c.* 33 : L., *w.* 35, 91 : Y., *f.* 25.
David, *w.* 37
Dirk Wannemaker, *c.* 35.
Dorotie, Dorothie, *m.* 1, 3, 47, 133.
Effie, *c.* 42.
Elisabeth, *m.* 25, 52, 75, 106, 117 ; *w.* 27, 35, 84.
Ellen Priscilla, *c.* 45.
Elsje, *w.* 78, 79.
Eva, *c.* 41 ; *w.* 115.
Fyke, *m.* 68.
Gardener, *f.* 33.
Geertje, *c.* 47, 52 ; *w.* 52.
Geesje, *m.* 9, 120 ; *c.* 50 ; *w.* 120.
Gerrit, *c.* 53.
Grietje, *m.* 119.
Hendrik, *c.* 56, 57, 58.
Hester Tebow, *gs.* ‡569.
Isaac, *f.* 22 ; *c.* 88 ; *w.* 10.
Jacob, *f.* 6, 41, 56 (2), 57, 58, 119, 126 ; *c.* 68, 75 ; *w.* 26, 58, 81, 83.
Jacomyntje, *m.* 53, 116.
Jacobus, *f.* 26 ; *c.* 66, 68, 78, 79 ; *w.* 11, 29, 35, 66, 68, 71, 72, 78, 103, 135 (2) ; *gs.* ‡452, ‡456 ; *mem.* 144.
James S., *f.* 76, 131 ; *gs.* ‡503.
Jan. *f.* 121, 130, 136 ; *c.* 82 ; *w.* 1, 25, 119.
Jane, *m.* 20, 22, 32, 76, 87, 125 ; *c.* 75 ; *gs.* ‡239 : Post, *gs.* ‡471.
Jannetje, Jannitje, Jannette, Jennet, Jenny, *m.* 15, 28, 33, 66, 88, 91, 109, 141 ; *c.* 56, 65, 66, 72 ; *w.* 68 ; *mem.* 143.

Rachel, *c.* 131; *gs.* ‡383.
Samuel, *f.* 29, 49, 66, 102; *c.* 130, 131; *w.* 78, 94: H., *gs.* ‡385.
BRICKELL, BRICKLE, BRICKER, Abraham, *w.* 8.
Ally, *m.* 61.
George, *f.* 61, 137.
Hiram, *c.* 61.
Letty, *m.* 137.
Polly, *w.* 8.
Thomas, *c.* 137.
BRICKMAN, Lodewyk, *f.* 120.
Marytje, *m.* 120.
Reinhart, *c.* 120.
BRIKKER, Francyntje, *w.* 94.
Hannes, *w.* 94.
BRINKERHOF, BLINKERHOF, Dirk, *c.* 35; *w.* 38, 111: S., *f.* 35.
Osseltje, *m.* 35; *w.* 38, 111.
BROWER, BROUWER, Aaltje, *m.* 78, 94.
Abram, Abraham, *f.* 82; *c.* 6, 13, 16; *gs.* ‡408: D., *f.* 6, 56, 91, 112.
Antje, *m.* 65, 91, 112; *c.* 14.
Catrina, Catriena, *m.* 16, 38, 115.
David, *c.* 38.
Elizabeth Hopper, *gs.* ‡408.
Hans, *c.* 56.
Isaac, Isack, *f.* 2; *c.* 78; *w.* 78.
Jacob, *f.* 99, 110; *w.* 113.
Jacobus, *c.* 65.
Jan. *f.* 115.
Jannetje, *c.* 82; *w.* 112.
Johannis, *c.* 71.
John, *f.* 16, 38, 72; *c.* 72.
Lea, *c.* 91.
Maria, Marytje, *c.* 2, 94, 99.
Nikolaas, *c.* 110.
Pieter, Petrus, *f.* 13, 14, 71; *c.* 112, 115; *w.* 13.
Rachel, *m.* 2, 13, 14, 71; *w.* 13, 78.
Tryntje, *m.* 72, 110.
Uldrick, *f.* 78, 94.
BROWN, Anna, *m.* 13; *c.* 13.
James, *f.* 13.
Mary, *gs.* ‡518.
BRUYN, Antje, Annatje, *m.* 96, 114; *w.* 26.
Coenraad, *f.* 96; *w.* 26.
Marten, *f.* 114.
Marytje, *c.* 96.
Pieter Post, *c.* 114.
BURGESS, Daniel, *f.* 38; *c.* 38.
Grietje, *m.* 38.
BUSH, BOSH, BOSCH, Bos, Aaltje, *m.* 127.
Abram, Abraham, *c.* 18, 19.
Andrias, *c.* 16.
Antje, Annatje, Anne, *m.* 14, 15, 30, 38, 39, 43, 50, 58, 66, 124, 127;
   c. 12, 14, 15, 18, 19; *w.* 38 (2), 114, 115.
Barend, *c.* 24.
Benjamin, *f.* 87; *c.* 23.
Catriena, *c.* 30.
Coenraad, *c.* 29, 31.
David, *c.* 36, 38, 39 (2).
Dirk, *f.* 14, 15, 30, 38, 43, 50, 58, 66; *c.* 38, 39; *w.* 38 (2), 114, 115.
Elisabeth, *m.* 18, 38, 59, 122; *c.* 43 (2); *w.* 29, 115.
Francyntje, *c.* 47.
Frone, Phrone, *m.* 12, 51, 115.
Grietje, *m.* 19, 31, 43, 122; *c.* 50, 51 (2), *w.* 50.
Hendrik, *f.* 29, 38, 39; *c.* 58, 59 (2), 60; *w.* 42, 51, 102.
Jacobus, *f.* 127.
Jan, *c.* 66.
Jannetje, *c.* 85.
John, *f.* 19, 39, 84; *c.* 38, 72, 84: Jr., *f.* 124: Henry, *c.* 87: I., *f.* 107.
Joshua S., *w.* 55.
Lena, Lenah, Leentje, *m.* 16, 24, 36, 47, 51, 59, 60, 72, 85, 107, 114
   (2), 115, 120, 128, 140; *w.* 14, 15, 127 (2).
Lisabeth, *w.* 55.
Lodewyk, Lodewyck, *f.* 16, 18, 24, 39, 47, 51, 60, 72, 85, 107, 114,
   115, 136; *w.* 14, 15, 102.
Magdalen, *m.* 18, 39, 136.
Margaret, *m.* 87; *c.* 107.
Maritje, *m.* 29, 38; *w.* 42.

Maria, *m.* 19, 39, 84, 107 ; *c.* 107 ; *w.* 51, 102.
Peter, Pieter, *f.* 12, 19, 31, 51, 114, 115, 122, 127 ; *c.* 114, 115 (2) ;
    w. 50 : C., *f.* 43.
Rachel, *c.* 124.
Rebecka, *m.* 23, 125 ; *c.* 120 ; *w.* 24, 89, 97 (2), 111, 118, 120.
Reinard, Reinhart, *f.* 18, 38, 59, 122 ; *c.* 122 ; *w.* 115.
Richard, *c.* 122.
Sara, Saartje, *c.* 125, 128.
Sam, Samuel, *f.* 23, 59, 114, 118, 125, 127, 128, 140 ; *c.* 127 (3) ; *w.*
    24, 89, 97 (2), 111, 120, 127 : Jr., *f.* 36, 120 : S., *w.* 127.
Trientje, *c.* 136.
Wybrech, *c.* 140.
BUSKERCK—see Van Buskirk.
BUTLER, Daniel Dash, *c.* 39.
Jane Ann, *m.* 39, 108.
Martha Sara, *c.* 108.
Thomas C., *f.* 39, 108.

"C"

CADMUS, CODMUS, Abram, Abraham, *c.* 5 ; *w.* 5, 15, 57, 58, 79 ; *gs.* ‡414,
    ‡435, ‡436.
Catriena, *w.* 15, 30, 58 : Gerritse, *gs.* ‡435.
Frederik, *f.* 5 ; *w.* 111, 126.
Hartman, *w.* 47.
Lea, *w.* 5, 47, 57, 79.
Saartje, *m.* 5 ; *w.* 111, 126.
CAEF, Christiaen, *w.* 95.
Maria, *w.* 95.
CAERLOG—see Carlock.
CALL, Deborah, *gs.* ‡566.
Jacob, *gs.* ‡565.
John A., *gs.* ‡566.
CAMPBELL, CAMPBEL, CAMPBLE, Abraham, *f.* 75, 84.
Archibold, *c.* 14.
Betsy, *m.* 87.
Caty, *m.* 31 ; *c.* 31.
Claartje, *w.* 29.
Elizabeth, *c.* 43.
Jacob Andrew Jackson, *c.* 87.
Jacobus, *c.* 84.
Jannetje, Jane, *m.* 14, 43, 75, 136, 141 (2) ; *c.* 75.
John, *f.* 14, 70 ; *c.* 70, 75 ; *w.* 136 (2).
Margrietje, *m.* 75, 84.
Samuel, *f.* 31, 87.
Steven, *w.* 29.
Tietje, *m.* 70 ; *c.* 136 ; *w.* 136 (2).
William, *f.* 43, 75, 136, 141 (2) ; *c.* 141 (2).
CARLOCK, CARLOUGH, CARLOGH, CAERLOG, CERALLAGH, CERALLACH, CERREL-
    LACH, KERLOGH, Abraham, *f.* 45, 86, 88 (2), 124, 125 ; *gs.* ‡558,
    ‡559, ‡560, ‡561, ‡562, ‡563.
Betsy, Betje, *m.* 76 ; *w.* 110.
Coenraad, *c.* 26.
Cornelius, *c.* 32 : Smith, *gs.* ‡546, ‡605.
Eleanor Lavinia, *gs.* ‡563.
Elisabeth, *m.* 32, 76 ; *w.* 15
Eliza, *gs.* ‡546 : Ann, *c.* 45 : Lozier, *gs.* ‡571 : Post, *gs.* ‡555.
Ellen, *c.* 45.
George, *f.* 122.
Grietje, *m.* 26.
Henry, Hendrik, *f.* 26 ; *gs.* ‡564.
Hermanus, *w.* 58.
Jacob, *f.* 45 ; *c.* 76.
Jacobus, *c.* 69.
Jane, Jannitje, *m.* 122 ; *gs.* ‡403.
Jeremiah, *f.* 32, 76 (2) ; *c.* 76, 86, 88 ; *gs.* ‡546, ‡562, ‡571, ‡572.
Johannis, *f.* 72.
John, *f.* 68, 110, 124 ; *c.* 68 : Jacob, *c.* 88.
Jure, *c.* 72 ; *w.* 72.
Lena, Leentje, *m.* 68, 72, 110.
Maria, *m.* 45 (2), 69, 86, 88 (2), 124 (2), 125 ; *w.* 58 ; *gs.* ‡558, ‡559,
    ‡560, ‡561, ‡562, ‡563.
Nicolaas, *f.* 69 ; *c.* 110.
Rachel, *c.* 125 : Catherine, *c.* 124 ; *gs.* ‡560 : Jane, *c.* 124.
Robert, *c.* 122.

Sara, *w.* 72.
CARNS, CAIRNS, Cornelis, *c.* 27.
    David, *f.* 140; *w.* 27.
    Dorothie, *c.* 36.
    Douglas, *f.* 27, 36; *w.* 139.
    Elisabeth, *m.* 140.
    Geesje, *m.* 27, 36; *w.* 139.
    William, *c.* 140.
CERALLAGH, CERALLACH, CERRELLACH—see Carlock.
CHAPMAN, Christiana, *gs.* ‡233.
    George Warren, *gs.* ‡233.
    John Warren, *gs.* ‡233.
CHAPPLE, Maria, *m.* 103; *c.* 103.
    Thomas, *f.* 103.
CHRISTIE, CHRISTE, Abigail, *m.* 7, 8, 35.
    Andries, *f.* 7, 8, 35.
    Antje, Annatje, *c.* 7, 8, 9; *w.* 15, 16.
    Bethsie, *m.* 9.
    David, *c.* 35, 36; *w.* 35, 36 (2).
    Elisabeth, *m.* 36.
    James, *f.* 9.
    John, *f.* 36; *w.* 15.
    Willem, *w.* 16.
    Wybrech, *w.* 35, 36 (2).
CHRISTOPHER, CHRISTOPHEL, CURISTOPHER, Aaltje, *m.* 17, 59, 71; *c.* 18, 19.
    Abraham Quacenbush, *c.* 20.
    Anna, *c.* 17.
    Caty, *c.* 31 (2).
    Charity Ann, *c.* 31.
    Eva, Eve, Eefje, Effy, Efy, *m.* 18, 31, 75, 76, 93, 117.
    Geesje, *m.* 19, 31, 107.
    Hendrik, *c.* 59.
    Jacob, *f.* 19, 20, 31 (2), 107, 131; *c.* 76.
    Jenny, *c.* 71.
    John, *f.* 17, 59, 71; *c.* 75.
    Joseph, *f.* 18, 31, 75, 76, 93, 117.
    Kizia, Kaziah, *m.* 20, 31, 131.
    Levina, *c.* 93
    Mary, *c.* 107.
    Peter, *c.* 117.
    Stephen, *c.* 131.
CLASE, Jan, *w.* 49.
CLEA, Christiaan, *f.* 139.
    Maria, *m.* 139.
    Wilhelm, *c.* 139.
CLEARWATER, CLAARWATER, Frederick, *f.* 53, 76, 84, 123, 142.
    Garrit, *c.* 53.
    Hetty, Hester, *m.* 53, 76, 84, 123, 142.
    John Hopper, *c.* 76.
    Joseph, *c.* 84.
    Rachel, *c.* 123.
    William Rathbone, *c.* 142.
CLENDENNY, John, *c.* 69.
    Osseltje, *m.* 69.
    Walter, *f.* 69.
CLERK, CLERCK, Elisabeth, *w.* 105.
    Hermanus, *c.* 57.
    Jacobus, *w.* 135: D., *f.* 57.
    Neeltje, *m.* 57.
    Trientje, *w.* 135.
    William, *w.* 105.
COCKROW, Jannetje, *c.* 83.
    Josie, *c.* 64.
    Lisabeth, *c.* 90.
    Niklaas, *f.* 64, 83, 90, 119.
    Pietertje, *m.* 64, 83, 90, 119.
    Rachel, *c.* 119.
COEL—see Cole.
COERTEN, COERTE, Arie, *w.* 78.
    Catrina, *m.* 92.
    John, *f.* 92.
    Lena, *c.* 92; *w.* 78.
COLE, COEL, COOL, Abraham, *f.* 19, 71; *c.* 19.
    Adriaan, *f.* 24, 42, 59.
    Annatje, Antje, *m.* 19, 71; *w.* 59.
    Barend, *c.* 24.

Albert, *c.* 19.
Cornelia, *c.* 29.
Cornelius, *f.* 47, 107.
Elisabeth, *w.* 69: Blauvelt, *gs.* ‡583.
Frederik Van Rypen, *c.* 47.
George, *c.* 51.
Jacob, *f.* 29, 71; *c.* 69; *w.* 69.
Jacobus, *f.* 74; *c.* 71; *w.* 71.
James, *f.* 19, 136.
Johannis, *f.* 69; *w.* 100.
John, *f.* 51.
Joseph, *c.* 74.
Margaret, Margrietje, *m.* 19, 51, 69, 74, 136; *w.* 100.
Maria, *m.* 29, 71; *c.* 107.
Peter, *f.* 132 (2).
Samuel, *c.* 132.
Stephen, *c.* 132; *gs.* ‡582, ‡583.
Trientje, *c.* 136.
CUYPER—see Cooper.

"D"

DATOR, DATER, DATIE, DATEY, DAYTOR, DETE, DETOR, DIETER, Abraham, *f.* 100, 109, 114; *w.* 58, 70.
Adam, *f.* 42, 103, 104.
Elisabeth, *c.* 42.
Hannah, *m.* 100, 114; *c.* 58; *w.* 58, 70.
John, *f.* 58, 102.
Margrietje, *c.* 100, 102, 103.
Maria, *m.* 109.
Mary Catherina, *c.* 109.
Matheus, *c.* 104.
Polly, *m.* 58, 102; *c.* 114.
Rosina, *m.* 42, 104.
Syntje, *m.* 103.
DAVENPOORT, DEVENPOORT, Catrina, *c.* 27.
Grietje, *m.* 111.
Jacob, *w.* 118.
Lea, *m.* 27; *c.* 90; *w.* 118.
Leendert, *f.* 127.
Lisabeth, *w.* 111.
Mary, *m.* 111, 127.
Nathaniel, *f.* 111.
Omphre, *f.* 90; *c.* 111; *w.* 111.
Pieter, *f.* 27.
Sara, *c.* 127.
Willemina, *m.* 90.
DAVIDS, Class, *f.* 66.
Isaac, *c.* 66.
Richard, *w.* 100.
DAVIS, Charles De Buard, *c.* 33.
Egbert, *c.* 41.
James, *f.* 33.
Johannis, *c.* 65 (2).
Lisabeth, *c.* 91.
Maria, Marytje, *m.* 65, 91.
Nancy, *m.* 33.
Nellie, *w.* 51.
Niklaas, *f.* 41, 65 (2), 91.
Pieter, *w.* 51.
DAY, Harriet, *c.* 60.
Jenny, *m.* 60, 84, 131.
Julian, *c.* 84.
Sally, *c.* 131.
William, *f.* 60, 84, 131.
DEBAUN, DEBAAN, DEBAEN, DUBAAN, DUBAEN, DUBEAN, Aaltje, *m.* 18, 60, 70; *w.* 17, 69.
Abigail, *m.* 116.
Abram, Abraham, *f.* 8, 37, 52; *c.* 4, 8, 18 (2), 19; *w.* 23, 81, 82; *mem.* 145.
Albert, *f.* 105, 116.
Andries, Andrias, *f.* 17, 30, 46, 67, 69, 104; *c.* 4 (2); *w.* 16, 70, 72; *mem.* 144.
Angonietje, *c.* 12.
Antje, Annatje, *m.* 18, 23, 31; *c.* 6, 14 (2), 16 (2), 17; *w.* 14 (2), 16, 17, 37 (2), 67.

Margrietje, *c.* 103 (2).
Moses, *f.* 30.
Nancy, *m.* 71.
Polly, *m.* 30.
DEE—see Dey.
DEFFENDORF, Dolle, *c.* 37.
    Elisabeth, *m.* 37.
    George, *f.* 37.
DEGRAFF, Henry, *f.* 117.
    Letty, *m.* 117.
    Peggy, *c.* 117.
DEGRAU, DEGREA, DUGRAU, DEGRAUW, Abel, *f.* 47, 78; *w.* **55.**
    Angonietje, *m.* 1.
    Arend, *f.* 1.
    Casparus, *c.* 25.
    Cornelis, *w.* 141: C., *w.* 47.
    Geertje, *c.* 47.
    Hannah, *m.* 1.
    Hattie, *w.* 141.
    Hermanus, *f.* 25; *c.* 56; *w.* 2, 25, 78.
    Jan, *f.* 77.
    Janneke, Jannitje, *m.* 25; *c.* 77, 78; *w.* 2, 25, **78.**
    John, *f.* 1.
    Klaes, *f.* 56.
    Lena, *m.* 77.
    Maaike, *m.* 47, 78; *w.* **55.**
    Molly, *c.* 1.
    N. N., *m.* 56.
    Willem, *c.* 1.
DEGROOT, Angonietje, *c.* 10.
    Annatje, *m.* 74.
    David, *f.* 10.
    Elsje, *m.* 10.
    Jacobus, *f.* 65, 70, 71, 72, 73, 130; *c.* 65, 70.
    Jannetje, *c.* 73.
    James, *f.* 74; *c.* 74: S., *f.* 116.
    John, *c.* 71, 72.
    Maria, *m.* 70, 71, 72, 73, 130.
    Naatje, *m.* 116.
    Peter, *c.* 116.
    Richard, *w.* 115.
    Santje, *w.* 115.
    Susannah, *c.* 130.
DEI—see Dey.
DELAMATER, DELAMARTER, Abraham, *f.* 74.
    Hannah Van Ryper, *gs.* ‡514.
    Isaac, *c.* 74; gs. ‡514.
    Sarah, *m.* 74.
DEMAREST, DEMARE, DEMAREE, DUMARE, DUMAREE, DUMAREST, Abigael, *c.*
    19.
    Abraham, *c.* 17; *w.* 17.
    Agnes, *m.* 45.
    Albert, *f.* 38, 60, 74, 106 (2), 115, 122, 129; *c.* 8: C., *f.* 8.
    Angenietje, *c.* 4.
    Annatje, Anna, Anne, Antje, *m.* 32, 38, 60, 74, 77, 85, 89, 106 (2), **115,**
      122, 129; *c.* 4, 8, 17; *w.* 8, 9, 12 (2), 113, 128: C., *w.* 4.
    Barend, *f.* 136.
    Belitie, *c.* 23.
    Benjamin, *f.* 4, 63, 130; *w.* 95.
    Barney, *f.* 47.
    Catriena, *m.* 46, 69, 70, 100; *c.* 31.
    Catherine Ann, *c.* 32 .
    Cornelia, *m.* 23, 104, 121.
    Cornelis, Cornelius, *f.* 89, 104; *c.* 29; *w.* 29 (2), 94, 95, 103; *gs.*
      ‡13, ‡14, ‡34; *mem.* 144: I., *f.* 91: J. *f.* 98.
    Daniel, *f.* 100, 130, 138; *c.* 34; *w.* 12: D., *f.* 23.
    David, *f.* 17, 29, 38, 102, 114, 129; *c.* 36, 38 (2); *w.* 4, 8, 34, 64:
      I., *w.* 79: P., *w.* 63: S., *w.* 138.
    Elisabeth, *m.* 29; *w.* 103.
    Eliza, *c.* 45.
    Feytje, *m.* 138.
    Frances, *c.* 47.
    Francyntje, *c.* 46.
    Garret Hopper, *c.* 52.
    Geesje, *m.* 29, 38, 52, 105, 115, 116, 129; *c.* 49.
    Gerrit, *c.* 48, 49, 52; *w.* 48.

Albert, *c.* 22.
Eliza Jane, *m.* 22, 62, 88.
Harman, Harmanus, *f.* 22, 88 ; *c.* 62.
Jan, *f.* 7.
John Quackenbush, *c.* 88.
DEY, DEE, DEI, Antje, *w.* 79.
Caty, *c.* 30.
Dirk, *f.* 125 ; *w.* 133 : D., *w.* 133.
Esther, Hester, *m.* 79, 112 (2), 134.
Francyntje, *m.* 128.
Ginny, *c.* 52.
Isaac, *f.* 98, 128 ; *c.* 71; *w.* 10 .
Jacob, *c.* 69.
Jacobus, *f.* 130.
Johannis, *c.* 79.
John, *c.* 74.
Maria, *c.* 98 ; *w.* 112.
Nancy, *m.* 30.
Peggy, *m.* 130.
Petrus, *c.* 112.
Philip, *c.* 112.
Polly, *c.* 114.
Salomon, Solomon, *f.* 52, 69, 71, 74, 114, 140 ; *w.* 1, 141.
Sally, Sara, Saartje, 52, 69, 71, 74, 114, 125, 140 ; c. 125, 130 ; *w.* 133, 141.
Susannah, *c.* 128.
Syntje, *m.* 98 ; *w.* 10.
Teunis, *f.* 79, 112 (2), 134 ; *c.* 134.
William, *f.* 30 ; *c.* 140.
DIETER—see Dator.
DILL, Dortie Gable, *m.* 103.
George, *f.* 103.
Maria, *c.* 103.
DOBBS, DOBS, DODDS, DODS, Abigael, *c.* 8.
Catriena, *c.* 29.
Eva, *m.* 73.
Jacob, *c.* 73.
Jacobus, *c.* 70, 73.
James, *f.* 29, 70 ; *w.* 73.
Lea, *w.* 140.
Mary, Maria, *m.* 29, 70 ; *c.* 96, 97 ; *w.* 73.
Rachel, *m.* 8, 73, 96, 97, 120, 134, 139 ; *c.* 120 ; *w.* 98, 122.
Thomas, *f.* 73 (2) ; *c.* 134 ; *w.* 122.
Walterus, *c.* 139.
William, Willem, *f.* 8, 96, 97, 120, 134, 139 ; w. 98.
DOREMUS, DEREMES, DEREMUS, DOREMES, DREMES, DREMUS. DUREMES, DU-REMUS, Aagje, *m.* 26.
Aaltje, *c.* 3.
Abby, Abigael, *m.* 16, 19, 38, 75.
Abram, Abraham, *f.* 24 ; *c.* 8, 18.
Andrew, Andreas, *f.* 16, 19, 38, 73, 75 ; *c.* 10.
Annatje, Antje, *m.* 24 ; *c.* 2, 16, 17 ; *w.* 19.
Ariaantje, *c.* 19.
Belitje, *w.* 5, 83.
Betsy, *m.* 44.
Catrina, *c.* 24, 26 ; *w.* 26.
Caty Ann, *c.* 32.
Cornelis, Cornelius, *f.* 3, 34 ; *w.* 78 : A., *f.* 44 : H., *f.* 119.
David, *f.* 99 ; *c.* 34, 38.
Ebbe, *m.* 73.
Eegje, *w.* 119.
Elizabeth, *gs,* ‡311 : Jemima, *c.* 44.
Geesje, *m.* 2, 55 ; *w.* 4, 49.
George, *c.* 54 : Jr., *f.* 32, 54, 108.
Ginny, *c.* 52.
Grietje, *m.* 112.
Hannis, *f.* 10.
Harriet, *m.* 32, 54, 108.
Hendrik, *f.* 26, 112 ; *c.* 55 ; *w.* 11, 57, 119.
Hessel, *f.* 2, 55 ; *w.* 4, 49.
Jacob Conklin, *c.* 86.
Jacobus, James, *f.* 17, 18, 52, 73, 75 ; *w.* 73.
Jan, *w.* 5, 83.
Jannetje, *m.* 8, 10 ; *c.* 75 ; *w.* 14, 16, 70.
Johannes, *f.* 8 ; *c.* 73 ; *w.* 14, 16, 70.
John, *c.* 73.

Jores, *w.* 19.
Jost, *c.* 79.
Lea, *m.* 99.
Margaret, *c.* 99, 108 ; *w.* 11.
Peggy, *m.* 86.
Polly, *m.* 17, 18, 52, 73, 75 ; *w.* 73.
Pryntje, *c.* 112.
Ralph, *f.* 86.
Rachel, *m.* 3, 34, 119 ; *w.* 78.
Thomas, *w.* 112.
DOTY, Aaron, gs. ‡519.
Jacob L., *gs.* ‡519.
Rachel, *gs.* ‡519.
DOUGHTY, Margrieta, *c.* 105.
Mary, *m.* 105.
Robert, *f.* 105.
DREMES, DREMUS—see Doremus.
DUBAAN, DUBAEN, DUBEAN—see Dubaun.
DUBOU, DUBOUW—see Debow.
DUGRAU—see Degrau.
DUREMES, DUREMUS—see Doremus.
DUREST, DERIST, Christina, *c.* 141.
Elisabeth, *m.* 71, 141 (2).
Jacob, *c.* 71.
Leashon, Lison, Lieshon, *f.* 71, 141 (2).
Wollem, William, *c.* 141 (2).
DURYEA, DURIE, DUREA, DERYEA, DERYEE, DURYIE, DURJEE, DURYEE, Albert,
    f. 39 ; *w.* 8.
Angonietje, *m.* 39.
Annatje, *m.* 42 ; *c.* 12, 16.
Catriena, *m.* 43, 72, 129 ; *w.* 30, 129, 136.
Cathalyntje, *w.* 50, 51.
Charity Westervelt, *gs.* ‡68.
Daniel, *f.* 56, 111 ; *w.* 134.
David, *f.* 34, 72, 83, 106 ; *c.* 39 ; *gs.* ‡68.
Dirk, *c.* 35.
Elisabeth, *c.* 42, 43.
Geertje, *m.* 72, 83, 106.
Geesje, *m.* 106.
Gerrit, *w.* 50, 51.
Hannah, *gs.* ‡469.
Hendrika, *c.* 56.
Jacobus, *w.* 49.
Jan, *f.* 42, 103, 128 ; *c.* 70 ; *w.* 70, 111, 121 : D., *f.* 125 : J., *w.* 78 : P.,
    f. 90 ; *w.* 126.
Jannitje, *m.* 90. 125 ; *c.* 72 (2) ; *w.* 126.
Joannes, *c.* 83.
John, *f.* 16, *w.* 122 ; *gs.* ‡469 : I., *f.* 110.
Lea, Leah, *c.* 92 ; *w.* 8.
Leitje, *m.* 110.
Lisabeth, *c.* 90.
Maria, *c.* 103.
Nancy. *c.* 110.
Osseltje, *m.* 12, 70, 92, 115.
Peter, Petrus, *f.* 12, 70, 92, 115 ; *c.* 111, 115.
Rachel, *m.* 16, 103, 128 ; *w.* 70, 121, 122.
Samuel, *f.* 43, 72, 129 ; *c.* 125 ; *w.* 30, 129, 136.
Sara, *c.* 128, 129 : Martyntje, *c.* 106.
Vrouwtje, *m.* 35, 56, 111, 134.
Wyntje, *w.* 78.
DYKMAN, Cornelia, *w.* 98.
Dirk, *w.* 98.
Jan, *w.* 48.
Jannitje, *w.* 48.

"E"

EATHEN, Maria, *w.* 98.
Richard, *w.* 98.
EARL, EARLE, Abigail, Abby, 37, 42 (2), 70, 91 ; *c.* 19 ; *w.* 59 ; *gs.* ‡50.
Daniel Blauvelt, *c.* 40.
Doosje, *c.* 37.
Edward, *f.* 37, 42 (2), 70, 91 ; *c.* 44 (2) ; *w.* 59 ; *gs.* ‡49.
Elisabeth, *c.* 42.
Enoch, *c.* 42.

Gerrit, *f.* 19, 44, 107 : E., *f.* 93.
Hannah, *c.* 61.
Jacob, *f.* 40, 44, 61, 86, 100 ; *c.* 70. 86 ; *gs.* ‡51 : T., *w.* 27.
Lena, *c.* 91.
Lewis, *c.* 93.
Lisabeth, *c.* 89.
Machtel, *m.* 89 ; *w.* 25, 80.
Maria, *m.* 40, 44, 61, 86.
Mary Ann, *c.* 107.
Myntje, *c.* 100.
Rachel, *m.* 100.
Sally, Salla, *m.* 19, 44, 93, 107.
Sylvester, Silvester, *f.* 89 ; *w.* 25, 80.
ECKER, ECKERT, ECKHART, EKKER, Abram, Abraham, *f.* 92 ; *w.* 77.
Cornelius, *f.* 38, 74, 99.
David, *c.* 38.
Jacobus, *c.* 74.
Jan, *w.* 99.
John, *c.* 72 ; *w.* 72.
Lea, *c.* 92.
Margrietje, *m.* 74.
Maria, *m.* 72 ; *c.* 95, 99.
Marytje, *m.* 38, 95, 111 ; *w.* 34 (2).
Matje, *w.* 77.
Paulus, *f.* 72.
Petrus, *c.* 111.
Samuel, *w.* 34.
Thomas, *f.* 95, 111 ; *w.* 34.
Tryntje, *m.* 92.
William, *w.* 140.
ECKERSON, ECKERSEN, EKKERSON, ECKENSEN, ECKERSE, ECKERSE, ACKER-
SON, Aaron, *f.* 18, 39.
Abraham, *f.* 38 ; *c.* 17.
Angenietje, Angonietje, *m.* 6, 7, 96, 113, 133 (2), 137 ; *c.* 7, 12, 13,
16, 17, 18 ; *w.* 12 (2), 13, 15, 16, 17, 35, 37 (2), 38, 67 ; *mem.*
145.
Annatje, Ann, *m.* 67 (2), 88, 92, 100, 131 ; *c.* 6, 12, 14, 18 (2) 19 ;
w. 17, 114 ; *mem.* 145.
Carl, *f.* 137.
Catriena, Catryntje, Caty, *m.* 12, 29, 39, 68, 122, 128, 135, 141 ; *c.*
29 ; *w.* 58, 122 ; *mem.* 144.
Charity, *c.* 30.
Cornelia, *m.* 66, 70, 98, 113, 134 ; *c.* 30 (2), 31 (2) ; *w.* 29, 30, 135,
136 ; *mem.* 145.
Cornelis, Cornelius, *f.* 18, 29, 68, 141 ; *w.* 58, 119 : J., *f.* 88.
Daniel, *c.* 39.
David, *f.* 6, 7, 30, 39, 75, 76, 95, 107, 113, 133 (2) ; *c.* 37, 38, 39 (3) ;
w. 12 (2), 13, 15, 16, 17, 35, 37 (2), 38, 67, 80 ; *mem.* 145.
Dirk *f.* 81, 96.
Dorkus, *c.* 38.
Edward, *f.* 12, 30, 43, 50, 66, 104, 122, 128, 130, 135 ; *mem.* 144:
P., *f.* 12 ; *w.* 12.
Elisabeth, *c.* 43.
Garret, Gerrit, *f.* 92, 131.
Geertje, *m.* 17, 18, 19, 39, 110 ; *w.* 73.
Grietje, *m.* 39, 107 ; *c.* 50.
Hannah, *c.* 61.
Hendrik, *c.* 58.
Hetty, *m.* 12, 30, 43, 104, 130 ; *w.* 12.
Jacob, *f.* 67, 119, 130, 133 ; *c.* 63, 74 ; *w.* 17, 66 (2), 82, 103, 114,
122, 126, 127, 134 ; *mem.* 145 : S., *f.* 31 : T., *f.* 133 ; *w.* 63.
James, Jacobus, *f.* 105 ; *c.* 71.
Jannetje, *m.* 133 ; *c.* 66, 76 ; *w.* 63, 134.
Jan, *f.* 97, 98, 110, 126, 133 ; *c.* 67, 81 ; *w.* 28, 65, 67, 69, 70, 102.
Jenny, *c.* 66.
Johannis, *c.* 68, 69.
John, *f.* 17, 18, 19, 39, 61, 110 ; *c.* 67, 70, 73, 88 ; *w.* 70, 73, 135 : J.,
w. 26.
Joseph, *c.* 75.
Katelyntje, *m.* 18.
Lea, Leah, *m.* 31, 119, 130 ; *c.* 92, 93.
Lena, *m.* 133 ; *w.* 28, 70.
Margaret, Margrietje, *m.* 31, 39, 106, 116, 136 ; *c.* 100, 104.
Maria, *m.* 16, 30, 37, 58, 69, 75, 76, 96, 103, 115, 126 ; *c.* 96, 98 (2),
103, 104, 106 (2), 107 ; *w.* 26, 69, 70, 96, 97, 98, 102, 103, 106, 122,
126, 133 (4), 134 ; *mem.* 145.

FOLIE, FOLLY, Adam, *c.* 14.
   Antje, *m.* 14, 16.
   Peter, *c.* 116.
   Willem, *f.* 14, 116.
FORSHEA, FORSHUER, FORSHUR, FURSHEUR—see Verschuer.
FOSTER, Ann, *m.* 122.
   Henry, *f.* 122.
   Rachel, *c.* 122.
FOX, Jane Bogert, *gs.* ‡239.
   John, *gs.* ‡239.
   Margaret, *gs.* ‡597.
FREDERICK, FREDERIKS, FREDERIKSE, FRERIKSE, VRERIKSE, VRERICKSON,
   VREDRIKS, Abraham, *f.* 103.
   Catrina, *c.* 28 ; *w.* 28.
   Coenraad, *f.* 28 ; *w.* 94.
   Elisabeth, *m.* 28, 103 ; *c.* 43.
   Grietje, *m.* 115.
   Hendrik, *f.* 115, 135, 141 ; *w.* 58, 69.
   Hette, *w.* 58..
   Isaak, *f.* 100 ; *w.* 59.
   John, *f.* 102.
   Margrietje, *m.* 141 ; *c.* 103 ; *w.* 94.
   Maria, *m.* 100, 102, 135 ; *c.* 100, 102 ; *w.* 59, 69.
   Pieter, *c.* 115.
   Robert, *w.* 28.
   Tryntje, *c.* 135.
   William, *f.* 43 ; *c.* 141.
   Wyntje, *m.* 43.
FREELAND, John *c.* 84.
   Margaret, *m.* 84.
   Tunis, *f.* 84.
FREEMAN, Francis, *f.* 60.
   Hassel, *c.* 60.
   Mary, *m.* 60.
FURDON, Abraham, *f.* 132.
   Louisa, *m.* 132.
   Stephen, *c.* 132.

"G"

GABLE, Dortie *m.* 103.
GALLEWE (Galloway), Isaak, *c.* 125.
   John, *f.* 125.
   Lea, *m.* 125.
GARDENIER, GARDINER, GARDNER, Aaltje, *m.* 125.
   Annatje, *c.* 9.
   Barend, *c.* 23.
   Hans, Johannis, Jan, *f.* 9, 23, 63.
   Jacob, *f.* 130 ; *c.* 63.
   Jacomyntje, *m.* 9, 23, 63.
   Josiah, *f.* 101, 124.
   Maria, *m.* 130 : Jane, *c.* 101.
   Peggy, *m.* 101, 124.
   Rachel Catharine, *c.* 124.
   Sarah, *c.* 130.
   Thomas, *f.* 135 ; *c.* 135.
GARRISON, GARRETSON, GARRITSE, GARRITSON, GERRETSEN, GERRITSE, GER-
   RITSEN, GERRITSON, Aaron, *c.* 19.
   Abram G., *w.* 9.
   Abraham, *c.* 4.
   Albert, *f.* 19, 84, 108 ; *c.* 11 ; *gs.* ‡420.
   Anne, Antje, *m.* 109 ; *c.* 12, 18 ; *w.* 31.
   Caty, Cate, Catharina, *c.* 31 (2), 32 ; *gs.* ‡435.
   Effie, *m.* 134
   Eliza, *gs.* ‡364.
   Gerrebrand, *f.* 138.
   Gerrit, *w.* 97 : A., *w.* 98 : C., *w.* 120.
   Grietje, *w.* 97.
   Hannis, *f.* 66.
   Hendrik, *f.* 4.
   Hessel, *f.* 84 ; *c.* 58 (2) ; *w.* 58.
   Jacob, *f.* 18, 31 (2), 107 ; *w.* 4 : I., *f.* 84, 131.
   Jemima, Jacomyntje *m.* 19, 84, 108 : Ackerman, *gs.* ‡420.
   Johannis, *f.* 11, 12, 58, 115, 127 ; *c.* 66 ; *w.* 68, 73 : H., *f.* 58 ; *mem.* 14**3**
   John, *c.* 84 (3) : H., *f.* 109.
   Lea, *w.* 9.

Helena, *mem.* 144.
Johannis, *c.* 71.
Judik, *w.* 50.
Lena, *c.* 92; *w.* 92, 110.
Magdalen, *w.* 110.
Margreitje, *m.* 28; *w.* 30, 98, 116; *gs.* ‡103.
Maria, *c.* 99.
Marretje, etc., *m.* 50; *c.* 106; *w.* 23.
Nicholas, Klaas, *f.* 50; *c.* 110; *w.* 23, 92, 110 (3); *mem.* 144.
Trientje, *w.* 134.
William, *f.* 30, 43, 71, 92, 106, 110; *w.* 98 (2), 136.
HALL, Caroline, *c.* 32.
Eliza Jane, *c.* 44.
Frederik, *c.* 47.
James, *c.* 86.
Jane, *m.* 32, 44, 47, 86.
William, *f.* 32, 44, 47, 86.
HAMMOND, HAMMON, David, *w.* 77: Henry, *c.* 40.
Garrit, *c.* 54.
Martha Esther, *c.* 101.
Mary Elisabeth, *c.* 101.
Marytje, *w.* 77.
Patty, *m.* 40, 54, 101 (2), 124.
Rachel Ann, *c.* 124.
Thomas, *f.* 40, 54, 101 (2), 124.
HARING, HAARING, HARRING, HERRING, Aaltje, *w.* 68.
Abraham, Abram, *f.* 75, 130; *w.* 94, 95: A., *w.* 95: C., *w.* 8: John, *c.* 22.
Antje, Annatje, *m.* 44, 140; *c.* 18.
Ariaantje, *c.* 9.
Catrina, *w.* 8, 26.
Cattelyntje, *gs.* ‡43.
Christiana, *c.* 26.
Cornelis, *f.* 50; *w.* 26, 68: A., *f.* 140.
David, *f.* 70, 136.
Elisabeth, *m.* 52, 75; *c.* 44; *w.* 67.
Eliza, *m.* 22.
Femmetje, *m.* 18, 52, 130.
Fytje, *w.* 74.
Garrit, *f.* 59; *c.* 50.
Geertje, *c.* 52.
Grietje, *c.* 52.
Hetty, *c.* 59.
Isaac, *f.* 44; *c.* 67; *w.* 103.
Jacob, *f.* 18, 52, 130.
Jan, John, *f.* 22, 67; *c.* 75; *w.* 67, 74: D., *f.* 9.
Jannitje, *m.* 67.
Joost, Joseph, *c.* 70, 75.
Lea, *m.* 26.
Lisabeth, *m.* 9.
Margrietje, *m.* 75, 130.
Maria, *m.* 59; *w.* 103.
Martyntje *w.* 94, 95; *gs.* ‡478.
Marytje, *w.* 95.
Peter, Petrus, *f.* 52, 75: A., *w.* 8.
Sarah, *c.* 130.
Stephanas Goetsius, *c.* 130.
Tryntje, *m.* 70, 136; *c.* 136.
Willem, *c.* 140.
HARMANUS, Geertje, *c.* 47.
Nix, *f.* 47.
HARMUTMAN, Geertrui Venniceman, *m.* 88.
Job, *c.* 88.
Peter, *f.* 88.
HARRIS, HARRES, HERRES, Annatje, *m.* 59, 75, 84.
Charles Augustus, *c.* 34.
Cornelius, *c.* 31.
Dorothy, *c.* 39.
Edward, *f.* 34.
George, *c.* 54.
Grietje, *m.* 68.
Hannah, *m.* 31, 39, 54, 86, 111.
Henry, Hendrik, *f.* 54, 86; *c.* 59, 60.
Hester, *m.* 60.
Isaac, *f.* 31, 39, 59, 75, 84, 111; *c.* 86.
Jacob, *f.* 60; *c.* 84.

HOGENKAMP, Elisabeth, *m.* 96.
   Garret, *w.* 130.
   Helena, *w.* 96.
   Jan, *f.* 96.
   Lena, *w.* 95.
   Myndert, *c.* 96; *w.* 95, 96.
   Sarah, *w.* 130.
HOLDEROM, HOLDRUM—see Halderom.
HOLSTEAD, Anna, *w.* 66.
   Jacob, *w.* 66.
HOMS, Debra, *m.* 139.
   Jan Jr., *f.* 139.
   Wyntje, *c.* 139; *w.* 139.
HOOGLAND, Keetje, *w.* 46.
   Rebeckah, *gs.* ‡466.
HOPPER, HOPPE, HOPPEN, Aaltje, *m.* 36, 37, 49, 51, 52, 91, 102, 140; *c.* 3, 7, 13, 139; *w.* 16, 49, 57, 59, 64 (2), 92, 141; *mem.* 144.
   Abigail, *c.* 2, 7; *w.* 48.
   Abram, Abraham, *f.* 11, 29, 48, 51, 64, 65, 80, 102, 103, 121; *c.* 3, 4, 6 (2), 13, 14, 16, 17, 18 (4); *w.* 2 (2), 3, 6 (2), 11, 12, 13, 15, 95, 103, 120; *mem.* 143; *gs.* ‡496: H., *f.* 7, 10, 56, 57, 139 (2); *w.* 11, 12, 16, 56, 65: I., *w.* 13; *mem.* 144: J., *w.* 51.
   Albert, *f.* 4, 7, 41, 43, 48, 52, 53, 65, 78, 82, 94, 97, 118, 131; *c.* 7, 10, 11, 12 (2), 13, 16 (2), 17, 19, 20 (2), 21 (2), 22; *w.* 7, 8, 10, 118 (2), 119, 133; *gs.* ‡606: Jr., *c.* 20: G., *f.* 32, 61, 85, 137; *w.* 12; *gs.* ‡392, ‡393: H., *f.* 107.
   Andries, Andrew, Andreas, Andrias, *f.* 9, 16 (2), 18, 19, 31, 37, 52, 55, 74 (2), 75 (2), 91, 105, 106, 107, 116, 118, 128; *c.* 4 (2), 5, 7 (2), 8, 10, 11 (2), 17, 18 (2), 19 (2), 20, 21; *w.* 4, 11, 13, 15, 50, 68, 100, 114; *mem.* 144: A., *f.* 6, 7, 65, 82, 97, 116, 126; *w.* 7; *gs.* ‡488: C., *f.* 53, 117: G., *f.* 49, 57 (2); *w.* 48: H., *f.* 32, 44, 53, 60, 131; *w.* 5: I., *f.* 41, 49; *w.* 7; *gs.* ‡301: J., *f.* 4, 57; *gs.* ‡99: P., *f.* 20 (2), 61 (2), 89, 107: W., *w.* 140.
   Antje, Annatje, Anne, Anny, *m.* 7 (2), 10 (2), 16, 18, 20 (2), 26, 31, 48, 49 (2), 53 (2) 56, 57, 61 (2), 64, 65, 74, 75, 77, 78, 80, 89, 94, 95, 99 (2), 106, 107, 116, 117, 120, 133, 136, 139 (3); *c.* 4 (2), 9, 10, 11, 12, 18, 19 (2); *w.* 5, 7, 8, 10, 11 (2), 12 (3), 13, 16, 49, 50, 56 (2), 57 (2), 65, 80, 115, 116, 133, 139; *mem.* 143, 144; *gs.* ‡497, ‡581.
   Arie, *c.* 12.
   Ariaantje, *c.* 5.
   Betsey, *m.* 20, 62.
   Carolina, *c.* 32.
   Cathalyntje, Caty, Catrina, Catrintje, Catherine, Catherina, *m.* 2, 12, 22, 50, 51, 62, 86, 99, 108, 121, 124, 128; *c.* 26, 31, 32 (3), 33; *w.* 13, 69, 100 (2), 104, 114, 118: Ann, *c.* 31; *gs.* ‡504: Cooper, *gs.* ‡386.
   Charity, Charette, *m.* 16, 54, 74, 75, 92, 106.
   Chatrine, *gs.* ‡324.
   Christian, *c.* 32.
   Cornelia, *c.* 25, 30.
   Cornelis, Cornelius, *c.* 28, 29: A., *f.* 21, 62.
   David, *f.* 4, 5, 7, 25, 54, 56; *c.* 37 (2), 38; *w.* 26, 36, 37 (2), 113; *mem.* 145: G. *f.* 108: Henry, *c.* 40.
   Derrick, Dirk, *c.* 36; *gs.* ‡150.
   Dirkje, *w.* 52, 53.
   Dolly, *c.* 39.
   Elisabeth, *m.* 13, 18 (2), 19, 21, 28, 29, 32, 41, 43, 52, 53, 69, 71 (2), 76, 107, 116, 120, 121; *c.* 41 (2), 43 (5), 44, 45, 91; *w.* 7, 15, 41, 64, 68, 103; *mem.* 144 (2); *gs.* ‡81, ‡363, ‡408: A., *gs.* ‡78: Ackerman, *gs.* ‡99.
   Eliza, Ann, *m.* 44; *c.* 46: Jane, *c.* 45; *gs.* ‡611: Maria, *c.* 44.
   Ellen, *m.* 61, 67: Winters, *gs.* ‡391.
   Elsje, *m.* 4, 81, 94, 118; *w.* 46, 47, 48 (2), 81, 89, 138; *mem.* 143.
   Esther, *m.* 136.
   Frederik, *c.* 47.
   Futje, *w.* 83.
   Fytje, *m.* 11, 43, 57.
   Garrit, Gerrit, *f.* 2, 4, 11, 17, 18 (2), 38, 44, 50, 53, 66, 91, 94, 99, 105, 110, 123, 130, 135; *c.* 48 (5), 49 (2), 50 (3), 51 (3), 52 (2), 53 (5), 54 (3); *w.* 48 (2), 50, 51, 52 (2), 53 (2), 67, 89, 104, 138; *mem.* 143 (2); *gs.* ‡144, ‡146, ‡148, ‡548: A., *f.* 20, 21, 33, 44, 48, 61, 86, 99, 118, 121, 125; *w.* 48, 49 (2), 57 (2), 100 (2); *gs.* ‡386, ‡387: H., *f.* 7, 10, 26, 39, 80, 120, 137; *w.* 12, 49, 56, 57, 133; *f.* 13, 81; *w.* 47, 67; *mem.* 143; *gs.* ‡300; *f.* 12, 58, 64, 65, 69, 71; *w.* 46, 81: Jan, *f.* 118: W., *f.* 140: Wm., *f.* 67.

Tryntje, Trientje, *m.* 4, 49, 57, 91; *c.* 133 (2), 135, 137; *w.* 2, 5, 50, 71, 80.
Tyna, *m.* 108; *c.* 136, 137; *w.* 52.
Wibie, Whiby, Wybee, Wiiby, *m.* 20, 40, 45, 54, 117 : Voorhis, *gs.* ‡610, ‡611.
Willem, *f.* 48, 77, 78, 94, 95; *c.* 139, 140; *w.* 7, 8, 80, 133, 139.
Wyntje, *m.* 3, 56; *c.* 139 (3), 140; *w.* 3, 4, 6, 48, 55, 56, 79, 80, 139.
HORN, Abraham, *c.* 114.
    Andries, *f.* 39; *c.* 13.
    Catrina, *c.* 28.
    David, *c.* 37, 39.
    Ebby, *m.* 103.
    Elisabeth, *c.* 41.
    Femmetje, *m.* 14, 41.
    Jacob, *f.* 14, 41; *gs.* ‡468.
    Joseph, *f.* 13, 28, 37, 103; *c.* 39; *w.* 100.
    Maria, Marytje, *m.* 13, 28, 37, 39; *c.* 103.
HORSBROOK—see Hasbrook.
HOVER, Benjamin, *f.* 24, 62, 85, 108; *c.* 24.
    Hannah, *c.* 62.
    Jemima, *m.* 24, 62, 85, 108.
    Joseph, *c.* 85.
    Margaret, *c.* 108.
HULDRUM—see Halderom.
HUNTER, Jannetje, *c.* 83.
    Mollie, *m.* 83.
    Robert, *f.* 83.
HUTCHINSON, HUTCHISON, Eliza M., *gs.* ‡389.
    Henry, *c.* 61.
    Mary Matilda, *gs.* ‡388.
    Matilda Brevoort, *gs.* ‡388, ‡389, ‡390.
    Pardon, *f.* 61; *gs.* ‡388, ‡389, ‡390.
    Tyna, *m.* 61.
HUYLER, Cornelis, *m.* 95.
    Grietje, *w.* 97.
    Jan, *w.* 97.
    Margrietje, *c.* 95.
HUYSMAN, Jan, *w.* 79.
    Marietje, *w.* 79.

"I"

IESTERLI, USTERLI, Catrientje, *c.* 25.
    Gouda, *m.* 25, 133.
    Marte, *f.* 25, 133.
    Thomas, *c.* 133.

"J"

JACOBUSSE, Antje, *c.* 7.
    Brand B., *f.* 7.
    Geertje, *m.* 7.
    Lydia, *m.* 121, 128.
    Rachel, *c.* 121.
    Roelof, *f.* 121, 128; *w.* 113.
    Sara, *c.* 128.
    Susannah, *c.* 128.
JANSE, JANSEN, Aaltje, *c.* 12.
    Abraham, *f.* 12, 13, 24, 135; *c.* 13.
    Barend, *c.* 24.
    Elisabeth, *m.* 12, 13, 24, 135.
    Fytje, *m.* 68.
    Johannis, *f.* 68; *c.* 68.
    John, *mem.* 145.
    Sophia, *mem.* 145.
    Tietje, *c.* 135.
JENKINS, JENKENS, JINKINS, GINCKINS, Annatje, *m.* 57, 92.
    Dorothy, *m.* 54.
    Elisabeth, *m.* 102.
    Gerrit, *f.* 102; *w.* 99 : Van Wagoner, *c.* 54.
    Hannes, *c.* 57.
    Jacobus, *c.* 79.
    Jacomyntje, *m.* 79.
    John, *f.* 79.

Grietje, *m.* 4; *c.* 49; *w.* 49.
Hendrikje, *m.* 49.
Isaac, *w.* 66: N., *f.* 49.
Jane, *m.* 109.
Margaret, *c.* 109.
Nicasie, *f.* 4; *w.* 49.
Roelof, Ralph, *f.* 20: R., *f.* 109.
KNEGHT, KNEGT, Coenraad, *f.* 41, 103; *w.* 105 (2).
  Elisabeth, *c.* 41.
  Margrietje, Grietje, *m.* 41, 103; *w.* 105 (2).
  Martienus, *c.* 103.
KOGH, KOUGH, COGH, COUGH, COCH, Albert, *f.* 105.
  Anna Maria, *w.* 25.
  Casper, Casparus, *f.* 25, 30, 32, 44, 108, 117, 126, 134; *c.* 25, 28, 31, 32; *w.* 114; *mem.* 143; *gs.* ‡489: Jr. *f.* 31; *gs.* ‡489, ‡490: C., *f.* 28.
  Elias, *w.* 25.
  Elisabeth, *c.* 44.
  Grietje, *w.* 30.
  Jacob, *w.* 95, 97, 128.
  Jasper, Jr., *f.* 123.
  Lidea, *m.* 25, 126, 134; *mem.* 143: Terhune, *gs.* ‡490.
  Margrietje, *m.* 28, 105.
  Maria, Mary, *c.* 108; *w.* 95, 97, 114, 128; *gs.* ‡487.
  Marytyntje, *c.* 105.
  Peggy, *c.* 117.
  Rachel, *c.* 123.
  Sara, *w.* 28.
  Steven, *c.* 126.
  Trientje, *c.* 134.
  Tyna, *m.* 31, 32, 44, 108, 117, 123; *gs.* ‡ 489, ‡490.
KOOL, Abram, *f.* 99.
  Barend, *w.* 4.
  Catriena, *m.* 118.
  Christina, *w.* 4.
  Grietje, *c.* 99.
  Hannes, *f.* 118.
  Isaak, *c.* 79.
  Jacob, *f.* 79.
  Lea, *w.* 90.
  Leendert, *w.* 90.
  Rachel, *m.* 79; *c.* 118.
KOM—see Van Blercom.
KONKELE—see Conklin.
KONING, Johannis, *w.* 68.
  Rachel, *w.* 68.
KOUGH—see Kogh.
KRIM—see Crim.
KROM, Catriena, *m.* 90; *w.* 100.
  Elisabeth, Lisabeth, *c.* 90; *w.* 28.
  Grietje, *m.* 78.
  Hendrick, *f.* 78.
  Isaak, *c.* 78.
  Teunis, *f.* 90; *w.* 100.
KUYPER, Abram, *f.* 6; *c.* 6.
  Catharina, *c.* 25.
  Cornelis, *f.* 25.
  Mettie, *m.* 25.
  Sara, *m.* 6.

"L"

LABACH, LABBAGH, Jan. *f.* 121.
  Lena, *m.* 104.
  Maragrietje, *m.* 121.
  Maretje Yeomans, *c.* 104.
  Maria, *mem.* 145.
  Rachel, *c.* 121; *w.* 2.
LACKY, Catharine, *m.* 54.
  Garrit Banta, *c.* 54.
  James, *f.* 54.
LANE, Betsie, *m.* 138.
  Henry, *f.* 138.
  William Henry, *c.* 138.
LAROI, LAROY, LAROE, LARUE, Arie, *w.* 138.
  Annatje, *m.* 98.

Pieter, *f.* 8, 83; *w.* 57.
Rachel, *m.* 44, 59, 73; *c.* 120; *w.* 130: Ann, *c.* 124.
Stephen, Steven, *f.* 59, 73; *c.* 126, 130, 131; *w.* 128, 130.
LYDECKER, LEYDECKER, Albert G., *f.* 107.
　Caty, Catharina, *m.* 44, 53, 60, 108.
　David, *f.* 45, 54; *gs.* ‡480a: G., *f.* 62.
　Elisabeth, Lisbeth, *c.* 44; *w.* 23, 125.
　Evelina Amelia, *c.* 45; *gs.* ‡480a.
　Hester Maria, *m.* 62.
　Garret, Gerrit, *f.* 70, 105, 122; *c.* 53, 54; *gs.* ‡478, ‡479, ‡480.
　Henry Hooper, *c.* 60.
　Jannetje, *m.* 107.
　John, *c.* 70: G., *f.* 44, 53, 60, 108.
　Maria, *m.* 105, 122.
　Mary Van Riper, *gs.* ‡480.
　Martyntje, *m.* 70; *c.* 105, 107: Haring, *gs.* ‡478.
　Mathilda, *c.* 108.
　Richard, *c.* 122.
　Susan, *m.* 45, 54, 62; *gs.* ‡480a.

"M"

MABIE, MABE, MABEE, MABEY, MABY, MAEBIE, MAYBE, MEABY, MEBE, ME-
　　BIE, MEEBE, Aaltje, *m.* 83.
　Aaron, *gs.* ‡573.
　Abraham, *f.* 85, 92, 131, 136; *c.* 13, 18; *w.* 97, 104.
　Annatje, *c.* 16.
　Casparus, *c.* 24; *w.* 24.
　David, *c.* 37.
　Ellen M., *gs.* ‡573.
　Femmitje, *m.* 81.
　Fytje, *w.* 46.
　Ginny, *m.* 74.
　Hannes, *f.* 81.
　Isaac, *f.* 13, 69; *w.* 14, 46.
　Jacob, *c.* 81.
　Jan, John, *f.* 37, 65, 66, 113; *c.* 69, 74, 83; *w.* 8, 9, 68, 120.
　Jannetje, *m.* 16, 18, 73, 92, 95, 104, 116; *c.* 65, 73, 85; *w.* 65, 73, 113,
　Johanis, *c.* 66.
　Joost, *w.* 70.
　Lea, *m.* 37, 65, 66, 113; *c.* 92 (2); *w.* 8, 9, 68, 120.
　Maria, Maritje, *m.* 92, 136; *c.* 104; *w.* 97, 104.
　Myndert, *c.* 95.
　Peter, Pieter, *f.* 16, 18, 24, 73, 74, 92, 104, 116; *c.* 113, 116; *w.* 65, 77.
　　113 (2): Jr., *f.* 95; *w.* 83.
　Rachel, *m.* 24; *w.* 77.
　Sara, Sally, *m.* 13, 69; *c.* 131; *w.* 14.
　Sichey, Sechy, *m.* 85, 131.
　Trientje, *c.* 136; *w.* 70.
　William, *f.* 83; *w.* 73.
　Willempje, *w.* 24.
MACDANNEL, MACDANEL, MAGDANEL, MCDANNEL, MACKENNEL, Catrina,
　　Trientje, *m.* 26, 35, 82; *w.* 90.
　Cornelis, *f.* 26, 35, 63, 82; *c.* 26; *w.* 90.
　Daniel, *c.* 35.
　Jacob, *c.* 82.
　Jan, *c.* 63.
MACELESE—see Merseles.
MACLAIN, Andrew, *c.* 19.
　Dorothy, Dolla, *m.* 19, 123.
　Rachel, *c.* 123.
　William, *f.* 19, 123.
MARCELESSE—see Merseles.
MARIE, Abram, *c.* 8.
　Jan, *f.* 8.
　Lea, *m.* 8.
MARINUS, MARINES, MORINUS, Catharina Maria, *c.* 34.
　David, *c.* 40; *w.* 135.
　Eliza, *m.* 40: Jane, *m.* 34.
　Harmanus, *f.* 34.
　John, *w.* 30: D., *f.* 40.
MARKS, Anny, *m.* 76.
　Hendrik, *f.* 76.
　John, *c.* 76.
MASSACRE, MASSEKER—see Messiker.

Thomas, *f.* 138.
Willem, *c.* 138.
MILRIEN, Margriet, *w.* 96.
MILTENBERRI, MELTENBERRIE, Crastina, *c.* 27.
Joannes, *c.* 64.
Lisabeth, *m.* 27, 64.
Luwis, Lewis, *f.* 27, 64; *w.* 11.
MITCHELL, Elizabeth, *gs,* ‡406.
MOLGRAF, Boljer, *f.* 50.
Christien, *m.* 50.
Grietje, *c.* 50.
MOORE, MORE, Anna, *c.* 16.
Jane, Jennie, Jannitje, *m.* 16, 141; *c.* 78; *w.* 45.
Jeremias, Jeremiah, *f.* 78, 138.
Johannis, *w.* 65.
John, *f.* 16, 67, 141; *w.* 140.
Joseph, *c.* 67.
Lisabeth, *m.* 78, 138.
Maria, Marytje, *m.* 67; *w.* 65, 140.
William, Wilms, *c.* 138, 141.
MORINUS—see Marinus.
MOUNT, Rachel, *m.* 127.
Richard, *f.* 127.
Susannah, *c.* 127.
MOURUSSE (MORRIS?), MAURUSSEN, MAURISSEN, MAURUS, MOURESE,
    MOURESEN, MOURISON, MOURUS, MOWERSON, Abraham, *f.* 87,
    88; *c.* 19.
Brechje, Bridget, *c.* 23: Maria, *c.* 24.
Catrina, *c.* 26.
Dirk, *f.* 95.
Elisabeth, *m.* 23; *c.* 44.
Eliza, *m.* 24, 87.
Grietje, *m.* 72.
Isaac, *c.* 63; *w.* 63.
Jacob, Jacobus, *f.* 19, 26, 63, 117; *c.* 64, 72, 88; *w.* 64.
John, *c.* 73: Andrew, *c.* 87: D., *f.* 24, 87: Jacob, *c.* 87.
Lena, *m.* 26, 63.
Margreitje, *m.* 73.
Marytje, Mary, *m.* 19, 117; *c.* 95; *w.* 63, 95.
Mourus, Maurits, *f.* 64; *w.* 83.
Nathaniel, *f.* 23.
Patty, *c.* 117.
Peggy, *m.* 44.
Pieter, *f.* 44, 72, 73; *w.* 95.
Rachel, *m.* 87, 88, 95.
Tryntje, *m.* 64; *w.* 64.
MUYSINGER, MUYSEGER, MUYSENER, MUISEGER, Catriena, *m.* 103; *w.* 55.
Coenraad, *f.* 103; *w.* 55.
Jacobus, *c.* 68; *w.* 68.
John, *w.* 103.
Lena, *w.* 68.
Margrietje, *c.* 103.
Marytje, *w.* 1.
Niklaas, *w.* 1.
Peggy, *m.* 68.
Petrus, *f.* 68; *w.* 114.
MYER, MEYER, MYERS, MYRES, Aaltje, *c.* 10.
Abigail, *m.* 8, 99.
Abram, *f.* 78; *c.* 2, 11; *w.* 2.
Adolf, *w.* 89, 112.
Andrew, *f.* 27.
Annatje, *c.* 8.
Ariaantje, *m.* 96, 97, 119; *w.* 42, 48, 97, 100, 128.
Betsy, *m.* 86, 137 (2).
Brechje, *m.* 29, 42.
Catrientje, *m.* 78.
Cornelia, *c.* 27; *w.* 27.
Cornelis, *f.* 119; *c.* 25, 29; *w.* 27, 48, 94, 97, 128: M., *f.* 96, 97.
David, *c.* 36.
Ebbi, *w.* 49.
Elisabeth, *m.* 123; *c.* 42.
Ellie, *m.* 46.
Fytje, *c.* 46.
Geertje, *m.* 2, 129; *w.* 115.
Gerrebrecht, *m.* 10, 36.
Hannes, *f.* 94: C., 65, 95, 119, 133: I., *f.* 25: M., *f.* 89.
Jacob, *f.* 99; *c.* 78; *w.* 49, 97: D., *f.* 8, 46.

Maria, *m.* 102.
Matthew, *f.* 53, 106, 123.
Rebeckah, *c.* 123.
OUTWATER, Belitie, *w.* 23.
Pieter, *w.* 23.

"P"

PAKE, Betsy, Elisabeth, *m.* 33, 77, 101.
Catharine Ann, *c.* 33 : Hopper, *gs,* ‡504.
John, *c.* 77 ; *gs.* ‡504.
Maria, Elizabeth, *c.* 101.
Martin, *f.* 33, 77, 101.
PARRELMAN, PARLMAN, PARLEMAN, Aimy, *c.* 52.
Antje, Anne, *m.* 38, 94, 97 ; *w.* 48, 49, 79.
David, *c.* 38.
Gilbert, *c.* 52.
Han Jurry, *f.* 83.
Isaac, *c.* 83.
Jacobus, Cobus, James, *f.* 38, 52, 82, 97 ; *c.* 82 ; *w.* 48, 49.
Margriet, *c.* 94, 97.
Maria, *m.* 83.
Ned., *w.* 79 : D., *f.* 94.
PAUL, PAULISFELT, PAULUS, PAULUSSE—see Pulisfelt.
PECKER, Catriena, *c.* 29.
Coenraad, *f.* 115.
Elisabeth, *m.* 95.
Jacob, *f.* 95, 112.
Johannis, *w.* 14.
Klaartje, *m.* 115.
Lena, *w.* 14.
Maria, *c.* 95.
Phillipus, *c.* 112.
Pieter, *c.* 115.
Sally, *m.* 29 ; *w.* 141.
William, *f.* 29 ; *w.* 141.
PEEK, PEECK, David, *f.* 63.
Jacobus, *c.* 63 ; *w.* 63.
John, *w.* 71.
Maria, *w.* 71.
Sarah, *m.* 63.
Willempje, *w.* 63.
PERHEMEUS—see Polhemus.
PERKHOFF, Geesje, *c.* 50.
Hendrik, *f.* 50.
Polly, *m.* 50.
PERRY, PERRIE, PERRI, Annatje, *m.* 8, 26, 40 ; *c.* 8 ; *w.* 13, 65, 98.
Catrina, Catharina, *c.* 26 (3) ; *gs.* ‡106.
Cecilia, *c.* 29.
Charity, *m.* 29, 92, 114, 128.
Cobus, Jacobus, *f.* 8, 26, 40 ; *w.* 13, 65, 66, 98.
Daniel, *f.* 26 (2), 35, 64, 65, 73, 101, 109, 113 ; *c.* 35, 37 ; *w.* 8, 37 (2), 71, 72, 73 : D., *f.* 102, 133, 142.
Dirkje, *m.* 103.
Elisabeth, *c.* 40.
Grietje, *w.* 64.
Isaac, *c.* 64 ; *w.* 26, 64.
Jannetje, Jannitje, *m.* 26 (2), 35, 64, 65, 113 ; *c.* 65, 73 ; *w.* 8, 37 (2), 71, 72, 73.
Johannis, *f.* 103.
John, Jan. *f.* 29, 92, 114, 128 ; *c.* 74 ; *w.* 35.
Lidea, *c.* 92.
Lisabeth, *w.* 35, 113.
Margrietje, Margaret, *m.* 37, 74, 115 ; *w.* 26 : Catharine, *c.* 101, 102.
Maria, *c.* 103, 113 : Cooper, *c.* 109.
Peter, Pieter, *f.* 37, 74, 115 ; *c.* 113, 115 ; *w.* 113.
Polly, *c.* 114.
Sarah, Sally, *m.* 73, 102, 109, 133, 142 ; *c.* 128 : Margaret, *c.* 133.
William Henry, *c.* 142.
PERVO, Gerrit Hopper, *c.* 52.
Hendrik, *f.* 52.
Polly, *m.* 52.
PETERSON, PIETERSE, PIETERSEN, PIETERSON, PIETERIE, Andries, *c.* 6 ; *w.* 6.
Barend, *c.* 23.
Elisabeth, *m.* 1.
John, Jan, *f.* 110 ; *c.* 63.
Lena, *m.* 137.

POTTER, Adam, c. 14.
  Caty, Catriena, c. 28, 30.
  Dolle, c. 38.
  Grietje, c. 52.
  John, f. 14, 28, 30, 38, 52, 129.
  Maria, m. 14, 28, 30, 38, 52, 129.
  Samuel, c. 129.
POULISSON, POULISVELT, POULUSSE—see Pulisfelt.
POURHEMIUS—see Polhemes.
PREVOO, Grietje, w. 99.
  Johannis, w. 99.
PULISFELT, PULISVELT, PULESVELT, PAULISVELT, PAUL, PAULUSSE, PAULUS,
    PIELESFELT, PIELISFELT, PILESFELT, PILESVELT, PILISFELT, POELIS-
    FELT, POELISVELT, POULISVELT, POULUSSE, POULISSON, POWEL,
    PULLES, PULIS, PULUS, Abram, c. 6; w. 140.
  Andries, f. 10, 83; c. 10; w. 3 (2).
  Antje, c. 3, 16; w. 3 (2).
  Cathalyntje, Catriena, m. 27; w. 140.
  Coenraad, f. 26, 97, 140; c. 27, 28; w. 41.
  Christiaan, w. 27, 41, 96.
  Charitie, m. 38.
  Claartje, w. 27.
  Claasje, m. 122.
  Cornelis, m. 82, 83, 96, 113; c. 29; w. 58.
  Cornelis, c. 26, 27; w. 26 (2).
  David, c. 36, 38; w. 24.
  Elisabeth, m. 27, 28, 103, 140; c. 44; w. 67, 100; mem. 144.
  Eva, m. 26, 97; c. 41 (2).
  Geertje, c. 49.
  Hendrik, f. 27, 82, 96, 113; c. 58 (2); w. 58, 114.
  Jacobus, Cobus, f. 82; w. 8, 66, 82, 83, 135.
  Jannetje, c. 76.
  Johannis, Hannis, f. 3; c. 82 (2), 83.
  John, Jan, f. 28, 38, 58, 104, 122, 135; w. 67; mem. 144.
  Klaasje, m. 58, 104, 135.
  Lisabeth, m. 6, 36, 49, 96.
  Margrietje, c. 97, 105.
  Maria, Marytje, m. 3, 44; c. 96 (2), 103, 104, 106; w. 96, 114 (2).
  Nancy, Nansje, Nense, Nanny, m. 16, 29, 58, 76, 105, 106, 115, 136.
  Pieter, Peter, Petrus, f. 16, 29, 58, 76, 103, 105, 106, 115, 136; c.
    26, 113, 115; w. 36, 100, 113, 114 (2).
  Rebecka, c. 122.
  Sally, w. 114.
  Teunis, c. 135.
  Tittie, Tietje, Titie, m. 82; w. 8, 66, 82, 83, 135.
  Trientje, c. 136.
  Willem, William, f. 6, 27, 36, 44 49, 96 140.
PYPER, David, f. 89.
  Jan, c. 89.
  Lodewyk, c. 89.

"Q"

QUACKENBUSH, QUACKENBOSH, QUACKENBOS, QUACKINBUSH, QUACKINBOS,
    Abram, Abraham, f. 8, 101, 118; c. 17, 21; w. 26, 31, 121; mem.
    144.
  Ann, Annatje, m. 109, 124, 132; c. 17 (3); mem. 145: Elisabeth, c. 8.
  Barend, f. 17, 52, 69; c. 23.
  Catrina, m. 17, 26, 52, 69; c. 26, 33.
  Cornelius, c. 33.
  David, f. 38, 109, 124, 132; c. 38, 39.
  Elisabeth, w. 17.
  Geertje, c. 52.
  Gerritje, m. 8; w. 26.
  Grietje, m. 127.
  Hannes, f. 23.
  Hendrikje, m. 17.
  Jacob, f. 105, 123; c. 84; gs. ‡520, ‡521.
  Jannitje, m. 121; c. 84.
  John, f. 75, 124; c. 76 (2), 85; w. 17; mem. 145: I., f. 84, 85: J.,
    f. 21, 33 (2), 39, 108, 132; gs. ‡522, ‡523.
  Johannis, c. 69.
  Leendert, f. 121.
  Margrita, Margrietje, Margaret, m. 23; c. 105; w. 105: Ann, c. 101.
  Maria, Mary, m. 17 (2), 38, 75, 76, 84, 105, 123; c. 108; gs. ‡520:
    Ann, c. 109.
  Martin, c. 107.

Rose, Catrina, *w.* 28.
  Jan. *w.* 28.
Rosegrant, Andrew, *c.* 20.
  Cornelia, *m.* 20, 44, 53, 75.
  Eliah, Elijah, Eliza, *f.* 20, 44, 53, 75 ; *c.* 44.
  George Puffern, *c.* 53.
  John, *c.* 75.
  Sarah, *m.* 130.
  Simeon, *f.* 130 ; *c.* 130.
Rotan—see Rutan.
Row, Rouw, Elisabeth, *m.* 114 ; *c.* 44.
  Henry, *c.* 62.
  Jane, *m.* 44, 62, 77, 142.
  John, *c.* 77.
  Maria, *m.* 115, 140.
  Philip, *g.* 115, 140.
  Peter, Petrus, *f.* 44, 114 ; *c.* 114, 115 : Jr., *f.* 62, 77, 142.
  William, *c.* 140, 142.
Rutan, Rotan, Ratan, Retan, Aaltje, *m.* 3, 34, 55, 98.
  Abram, Abraham, *f.* 18, 59, 72, 78, 129, 130, 137, 141 ; *c.* 3, 7 (2), 15, 16, 20 ; *w.* 1, 2, 3, 5, 6, 7, 11, 14, 26, 35, 72, 91, 105, 128 ; *mem.* 143 ; *gs.* ‡21, ‡22 : D., *f.* 20, 123 : W., *w.* 7, 8, 126,139.
  Albert, *c.* 8.
  Antje, *c.* 18.
  Caartie, *w.* 2.
  Cathalyntje, *m.* 7.
  Daniel, *f.* 16, 67, 121, 134 ; *c.* 34 : D., *f.* 94 ; *w.* 34.
  David, *c.* 1, 34 : W., *f.* 98.
  Dennis D., *w.* 55.
  Elisabeth, *m.* 127 ; *gs.* ‡494.
  Harmen, *w.* 126.
  Hendrik, Henry, *c.* 59 ; *gs.* ‡494.
  Jacob W., *f.* 98.
  Jacobus, Cobus, *f.* 8, 26, 66 ; *c.* 72 ; *w.* 6, 68, 71, 127, 129, 139 ; *mem.* 144.
  Jan, John, *f.* 15, 71, 128, 129, 135 *c.* 66 ; *w.* 67 : H., *gs.* ‡494.
  Jannetje, *m.* 7, 16, 67 (2), 71, 121, 135 ; *c.* 71 ; *w.* 6, 67.
  Johannes, Hannes, *f.* 3, 34, 55, 67 ; *c.* 55, 67 (2), 78 ; *w.* 11 : A, *f.* 127 : P. *f.* 7.
  Lea, Leah, *m.* 20 ; *w.* 55.
  Lybetje, *m.* 1.
  Lydia, *m.* 18, 123, 130, 137, 141.
  Margrietje, Grietje, *m.* 98 ; *w.* 7, 8, 11, 14, 91, 105, 126, 139 ; *mem.* 143 : Rytan, *gs.* ‡22.
  Maria, Marytje, *m.* 34, 59, 129 ; *c.* 94, 98 (2) ; *w.* 72, 96, 128.
  Paulus, *f.* 1 ; *w.* 6.
  Pieter, *f.* 7.
  Rachel, *m.* 15, 128, 129 ; *c.* 121, 123.
  Saartje, Sara, *m.* 78 ; *c.* 26, 127, 128, 129 ; *w.* 1, 3, 5, 6, 7, 26, 35.
  Santje, *m.* 134 : A., *w.* 111.
  Susan, Susannah, *m.* 94 ; *c.* 129, 130 ; *w.* 34 ; *gs.* ‡522.
  Tryntje, *c.* 134, 135, 137 ; *w.* 128.
  Vroutje, *w.* 97.
  Willempje, *m.* 8, 26, 66, 72 ; *c.* 141 ; *w.* 6, 68, 71, 127, 129, 139, 141 ; *mem.* 144.
  William, Willem, *f.* 34 ; *w.* 96, 97.
Ryerse, Ryer, Ryers, Reyer, Ryerson, Antje, *m.* 118 ; *w.* 95.
  Barend, Barney, *f.* 76, 131 ; *c.* 23.
  Betje, *m.* 80 ; *w.* 1.
  Catriena, Cathalyntje, *w.* 37, 96.
  Dirk, *f.* 80 ; *w.* 125 : F., *f.* 80.
  Elisabeth, *c.* 42.
  Frans, *c.* 46.
  Hannes, *w.* 78 : F., *f.* 80 : W., *f.* 46.
  Hessel, *w.* 37.
  Jacob, Jacobus, *f.* 1 ; *c.* 68 ; *w.* 96 : Demarest, *c.* 75.
  Jan, John, *f.* 23, 42, 75, 77, 82, 118, 125, 126, 127, 129 (2) ; *c.* 76, (2), 77 ; *w.* 68, 72, 126 : R., *f.* 122.
  Jannetje, *c.* 80, 82.
  Johannis, *c.* 80 : R., *w.* 96.
  Joris, *c.* 80 : F., *f.* 95.
  Lena, *m.* 80 ; *w.* 46.
  Lisabeth, *m.* 96.
  Maria, Marytje, *m.* 1, 23, 42, 46, 68, 80, 95, 102, 127, 129 (3) ; *c.* 96 ; *w.* 68, 72, 78, 96, 100.
  Marten, Marte, *f.* 118 ; *c.* 95 : F., *w.* 95.

Michael, *c.* 102 : R., *f.* 76.
Polly, *m.* 75, 122 ; *gs.* ‡399.
Rachel, *c.* 118.
Rebecka, *c.* 1.
Ryer, Reyer, Reier, *f.* 68, 102, 129 ; *c.* 118, 122 ; *w.* 1, 100 : J., *f.* 96.
Sarah, *m.* 76, 131 ; *c.* 125, 129 : Jane, *c.* 131.
Susanna, Sunna, *m.* 77, 82, 118, 125 ; *c.* 126 ; *w.* 126.
Sukee, Soike, Soecke, *m.* 126 ; *c.* 127, 129.
Syntje, *c.* 129.
Teunis, *w.* 46.
Tryntje, *m.* 76.
RYKER, RYKE, Abraham, *c.* 8.
Cornelis, *c.* 27.
Crestina, Crastina, *m.* 63 ; *w.* 57.
Grace, *m.* 8.
Hendrik, *f.* 8, 63 ; *w.* 57, 90.
Jannetje, *m.* 70 ; *c.* 63, 70.
Johannis, *f.* 70.
Lea, *m.* 27.
Pieter, *f.* 27.

"S"

SABRISKA—see Zabriskie.
SALOMONSE, Antje, *w.* 3.
SARVENT—see Servent.
SCHOEMAKER, SCHOENMAKER, SHOEMAKER, Anna Margriet, *c.* 96.
Battius, *w.* 68.
Betsy, *w.* 24, 100.
Catryn, *m.* 96.
Grietje, *w.* 68.
Lodewyk, *f.* 96.
SCHOERTERS, SCHYOERT, SCHYOURT—see Syourt.
SCHUYLER, Adonia, *f.* 12, 29, 41.
Anna, *w.* 112.
Arend, *c.* 12.
Cornelis, *c.* 29.
Elisabeth, *m.* 12, 29, 41 ; *c.* 41.
Isaak, *w.* 79.
Philip, *w.* 112.
Pieter P., *w.* 112.
SCISCO—see Sisco.
SECOORT, Adolf, *w.* 2.
Maragriet, *w.* 2.
SEDMAN—see Sidman.
SEE, John, *f.* 73 ; *c.* 73.
Polly, *m.* 73.
SENDEL, Christoffel, *w.* 40.
Rebecka, *w.* 40.
SERVENT, SARVENT, Annatje, *m.* 100 ; *w.* 12 (2).
Catrina, *c.* 28, 100.
Geertrui, *w.* 113.
Grietje, *m.* 51 ; *c.* 51 ; *w.* 58.
Hendrik, *w.* 113.
Jacob, Jacobus, *f.* 28, 81, 100 ; *c.* 81 ; *w.* 12 (2).
Jan, John, *f.* 51, 99 ; *w.* 58.
Margreitje, *m.* 99.
Maria, *c.* 100.
Martha, *c.* 99.
Polly, *m.* 28.
Trientje, *m.* 81.
SHARP, Elisabeth, *m.* 42, 58, 103 ; *c.* 42.
Hester, *c.* 58.
Matheus, *c.* 103.
Morris, *f.* 42, 58, 103.
SHEDDEN, Agnes, *gs.* ‡545.
SHERWOOD, Anna, *m.* 72.
Isaak, *f.* 72 ; *c.* 72.
SHOEMAKER—see Schoemaker.
SHUART, SHULTERS, SHURTE—see Syourt.
SICKELSEN, Henricus, *c.* 58.
Jacobus, *f.* 58.
Maria, *m.* 58.
SIDMAN, SEDMAN, Angonietje, *m.* 5, 81, 89, 95 ; *c.* 5 ; *w.* 4, 78.
Jannetje, *m.* 102.
John, *c.* 81.

Lisabeth, *c.* 89.
Marytje, Maria, *c.* 95, 102.
Samuel, Samme, Sam, *f.* 5, 81, 89, 95, 102 ; *w.* 4, 78.
SISCO, SCISCO, Elisabeth, *m.* 42, 73 (2), 115, 129, 130 (2) ; *c.* 42.
  Isaac, *c.* 73.
  John, *c.* 73.
  Polly, *c.* 115.
  Semme, *c.* 129.
  Solomon, *c.* 130.
  Susannah, *c.* 130.
  William, Willem, *f.* 42, 73 (2), 115, 129, 130 (2).
SJOERT—see Syourt.
SLINGERLAND, Abram, *c.* 55.
  Casparus, *c.* 25.
  Hendrik, *c.* 55.
  Hendrika, *m.* 25.
  Teunis, *f.* 25, 55.
SLOT, SLODT, Helena, *c.* 58.
  Isaac, *f.* 58, 69, 99 ; *c.* 79.
  Jacob, *c.* 69.
  Johannis, *c.* 78.
  Lea, *m.* 58, 69, 99.
  Lisabeth, *c.* 90.
  Marytje, etc., *m.* 78, 79, 90, 96 ; *c.* 96, 99 ; *w.* 94, 99, 125.
  Steven, *f.* 78, 79, 90, 96 ; *w.* 94, 99, 125.
SMITH, SMIT, SMYTH, Aaltje, *c.* 13.
  Abbott, *f.* 71.
  Abraham, Abram, *f.* 13, 111 ; *c.* 19.
  Adeline, *gs.* ‡47.
  Albert, *f.* 13, 50 ; *c.* 13.
  Anny, Anne, Annatje, Antje, *m.* 116, 130 ; *c.* 9, 12.
  Catriena, Caty, *m.* 44, 72, 102, 111, 122 ; *c.* 27 ; *w.* 71.
  Charles, *c.* 32.
  Cornelis, Cornelius, *f.* 43 ; *c.* 29 ; *w.* 97, 99, 125 : A., *f.* 106.
  Daniel, *f.* 35.
  David Ackerman, *c.* 39.
  Dunken, *c.* 35.
  Edward, *f.* 116, 130 ; *c.* 43.
  Elisabeth, *c.* 42, 44 ; *w.* 102.
  Femmetje, *c.* 47.
  Frans, *w.* 9.
  Geertje, *m.* 19, 47, 104, 116.
  George, Jores, *f.* 19, 47, 104, 116.
  Gerrit, *f.* 29, 52, 58 ; *c.* 50 ; *w.* 50.
  Grietje, *m.* 9, 13, 42 ; *w.* 10.
  Hannes, *w.* 23.
  Harmen, *c.* 62 : P., *f.* 32, 62.
  Henry, *f.* 59, 123.
  Hester, *w.* 50.
  Hetty, Hette, *m.* 29, 52, 58 ; *c.* 58, 59.
  Jacobus, Jacob, James, *f.* 27, 72, 102, 122 ; *c.* 71 ; *w.* 71.
  Jan, John, *f.* 12 ; *w.* 66, 102 : Jr., *f.* 124 : S., *f.* 39.
  Jane, Jannetje, *m.* 32, 62, 102, 106 ; *c.* 72 ; *w.* 102.
  Lena, *m.* 107.
  Maragrietje, *c.* 104, 107.
  Maria, Marytje, *m.* 43 ; *c.* 102 (2), 106 ; *w.* 97, 125.
  Nansje, *m.* 35.
  Omphre, *c.* 111.
  Patty, *m.* 39, 124.
  Pieter, Peter, Petrus, *f.* 42, 44, 102, 107 ; *c.* 116 (2) ; *w.* 102.
  Rachel, *m.* 27, 59, 123 ; *c.* 122, 123 : Ann, *c.* 124.
  Sara, *m.* 12.
  Susanna, *m.* 13, 50, 71 ; *c.* 130.
  Willem, William, *f.* 9 ; *w.* 10, 64.
SNYDER, SNIDER, Adam, *f.* 60, 107, 123 ; *c.* 12.
  Ally, Allena, *m.* 20, 53, 60, 86, 107, 117, 123, 124 (2), 137 ; *c.* 19.
  Andries, Andrew, Andreas, *f.* 17 ; *c.* 17, 19, 20, 21 ; *w.* 123 ; *gs.* ‡527.
  Anne, *c.* 86.
  Catherine, Catharina, Catriena, Caty, *m.* 19, 21, 33, 53, 60, 75, 76,
    84, 107, 117, 123 (2) ; *c.* 33 ; *gs.* ‡524, ‡527, ‡528, ‡529.
  Charity, *m.* 53, 61, 62, 86, 87, 93, 108 (2), 124, 137.
  Dolly, *w.* 19.
  Elisabeth, *w.* 41.
  Ellen, *m.* 108.
  Garrit, Gerrit, *f.* 19 (2), 21, 53, 75, 76, 84, 117, 123 ; *c.* 53 (3) ; *gs.*
    ‡525, ‡527, ‡528, ‡529.

Polly Ackerman, *gs.* ‡198.
Sarah, *gs.* ‡242.
Willem, *w.* 1.
STOR, Abraham P., *f.* 137.
Antje, *m.* 137; *c.* 3.
Geesje, *m.* 92.
Grietje *m.* 3; *w.* 49.
Jacob, *f.* 2, 3, 92; *w.* 49.
Jacomyntje, *w.* 72.
Lea, *c.* 92.
Machiel, *c.* 2.
Maragriet, *w.* 2.
P. Wannemaker, *m.* 2.
Pieter, *w.* 72.
Tyne, *c.* 137.
STORM, STOERM, STORMS, A., *gs.* ‡54, ‡55.
Aaltje, *m.* 4, 44, 78, 80, 94, 116, 118; *w.* 4, 13; *mem.* 144.
Abby, *m.* 62.
Abram, Abraham, *f.* 4, 78, 80, 93, 94, 118; *c.* 4, 7, 17, 19, 21; *w.* 4.
Albert, *c.* 21.
Angonietje, *c.* 5.
Antje, Annetje, *c.* 4, 19.
Belitje, *m.* 4.
Catriena, *w.* 73.
Caty Ann, *gs.* ‡86.
Coenradus, Conrad, *f.* 62, 127; *c.* 24, 30; *w.* 30, 98, 104; *gs.* ‡19, ‡20, ‡86: H., *f.* 21.
Cornelia, *m.* 5, 7, 24, 55, 125 (2), 126; *c.* 28; *w.* 28, 78; *mem.* 144.
Cornelius, *f.* 21, 61, 108; *c.* 30; *gs.* ‡612.
Elisabeth, *m.* 129; *c.* 44.
Hannes, *w.* 118.
Hendrik, Henry, *f.* 5, 7, 24, 30 (2), 55, 104, 116, 125 (2), 126; *c.* 55, 57, 60, 61, 62; *w.* 13, 28 (2), 57, 78; *mem.* 144; *gs.* ‡612: C., *gs.* ‡592, ‡593: H., *mem.* 144.
Hetty, *m.* 21; *gs.* ‡86.
Isaac, *f.* 19 (2), 64, 99, 110, 129; *c.* 69, 77, 80; *w.* 64.
Jacob, *f.* 60; *c.* 64; *w.* 64.
Jannitje, *w.* 64.
Johannis, *c.* 78.
John, *f.* 44, 69, 116; *w.* 73.
Leah, *m.* 60; *c.* 93.
Margrietje, Margaret, *m.* 17, 28, 30 (2), 104, 116, 129; *c.* 108; *gs.* ‡593.
Maria, Mary, Marytje, *m.* 69; *c.* 94, 104; *w.* 28, 30, 98, 104; *gs.* ‡19: Ackerman, *gs.* ‡20.
Metje. *c.* 99.
Niklaas, *c.* 110.
Peggy, *c.* 116 (2).
Rachel, *m.* 19 (2); *c.* 118; *w.* 118.
Sally, Saartje, Sara, *m.* 21, 61, 64, 108, 110; *c.* 129; *w.* 64; *gs.* ‡612.
Staats, *f.* 4, 17, 28, 57 (2), 77, 129; *c.* 125 (2); *w.* 125 (2).
Susannah, Susan, *m.* 77, 93; *c.* 126, 129; *w.* 125 (2).
STRAAT, STRAET, Catharina, *c.* 26.
Dirk, *f.* 26, 119.
Grietje, *w.* 83.
Jacobus, Jacob, *c.* 70; *w.* 26.
Jan, John, *f.* 68, 70, 128; *c.* 68; *w.* 83, 119.
Rebecka, *m.* 26, 119; *c.* 119.
Sara, *w.* 26.
Sukie, Soecke, *m.* 70, 128; *c.* 128.
Susanna, *m.* 68.
STUART—see Syourt.
STUDS, Elisabeth, *c.* 43.
Henry, *f.* 43.
Margaret, *m.* 43.
STULTZ, Henry, *f.* 74.
Jacob, *c.* 74.
Margaret, *m.* 74.
SUDDERLAND, Antje, *c.* 8.
James, *f.* 8.
Marietje, *m.* 8.
SURLIE, James, *f.* 90.
Lourens, *c.* 90.
Marytje, *m.* 90.
SWAN, Frances, *c.* 46.
Rachel, *m.* 46.
William, *gs.* ‡352.

TERHUNE, TERHUYN, TERHUEN, TERHUUN, Aaltje, *m.* 15, 66, 99; *c.* 3, 4;
   w. 14 (2), 17, 71; *mem.* 143.
Abigail, *c.* 3; *gs.* ‡443.
Abram, Abraham, *f.* 4, 9, 17, 48 (2), 54, 56, 63, 68, 69, 71, 92, 95,
   96, 104, 136; *c.* 9, 15 (2), 16, 17, 18, 21, 22; *w.* 5, 15, 37, 48, 96,
   99; *mem.* 143; *gs.* ‡477: Jr., *gs.* ‡337, ‡338: A., *f.* 32, 87, 124,
   139; *w.* 22, 33; *gs.* ‡576, ‡577, ‡578: Ab., *f.* 76: O., *f.* 102: Romine, *c.* 21.
Albert, Albertus, *f.* 15, 16, 19, 37, 59, 66, 72, 74 (3), 84 (2), 99, 103,
   116, 117, 136, 141; *c.* 2, 4 (2), 8, 9 (2), 10, 17, 20; *w.* 3, 4 (2), 6, 9,
   10, 14 (2), 17, 41, 42, 71, 90, 94 (3); *mem.* 145; *gs.* ‡269, ‡319: A.
   f. 3, 78, 94; *w.* 2, 3 (2), 8, 10, 23, 91, 139; *mem.* 143: G., *f.* 18,
   137: H., *w.* 47, 56: I., *f.* 130: S., *w.* 112.
Alexander, *c.* 22.
Alley, *gs.* ‡1.
Andrias, Andries, *f.* 92; *c.* 5, 7.
Angenietje, *m.* 17.
Antje, Anna, Anne, Annatje, *m.* 18, 19, 76, 92, 105, 123, 129, 136; *c.*
   6, 11, 16, 18, 19, 20; *w.* 4, 11, 72: Amelia, *c.* 22: Maria, *w.* 4, 94
   (2); *gs.* ‡318.
Betje, *w.* 8, 91, 139.
Casparus, *f.* 45, 54 (2), 62, 132; *c.* 30.
Catharina, Caty, *m.* 20, 21, 32, 39, 43, 54, 72, 87, 117 (2), 124, 128,
   130; *c.* 32; *mem.* 145; *gs.* ‡477: Westervelt, *gs.* ‡577, ‡578.
Charles, *c.* 34.
Clarence, *gs.* ‡398.
David, *f.* 30, 72, 77, 130; *c.* 26, 36, 39; *w.* 11, 26, 36 (2), 125, 126.
Dirk, *f.* 2, 3, 4, 5 (2), 8, 55, 81, 138; *c.* 37; *w.* 4, 63, 77; *mem.* 145:
   A., *f.* 4, 7, 94.
Egje, *m.* 16.
Elisabeth, Lisabeth, *m.* 3, 78, 94; *c.* 43; *w.* 3 (2), 4, 10, 41, 42, 90;
   mem. 145.
Eliza Jane, *c.* 44.
Ellen, *c.* 45: Zabriskie, *gs.* ‡337.
Eva, *m.* 129.
Garrit, *c.* 54 (2); *gs.* ‡600.
Geertje, Geertrui, *c.* 48 (2).
George Demarest, *c.* 54; *gs.* ‡578.
Getty, *m.* 45, 54 (2), 62, 132.
Gilliam, *w.* 105.
Hannah, *m.* 85, 131: Jane, *c.* 62.
Harmen, *f.* 75, 106, 136; *c.* 57.
Harriet, *gs.* ‡36.
Helena, Helen, *m.* 84: Jane, *c.* 62: Zabriskie, *gs.* ‡531.
Hendrik, Hendrikus, Henry, *f.* 59, 61, 83, 92, 102; *c.* 55, 56 (2), 59,
   61; *w.* 13, 15, 58, 59, 70, 91 (2), 99, 103; *mem.* 145; *gs.* ‡526: A.,
   mem. 143; *gs.* ‡142: D., *w.* 36: I., *f.* 93: J., *f.* 44: P., *f.* 21, 124:
   S., *gs.* ‡574, ‡575: Z., *f.* 22 (2), 34, 62, 117, 142.
Hendrika, Hendrikje, *c.* 56, 59.
Hester, *m.* 20.
I., *gs.* ‡317.
Isaac, *c.* 72.
Jacob, Jacobus, *f.* 15, 17; *c.* 63, 66, 68, 71, 74, 76, 84; *w.* 130.
Jacomyntje, *c.* 74.
Jan, John, *f.* 16, 43, 57, 105, 106, 128, 129; *c.* 65, 69, 74, 75, 77, 81,
   84, 88; *w.* 66, 72, 136; *mem.* 145: A., *w.* 65: Ackerman, *c.* 85: D.,
   w. 65: Nichousis, *c.* 83: Richard, *c.* 84: S., *f.* 129.
Jannetje, *m.* 9, 10, 11, 26, 65, 127, 128; *c.* 72; *w.* 13, 47, 58, 59, 70;
   mem. 143, 145.
Jasper, *c.* 87.
Jemima, *c.* 76.
Johannis, *c.* 78: A., *w.* 64.
Lea, *m.* 2, 3, 4 (2), 5 (2), 6, 7, 8, 9, 37, 55, 56, 72, 74, 81, 94, 138,
   141; *c.* 92 (3); *w.* 63, 77, 97; *mem.* 145.
Letitia, *c.* 93.
Lydia, *gs.* ‡490.
Margrietje, *w.* 105.
Maria, Marytje, Mary, *m.* 4, 9, 15, 21, 22 (2), 34, 48 (2), 56, 61, 62,
   63, 74, 83, 88, 95, 96, 117, 124, 139, 142; *c.* 94 (2), 95, 96, 99,
   102 (2), 104, 105, 106; *w.* 5, 48, 65, 94, 96, 99, 103, 130; *mem.*
   143; *gs.* ‡600, ‡601.
Martha, *gs.* ‡601.
Martin, Martha, *f.* 20 (2), 21, 39, 117 (2); *c.* 103.
Martynetje, Martina, *m.* 18, 74, 130, 137.
Matje, *c.* 106.
Patty, *c.* 117.

Hannes, *c.* 57.
Hendrik, *f.* 56, 57, 64, 81, 83, 91, 98 ; *c.* 56, 58 (2) ; *w.* 26, 58 (2).
Jacobus, *c.* 64, 83.
Jonathan, *f.* 8, 58, 64, 81, 97, 120 ; *c.* 81 ; *w.* 8, 67 : H., *f.* 58.
John, *c.* 64.
Martyntje, *w.* 106 : Westervelt, *gs.* ‡71.
Marytje, Maria, *c.* 91, 97.
Mettie, *c.* 98.
Polly, *m.* 58.
Rachel, *c.* 120.
Trientje, *m.* 8, 120 ; *w.* 8.
Willem, *w.* 81 ; *gs.* ‡71.
Willemyntje, *m.* 98.
TURNEUR, Grietje, *m.* 82.
    Jacobus, *f.* 82.
    Jacomyntje, *c.* 82.
TURSE, TWICE—see Toers.
TYSE, TICE, TISE, TYCE, TYSEN, TYSON, TEYSEN, Abraham, *w.* 100.
    Antje Worms, *m.* 1.
    Annatje, *m.* 128.
    David, *c.* 37.
    Filip, *f.* 1.
    Hendrik, Henry, *f.* 60, 100 ; *c.* 60.
    John, *f.* 37, 116, 128.
    Maragrietje, *c.* 100.
    Maria, *m.* 60, 100, 121.
    Pieter, Peter, *f.* 121 ; *c.* 1, 116.
    Rachel, *m.* 37 ; *c.* 121.
    Saartje, *c.* 128.

"U"

USTERLI—see Iesterli.

"V"

VALENTINE, VALENTYNE, VALENTYN, Abraham, *f.* 60 ; *c.* 11.
    David, *f.* 69, 72, 140.
    Elisabeth, Lisabeth, *m.* 75, 105, 123, 140 ; *c.* 91.
    Grietje, *m.* 11, 57, 91 ; *w.* 49.
    Hantice, *c.* 57.
    Hendrik, *f.* 103, 105 ; *c.* 60 ; *w.* 100, 114.
    Jacob, *f.* 11, 57, 91, 140 ; *c.* 69, 75 ; *w.* 49, 69.
    John, *f.* 75, 105, 123 ; *c.* 72.
    Liesje, *w.* 69.
    Margrietje, *c.* 100, 105 (2).
    Maria, *m.* 60, 103, 105 ; *c.* 103 (2) ; *w.* 103, 140.
    Mathys, *w.* 57.
    Metje, *m.* 100, 103, 128 ; *w.* 140.
    Peggy, *w.* 114.
    Rachel, *m.* 69, 72, 130 ; *c.* 123 ; *w.* 72.
    Sara, *c.* 128.
    Wiert, *f.* 100, 103, 128 ; *c.* 140 (2) ; *w.* 140.
VALLEAU, Elleanor, *gs.* ‡518.
VAN ALE, Cornelis, *f.* 65.
    Hendrik, *w.* 55.
    Johannis, *c.* 65.
    Lybe, *w.* 55.
    Susanna, *m.* 65.
VAN ALLEN, VAN ALEN, VAN AULEN, Angonietje, *m.* 71, 74, 135.
    Agness Bogert, *gs.* ‡454.
    Catharine, *gs.* ‡453.
    Eefje, Effie, *c.* 43 : Neefje, *m.* 1.
    Geertje, *m.* 43, 110.
    Gerrit, *f.* 1, 43, 110.
    Jacobus, *c.* 71.
    James, *gs.* ‡451.
    Jannitje, *w.* 1.
    John, Jan, *f.* 71, 74, 135 ; *c.* 74 ; *gs.* ‡451, ‡453.
    Lea, *c.* 1.
    Neesjen, *c.* 110.
    Thomas, *c.* 135.
    Willem, *w.* 1.
VAN BEECK—see Vanderbeeck.
VAN BLERCOM, VAN BLARCOM, VAN BLERCUM, VAN BLERKOM, VAN BLER-
    KUM, V. B. KOM, VAN VLERKOM, VAN VLERCOM, Aaltje, *m.* 90,
    95 ; *c.* 7 ; *w.* 25, 48.

Elisabeth, *m.* 75; *c.* 41.
Femmitje, *m.* 113; *w.* 98.
Geesje, *w.* 71.
Hannah, *c.* 61.
Hester, *m.* 63; *w.* 137.
I., *gs.* ‡227.
Jan, John, *f.* 12, 67, 75; *c.* 75; *w.* 66, 68, 71; gs. ‡219: J., *f.* 63.
Jennie, *w.* 16.
Johannis, *c.* 63, 67.
Joost, *f.* 27; *w.* 121.
Laurens, *f.* 41; *w.* 29, 100, 104.
Maria, Marytje, Molly, *m.* 11, 27, 41; *w.* 29 (2), 41, 68, 100, 104, 140.
Martyntje, *w.* 28.
Paulus, *c.* 113; *w.* 14.
Pieter, *f.* 16, 135.
Polly, *w.* 102, 121.
Rachel, *w.* 14.
Sara, Sally, Selle, *m.* 12, 16, 67, 135.
Thomas, *c.* 135; *w.* 41, 102, 140: A., *f.* 11.
Wynte, *gs.* ‡219.
VAN BUSSEN, Maregrit, *gs.* ‡144.
VAN BUSSUM, Mary, *gs.* ‡307.
VAN DALSEN, VAN DALSON, VAN DALSE, VAN DALSEM, Albert, *c.* 21.
Caty, *c.* 32.
Hendrik, *f.* 65.
Jan, John, *f.* 21, 32, 142; *c.* 65; *w.* 65.
Jane, *m.* 21, 32, 142.
William, *c.* 142.
VANDELINDE, Ariaantje, *c.* 3; *w.* 3, 134.
Dom. Benjamin, *f.* 3, 40; *w.* 23, 82.
Elisabeth, Lisabeth, *m.* 3, 40; *w.* 23, 82.
Ester, *c.* 40.
Hendrik, *w.* 3.
VANDERBEEK, VANDERBECK, VANDERBEAK, VANBEECK, A., *gs.* ‡95.
Aaltje, Altye, *m.* 12, 102; *gs.* ‡498.
Aaron, *f.* 55; *c.* 21.
Abigail, *m.* 67, 120, 140; *w.* 9, 69, 71, 92, 140; *mem.* 144: Terhune, *gs.* ‡443.
Abram, Abraham, *f.* 3, 5, 39, 79, 84; *c.* 5, 9, 12, 13 (2), 20, 22; *w.* 13 (2), 15, 102, 121, 126, 128, 129, 130; *gs.* ‡171, ‡172: C., *f.* 20, 31, 81, 117: J., *f.* 9, 44, 108, 119; *w.* 63, 65.
Agnes, *gs.* ‡74.
Ally, *c.* 20.
Andrew, Andreas, *f.* 61, 86 (2); *c.* 15, 20.
Angenietje, *c.* 12, 14, 15; *w.* 24; *gs.* ‡16.
Annatje, Ann, Antje, *m.* 12, 15, 52, 60 (2), 69, 71 (2), 72, 75, 78, 87, 105 (2), 111, 121 (2), 132, 138; *c.* 11, 18, 20; *w.* 3, 7, 9, 14, 25, 79, 113, 114; *mem.* 144.
Arie, Aurie, *f.* 11, 14, 18, 42, 104, 114, 116, 129; *c.* 4; *w.* 9.
Caty Ann, *c.* 33.
Coenraad, Coenradus, *f.* 12, 15, 33, 52, 71, 72, 75, 105, 111, 121; *c.* 3, 25; *w.* 3, 24; *gs.* ‡341, ‡343.
Cornelis, Cornelius, *f.* 13, 15, 73, 106; *c.* 31, 32.
Daniel, *c.* 39.
Dirk, *f.* 75 (2).
Doortje, *w.* 67, 121.
Ebbie, *m.* 91.
Eliza, *m.* 61; *c.* 44.
Elisabeth, *m.* 20, 31, 39, 47 (2), 62, 86 (2), 117; *c.* 42: Ackerman, *gs.* ‡510, ‡511, ‡512.
Femmetje, *w.* 79.
Frederik, *c.* 47 (2); *gs.* ‡510, ‡511.
Garrit Van Wagoner, *c.* 54.
Geesje, *c.* 52.
George, *f.* 47; *c.* 55; *gs.* ‡534, ‡535, ‡536, ‡537.
Getty, *c.* 54.
Grietje, *w.* 70.
H. Y., *gs.* ‡17.
Hannah, *m.* 20, 21, 54, 61 (2), 76, 84, 85, 117, 137; *c.* 61 (3), 62; *gs.* ‡510, ‡533, ‡534, ‡535, ‡613: Demarest, *gs.* ‡343: Young, *gs.* ‡537.
Harmen, Hermanus, *f.* 62, 71, 85, 93; *c.* 60 (2); *w.* 14.
Henry, *c.* 61, 62.
Henrietta, *c.* 61.
Hetty, *m.* 33.
Hillegond, *mem.* 144.

Catryntje, Caty, Catharina, *m.* 2; *c.* 32; *w.* 25, 36: Leah, *c.* 31.
Cornelis, Cornelius, *f.* 36 (2), 51, 136; *c.* 27, 32; *w.* 10, 35, 50; *mem.*
   144; *gs.* ‡437, ‡439, ‡440: G., *f.* 54, 132 (2); *gs.* ‡549.
Dirk, *f.* 2, 103; *c.* 35, 36 (2), 38 (2); *w.* 25 (2), 31, 38 (2), 136.
Elisa Blanch, *c.* 43.
Elisabeth, Lisabeth, *c.* 41, 45 (2), 90; *gs.* ‡238, ‡280, ‡281: Doremus,
   gs. ‡311.
Ellen, Eleanor, *m.* 45; *gs.* ‡238: Zabriskie, *c.* 44.
Geertje, *m.* 103.
Gerrit, Garret, *f.* 5 (2), 27, 32, 33, 54, 56, 85, 86, 131 (2); *c.* 49, 50,
   51 (2), 52, 54 (2); *w.* 4, 6; *gs.* ‡275, ‡276, ‡279, ‡312, ‡313,
   ‡549: C., *f.* 32, 76, 124: H., *f.* 31, 85: Henry, *c.* 54.
Hannah, *m.* 21, 61.
Harmen, *f.* 51, 71; *c.* 56, 61; *w.* 128.
Henry Hennion, *c.* 62.
Hester, *gs.* ‡271.
Jane, Jenny, *m.* 32, 33, 54 (2), 85, 86, 131 (2), 136; *gs.* ‡275, ‡276,
   ‡279, ‡549: Demarest, *gs.* ‡313: Voorhies, *gs.* ‡276.
John, Jan, *f.* 21; *c.* 71, 76, 87: B., *gs.* ‡280, ‡281, ‡311: Bogert, *c.*
   76: Buskirk, *c.* 85: H., *f.* 44, 61: Van Boskerk, *c.* 71: Voorhis,
   c. 86: Z., *f.* 22, 45, 54: Zabriskie, *c.* 85.
Johannis, *c.* 68.
Leah, *m.* 44.
Margrietje, Margaret, *m.* 51; *gs.* ‡281, ‡437.
Maria, Mary, *m.* 22, 38, 45, 54, 62, 71, 76, 104, 128; *c.* 99 103, 104,
   108; *w.* 31, 38, 42, 51; *gs.* ‡336: Bogert, *gs.* ‡84: Kough, *gs.* ‡487.
Polly, *m.* 35, 43, 49, 50, 52, 68, 90, 99, 134, 136, 137; *w.* 27.
Rachel, *w.* 4, 5; *gs.* ‡278.
Richard, *c.* 124; *gs.* ‡238, ‡280: A., *f.* 20, 45, 87, 132; *gs.* ‡273: C.,
   gs. ‡438.
Sara, Sarah, Saartje, Sierie, Sally, *m.* 5 (2), 27, 36 (2), 38, 41, 56,
   128; *c.* 128 (2), 131 (2), 132; *w.* 6, 10, 49, 50; *gs.* ‡272, ‡276,
   ‡279: Catherina, *m.* 22.
Sophia, *m.* 32, 124: Catharine, *c.* 132; *gs.* ‡440: Elisabeth, *c.* 132.
St., *m.* 76.
Susan, *m.* 132 (2); *gs.* ‡440.
Thomas, *f.* 35, 49, 90, 99, 134; *c.* 136, 137; *w.* 27, 35, 42; *gs.* ‡84.
Tryntje, *c.* 134; *w.* 25, 35 (2).
VAN EMBURGH, VAN IMBURGH, VAN IMBURG, Albert, *f.* 24, 62, 108; *c.* 14;
   gs. ‡369: H., *f.* 117.
Antje, Antie, *m.* 56, 134; *w.* 65.
Ariaantje, *w.* 5, 56.
Benjamin Zabriskie, *c.* 24.
Caty Ann, *c.* 32.
Hannah, *m.* 24, 62, 108, 117.
Hannes, *w.* 5, 56.
Hendrik, Henry, *f.* 14, 59, 69, 75, 116, 117, 122, 127; *c.* 56, 59, 60,
   62 (2): H., *f.* 62, 85, 86, 108; *gs.* ‡401, ‡402, ‡403.
Jacob Demarest, *c.* 85.
James, *c.* 86.
Jane Carlock, *gs.* ‡403.
John, Jan, *f.* 32, 56, 60, 134; *c.* 69; *w.* 41, 65, 69, 92; *gs.* ‡404: H.,
   f. 93, 108.
Joris, *c.* 75.
Lea, *w.* 41, 69, 92.
Levinah Zabriskie, *c.* 93.
Margaret, *c.* 108: Demarest, *gs,* ‡402.
Maria, *m.* 14, 69, 75, 116, 122; *c.* 108 (2).
Peggy, *m.* 62, 85, 86, 108.
Peter, *c.* 116.
Polly, *m.* 32, 59, 60, 93, 108, 117, 137; *c.* 117 (2); *gs.* ‡369.
Ralph Westervelt, *c.* 122.
Tryntje, *c.* 134, 137.
VAN ES, Jacob, *c.* 80.
Lisabeth, *m.* 80.
Syme, *f.* 80.
VAN GELDER, Abraham, Abram, *f.* 1; *w.* 25, 78, 119.
Antje, Annatje, *m.* 10, 36; *c.* 9, 10.
Catherine, *gs.* ‡461.
David, *c.* 36.
Hendrik, *f.* 10, 36.
Hittie, *c.* 57.
Jacobus, Cobus, *f.* 9, 120; *c.* 1; *w.* 1, 64.
Jannitje, *m.* 9, 120; *w.* 64.
Jonathan, *f.* 57, 119; *w.* 120; *gs.* ‡461.

Jan, John, *f*. 6, 36, 42, 63, 70, 72, 81; *c*. 63, 70, 86; *w*. 91: P., *f*, 64.
Jannitje, *m*. 6, 10, 36, 63, 64, 81; *c*. 64, 72; *w*. 91.
James, *c*. 84.
Johannis, *c*. 81.
Laurens, *w*. 11.
Letty Jane, *c*. 93.
Maritje, *w*. 13.
Pieter, *w*. 66.
Rachel, *c*. 123: Ann, *c*. 124.
Rosy, Rosamon, *m*. 40, 93, 124.
Tryntje, *m*. 42, 70, 72; *c*. 133.
VAN NOSTRAND, VAN OSTRAND, Anna, *gs*. ‡568.
Charratje Ann, *c*. 31.
Elisabeth, *c*. 44.
John, *f*. 31, 44; *gs*. ‡567, ‡568.
Maria, Polly, *m*. 31, 44.
VAN ORDEN, VAN ORDER—see Van Norden.
VAN RODEN, Jemimah, *c*. 76.
Tyna, *m*. 76.
William, *f*. 76.
VAN RYPER, VAN RIPER, VAN RYPEN, VAN RIPEN, VAN RYPE, Abigail, *m*.
57; *w*. 13, 51, 58, 59 (3); *mem*, 144.
Abraham, *f*. 34; *c*. 20; *gs*. ‡517.
Adriaan, *c*. 15, 19.
Angenietje, *c*. 15.
Antje, Anna, Annatje, *m*. 25, 34, 77; *c*. 13, 17, 18; *w*. 46, 92, 118;
gs. ‡517.
Caty, *m*. 20, 61, 108.
Catharine Maria, *c*. 34.
Cornelius, *f*. 17, 73, 106 (2); *c*. 25.
David Baldwin, *c*. 38.
Elisabeth, *m*. 17, 73, 106 (2).
Frederik, Vredrik, *f*. 15, 18, 19, 25, 38, 52, 59, 74, 77, 100, 125, 137;
c. 46, 138; *w*. 46, 118; *gs*. ‡515: G., *f*. 116.
Geertje, *m*. 13, 15, 67.
Gerrit, *f* 57, 138; *c*. 51, 52; *w*. 13, 51, 58, 59 (2), *mem*. 144.
Hannah, *c*. 61 *gs*. ‡514.
Harmen, Harme, Herman, *f*. 20, 46, 51, 61, 98, 108; *c*. 59; *w*. 40,
59, 67, 99, 100 (2), 138; *mem*. 145.
Hendrika, *c*. 57.
John, *c*. 67, 73, 74.
Johannis, Hannes, *f*. 13, 15, 67; *c*. 77; *w*. 77, 118.
Jurrien, *c*. 79.
Margriet, *m*. 79.
Maria, Mary, *m*. 15, 18, 19, 38, 46, 51, 52, 59, 74, 98, 100, 116, 137;
c. 98, 100, 106 (2), 108; *w*. 40, 59, 67, 98, 100 (2); *mem*. 145; *gs*.
‡480: Vanderbeek, *gs*. ‡516.
Peter, *c*. 116.
Rachel, *w*. 118.
Saartje, *m*. 125; *w*. 77.
Simeon, *f*. 79; *c*. 125.
Thomas, *c*. 137.
VAN SAUN, VAN SAAN, Betsey, *c*. 24.
Christina, *c*. 33.
Cornelius, *f*. 24, 84, 107, 123; *w*. 14.
Elsje, *m*. 54, 87, 93, 132.
Garrit Zabriskie, *c*. 54.
Hester, *w*. 14.
Isaac, *c*. 87 (2).
Jacob, *f*. 76, 84, 123; *c*. 76, 84 (2); *w*. 84: Jr., *f*. 85.
Jane, *m*. 33, 87.
John, *c*. 85: I., *f*. 93, 132: J., *f*. 87: S., *f*. 54.
Levina, *c*. 93.
Lucas I., *f*. 33, 87.
Margaret, *c*. 107.
Maria, *m*. 84.
Polly, *m*. 76, 85, 123.
Rachel, *m*. 24, 84, 107, 123; *c*. 123 (2); *w*. 84.
Sarah, *c*. 132.
VAN SCHYVEN, VAN SCHYVE, Abraham, *c*. 17.
Annatje, *c*. 3.
Dirk, *c*. 38.
Hannes, Hans, *f*. 3, 80, 96, 138; *w*. 79, 89.
Jan, *c*. 80.
Johannis, *c*. 70.
Maria, *c*. 96.

Janneke, *m.* 125 ; *c.* 125 ; *w.* 125.
John, *f.* 19, 61 ; *c.* 84, 85 : Henry, *c.* 86.
Lena, *w.* 95.
Lisabeth, *w.* 89.
Paulus, *f.* 64.
Robert, *f.* 84.
Simeon, *c.* 125 (2) ; *w.* 89.
Sylettje, *m.* 19.
Tryna, *m.* 84.
Vrouwtje, *m.* 125 ; *w.* 36, 125 (2), 138.
VAN ZEYL, VAN ZILE, VAN ZYL, VAN SILE, VAN SYL, Abraham, *f.* 115,
    140 ; *c.* 6.
Albert, *f.* 114, 115.
Catriena, Catharina, *m.* 80, 90.
Divertje, *c.* 34.
Egbert, *f.* 112 ; *c.* 40 ; *w.* 25, 26, 40, 41, 46.
Elisabeth, *m.* 114 (2), 115, 128 ; *w.* 67.
Hans, Hannes, Johannis, *f.* 90 ; *c.* 55, 80 ; *w.* 55, 80, 81, 140 : A., *f.*
    56, 80 ; *w.* 118 : J., *f.* 80.
Hendrik, *c.* 56.
Hermanus, *f.* 114 (2), 115, 128 ; *c.* 55 ; *w.* 65, 67.
Jakomyntje, *c.* 80.
Jannitje, *m.* 6, 34, 118 ; *w.* 81, 114.
Lena, *m.* 26, 40, 55 (2), 94 ; *c.* 90, 94 ; *w.* 55, 64, 65.
Marytje, *m.* 56 ; *c.* 94.
Pieter, Petrus, *f.* 6, 26, 34, 40, 55 (2), 94, 118 ; *c.* 112, 114 (2), 115 ;
    w. 64, 65, 81, 114.
Polly, *c.* 114, 115.
Rachel, *m.* 114, 115 (2), 140 ; *c.* 118.
Saartje, Sara, *c.* 26 ; *w.* 25, 26, 40, 46, 65.
Susannah, *c.* 128.
Trientje, Triena, *w.* 81, 118.
William, *c.* 140.
Willempje, *m.* 112.
VEEDER, Antje, *m.* 79.
Hermanus, *f.* 79.
Jacob, *c.* 79.
VEIL, Catharina, *c.* 29.
Enos, *f.* 29.
Nellie, *m.* 29.
VENNICEMAN, Geertrui, *m.* 88.
VERBURGH, Cornelia, *w.* 27.
Willem, *w.* 27.
VERSCHUER, VERSEUR, VERSCHEUR, VERSIEUR, VESEUR, VESIEUR, VOSEUR,
    VOCHIE, VOSUER, VOSUET, FORSHEA, FERSEUR, FERSHUIR, FESJEUR,
    FERSYEUR,? FESHEUR, FESYEUR, FESYOUR, FYRSHEUR, FORSHUER,
    FOCHI.
Abraham, *f.* 12, 15, 16, 68, 69, 102, 106, 116, 141 ; *c.* 5, 15 ; *w.* 15.
Annatje, Antje, *c.* 6, 7, 12, 16.
Barend, *f.* 7, 25, 81, 96, 97 ; *c.* 23 (2) ; *w.* 23 (3), 24, 46 (3), 47, 66,
    129, 134 ; *mem.* 144.
Catharina, Catrina, Catrientje, *c.* 25, 28 ; *w.* 25, 26 (2), 80, 81 ;
    mem. 144.
Cornelis, Cornelius, *f.* 27, 39, 43, 71, 74, 122, 140 ; *c.* 26 ; *w.* 28.
David, *f.* 136, 140 ; *c.* 35, 39 ; *w.* 140.
Elisabeth, *m.* 12, 15, 16, 68, 69, 102, 106, 116, 141 ; *c.* 43 ; *w.* 15.
Francyntje, *m.* 25, 81, 97 ; *w.* 23 (3), 24, 46 (3), 47, 129 ; *mem.* 144.
Hannes, *f.* 6, 23, 27, 112, 127, 139 ; *w.* 97.
Jacob, *c.* 68.
Jan, *c.* 80, 81 ; *w.* 25, 26 (2), 80, 81 : W., *f.* 28, 68.
Jannetje, *m.* 71, 140 ; *c.* 71, 81.
Johannis, *f.* 5 ; *c.* 68 ; *w.* 6, 69, 99, 102.
John, *c.* 69, 74 ; *w.* 74, 140.
Lena, *m.* 5, 6, 23, 27, 112, 127, 139 ; *w.* 6.
Lisabeth, *m.* 35, 81 ; *w.* 27, 139.
Magdalena, *c.* 97, 102, 106 ; *w.* 97.
Maragrietje, *w.* 69.
Maria, *m.* 23, 39, 43, 74, 80, 122, 136, 140 ; *c.* 96 ; *w.* 96 (2), 112,
    113.
Pieter, *f.* 23, 80 ; *c.* 112, 116 ; *w.* 96 (2), 112, 113.
Polly, *w.* 140.
Rebecka, *w.* 99, 102.
Rachel, *c.* 122.
Samuel, *c.* 127.
Syntje, *m.* 7, 96 ; *w.* 23, 134.
Trientje, *c.* 136 ; *w.* 28.

Pieter, *f.* 55, 102; *c.* 111; *w.* 24, 111: D., *f.* 94; *w.* 34.
Sara, *w.* 69, 70.
Susanna, Susan, *m.* 55, 111.
Willem, f. 109; w. 37.
WARD, WAARD, Abigael, *m.* 82.
Ann, *m.* 85, 117.
James, *f.* 85, 117.
Jenneke, *c.* 67.
John, *c.* 85.
Jones, *c.* 82.
Nancy, *m.* 67.
Pieter, *f.* 67; *c.* 117.
Samuel, *f.* 82.
WARENT, Antje, *c.* 9.
Elisabeth, *m.* 9.
John, *f.* 9.
WATKINS, Grietje, *w.* 51.
Pieter, *w.* 51.
WATSON, WATSENS, Elisabeth, *c.* 43.
John, *c.* 71.
Margrietje, Margaret, *m.* 43, 71, 102, 106, 116; *c.* 106; *w.* 104.
Maria, *c.* 102.
Peter, Petrus, *f.* 44, 71, 102, 106 ,116; *c.* 116; *w.* 104.
Sarah, *gs.* ‡472.
WEALER, Annatje, *w.* 8.
Jonathan, *w.* 8.
WELBER, Elisabeth, *m.* 93.
Henry, *f.* 93.
Laura, *c.* 92.
WENDYK—see Wortendyk.
WESLEY, Catharine, *m.* 54.
Garret, *f.* 54.
Guistica, *c.* 54.
WESSELS, WESSELLS, Ariaantje, *m.* 7, 23, 109 (2), 125; *c.* 7; *w.* 40, 96, 125.
Benjamin, *c.* 23.
Catharina, *m.* 101.
Joseph, Josie, *f.* 7, 23, 109 (2), 125; *w.* 40, 96, 125.
Mary Bogert, *c.* 101.
Nellie, *c.* 109.
Niklaas, *c.* 109.
Sara, *c.* 125.
Wessel, *f.* 101.
WESTERVELT, Aaltje, *m.* 18, 30, 39, 116.
Abraham, Abram, *f.* 14, 113, 120, 135; *c.* 2, 14, 19; *mem.* 143: R.,
    w. 41.
Adeline Smith, *gs.* ‡47, ‡48.
Agnes, *c.* 20, 21; *gs.* ‡45: Van Derbeck, *gs.* ‡74.
Albert, *f.* 17, 28, 30, 59, 72, 104, 135; *c.* 6, 20 (2); *w.* 106: P. *gs.*
    ‡203, ‡204, ‡205: R., *gs.* ‡551, ‡552.
Angonietje, Angenietje, *m.* 128; *c.* 4, 17 (2); *w.* 17, 102.
Antje, Annatje, *m.* 14, 65, 91, 96, 113, 119, 120, 135; *c.* 17; *w.* 9, 41,
    120; *mem.* 143 (2).
Arie, Aury, *c.* 18; *w.* 66.
Casparus, *f.* 4, 49, 79, 85, 113, 134; *c.* 29, 30; *mem.* 144; *gs.* ‡69,
    ‡70: J., *f.* 80.
Caty, *m.* 19, 76, 85, 106, 123, 131; *gs.* ‡365.
Cathalyntje, Catharine, *m.* 46; *c.* 28, 30; *w.* 66, 79; *gs.* ‡577: Har-
    ing, *gs.* ‡43.
Charity, *gs.* ‡68.
Cornelius: I., *w.* 47: J., *f.* 47.
Daniel, *f.* 115; *c.* 39; *mem.* 144; *gs.* ‡42, ‡48: Talman, *c.* 39.
Deter, *f.* 131.
Dorothea, *c.* 35.
Eefje, *w.* 80.
Elisabeth, *m.* 17, 35, 155; *mem.* 144; *gs.* ‡204: Ackerman, *gs.* ‡131.
Fytje, *c.* 46: D., *w.* 34.
Geertje, *c.* 49; *w.* 66.
Gerrit, *c.* 47.
Hannah Ackerman, *gs.* ‡130.
Henry, Hendrik, *f.* 18, 30, 39, 116; *c.* 59, 61, 62; *gs.* ‡47, ‡48, ‡202.
Hetty, Hatty, Hester, *m.* 75, 131: Van Dien, *c.* 60; *gs.* ‡271.
Hillegont, *w.* 1.
Jacob, Jacobus, *c.* 66, 74.
James, *c.* 76: Bogert, *c.* 86.
Jannike, Jannitje, *m.* 47; *c.* 1; *w.* 41, 47.
Jasper, *c.* 88.

Jacob, Jacobus, *f.* 43, 100, 121 (2), 136; *w.* 35, 68, 128.
Jannetje, *m.* 96, 118; *c.* 67, 71; *w.* 67, 70, 71, 82, 119, 120, 121 (2).
Jemyma, *w.* 7.
John, Jan, *f.* 46, 92, 103.
Johannis, *c.* 69, 73.
Margrietje, *m.* 39, 71, 121.
Marjeree, Majeri, Majere, Maseri, Macere, *m.* 35, 97, 126 (2); *c.* 97, 103; *w.* 127.
Maria, Mary, Marietje, *c.* 96, 99, 100, 104; *w.* 35, 73.
Marlena, *c.* 104.
Metje, *m.* 115; *c.* 92; *w.* 103.
Pieter, Petrus, *f.* 115; *c.* 115 (2); *w.* 103.
Rachel, *c.* 121, 122, 123.
Reinier, Rynier, Ryna, *f.* 7 (2), 15, 67, 69, 96, 104, 115, 118, 122; *c.* 118, 119, 120, 121 (2); *w.* 67, 70, 71, 82, 119, 120, 121 (2); *mem.* 144.
Sara, Sally, *m.* 100, 119, 121; *c.* 126, 127, 130 (2); *w.* 68, 118, 125, 128.
Sophia, *m.* 12, 15, 104, 120; *c.* 130; *mem.* 144.
Susannah, *c.* 126.
Titje, *c.* 136.
Vroutje, *w.* 138.
WORMS, Antje, *m.* 1.
WRIGHT, WRITE, WREYGHT, RITE, Aaltje, *m.* 5, 6, 56, 63; *c.* 13, 15, 16.
Abigail, *m.* 15, 72, 122, 141.
Abraham, *f.* 16; *c.* 6.
Albert, *f.* 13, 51, 141; *c.* 5.
Annatje, *m.* 16, 51, 141.
Geertje, *m.* 13; *c.* 51.
Hendrik, *c.* 56.
Jannitje, *c.* 72.
John, Jan, *f.* 15, 72, 122, 141; *c.* 63.
Rachel, *c.* 122.
Willem, William, *f.* 5, 6, 56, 63; *c.* 141 (2).

"Y"

YELVERTON, Anthony, *f.* 84, 131.
John Hopper, *c.* 84.
Rachel, *m.* 84, 131.
Sarah, *c.* 131.
YEOMANS, YOUMENS, YOOMENS, YOUMANS, Abby, *c.* 18.
Catriena, Caty, *m.* 29 (2), 42, 75.
Coenraad, *c.* 29.
Daniel, *f.* 42.
Elisabeth, *m.* 69, *c.* 42.
John, *f.* 18, 29 (2), 69, 75, 105; *c.* 69, 75.
Maretje, *c.* (?) 104.
Margrietje, *c.* 105.
Trientje, *m.* 18, 105.
YOUNG, Hannah, *gs.* ‡537.

"Z"

ZABRISKIE, ZABRISKE, ZABRISKA, ZABRISKO, ZABROWISKE, ZABROWISKIE, ZOBEREWISKE, ZOBRISKE, ZOBRISKIE, ZOWBROWISKE, SABRISKE, Aaltje, *m.* 2, 3, 17, 24, 52, 63, 72, 79, 94 (2), 116, 119, 138; *c.* 5 (2), 8, 11 (2), 13, 16, 17, 18; *w.* 2, 3, (3), 4, 5 (3), 7 (2), 8, 9, 24, 25, 48, 57, 78, 79, 80 (2), 83, 95, 96, 120.
Abram, Abraham, *f.* 9, 13, 14, 50, 58, 66, 76, 93, 122; 3, 8, 10, 12, 14, 20; *w.* 67; *mem.* 143; *gs.* ‡272: A., *f.* 20, 53, 65, 86, 91: C., *f.* 44, 108: J., *f.* 88, 105: Stephens, *c.* 21: Van Buskirk, *c.* 21.
Albert, *f.* 14, 16, 17, 24, 31, 52, 70, 72, 116, 129 (2); *c.* 3, 5, 9, 14, 17 (2), 19, 20, 21 (3); *w.* 1, 11, 23, 24, 66, 139; *mem.* 143; *gs.* ‡396, ‡397, ‡493: C., *f.* 94; *w.* 5, 9, 25, 48: H., *f.* 3, 77; *w.* 5, 9, 77, 80: I., *mem.* 143; *gs.* ‡56: J., *f.* 11, 48, 64, 67, 127; *w.* 23, 77, 89: Jan, *f.* 80: T., *w.* 110.
Aletta Levina, *c.* 21.
Andrew, Andries, Andreas, *f.* 11, 24, 80, 85; *c.* 10, 15, 20, 22; *w.* 10, 15, 29, 82 (2); *mem.* 143: A., *w.* 7: C., *f.* 22, 46, 88, 89: Hoppe, *c.* 22: I., *f.* 85, 137: J., *f.* 61, 80, 83, 85, 137; *w.* 7.
Antje, Annatje, Anne, *m.* 16, 18, 19, 20, 21, 22, 30, 45, 53, 60, 84, 85, 86, 87 (2), 93, 108, 110, 123, 141, 142; *c.* 2 (2), 4, 7, 9, 10, 16 (2), 18, 19, 20 (2), 22 (2); *w.* 16, 49, 52 (2); *mem.* 143, 144: Hopper, *gs.* ‡581: Maria, *c.* 21.
Belitie, *c.* 23 (2).

Maria, Marytje, Merya, Mary, *m.* 8, 9, 12 13, 14, 20, 25, 27, 28, 30, 31,
33, 41, 44, 45, 50, 51, 53, 58, 59, 64, 65, 66, 82, 85, 88, 91 (2), 95,
96, 101, 106, 108 (2), 109 (2), 126, 140; *c.* 82, 91, 94 (3), 95, 101,
(3), 105 (3), 106, 107 (3), 108 (2); *w.* 1, 3 (2), 9, 10, 15, 16,
28, 29 (2), 41, 49, 51, 56, 58, 59, 63, 64, 67, 79, 102 (2), 129;
mem. 143 (6); *gs.* ‡93, ‡153: Jane, *gs.* ‡199, ‡242: Martina, *c.*
101, 106: Van Dien, *gs.* ‡336: Westervelt, *gs.* ‡492.
Martha, *c.* 101, 107; *gs.* ‡397: Ann, *gs.* ‡367, ‡614.
Martyntje, *m.* 10, 19, 106; *c.* 95; *w.* 27, 127.
Mathilda Bogert, *c.* 107.
Metje, Matje, Mettie, *m.* 11, 14, 16, 67, 107, 129 (2); *w.* 110; *mem.*
143.
Myntje, *w.* 105.
Neesje, *m.* 47; *c.* 109; *w.* 24.
Nicholas, Niklaas, *f.* 16, 105; *c.* 109, 110; *w.* 109, 110, 119; *gs.* ‡154:
J., *gs.* ‡155, ‡156.
Patty, *m.* 21, 53, 62, 85, 87, 107, 123.
Peter, *c.* 116, 118: A., *f.* 21, 85, 86, 87, 108.
Polly, *m.* 10, 31, 58, 61, 85 (3), 107, 137 (2); *w.* 33.
R., *gs.* ‡18.
Rachel, *c.* 118, 119 (2), 120, 122, 123; *w.* 90, 109, 110, 119, 126; *gs.*
‡70: Ann, *m.* 88 (2), 101; *c.* 123, 124: Catharine, *c.* 124.
Rebecca, *gs.* ‡554.
Robert Post, *c.* 124.
Sara, Sarah, Sally, *m.* 21, 47, 60, 86, 87, 132; *c.* 126; *gs.* ‡199, ‡241,
‡588: Jane, *c.* 132; *gs.* ‡240, ‡602, ‡603, ‡614: Margaret, *m.* 22,
46, 88: Stevens, *gs.* ‡242: Van Dien, *gs.* ‡272.
Simon, Simeon, *c.* 129, 132: Demorest, *c.* 131.
Sophia, *c.* 132.
Steven, Stephen, Steve, *f.* 2, 78, 118; *c.* 127, 129; *w.* 26, 55, 118, 119,
126, 127, 133: A., *gs.* ‡28: I., *f.* 88: J., *f.* 45, 124, 137: T., *f.* 101:
Terhune, *c.* 130.
Susanna, *m.* 76, 93, 105, 122.
Thellitie, Thelletje, *m.* 3, 77; *w.* 5, 77, 80.
Thomas, *c.* 137; *gs.* ‡586: B., *f.* 88: Buskirk, *c.* 137 (2).
Tyna, Tina, Tiena, *m.* 21, 33, 34, 45, 82, 87, 118.
Tryntje, *m.* 2, 78, 118; *w.* 55, 118, 119, 126, 133 139.
Willempje, *m.* 27, 64, 98; *w.* 31.
William, *c.* 141 (2), 142.
Wyntje, *m.* 4, 5 (2), 10, 17, 48, 55, 64, 72, 90, 94, 105 (2), 119, 139
(2); *c.* 138, 139 (2), 140; *w.* 11, 48 (2) 58, 64, 65, 69, 129, 138
(2); *mem.* 143 (2).